Problems of Transnational Civil Procedure

Volume
I

AF776199

# Current Topics of International Litigation

Edited by

Rolf Stürner and Masanori Kawano

Mohr Siebeck

ISBN 978-3-16-149972-2

Die Deutsche Nationalbibliothek lists this publication in the Deutsche Nationalbibliographie; detailed bibligraphic data is available in the Internet at *http://dnb.d-nb.de*.

© 2009 by Mohr Siebeck, Tübingen.

This book may not be reproduced, in whole or in part, in any form (beyond that permitted by copyright law) without the publisher's written permission. This applies particularly to reproductions, translations, microfilms and storage and processing in electronic systems.

The book was typeset and printed by Gulde-Druck in Tübingen on non-aging paper and bound by Großbuchbinderei Spinner in Otterweier.

Printed in Germany.

# Preface

This first volume of a book series is the result of the international symposium "Current Topics of Transnational Civil Procedure", held on February 18–19, 2006 at the Nagoya Castle Hotel in Nagoya, Japan. The symposium was planned as part of an international research program sponsored by the Japan Society for the Promotion of Science from 2005 to 2010.

The main idea of this project is to develop and encourage methods of comparative study of civil procedure by establishing a personal network for the exchange of legal information. The purpose of such a personal network is the intensive discussion of common and differing features of proceedings in business litigation matters. In our globally integrated society, legal disputes are inevitably expanding beyond national borders. But in each jurisdiction, legal system and practice have developed their own different traditions. Such differences may sometimes cause special difficulties in transnational litigation. Therefore, it is necessary to promote harmonization of special rules of transnational civil procedure. This form of harmonization is very different from unification of law. Some visitors of this symposium were members of the Working Group of the joint project of the ALI and Unidroit "Principles of Transnational Civil Procedure" from 2000–2003. This present Japanese project takes the ALI/Unidroit Principles as a basis for continuing research and exchange. To further close and continuous cooperation between legal scholars with different legal backgrounds, we scheduled two international symposia annually, one in Japan and the other in varying European universities. This volume documents the first symposium of our project.

We would like to express our gratitude to all participating members who actively contributed to the symposium and who travelled the long way from Europe and the United States to Japan.

This volume was edited by the Institute for Business Litigation of Nagoya University at Freiburg University, Germany. The Institute was established to perform this project in collaboration with and the kind support of Freiburg University. We would also like to thank Dr. Natalie Konomi who organized the editing work for this book, Ms Tohko Hayakawa for her invaluable assistance and the Japan Society for the Promotion of Science for its kind financial support.

*Rolf Stürner*, Germany
*Masanori Kawano*, Nagoya, Japan
Freiburg/Nagoya, December 2008

# Contents

Opening of the Symposium
*Professor Shin-ichi Hirano, Professor Saburi Haruo,*
*Professor Masanori Kawano* . . . . . . . . . . . . . . . . . . . . . . . . 1

*Chapter 1*

Provisional Measures and Prohibitory Injunctions

*Masanori Kawano*
Provisional Measures for Prohibition of Actions –
New Tendencies in Japan . . . . . . . . . . . . . . . . . . . . . . . . 7

*Neil H. Andrews*
Accelerated Justice: Protective, Interim and Summary Procedures
in English Law . . . . . . . . . . . . . . . . . . . . . . . . 18

*Marco de Cristofaro*
Anti-suit Injunctions as a Tool for Governing Private Litigation . . . . 58

*Laura Ervo*
Some Comments on Civil Provisional Measures to Prohibit Specific
Actions According to Finnish Law . . . . . . . . . . . . . . . . 69

Discussion . . . . . . . . . . . . . . . . . . . . . . . . 81

*Chapter 2*

International Class Actions

*Peter L. Murray*
Class Actions in a Global Economy . . . . . . . . . . . . . . . . . . . . 95

*Rolf Stürner*
International Class Actions from a German Point of View . . . . . . . 107

*Laura Ervo*
Class Actions – Scandinavian Novelties . . . . . . . . . . . . . . . . . 118

Discussion . . . . . . . . . . . . . . . . . . . . . . . . 127

## *Chapter 3*
## Taking Evidence Abroad

*Nicolò Trocker*
Transnational Litigation, Access to Evidence and U.S. Discovery: Understanding American 'Exceptionalism' . . . . . . . . . . . . . . . . . 145

*Peter L. Murray*
Taking Evidence Abroad – Understanding American Exceptionalism 200

*Miklós Kengyel*
Taking Evidence Abroad – Hungarian Aspects . . . . . . . . . . . . . . . 214

*Laura Ervo*
Taking Evidence Abroad According to Finnish Law . . . . . . . . . . . 220

Discussion . . . . . . . . . . . . . . . . . . . . . . . . . . . . . . . 225

## *Chapter 4*
## Preclusive Effects of Foreign Judgments

*Rolf Stürner*
Preclusive Effects of Foreign Judgments – The European Tradition . . 239

*Laura Ervo*
Preclusive Effects of Foreign Judgments According to Finnish Law . . 256

Discussion . . . . . . . . . . . . . . . . . . . . . . . . . . . . . . . 262

Speakers' Profile . . . . . . . . . . . . . . . . . . . . . . . . . . . 275

# Opening of the Symposium

## Professor Shin-ichi Hirano, President of Nagoya University

Good morning ladies and gentlemen, distinguished guests. It is my great honour to have you here in Nagoya and to get together with you here in Nagoya city on this occasion of the International Symposium on Current Topics of Transnational Civil Procedure, which is the first symposium in a series of upcoming conferences to be held in Nagoya. On behalf of Nagoya University and on my own behalf, I would also like to take this opportunity to welcome you all to this symposium. A special welcome goes to those of you who have come from all over the world and outside of Nagoya. I believe some of you have not visited Nagoya before. Please relax and feel at home during your short stay in Nagoya and please enjoy this symposium.

Some of you I have already met during the opening ceremony of the Nagoya University Institute for Business Litigation in Freiburg. We opened the Institute in Freiburg on November 25th last year. I mentioned during my opening address then that the opening of the Institute was a very important milestone for us. Today I would like to point out that the holding of this symposium is another important milestone in the fruitful process of this project. I am aware that the theme of this symposium "Current Topics of Transnational Civil Procedure" is a matter of interest to many countries. I am, therefore, confident that the symposium will offer a good opportunity for the experts of various fields present to share experiences and formulate appropriate recommendations on how best to address the issues relating to this topic. It is now my pleasure and privilege to declare this first symposium open.

I wish you a good symposium and a happy and enjoyable stay in Nagoya, especially those of you who have travelled long distances to come to Nagoya. Thank you very much for attending, and I hope you have fruitful discussions and results. Thank you very much.

## Professor Haruo Saburi, Dean of the Graduate School of Law, Nagoya University

Welcome to Nagoya. In particular, I would like to extend my heartfelt welcome to the guests who have come all the way to Japan from Europe and America. I would like to say a few words regarding our sponsor. This symposium is the first international symposium of the special project titled "Establishing a new framework for realizing effective transnational business litigation", which we submitted in a proposal to the Japan Society for the Promotion of Science, for a grant towards creative scientific research. Also, regarding myself, I am a specialist in international law and international economic law and I consider the activities of WTO.

Nowadays, many social systems have collapsed and transnational company activities have been expanding. The market economy has been expanding horizontally as well as vertically with economic globalization. Since its birth, the WTO has been active in the legal resolution of various conflicts. The handling of conflicts by the WTO entails dealing with economic conflicts between nations. However, as the economy becomes globalized, it is more and more important to have a legal framework to resolve economic conflicts between private persons transnationally, which is quite clear even for a private person.

In order to have a clear understanding about the current status of transnational civil procedures, it is of great significance for us to have an international symposium with esteemed guests from Europe and the US. Despite economic globalization, there are differences in legal cultures and legal systems among different countries. Therefore, for future harmonization and mutual understanding, international or transnational civil procedural law is very important. This first symposium marks a beginning for this project. I believe the symposium is an important starting point towards the success of this project. I hope we have a fruitful discussion at this symposium and that we are moving towards a brighter future thanks to your cooperation.

Thank you very much.

## Professor Masanori Kawano, Nagoya University

Good morning, Ladies and Gentlemen. Welcome to Nagoya. I greatly appreciate the very warm greetings from Professor Hirano, President of our University and the Dean, Professor Saburi. Many friends and distinguished scholars from around the world are here today. This is the first symposium for our project. Although the preparation period was very short, fortunately many participants who came here to attend are also good friends. It is my pleasure and honour to be holding such a very interesting symposium.

Before we start our symposium, I would like to explain our project briefly. You have all heard about it by now. It is an international cooperative project for the discussion of current problems in transnational litigation, especially in the field of business disputes. Recently, there have been, on the one hand, tendencies towards economic globalization and calls for harmonization of national legal systems, especially transnational litigation systems. On the other hand, it is not so easy to harmonize transnational litigation systems. Harmonization also entails retaining and respecting the special characteristics and legal history and legal cultures of each country. It is not easy to realize this.

For that purpose, we would like to encourage and further promote mutual understanding, international studies, and cooperation. Unfortunately, until now, we did not have such opportunities. For a long time, of course, we discussed comparative studies for the previously mentioned purposes. But for those purposes, we mainly used books or printed materials. As you know, printed materials are not always up to date, so if you are looking for information on actual problems, it is necessary to discuss with each other. This is why I think that we have to establish human relationships or human networks for that purpose. This is the main reason why I wanted to establish this project. It is a five-year project and this is the first symposium. My plan is to have such a 'get-together' at least once a year in Nagoya. But, in addition, I would like to have such a symposium, for example in Freiburg, Germany, perhaps in September of this year (2006), which I am discussing with my colleagues.

Unfortunately, one professor from Lyon, Professor Ferrand, could not attend today's symposium, but she promised me that she would hold a similar symposium in Lyon next year. I would like to discuss certain international problems not only in Japan, but also in Europe, for example. Moreover, in Europe and the United States, there is no good information available on the Japanese system. Therefore, another goal is to give some information about the Japanese legal system to our foreign colleagues. These are the first steps of our project.

Fortunately for this symposium, we have many guests from foreign countries. Here I would like to, very briefly, introduce some members. First of all, I would like to introduce our colleagues: Professor Stürner from Germany, Professor Murray from Harvard in the United States, Professor Trocker from Florence, Italy, Professor Kengyel from Hungary, Professor Andrews from Cambridge in England, and Professor Ervo from Finland. They are the 'permanent staff' of our project. We already discussed future cooperation in a meeting last night. We would like to start our international cooperation from this year and continue for five years.

Thank you very much for your attention.

*Chapter 1*

# Provisional Measures and Prohibitory Injunctions

# Provisional Measures for Prohibition of Actions – New Tendencies in Japan

*Masanori Kawano*

*Contents*

I. Introduction . . . . . . . . . . 7
II. Need for immediate remedies for resolving new kinds of disputes . . . . . . 8
III. A recent business case . . . . . . . . . . 12
IV. Characteristics of Japanese procedure of provisional measures . . . . . . . . 13
V. Transnational aspect of business disputes and provisional remedies . . . . . 16
VI. Final considerations. . . . . . . . . . 16

## I. Introduction

Timeliness of legal remedies is one of the most important aspects of effective justice. Delayed legal remedies mean sometimes non justice and are regarded as the same of it's deny. In the most countries timeliness of remedies has been and is always a subject of discussion of legal reform and amendment of legislation and practice. The ordinary system of civil justice, however, because of its nature to provide fair procedure, contains inevitably some time consuming formality with full procedural equipments. In most jurisdictions, therefore, parallel or followed by ordinary civil procedure, provisional remedies before ordinary judgments have been developed and provided for applying to the immediate and adequate relief required urgently.[1] Without such provisional remedies civil justice can not satisfy social needs for resolving different kinds of urgent disputes swiftly. But they can perform their task only when the instruments work well. Effectiveness and satisfaction of such legal remedies can be proved mainly by their real social function and satisfaction of the need for them.

Compared with ordinary civil procedures, such provisional procedures are composed of special summary procedures. Our discussions should be focused

[1] General view of provisional measures in European countries, see, *Stürner*, Einstweiliger Rechtsschutz, Generalbericht, in *Storme* ed., Procedural Laws in Europe, 2003, p. 143; as to the new movement in Europe see, *Andrews*, Toward an European protective order in civil matters, in *Storme* ed., Procedural Laws in Europe, 2003, p. 267.

only on the judicial orders for prompt remedies to regulate legal relationship between parties before judgment. They are such instruments as *Hozen Shobun* in Japan, Einstweiliger Rechtsschutz in Germany[2], Preliminary Injunctions or Temporary Restraining Orders in the USA[3] or Injunctions in England[4]. Here "Provisional measures" will be used as a general term for describing such procedures.[5]

Provisional measures are provided in most jurisdictions as a legal remedy for securing and preserving realization of following judgments rendered by courts with ordinary procedures. In the European countries they have common roots, but the present features differ slightly from country to country.[6] Generally speaking, they are provided not only arrest for the money judgments, but also provisional measures for sequestering individual property. Provisional measures for regulating legal relationships between parties are provided, too. The last measures can be applied to many different kinds of urgent dispute. In our current social life there are many legal disputes which require temporal decisions for making peaceful relationships between disputing parties even temporally. Provisional measures for regulating temporal legal relationships, *einstweilige Verfügung auf Handlung* or *Unterlassung*, can have some direct function on the legal and social relationship between disputing parties. They invoke social attention to the judicial remedies.

My presentation will focus mainly on the new developments of the provisional measures especially for prohibiting from some actions of opponents in Japan. They relate to some business cases in which provisional measures were applied to the dispute between mega banks in Japan. They suggest some new tendencies of applying provisional measures as an instrument for resolving business disputes and deciding important business policies.

## II. Need for Immediate Remedies for Resolving New Kinds of Disputes

### 1. *Japanese system of provisional measures*

In Japan the provisional measures were provided in the Code of Civil Procedure of 1890 which was the first modern code of civil procedure based on the German Code of Civil Procedure of 1877. Provisional measures were provided in "Book 6 Coercive Enforcement". They were provided as a part of civil enforce-

---

2 *Baur/Stürner/Bruns*, Zwangsvollstreckungsrecht, 13. Aufl. 2006, Rdnr. 50.1.

3 *James/Hazard/Leubsdorf*, Civil Procedure, 5th ed., 2001, p. 338.

4 *Andrews*, English Civil Procedure, 2003, 18.41, 18.44 (Classification of injunction).

5 Brussels I Regulations Section 10 uses "Provisional, including protective, measures".

6 As to the common roots of provisional measures of regulations in European countries, *Stürner*, Einstweiliger Rechtsschutz Generalbericht, op. cit. note 1, p. 169.

ment, and attached part of it. They were regulated by only 26 simplified provisions. Before the Second World War provisional measures were not popularly applied, and consequently they were paid scant attention from academic world. There was no successful attempt to encourage to use them, nor to prove their problems or to amend them. They kept their original features for about 90 years.

First in 1979, the provisions relating to the enforcement in the Code Civil Procedure were totally amended and were divided from the Code of Civil Procedure and established as an independent form as the Code of Civil Enforcement. As to the provisional measures, however, only the part of their execution was moved into this new Code of Civil Execution, but without substantive changes, and other parts of them remained in the Code of Civil Procedure. The consequence of this reformation was somewhat grotesque: Procedures of provisional orders and their enforcement were separately provided in different codes.

In 1989 regulations of provisional measures were totally rearranged and were provided as a form of independent code. The new code, "Code of Civil Provisional Remedies, or *Minji Hozen-hoh* promulgated in 1989, came into force on January 1, 1991. This code contains 67 articles and provides also attached Rules of Civil Provisional Remedies with 48 articles.[7] This Code is a general code for provisional measures applied to normal civil cases, for which civil procedures are regarded as main procedures.

The Japanese system of provisional measures based originally on the German system[8] was changed by the new Code of 1989. Fundamental structure and characteristics of German system remain. They are composed of previous tentative orders by the court and their enforcement procedures. They can be applied to freeze the defendant's property to secure successful enforcement of money judgments and to secure individual objectives of litigation to prevent to be dismissed. They can be applied to regulate the temporal legal relationships. These provisional measures for regulating a legal situation or *status quo* have had a different function: They decide the legal relationship tentatively. But they have a real function to decide it definitely by the interference of the court order, even though they were reserved the subsequent examination by the ordinary procedures. Sometimes because of the radical interference by them and of the definite changes of urgent situations between disputing parties, they make no use of reexamination in the following ordinary procedure. By considering such radical influences there have been such practical tendencies that they were ordered after the time consuming examination by the court. But such a practice

---

[7] According to Article 77 of the Japanese Constitution, Supreme Court is given a rule-making power relating to the procedural matters.

[8] Book 8 Chap. 5 of the German Code of Civil Procedure of 1877.

was contrary to their original functions of the provisional measures. They should be changed to rehabilitate their original functions as a timely remedy.

## 2. *Case Developments of Provisional Measures in Japan*

Before the Second World War provisional measures were not popular and were not used frequently in Japan. Such situations were changed just after the end of the Second World War in Japan. At the time, because of the social and economic confusion after the total destruction, there occurred many new and serious daily disputes which required immediate solution. They were brought to courts and provisional measures especially for tentative regulation have been applied. Depending on the changing situations in Japanese society, provisional measures have been applied to the various types of disputes:[9]

First, at the time just after the end of World War II and until the 1960s, there were many disputes relating to housing problems and labor relationships. Because of scarcity of houses in Japan provisional measures for evacuation of houses were applied frequently. At the time labor relations were not sure and the workers were not paid satisfactorily. There were many labor disputes. In labor cases petitioners who were discharged of their positions have applied provisional measures for securing their *status quo*.

Secondly, from the 1970s, there were many disputes relating to construction and to nuisance cases. In these times the Japanese economy has been rehabilitated immediately and developed very actively. But they brought some shadow sides, too: Constructions of high buildings destroyed the situation of surrounding neighbors seriously. They applied provisional measures for prohibiting from further construction. Active economic activities brought nuisance and pollution of water, noise, shock, ground subsides and bad smell etc. There were many cases to apply provisional measures for prohibiting from such harmful economic activities.

In such cases of provisional measures, courts examined cautiously because of their serious influences on the social relationships between disputing parties. So the examination had been made sometimes by oral hearings like an ordinary civil procedure. Under the old system the decision of courts in such cases had to be rendered only by the form of judgment.[10] The procedures were operated similar to the ordinary procedure of the main litigations. It was called the shifting phenomenon of provisional measures into ordinary procedure.

As a consequence of the old system of Japanese procedure of provisional measures their examination required long time. They were criticized because of

[9] Generally, *Takeshita/ Fujita* ed., Minji hozen-hou (Law of Civil Provisional Measures), 1997, p.2.

[10] Old Code of Civil Procedure Art.741 Sub.2, § 922 ZPO: Court Decision should be given in the form of judgment, if the examination was rendered after oral hearing, otherwise by a simple order.

their delay and ineffectiveness as an immediate dispute resolution system. There were many arguments and social call for their reform. Especially to change the procedure for provisional orders to promote and to realize speedy examination was urgent. The codification of civil provisional measures for revised procedure was an effort to change situations of provisional measures radically and to realize timely and effective remedies by provisional measures in Japan. It was the first step of an attempt to realize the effective civil justice and the following changes of the civil justice system in Japan.

### 3. *General Characteristics of Japanese Revised Provisional Measures*

Because of the necessity to establish effective provisional measures the Code of Civil Provisional Remedies was promulgated.[11] The new Code purported to promote effectiveness of provisional measures by establishing speedy and proper procedures by removing temptation to the time consuming examination for orders.

(1) General structure of the Japanese system of provisional measures remains. It is divided into two parts, provisional order and its enforcement, and it provides following types of provisional orders, like the former Code and those of the German system:[12]

1. Provisional attachment for the following enforcement of money judgment to preserve defendant's assets.
2. Provisional orders for protecting the objectives refraining from disposal by the defendant. This order will be issued to preserve the specific objectives of the litigation for securing following enforcement.
3. Outside the normal remedies to preserve possibilities of the following enforcement, there is a provisional measure to preserve *status quo*.

(2) The main point of amendments in the new Code was procedure for provisional orders. It provides purified summary procedures and all court decisions will be rendered by the form of simple order ("Kettei" or *Beschluß*) without exception. Under the old system because of difficulties of cases sometimes oral hearings were hold, but once there was an oral hearing the decision of the court should be "Judgment".[13] Under the new Code, application can be proved without oral hearings, or discretionally by oral hearing. Even in latter cases the decision of the court should be rendered by the simple court order (*Beschluß*).[14]

---

[11] The Code was passed on December 15, 1989 and was promulgated on December 22, 1989.

[12] Generally, *Murray/Stürner*, German Civil Justice, 2004, p. 433 ff.

[13] Art. 742 sec.1 of Japanese old Code of Civil Procedure.

[14] Art. 3 of new Code of Civil Provisional Remedies.

Under the new Code procedures of objection[15] and in appellate instance their decisions are rendered by the simple order, too. It was a legislative answer to resolve practical difficulties which suffered the procedure of Japanese provisional measures: Delay of procedure, especially based on the oral hearings which were necessary in the appellate instance and the order was made once by oral hearings in the original instance. Under the new Code the law makers tried to eliminate the matters which were argued as causes of delay to prove cases. Courts changed their attitude to the provisional measures and tried to examine pending cases swiftly and to give orders timely. Such attempts were accepted socially and they brought good echoes.

## III. A Recent Business Case

### 1. *New waves in business disputes*

In the last decade in Japan there have been observed some symptoms or waves of changing application of provisional measures. They were relating to the changing situation of the Japanese business world. For long time they provided in Japanese business world a tendency and tradition that Japanese business entities avoided to file cases with courts for resolving their business disputes. Especially big business entities have avoided publicly opened resolution before courts. One of the reasons of such behaviors was hidden arrangements by the Japanese administrative powers. They have arranged the relationships between big business entities by administrative instruction. One good example was the banking sector. Because of the serious social and economic influences of bank activities there have been strong arrangements by the Japanese financial ministry. But in the last two decades due to the developing deregulation such arrangement by administrative powers was blamed and such instructions were abandoned. Banks should decide their economic policy by themselves and there was no authoritative moderator for arranging their opposing policies. There occurred inevitably some disputes. They should be required to resort to courts for resolving their legal and business disputes by fair decision of courts. They imposed serious responsibility to courts for establishing orders timely and fairly.

### 2. *UFJ Bank Group v. Sumitomo Trust Bank*

One of the legal disputes paid attention publicly was the dispute between Japanese mega-banks relating to the contract of their merger.

---

[15] In this procedure it is required to have an oral hearing or hearings of adverse parties to avoid surprise, Art. 29 new Code of Civil Provisional Remedies.

For long time of the Japanese economic depression, one of the most important problems was how to deal with the mass bad loans which could be a cause for the endangered future of mega banks themselves. The *UFJ Bank Group* (*UFJ*) suffered substantially and decided to sell its trust branch and planned to increase capital for recovering the financial situation by themselves. *UFJ* negotiated with *Sumitomo Trust Bank* (*Sumitomo*) for selling the trust division of the *UFJ*. May 21, 2004 they reached the fundamental agreements. But just after that day, the *UFJ* faced some serious problems and realized the impossibility of self recovery. So *UFJ* gave up the negotiation with *Sumitomo* and decided to negotiate with the *Mitsubishi Tokyo Financial Group* (*Mitsubishi*).

June 16, 2004 *Sumitomo* filed with the Tokyo District court provisional measures against *UFJ* for prohibiting negotiations with *Mitsubishi* because of the fundamental agreements. In the agreements there was a provision relating to the monopolized negotiation with *Sumitomo*. The first decision by the Tokyo District Court was ordered on July 27, which agreed the validity of the clause on the monopolized negotiation with *Sumitomo* and ordered to refrain from negotiation with *Mitsubishi*. Against this first decision, *UFJ* filed a motion the next day. August 4, the Tokyo District Court decided the case and did not accept the motion and affirmed the decision. On the same day *UFJ* filed now with the Tokyo Appellate Court a *Kokoku* appeal. August 11, the Tokyo Appellate Court decided the case and reversed the decision on the ground that the fundamental agreement did not have validity because of the destruction of their *bona fide* relationships and it was not possible to keep their relationship for establishing final agreements. *Sumitomo* filed a special appeal for admission with the Supreme Court. August 30, the Supreme Court decided finally to reject the appeal of *Sumitomo*.[16]

This dispute was decided within very short time as one-and-a-half months from the beginning of court procedure in Inferior to the final order by the Supreme Court. The decisions have very serious influences and impacts on business activities of the leading banks. It shows that the judicial decisions could have functions to intervene into business activities and to have leading roles in the business world, which requires immediate decisions.

## IV. Characteristics of Japanese Procedure of Provisional Measures

The *UFJ* case shows that the Japanese System of provisional measures recovered their possibilities as immediate remedies. It must be an effect of the recent amendments of the system.

[16] Order of the Supreme Court on August 30, 2004, *Saikousai Minnshuh*, Report of the Supreme Court Decisions, Vol. 58 No.6. p. 1763.

One of the most significant points which can be observed in the recent developments in Japanese provisional measures cases is that the Japanese big business entities resorted to court for resolving their business disputes immediately. In business activities it is required to get decision immediately; otherwise they loose their business chance. On the other hand if the dispute is complex and serious, some credible and persuasive dispute resolution is required. It is sure that the court decision is fair and sometimes reasonable and understandable to all people who have interests in business activities. Especially in corporate cases it is necessary that the dispute resolution should be fair and reasonable and persuasive to the stock holders; otherwise they would sue the responsible persons of the unreasonable dispute resolution by stock holder's representative suit.[17] But if they can not trust the feasibility of the immediate decisions by courts, it is risky to use them easily. For long time there has been such prejudice of public that the Japanese court decision could be rendered after long proceedings. In this business between two Japanese leading mega- bank-case we can point out some important changes of social evaluation to the revised Japanese system of provisional measures.

On the one hand, as mentioned, one of the key points by which such immediate procedure of provisional measures could be realized in Japan was the introduction of simplified procedure. Provisional Measures should be ordered through summary procedures and their results should be rendered by simple order by the court. Their examination should be provided by the simplified proof of the matters. In the new system the possibilities of time consuming procedure have been abolished and replaced with summary procedures consequently.

But on the other hand, the case was serious and sensitive. In the cases of business disputes, provisional orders play decisive effects on the relationship between disputing parties. It is true that even the provisional measures for regulating legal relationship subordinate to the following "main litigation", regarded as a fundamental characteristic of provisional measures. Under the German system of civil procedure provisional measures have been regarded "provisional or tentative" remedies until the time that a final judgment will be rendered. *Leipold*[18] explained the necessity of provisional measures of the German system as follows: Final legal protection by ordinary judgment can not be rendered immediately, because the procedures require necessary long period. The task of provisional measures is to bridge such time span. He pointed out consequently that in all cases the purpose of provisional measures was devoted to the *intermediary* regulation.[19] The fundamental principle of subordination of provisional measures to the main litigation is accepted in the Japanese new

[17] See, Art. 847 Code of Corporation.
[18] *Leipold*, Grundlagen des einstweiligen Rechtsschutzes, 1971, p. 83.
[19] *Leipold, op. cit.*, p. 84.

Code, too.[20] But in such business cases as mentioned above the relationships between disputing parties can be decided by the provisional orders definitely. In the UFJ case a main litigation followed. But it was the law suit to resort the damages by breach of contract, and it was a subordinate nature. Here can be seen the converted role of provisional measures and following "main" litigation.

For the order of the provisional measures for *status quo* the oral hearing or the fixed date for hearing of the opponent should be required for securing procedural fundamental rights of opponents because of the potential possibilities of damages by the measures against him.[21] By such oral hearing the court can hear directly the main issues and legal arguments from both parties. It is very useful for their immediate decision.

In the procedure of provisional measures there are two main requirements which should be met by the applicant:

One is the requirement that the applicant has a substantive right which justifies the measures. As to the requirement there is some discussion whether it is necessary for the provisional measures. Sometimes it is not so easy to clarify the substantive right. Like in Germany[22] and in England, there are arguments in Japan[23] which assert not to require the substantive right as a fundamental condition for the provisional measures especially for *status quo*.

The second requirement is the "necessity" of the provisional measures. This is the cardinal requirement for the provisional measures especially for the status quo. If the applicant can not satisfy to show such urgent circumstances, the court can not render the provisional order required by him.

In the business cases it is clear that the relief by the court should be given immediately, but the legal situation should be proved carefully and sometimes the court required some legal decision based on professional consideration of the business law.

---

[20] Art. 37 sub. 1 Code of Civil Provisional Remedies provides: "The court rendered a provisional order should order on the petition of debtor to the creditor that he should file main claim within reasonable period and to present a document which shows the filing and falls the claim already filed the document shows the fling should be presented to the court." Art. 37 subs. 3 of Code of Civil Provisional Remedies provides: "If the creditor did not present the document within the period ordered on the sub. 1, the court should on the petition of debtor withdrawal the rendered order of provisional measure."

[21] Art. 23 IV Code of Civil Provisional Remedies.

[22] *Leipold, op cit*, p. 88.

[23] *Hasebe, Karino kyuusai niokeru Shinnrino Kouzou* (Legal Structure of Examination in Provisional Remedies), Hoh-kyou, Bd. 101. No. 10, p. 1495.

## V. Transnational Aspect of Business Disputes and Provisional Remedies

The Japanese system of provisional measures has redressed by the new Code its function as immediate remedies. But in the business world litigations in court were not popular for their business dispute resolutions. Especially provisional measures were not applied for their immediate dispute resolution. Recently there can be seen some changes of environment of the Japanese business world; one is the increase of corporate litigations and the other is their international integration.

Since last decade corporate litigations have been filed increasingly. They were law suits of stock holder's representative suit. They made on one hand corporate litigation as popular equipment for controlling corporate activities. It is necessary to decide some problems by court procedure as a fair and reliable dispute resolution. Provisional measures could be resorted for immediate dispute resolution if they were possible to resolve cases timely.

On the other hand, Japanese business has been integrated in the transnational cooperation and investigation. There are disputes with transnational aspects. In such context one of the problems is whether provisional measures should be internationalized. Except some examples[24], traditionally provisional measures do not have cross-border effects. But in our international committee it is required to develop some cooperative measures for the immediate remedies, especially in the aspects of transnational business activities. For realizing such transnational provisional measures especially for *status quo*, the procedure for the provisional measures should be reconsidered and international harmonization of provisional measures could be realized.[25]

## VI. Final Considerations

An ordinary civil procedure requires inevitably some period for the final judgment by time-consuming and sometimes complex proceedings, which are regarded as indispensable nature for final judgment by the court. But such requirements could be a difficulty for asserting business cases before the court. Immediate remedies should be provided especially for the business disputes. In the business world, timeliness of decision or of their dispute resolution is one of the fundamentals for their vital activities. If the civil justice could be applied for resolving business disputes it must be conformed to their requirements. Timeli-

[24] E.g., world wide freezing injunction in England.
[25] No. 17 of ALI/ Unidroit Principles of Transnational Civil Procedure.

ness of legal remedies is one of the indispensable parts. For the immediate dispute resolution the role of provisional measures is dominant.

Expanding business requires adequate dispute resolution systems with transnational aspects. Whether provisional remedies should be transnationally rearranged, should be considered, but carefully. Even in the transnational business activities immediate dispute resolution should be provided. Otherwise business activities in the transnational dimension must be very risky. Promoting effective legal remedies in the transnational situations, harmonized transnational provisional measures should be established. Profound gaps between globalization of economic activities, technological developments for the swift exchange of information, transportation and our legal devices by which we have to resolve new disputes should be filled. Provisional measures should prove their real efficiencies and feasibilities as an immediate legal remedy in transnational aspects, too.[26]

[26] See, *Schack*, Internationales Zivilverfahrensrecht, 4. ed., 2006, No. 412 and 413.

# Accelerated Justice: Protective, Interim and Summary Procedures in English Law

*Neil H. Andrews*

*Contents*

1. Introduction . . . . . 18
2. Protective Relief . . . . . 19
   A. Preservation of Assets: Freezing Injunctions . . . . . 20
   B. Preservation of Evidence: Search Orders . . . . . 30
   C. Protection of Defendant: Security for Costs . . . . . 35
3. Interim Relief . . . . . 38
   A. Interim Payments . . . . . 38
   B. Interim Injunctions . . . . . 40
   C. Preliminary Issues . . . . . 46
4. Accelerated Forms of Final Judgment . . . . . 47
   A. Summary Judgment . . . . . 47
   B. Striking Out Claims or Defences . . . . . 51
   C. Default Judgment . . . . . 55

## 1. Introduction

The terminology of protective, interim, conservatory, and provisional orders is confused.[1] The author has chosen, therefore, to present a range of pre-trial procedures some of which are protective, some are interim, and some involve final judgment on the substance, but by a summary procedure without oral evidence at trial. These topics can be conveniently grouped under the heading 'accelerated justice'.

[1] On these topics, see Neil Andrews, *The Modern Civil Process*, 2008, Ch.'s 4 and 5; for other references, see Neil Andrews 'Provisional and Protective Measures: Towards an Uniform Provisional Order' (2001) Uniform L Rev (Rev dr unif) vol VI at pp 931, at 933-5; and for the position in international commercial arbitration, A Redfern, 'Interim Measures' in LW Newman and RD Hill (eds) *The Leading Arbitrators' Guide to International Arbitration* (Bern, 2004), at 217ff; see also Stephen Goldstein, 'Revisiting Preliminary Relief in Light of the ALI/UNIDROIT Principles and the New Israeli Rules' in *Studia in honorem: Pelayia Yessiou-Faltsi* (Athens, 2007) 273–96.

English law provides three main types of accelerated justice:[2] 'protective relief': namely, ancillary protection of the claimant or defendant (in this paper we will consider freezing injunctions, search orders, and security for costs orders); secondly, interim judgment (whether payment or injunction); thirdly, final judgment by an accelerated or summary mode. As for this last category, the four main forms are:

(i) *summary judgment* (under CPR Part 24) is awarded if the claimant or defendant has 'no real prospect' of success at trial;
(ii) the court can *strike out* a 'statement of case', whether a claim, defence, reply, or counterclaim, or any part of one, if it 'discloses no reasonable grounds for bringing or defending the claim ... is an abuse of the court's process ... or [because of a party's] failure to comply with a rule, practice direction or court order.'
(iii) *judgment by default* takes place when the defendant fails to defend or indicates that he is unwilling to defend;
(iv) *small claims procedure* concerns relatively modest claims for less than £5000 (or less than £1000 if the claim is for personal injury) [small claims will not be discussed here].

## 2. Protective Relief

Protective protection of the claimant's interests takes several forms: orders for the freezing of the defendant's assets (freezing injunctions, formerly *Mareva* injunctions), for the seizure and preservation of evidence (search orders, formerly *Anton Piller* orders). These are more commonly applied before trial and usually 'without notice' to the defendant, that is (to use the former terminology), they are awarded *ex parte*. Another form of protective relief is an order for security of costs against a claimant. This order protects the defendant against the risk that the claimant might be unwilling or unable to pay the defendant's costs if the action ends with a costs order in favour of the defendant. These various forms of protective relief will now be examined.

[2] For US material J Resnik and O Fiss *Adjudication and Its Alternatives* (Foundation Press, New York, 2003) 813ff.

## A. Preservation of Assets: Freezing Injunctions[3]

### Nature

Formerly known as *Mareva* injunctions, these have been re-named 'freezing injunctions'.[4] The injunction's function is to preserve assets from dissipation pending final execution against the defendant. A freezing injunction does not give the applicant any proprietary interest in the defendant's assets.[5] This injunction is an *in personam* order which compels a defendant to refrain from dealing with his assets. It also imposes a collateral restraint upon non-parties, such as the defendant's bank.

The injunction commonly applies to the defendant's bank account or other liquid assets. The order normally provides that a portion of those assets, above a protected sum, should remain 'unfrozen'. The defendant is permitted to satisfy his ordinary domestic or business expenses, and to pay for legal advice when resisting the order.[6]

The injunction operates at first 'without notice' (*ex parte*), usually before the main proceedings against the defendant have commenced. Its essence is a surprise procedural strike, but the merits of the order are reviewed at an *inter partes* hearing, when the court must decide whether it should be continued or discharged.

---

[3] The leading work is S Gee, *Commercial Injunctions* (2004); see also N Andrews *English Civil Procedure* (Oxford UP, 2003), ch 17; *Zuckerman on Civil Procedure* (2006) 9.139ff; IS Goldrein (ed), *Commercial Litigation: Pre-emptive Remedies* (International Edition, 2005) ch 2; for extensive bibliographical details on this topic, see N Andrews *English Civil Procedure* (Oxford UP, 2003), 17.01 at n 7 and Neil Andrews 'Provisional and Protective Measures: Towards an Uniform Provisional Order' (2001) Uniform L Rev (Rev dr unif) vol VI at pp 931–49, at n 4 (this article contains analysis of a possible 'blue-print' for an international code or practice relating to freezing relief, preservation of evidence, and asset disclosure orders); for another valuable discussion, concerning the position in international commercial arbitration, A Redfern, 'Interim Measures' in LW Newman and RD Hill (eds) *The Leading Arbitrators' Guide to International Arbitration* (Bern, 2004), 217–43, and on the same context see M Mustill and S Boyd's *Commercial Arbitration* (2002, Companion Volume, London) at 314–6, 323–4, considering, respectively, ss 39, 44, Arbitration Act 1996; see also on those provisions the Departmental Advisory Committee (on the Arbitration legislation), on clauses 39, 44 (the report is reproduced in *Russell on Arbitration* (2003), appendix 3); the arbitral tribunal has power under s 39, 1996 Act, but only if the parties consent, to make a 'provisional' decision on the substance of the case, for example for an interim payment; the High Court has power under s 44, 1996 Act, to award (ex parte) freezing relief or a search order in support of pending or contemplated arbitration proceedings, if the matter is 'urgent'; therefore, the arbitral tribunal itself lacks power to award ex parte freezing relief or search orders.

[4] CPR 25.1(1)(f) renames the injunction.

[5] *Cretanor Maritime Co Ltd v Irish Marine Maritime Ltd* [1978] 3 All ER 164, CA; *Capital Cameras Ltd v Harold Lines Ltd* [1991] 1 WLR 54; *Flightline v Edwards* [2003] 1 WLR 1200, CA.

[6] PD (25); for examination of the legal expenses exception, *United Mizrahi Bank v Doherty Ltd* [1998] 1 WLR 435.

An application for a freezing injunction can be made, however, at any of the following stages: in anticipation of proceedings (whether the main proceedings will be in England or elsewhere); after commencement but before judgment on the substance of the dispute; and after judgment.[7] A person can only make repeated applications for 'without notice' relief on the same facts if either he uncovers new evidence or there is a justifiable change of argument. Otherwise, an unsuccessful applicant can only appeal.[8] However, issue estoppel does not arise from an unsuccessful application for 'without notice' relief.[9]

Most freezing injunctions are awarded by the High Court rather than the county courts.[10]

Freezing injunctions, although introduced by the courts, were ratified by Parliament.[11] Part 25 of the CPR now provides the standard form applicable to such injunctions.[12]

*Ancillary Disclosure Orders*

Freezing injunctions are supported by an ancillary disclosure order. This compels the respondent to disclose details of his assets in England (or, where appropriate, elsewhere),[13] whether or not in his own name, and whether or not solely owned.[14] Cross-examination of a respondent on the accuracy of this disclosure is possible even though the respondent has already disclosed an amount of assets sufficient to cover the applicant's substantive claim.[15]

A person (including non-parties, see next paragraph) who is subject to such an ancillary order can sometimes invoke the privilege against self-incrimination and refuse to provide information.[16]

Although in general a non-party is under no obligation to disclose information to a party before trial (the so-called 'mere witness rule'), such a non-party

---

[7] Eg, post-judgment, *Flightwise Travel Service Ltd v Gill The Times* 5 December 2003, Neuberger J; [2003] EWHC 3082 (Ch).

[8] *Laemthong International Lines Co Ltd v ARTIS* [2005] 1 Lloyd's Rep 100; [2004] 2 All ER (Comm) 797, Colman J at [24].

[9] Ibid at [65].

[10] PD (25): Masters or District judges to make such orders only in special cases.

[11] S 37(3), Supreme Court Act 1981.

[12] PD (25).

[13] *Derby & Co Ltd v Weldon (No 1)* [1990] Ch 48, CA; *Derby & Co Ltd v Weldon (Nos 3 & 4)* [1990] Ch 65, 86, 94–5, CA; *Bank of Crete SA v Koskotas* [1991] 2 Lloyd's Rep 587, CA; LA Collins (1989) 105 LQR 262, 286ff; C McLachlan "The Jurisdictional Limits of Disclosure Orders: Transnational Fraud Litigation" (1998) ICLQ 3–49.

[14] PD (25); *AJ Bekhor & Co Ltd Bilton* [1981] 1 QB 923, CA; *A* v *C (Note)* [1981] 1 QB 956, Goff J; *Bankers Trust Co* v *Shapira* [1980] 1 WLR 1274, CA.

[15] *Motorola Credit Corpn* v *Uzan (No 2)* [2004] 1 WLR 113, CA [138] to [147], per Millett LJ.

[16] *"SONANGOL" v Lundqvist* [1991] 2 QB 310, CA.

can be compelled to provide certain information if he has assisted, albeit innocently, another's wrongdoing.[17]

*Dangers of 'Without Notice' Proceedings*

Freezing injunctions[18] must be handled with the utmost care because they are available upon an application 'without notice' (formerly denoted as *'ex parte'* injunctions). The respondent initially has no opportunity to contradict the applicant's submissions.

*Threshold Criteria for the Grant of Freezing Injunctions*[19]

The following conditions must be satisfied before a freezing injunction can be awarded.

*'Good, Arguable Case'.* First, the applicant must show a good arguable case that he is entitled to damages or some other underlying relief. This is a low threshold: but the House of Lords in 2007 held that a freezing injunction had been invalidly awarded when the applicant had made no attempt at all to indicate the nature of its substantive claim.[20]

*Cause of Action Has Accrued.* The court must also be satisfied that the underlying cause of action has 'accrued'. This means that the respondent has already committed a breach of duty or a debt obligation has arisen. Such liabilities cannot be merely anticipated.[21]

---

[17] On the 'mere witness' rule, see *Norwich Pharmacal Co v Customs and Excise* [1974] AC 133, HL and its *sequelae*, particularly, in the present context, *Bankers Trust Co v Shapira* [1980] 1 WLR 1274, CA, *Arab Monetary Fund v Hashim (No 5)* [1992] 2 All ER 911, Hoffmann J.

[18] And search orders, on which see Section 2 B below.

[19] *Flightwise Travel Service Ltd v Gill The Times* 5 December 2003, Neuberger J; [2003] EWHC 3082 (Ch) at [18] to end, contains a good re-statement of various forms of protection aimed at ensuring that freezing relief is applied fairly.

[20] *Fourie v Le Roux* [2007] UKHL 1; [2007] 1 WLR 320; on the level of proof, *Ninemia Maritime Corpn v Trave* [1983] 2 Lloyd's Rep 600, *per* Mustill J (approved [1983] 1 WLR 1412, CA, *per* Kerr LJ); cf the more demanding test applicable to interim payments; on different perceptions of an applicant's claim by successive Commercial Court judges, see the facts of *Laemthong International Lines Co Ltd v ARTIS* [2005] 1 Lloyd's Rep 100; [2004] 2 All ER (Comm) 797, Colman J.

[21] *Veracruz Transportation Inc v VC Shipping Co Inc ('The Veracruz')* [1992] 1 Lloyd's Rep 353, CA, noted LA Collins (1992) 108 LQR 175–81 (expressing the hope that the House of Lords might reverse this decision); *Zucker v Tyndall Holdings plc* [1992] 1 WLR 1127, CA, noted R Harrison (1992) New LJ 1511-2; *Dicey. Morris and Collins on the Conflict of Laws* (14th edn, 2006) 8-009 (also 8-022ff) also criticize e the *Veracruz* case, noting also Lord Nicholls' doubts in the *Mercedes Benz* case [1996] AC 284, 312, PC (in a dissenting judgment on another aspect), and preferring contrary Australian authority, *Patterson v BTR Engineering (Australia) Ltd* (1989) 18 NSWLR 319, NSWCA; W Kennett, *The Enforcement of Judgments*

*Real Danger of Dissipation.* There must also be a real risk that the respondent's assets will be removed or dissipated unless the injunction is granted.[22] The court must be satisfied that there is clear and strong evidence of such a risk.[23]

'Dissipation' includes any act of alienation or charging of property,[24] with the exception of innocent transactions made in the ordinary course of business.[25] However, dissipation need not be unconscionable or heinous. It is enough that the court is satisfied that the applicant's eventual judgment will go unsatisfied unless a freezing injunction is granted.[26]

*Scope of Assets.* The order can include assets in the defendant's name, even if he is the trustee or nominee for a third party.

*Freezing Injunction Essential.* The court must also be satisfied that the applicant will be unable to receive satisfaction of the claim unless he receives an injunction.[27] The court will take into account whether the applicant already has adequate security against such a risk.[28]

*Assessment of Harm to Respondent.* The injunction must be necessary and a fair response, on the facts:

> '... the court [must be] satisfied that any damage which the respondent may suffer through having to comply with the order is compensatable under the cross-undertaking or that the risk of uncompensatable loss is clearly outweighed by the risk of injustice to the applicant if the order is not made.'[29]

---

*in Europe* (Oxford UP, 2000), 161, n 97, notes that the *Veracruz* position is not adopted in Austria, Germany, or to an extent Belgium.

[22] *Refco Inc v Eastern Trading Co* [1999] 1 Lloyd's Rep 159, 171, CA, *per* Morritt LJ (no such risk on the facts).

[23] *Laemthong International Lines Co Ltd v ARTIS* [2005] 1 Lloyd's Rep 100; [2004] 2 All ER (Comm) 797, Colman J at [60], citing *Thane Investments Ltd v Tomlinson* [2003] EWCA Civ 1271.

[24] Dispositions, pledges, charges; in *CBS UK Ltd v Lambert* [1983] Ch 37, 42, CA, *per* Lawton, LJ and in *Z Ltd* v *A-Z* [1982] 1 QB 558, 571, CA, *per* Lord Denning MR, both cited the words "otherwise dealing with" in s 37(3), Supreme Court Act 1981.

[25] PD (25).

[26] *Ketchum International plc v Group Public Relations Holdings Ltd* [1997] 1 WLR 4, 13, CA; *Commissioner of Customs & Excise v Anchor Foods Ltd* [1999] 1 WLR 1139 (if D's proposed transaction is *bona fide*, the court's discretion to grant injunction should be exercised very circumspectly); this factor was not satisfied in *Re Q's Estate* [1999] 1 All ER (Comm) 499, Rix J.

[27] *Etablissements Esefka International Anstalt v Central Bank of Nigeria* [1979] 1 Lloyd's Rep 445.

[28] *Refco Inc v Eastern Trading Co* [1999] 1 Lloyd's Rep 159, 171, CA, *per* Morritt LJ.

[29] *Re First Express Ltd The Times* 8 October, 1991, *per* Hoffmann J.

### *Undertakings by Applicant*[30]

The injunction's standard provisions require the applicant, *inter alia*, to:

indemnify the respondent if the injunction is wrongly granted; and the applicant should provide a guarantee to support this undertaking;[31] the court can order the applicant to provide a guarantee bond in case it becomes necessary to compensate the respondent by invoking this cross-undertaking;[32]

indemnify the reasonable costs of any non-party complying with the order, or compensate for any loss caused by the order (subject to the court's control), whether or not the injunction is properly granted; and

issue and serve his claim form straightaway, unless this is inappropriate because the main proceedings are to take place, or are pending, in another jurisdiction;

swear an affidavit confirming what was said to the Court by the applicant's lawyers;

serve details on the respondent for the return date and supporting documents to be considered on that occasion; and

inform all interested persons promptly if the order ceases to have effect, for whatever reason;

the applicant also undertakes to return to court;[33] at this 'with notice' hearing (formerly described as the'*inter partes* review'), the court can re-consider the merits of the injunction and whether to continue it.

### *The Duties of the Court and Applicant*

'Without notice' relief is exceptional and cannot be granted 'on the nod'.[34] An applicant must reveal to the court all material considerations and facts.[35] He should take reasonable steps to investigate matters.[36] The applicant's lawyers'

---

[30] PD (25).

[31] Ibid.

[32] Ibid.

[33] Ibid.

[34] *Memory Corporation plc v Sidhu* (No 2) [2000] 1 WLR 1443, 1460, CA; on the problem of multiple applications before different judges on essentially the same facts, *Laemthong International Lines Co Ltd v ARTIS* [2004] 2 All ER (Comm) 797, Colman J, or at [2005] 1 Lloyd's Rep 100.

[35] PD (25); leading case are: *Brink's Mat Ltd v Elcombe* [1988] 1 WLR 1350, CA; *Lloyds Bowmaker Ltd v Britannia Arrow Holdings plc* [1988] 1 WLR 1337, CA; *Behbehani v Salem* [1989] 1 WLR 723, CA; and (an important survey) *Memory Corporation plc v Sidhu (No 2)* [2000] 1 WLR 1443, 1453-6, CA, *per* Robert Walker LJ; *Re S (A Child) (Family Division: Without Notice Orders)* [2001] 1 WLR 211, 219, 222–3 Munby J; *Knauf UK GmbH v British Gypsum Ltd* [2002] 1 WLR 907, CA.

[36] *Bird v Hadkinson The Times* 7 April, 1999.

(counsel and solicitor) must also refrain from misleading the court. They too must make full and frank disclosure.[37]

Failure to make full disclosure will normally cause the injunction to be summarily set aside. However, the court might excuse an innocent failure to disclose if either of two conditions is met: first, the failure probably made no difference to the decision to grant the injunction;[38] or if, taking into account the context of the case, the interest in providing freezing relief, especially to combat fraud, outweighs this aspect of procedural fairness.[39]

*Variation of the Freezing Injunction*

The respondent has 'a right to ask the Court to vary or discharge' the injunction.[40]

*Satisfaction or Security*

The injunction will cease to apply if the respondent pays into court a sum specified in the injunction or provides security as agreed with the applicant's lawyers.[41]

*Freezing Injunctions and Contempt by the Respondent*[42]

A respondent will be in contempt of court if he breaches an injunction:[43] if his breach is aggravated ('contumacious'), he can be fined, imprisoned or, in the case of a company, suffer sequestration of assets. Contempt by a respondent requires only gross or prolonged negligence, for example, where a company or other complex body fails to ensure that its officers, employees or agents comply with the order.[44]An applicant will also be in contempt if he fails to satisfy the

---

[37] *Memory Corporation plc v Sidhu (No 2)* [2000] 1 WLR 1443, 1455, CA, *per* Robert Walker LJ.

[38] *Brink's Mat Ltd v Elcombe* [1988] 1 WLR 1350, 1358, CA; *Lloyds Bowmaker Ltd v Britannia Arrow Holdings plc* [1988] 1 WLR 1337, 1347, CA (these two statements were cited in *Memory Corporation plc v Sidhu (No 2)* [2000] 1 WLR 1443, 1454 CA); *Behbehani v Salem* [1989] 1 WLR 723, CA; *Gulf Interstate Oil Corpn LLC v Ant Trade & Transport Ltd of Malta ('the Giovanna')* [1999] 1 Lloyd's Rep 867; in *Laemthong International Lines Co Ltd v ARTIS* [2005] 1 Lloyd's Rep 100; [2004] 2 All ER (Comm) 797, Colman J at [64] held that a failure to reveal a comment made by another judge in an earlier and unsuccessful 'without notice' application did not satisfy this 'decisive influence' test ...

[39] *Marc Rich & Co Holdings GmbH v Krasner* (CA, unreported, 17 January, 1999).

[40] PD (25).

[41] PD (25).

[42] The Court of Appeal in *Motorola Credit Corpn v Uzan* (No 2) [2004] 1 WLR 113, CA [45]-[58], [148]-[156] reviewed many of these matters.

[43] *Federal Bank of the Middle East Ltd v Hadkinson* [2000] 2 All ER 395, 411, CA.

[44] *Z Bank v D1* [1994] 1 Lloyd's Rep 656, Colman J, consistent with *dictum* of Steyn LJ in *Guildford BC v Valler The Times* 15 October, 1993, CA; on the duty to respond to an order for information, *Bird v Hadkinson The Times* 4 March, 1999, Neuberger J (respondent to answer accurately after exercising reasonable care).

numerous undertakings given or implied when the order was granted (see above).

*Impact of Freezing Injunctions upon Non-Parties*

*Basic Limits of Freezing Injunctions.* Freezing injunctions do not confer proprietary rights upon successful applicants.[45] More generally, non-parties are not to be unreasonably inconvenienced by these orders. It follows that they can apply to the court to authorise the respondent to pay a pre-existing debt. Nor does the injunction prevent a non-party from honouring its contractual obligations owed to other non-parties.[46] Furthermore, the injunction should not apply to property which is manifestly owned by a non-party. However, injunction can apply to property jointly owned by the respondent and a non-party[47] or where the latter has acquired the relevant assets from the respondent in suspicious circumstances.[48]

*Duty of Non-Parties Not to Obstruct a Freezing Injunction.* Once notified, a non-party is obliged not to act inconsistently with the terms of the injunction.[49] It is common to notify the respondent's bank(s) of the injunction even before he receives notice. The bank must then refrain from undermining the injunction's efficacy by continuing to honour its client's cheques and instructions, except where such dealings are permitted by the order.[50]

A non-party, such as the respondent's bank, will be in contempt if it deliberately or 'knowingly' acts, or omits to act, with the result that the injunction is undermined, or if it aids and abets the respondent's primary breach of the order.[51] The courts are, however, mindful that it would be unrealistic and even oppressive to require such a non-party bank to inquire closely into the propriety of every transaction conducted by its client. The standard order makes this clear:

'No bank need enquire as to the application or proposed application of any money withdrawn by the Respondent if the withdrawal appears to be permitted by this Order.'[52]

---

45 *Cretanor Maritime Co Ltd v Irish Marine Maritime Ltd* [1978] 3 All ER 164, CA; *Capital Cameras Ltd v Harold Lines Ltd* [1991] 1 WLR 54; *Flightline v Edwards* (2003) [2003] 1 WLR 1200, CA.

46 *Galaxia Maritime SA v Mineralimportexport* [1982] 1 WLR 539, CA.

47 *SCF v Masri* [1985] 1 WLR 876, CA; injunctions can be granted against joint bank accounts, PD (25).

48 An instructive case is *Mercantile Group (Europe) AG v Aiyela* [1994] QB 366, CA (spousal transfer).

49 PD (25).

50 *Z Ltd v A* [1982] QB 558, CA.

51 PD (25); *Z Ltd v A* [1982] QB 558, 567, CA, *per* Eveleigh LJ; cf, consistently, *Re Supply of Ready Mixed Concrete (No 2)* [1995] 1 AC 456, HL; and *Att-Gen v Newspaper Publishing plc* [1997] 3 All ER 159, 169, CA.

52 PD, (25); *Ryan v Friction Dynamics Ltd The Times* 2 June, 2000, Neuberger J.

Non-parties are entitled to an indemnity from the applicant for expenses incurred in respecting or carrying out the injunction, for example, the expense incurred by a bank when searching its records to find the respondent's account(s).[53]

### *Non-Party's Only Duty of Care is to the Court*

The non-party is only liable to the court, in accordance with the contempt of court principle, just mentioned. In *Customs & Excise Commissioners* v *Barclays Bank plc* (2006) the House of Lords[54] (reversing the Court of Appeal) held that the non-party (a bank) owes no duty of care to the recipient of freezing relief. The facts were as follows. The bank had mistakenly transferred funds covered by these injunctions after receiving notification of the relevant order. As a result, the claimants could only recover a small percentage of their debts from the respondent creditors. And so the claimants alleged that the bank owed a duty of care in the tort of negligence to apply the freezing injunction properly applied to its customer's accounts (the bank's customer being the defendant, and debtor, in the main proceedings). Lord Bingham gave various reasons for denying such a duty. Perhaps the most telling point was this:

> '... it cannot be suggested that the customer owes a duty to the party which obtains an order, since they are opposing parties in litigation and no duty is owed by a litigating party to its opponent [citing authorities]. It would be a strange and anomalous outcome if an action in negligence lay against a notified party who allowed the horse to escape from the stable but not against the owner who rode it out.'

### *Freezing Injunctions and Foreign Assets*[55]

Freezing injunctions can apply to assets located outside England and Wales. 'Worldwide' freezing injunctions are now commonly granted by the English courts.[56] The applicant can gain both attachment of foreign assets and an order compelling the respondent to provide information relating to such assets. The disclosure order can operate on a worldwide basis even where the attachment

---

[53] PD (25); earlier, *Searose Ltd v Seatrain (UK) Ltd* [1981] 1 WLR 894, CA.

[54] [2006] 3 WLR 1, HL; [2006] UKHL 28 (reversing [2004] EWCA Civ 1555; [2005] 1 WLR 2082).

[55] C McLachlan, "Extraterritorial Court Orders Affecting Bank Deposits" in Meessen (ed), *Extraterritorial Jurisdiction in Theory and Practice: Symposium Held at Dresden on 8–10 October 1993* (Deventer, 1996).

[56] PD (25); *Babanaft Co SA v Bassatne* [1990] Ch 13, CA; *Republic of Haiti v Duvalier* [1990] QB 202, CA; *Derby & Co v Weldon* (No 1) [1990] Ch 48, CA; *Derby & Co Ltd v Weldon (Nos 3 & 4)* [1990] Ch 65, CA; LA Collins, "The Territorial Reach of *Mareva* Injunctions" (1989) 105 LQR 262–99; LA Collins, ch's VIII and IX, in *Essays in International Litigation* (Oxford UP, 1993); *Dicey, Morris and Collins on the Conflict of Laws* (14th edn, 2006) 8-011 ff; D Capper, "Worldwide *Mareva* Injunctions" (1991) 54 MLR 329–48; A Malek and C Lewis "Worldwide Injunctions – The Position of International Banks" (1990) LMCLQ 88; Rogers [1991] LMCLQ 231.

element of the same injunction is confined to assets situated in England.[57] It has also been suggested that a post-judgment disclosure order can operate without an attachment of assets.[58]

It has been suggested that the power to order disclosure is of greater practical and tactical importance than the main freezing injunction.[59] The English freezing injunction is here really a 'holding operation' to give the claimant time to apply to the relevant foreign court(s) for appropriate supplementary or substantive relief.[60]

To prevent oppressive proceedings, an applicant cannot make a related application for enforcement of a world wide English freezing order in a foreign jurisdiction without first obtaining the English court's permission. The Court of Appeal in *Dadourian Group International Inc v Simms* (2006) enumerated eight principles in this regard. For reasons of space, these will not be recited here.[61]

Non-parties resident in other jurisdictions are protected by the following provision (the so-called, '*Babanaft* proviso'):[62]

> 'The terms of this Order do not affect or concern anyone outside the jurisdiction of this Court until it is declared enforceable or is enforced by a Court in the relevant country and then it shall affect him only to the extent it has been declared enforceable or has been enforced *unless* such person is:
>
> (i) a person to whom this Order is addressed or an officer of or an agent appointed by a power of attorney of such a person; or
>
> (ii) a person who is subject to the jurisdiction of this Court and (a) has been given written notice of this Order at his residence or place of business within the jurisdiction of this Court and (b) is able to prevent acts or omissions outside the jurisdiction of this Court which constitute or assist in the breach of the terms of this order.'

### *Foreign Assets, Non-Parties and Conflict Between the English Freezing Injunction and Foreign Law*

The Court of Appeal in *Bank of China* v *NBM LLC and Others* made the following amendment (the so-called, '*Baltic* proviso') to freezing injunctions which have extra-jurisdictional effects:[63]

---

[57] *Gidrxslme Shipping Co Ltd v Tantomar-Transportes Maritimos Lda* [1994] 4 All ER 507, 519, Colman J.

[58] *ibid*, 519–20, *per* Colman J; if the freezing relief is sought *pre*-judgment, it seems the freezing element is a *sine qua non* for the disclosure order: *Grupo Torras SA v Sheikh Fahad Mohammed Al-Sabah* CA, unreported, 16 February, 1994), summarized (1994) New LJ 942; for other developments, K Lloyd (1994) New LJ 1482 and 1556.

[59] *Credit Suisse Fides Trust SA v Cuoghi* [1998] QB 818, 827–8, CA, *per* Millett LJ.

[60] *Babanaft International Co SA v Bassatne* [1990] Ch 13, 41, CA, *per* Nicholls LJ.

[61] [2006] EWCA Civ 399; [2006] 1 WLR 2499; [2006] CP Rep 31 at [25] with commentary on each at [26] ff; noted T Rutherford (2006) NLJ 837.

[62] Reformulated in PD (25); this protection originated in *Babanaft Co SA v Bassatne* [1990] Ch 13, CA).

[63] [2002] 1 All ER 717, CA; noting the proviso's genesis in *Baltic Shipping v Translink*

'It is further ordered and directed that nothing in this order shall, in respect of assets located outside England or Wales, prevent [the non-party bank] or any of its subsidiaries from complying with:

1. What it reasonably believes to be its obligations, contractual or otherwise, under the laws and obligations of the country or state in which those assets are situated or under the proper law of any bank account in question; and

2. Any orders of the courts of that country or state provided reasonable notice of any application for such an order by [the non-party bank] or any of its subsidiaries (to the extent such notice is permitted by the criminal law of such country or state), is given to the claimant's solicitors.'

### *English Protective Relief in Support of Primary Litigation in Another EU Member (or Lugano Contracting) State*[64]

The English High Court can grant freezing injunctions and connected orders for disclosure of assets in support of substantive proceedings throughout the world, whether or not the relevant foreign jurisdiction which is, or will be, entertaining the main claim is affiliated to the Brussels or Lugano regimes.[65]

### *Relevant Factors When Considering Whether to Support Foreign Proceedings*

In *Motorola Credit Corpn v Uzan (No 2)* the Court of Appeal, having reviewed the leading authorities, identified five factors:[66]

'whether the making of the [English supportive] order will interfere with the management of the case in the primary [foreign] court, e.g., where the order is inconsistent with an order in the primary court or overlaps with it';

secondly,

'whether it is the policy in the primary jurisdiction not itself to make worldwide freezing/disclosure orders';

thirdly,

'whether there is a danger that the orders made will give rise to disharmony or confusion and/or risk of conflicting inconsistent or overlapping orders in other jurisdictions, in

---

*Shipping Ltd* [1995] 1 Lloyd's Rep 673, Clarke J; the proviso is now incorporated into PD (25).

64 *Dicey, Morris and Collins on the Conflict of Laws* (14th edn, 2006) 8-024; G Maher and BJ Rodger, "Provisional and Protective Remedies: The British Experience of the Brussels Convention" (1999) 48 ICLQ 302 (a detailed account; also examining Scots decisions).

65 S 25, Civil Jurisdiction and Judgments Act 1982; The Civil Jurisdiction and Judgments Act 1982 (Interim Relief) Order 1997, (SI 1997, No 302) (the 1982 Act, s 25, gives effect to the United Kingdom's obligation to effectuate Article 24 of the 1968 Brussels Convention (now Article 31 of the Brussels I Regulation); from 1 April, 1997, the English High Court's jurisdiction to grant interim relief under the 1982 Act was extended in two important respects: to include non-Convention and non-Member countries; and to apply to civil proceedings outside the rather restricted scope of Article 1 of the Brussels Convention and its successor, the 'Brussels I Regulation'-'civil or commercial matters'.

66 [2004] 1 WLR 113, CA at [115].

particular the courts of the state where the person enjoined resides or where the assets affected are located. If so, then respect for the territorial jurisdiction of that state should discourage the English court from using its unusually wide powers against a foreign defendant';

fourthly,

'whether at the time the order is sought there is likely to be a potential conflict as to jurisdiction rendering it inappropriate and inexpedient to make a worldwide order';

fifth,

'whether in a case where jurisdiction is resisted and disobedience to be expected, the court will be making an order which it cannot enforce.'

On the facts of the present decision this last factor justified discharging freezing relief aimed at two co-defendants resident in Turkey, and who did not have assets in England.[67] However, the remaining co-defendants did have residential and proprietary connexions with England, and so the court maintained freezing relief against these.[68]

*'Bayer v Winter' Orders*

The English courts can restrain a defendant from leaving the jurisdiction and compel him to surrender his passport.[69]

### *B. Preservation of Evidence: Civil Search Orders*[70]

*Nature*

The civil search order (formerly known as an *Anton Piller* order) enables the applicant to swoop like a hawk upon the defendant and seize vital evidence be-

---

[67] Ibid at [125]–[126].

[68] Ibid at [127] and [128].

[69] Neil Andrews, *Principles of Procedure* (1994), 8–50 to 8–053; *Dicey, Morris and Collins on the Conflict of Laws* (14th edn, 2006), paras 8–010, 19–022; leading modern cases are *Bayer v Winter (No 1)* [1986] 1 WLR 497, CA, *Re Oriental Credit* [1988] Ch 204; *Lipkin Gorman v Cass The Times* 29 May, 1985; *Al Nakhel for Contracting and Trading Ltd v Lowe* [1986] QB 235, Tudor-Evans J (decided 2 says before the *Bayer* case); *Allied Arab Bank v Hajjar* [1988] QB 787, Leggatt J; the court has a statutory power in the case of a bankrupt, s 333, Insolvency Act 1986, on which see *Morris v Murjani* [1996] 1 WLR 848, CA; for academic discussion, see L Anderson, 'Antiquity in Action ...' (1987) 103 LQR 246; and case notes by C Harpum [1986] CLJ 189 and Neil Andrews [1988] CLJ 364; for Israeli abandonment of this protective remedy, Stephen Goldstein, 'Revisiting Preliminary Relief in Light of the ALI/UNIDROIT Principles and the New Israeli Rules' in *Studia in honorem: Pelayia Yessiou-Faltsi* (Athens, 2007) 273–96; in South Africa, civil orders restraining prospective defendants from fleeing the jurisdiction ('arrest *tamquam suspectus de fuga*') have a long tradition: Wouter de Vos (Rhodes University) report to the Brazil (2007) World Congress (South African national report on the 'pre-action phase', forthcoming).

[70] Re-named as such, CPR 25.1(1)(h); the standard order is prescribed by PD (25); S Gee, *Commercial Injunctions* (2004); Neil Andrews, *English Civil Procedure* (2003) ch 17; *Zucker-*

fore it can be conveniently lost or destroyed. These orders have been found useful in tackling breaches of intellectual property rights and confidentiality. They are not nearly as common as freezing injunctions (discussed above).

Search orders are ancillary injunctions requiring the respondent to permit the applicant to inspect premises and to remove or secure evidence of any alleged wrongdoing. The order is made *ex parte*, that is, 'without notice' to the respondent. The order authorises a limited number of persons, normally a solicitor acting for the applicant, to enter the respondent's premises within normal working hours and to search for evidence, property or other material falling within the categories of the order. After the respondent is served with the order, he has a short period within which to consult a lawyer, and immediately becomes subject to an obligation to comply with the order, otherwise she will be in contempt of court.[71] Subject to that pause, the applicant is entitled to remove the material so that it can be safeguarded, or at least take copies, samples, or other records made.[72]

A search order can be granted before or after the main proceedings have commenced, or even after judgment.[73] When granted in anticipation of the main proceedings, the applicant must undertake to commence and serve notice of the main action without delay.[74] Only the High Court can issue such an order.[75]

*Genesis of Search Orders*

The jurisdiction emerged in 1974 as a judicial application of the wide statutory power to grant injunctions contained in the Supreme Court Act 1981[76], as well as an instance of the court's 'inherent jurisdiction'. It was first applied in *EMI Ltd* v *Pandit.*[77] The Court of Appeal quickly ratified the innovation in the eponymous decision, *Anton Piller* v *Manufacturing Processes.*[78] In one of his autobiographical works, Lord Denning provided a vivid account of the birth of *Anton Piller* relief.[79] The jurisdiction has now been placed on a statutory basis.[80]

---

*man on Civil Procedure* (2006) 14.175 ff; IS Goldrein (ed), *Commercial Litigation: Pre-emptive Remedies* (International Edition, 2005) ch 3.

[71] PD (25).

[72] S 7(4)(b), Civil Procedure Act 1997.,

[73] On this last situation, *Distributori Automatici Italia SpA v Holford General Trading Co Ltd* [1985] 1 WLR 1066.

[74] PD (25).

[75] S 7(8), Civil Procedure Act 1997.

[76] S 37(1), 1981 Act.

[77] [1975] 1 WLR 302.

[78] [1976] Ch 55, CA.

[79] Lord Denning, *The Due Process of Law* (1980) 123–130.

[80] S 7, Civil Procedure Act 1997, following recommendation of a Committee of Judges appointed by the Judges' Council, "Anton Piller Orders: A Consultation Paper" ("The Staughton Committee"), Lord Chancellor's Department, November 1992; for comment, M Dockray &

*Controversial Relief*

Search orders come within a whisker of infringing the constitutional prohibition upon speculative search warrants of premises. Lord Denning employed the theory of the respondent's consent to justify this departure from constitutional practice.[81] After statutory ratification of these orders in 1997, the emphasis on requiring the owner's consent diminished.[82] Thus the order is now directed at 'any person' and requires him 'to permit any person described in the order ... (a) to enter premises in England and Wales ...'[83] Lord Mackay LC (a former Lord Chancellor) explained in Parliament in 1996 that:

> 'The main purpose of [this clause] is to dispense with the fiction that the entry on the premises is with the consent of the owner/respondent ... [The clause] will have the effect that in future it is more clearly the court order which is the basis of the requirement to permit entry, not the implied consent of the owner.'[84]

*Search Orders and the European Convention on Human Rights*

In *Chappell* v *UK* the European Court of Human Rights considered a challenge under Article 8 of the Convention to the execution of a civil search order upon domestic premises.[85] Although the court found no breach in the present case, its comments led to intensification of English controls upon these orders.

*Criteria for the Award of Search Orders*

In the Judges' Council report into these orders, it was said that search orders rest upon: 'The overriding principle ... of necessity. No such order ought to be made unless it is necessary in the interests of justice. No such order ought to be made in wider terms than is necessary to achieve the legitimate object of the order.'[86]

The following criteria govern the decision whether to make an order: (1) a search order must not be used as a means of fishing for a cause of action;[87] (2) the applicant must have a very strong *prima facie* case on the substance of the

---

K Reece Thomas, (1998) 17 CJQ 272); see also s 72, Supreme Court Act 1981 (privilege against self-incrimination; s 7(7), Civil Procedure Act 1997 Act, also acknowledges this privilege).

[81] *Anton Piller KG v Manufacturing Process Ltd* [1976] Ch 55, 60, CA.

[82] S 7, Civil Procedure Act 1997, following recommendation of a Committee of Judges appointed by the Judges' Council, "Anton Piller Orders: A Consultation Paper" ("The Staughton Committee"), Lord Chancellor's Department, November 1992; for comment, M Dockray & K Reece Thomas, (1998) 17 CJQ 272.

[83] Ibid.

[84] *Hansard*, vol 576, col 900, 19 December, 1996.

[85] (1990) 12 EHRR 1 and (1989) FSR 630, ECHR; *Chappell v UK* was considered by a South African court in *Dubelstein v Hildebrandt* 1996 (3) SA 42.

[86] Report into "Anton Piller Orders" (a Consultation Paper, Lord Chancellor's Department, 1992) para, 2.3.

[87] *Hy-trac v Conveyors International* [1983] 1 WLR 44, CA.

main complaint;[88] (3) there must be a very serious risk of damage to the applicant's interests unless this special order is granted;[89] (4) the court must be satisfied both that the respondent possesses relevant material and that he will destroy this material unless subjected to a surprise search;[90] (5) 'the harm likely to be caused by the execution of the ... order to the respondent and his business affairs must not be excessive or out of proportion to the legitimate object of the order.'[91]

*Disclosure Order Ancillary to Search Order*

A standard feature of search order practice is that the respondent is ordered to reveal the identity of co-wrongdoers.[92] The applicant can use information concerning non-parties to launch separate or related proceedings against those co-wrongdoers.[93] But he must not disclose these details to other non-parties, such as the Police, Customs and Excise and the Inland Revenue.[94]

*Controls Upon Execution of Search Orders*

A criminal search warrant and a civil search order should not be simultaneously executed at the same premises, because that would be oppressive.[95]

Search orders and freezing injunctions share many procedural features (see discussion above of the applicant's duty to make full disclosure of material facts before receiving the order and his undertaking to indemnify the respondent if the order is later held to have been wrongly granted). The standard order also contains numerous provisions aimed at controlling the process of executing these orders, especially the seizure of material.[96] There should be an independent and supervisory solicitor present to ensure fair-play and prevent oppression.[97] He must not be an employee or member of the applicant's firm of solicitors and should be suitably experienced.[98]

---

88 *Anton Piller KG v Manufacturing Processes Ltd* [1976] Ch 55, 62, CA, *per* Ormrod LJ.

89 Ibid.

90 Ibid, at 59–60, *per* Lord Denning: "grave danger that vital evidence will be destroyed".

91 Criterion proposed by the report into 'Anton Piller Orders', (Consultation Paper, Lord Chancellor's Department, 1992), para 2.8, following *Columbia Picture Industries v Robinson* [1987] 1 Ch 38, 76, and *Lock International plc v Beswick* [1989] 1 WLR 1268, 1281.

92 PD (25); earlier, *EMI Ltd v Sarwar & Haider* [1977] FSR 146; and see s 7(5), Civil Procedure Act 1997.

93 *Sony Corpn v Anand* [1981] FSR 398.

94 *Customs & Excise Commrs v AE Hamlin & Co* [1984] 1 WLR 509 (but Falconer J gave permission for the information to be used by a non-party); *EMI Records Ltd v Spillane* [1986] 1 WLR 967 and [1984] FSR 403 (in both cases permission for such use was refused).

95 PD (25).

96 Ibid; for earlier comment see, *Columbia Picture Industries Inc v Robinson* [1987] Ch 38.

97 PD (25); eg, *IBM v Prima Data International Ltd* [1994] 1 WLR 719, 724–5.

98 PD (25); for a rogue execution of a civil search order, where the supervisory solicitor

The applicant's solicitor and the supervisory solicitor can enter the premises while the respondent contacts and consults his lawyers. The respondent is also allowed to gather up material protected by legal professional privilege or the privilege against self-incrimination. Statutory provisions partially override the latter privilege in the context of offences under the theft legislation or in respect of protection of rights in intellectual property.[99] Subject to these qualifications, privileged material will be excluded from the search. This material will be checked and held safely by the supervisory solicitor.[100] No searching can begin until this process of consultation has taken place. However, the respondent can delay the search on this basis for a maximum of two hours.[101]

It is oppressive to execute a search order at the weekend, or before 9.30 am or later than 5.30 pm during a weekday.[102] The premises searched can be commercial, business or domestic premises, or a 'vehicle'.[103] These premises etc must be situated in England and Wales.

### *Setting Aside an Search Order*

The respondent can apply to the court for the order to be discharged or varied at the 'with notice' review, that is, on the 'return day'[104] specified in the main order. The defendant need not wait until then and can apply 'at any time' to have the order varied or discharged.[105]

### *Pre-Litigation Destruction of Documents or Other Evidence*

Sometimes a prospective defendant, sensing that litigation is imminent, will willfully destroy documents, delete e-mails, or take other steps to destroy evidence. Is the legal system powerless to respond to such 'spoliation' (as it is known in some jurisdictions?) This question was briefly examined at first instance in an English decision in *Douglas* v *Hello! Ltd* (2003).[106] The judge approved an Australian decision, which he summarised as follows: 'the criterion

lacked sufficient experience, *Gadget Shop Ltd v Bug.Com Ltd* [2001] CP 13, Rimer J, noted L Mulcahy, *Human Rights and Civil Practice* (2001), para 10.62.

99 Neil Andrews, *English Civil Procedure* (2003) 29.24 to 29.28 and (on possible reform) 29.56ff; B Thanki (ed), *The Law of Privilege* (2006) ch 8 and *Zuckerman on Civil Procedure* (2006) ch 17; see now Fraud Act 2006, s 13, on which Kensington v. Congo [2007] EWCA Civ 1128; [2008] 1 WLR 1144.

100 PD (25).

101 PD (25).

102 Ibid.

103 S 7(8), Civil Procedure Act 1997.

104 PD (25).

105 PD (25).

106 *Douglas v Hello! Ltd* [2003] 1 All ER 1087 (brief note); [2003] EWHC 55 (Ch), at [86].

for the Court's intervention ... is whether that [pre-action] destruction or disposal amounts to an attempt to pervert the course of justice ...'[107]

The Australian court held that destruction of documents or other evidence before the commencement of litigation might attract a sanction (in addition to the court henceforth drawing adverse inferences against that person) if that conduct amounts to an attempt to pervert the course of justice. The court left open the possibility that criminal contempt of court might also.[108]

### *C. Protection of the Defendant: Security for Costs*[109]

#### *Introduction*

A defendant can seek an order for security for costs against a claimant. The purpose of such an order is to protect the defendant against the risk that the claimant might not pay the defendant's costs if the claimant eventually becomes liable, or agrees as a term of settlement, to pay the defendant's costs. In fact security for costs is aimed at meeting one of three problems: that the claimant lacks sufficient funds; that he is a shifty litigant manifestly disposed to avoid liability for costs; that the procedural chase against the claimant would be uncertain and difficult because the foreign jurisdiction where he resides does not provide a straightforward and dependable system for enforcing an English costs order.

The security might take the form of a payment into court, or a banker's guarantee, or some other undertaking. A claimant who fails to comply with such an order will find either that the action is stayed until security is given or even that the action is struck out.

#### *Basic Rules*

There is no general right to security for costs: grant of security for costs is discretionary: it is never available automatically. CPR 25.13(1) states:

> 'The court may make an order for security for costs ... if (a) it is satisfied, having regard to all the circumstances of the case, that it is just to make such an order.'

An impecunious claimant resident in England or one of the Brussels or Lugano States cannot be made to provide such security simply on the basis of his inability to pay costs. To impose security against such a claimant would bar his access to justice.

---

[107] *British American Tobacco Australia Services Ltd v Cowell & McCabe* [2002] VSCA 197, esp at [173] to [175] (Supreme Court of Victoria, Australia).

[108] [173].

[109] Neil Andrews, *English Civil Procedure* (2003) ch 37; MJ Cook *Cook on Costs 2006* (2006) ch 13; P Hurst *Civil Costs* (4th edn, 2007) ch 15; *Zuckerman on Civil Procedure* (2006) 9.182ff; IS Goldrein (ed), *Commercial Litigation: Pre-emptive Remedies* (2005) ch 4; *Dicey, Morris and Collins on the Conflict of Laws* (14th edn, 2006), 8-092ff.

CPR 25.13(2) specifies six grounds (listed below). The defendant must establish any one of these grounds and then further satisfy the court that security should be awarded in exercise of its discretion (on the latter, see text below):

(1) the claimant is resident out of the English and Welsh jurisdiction but not resident in a Member State of the European Union or a Lugano Convention Contracting State; or
(2) the claimant is a company or other body (whether incorporated inside or outside Great Britain) and there is reason to believe that it will be unable to pay the defendant's costs if ordered to do so; or
(3) the claimant has changed his address since the claim was commenced with a view to evading the consequence of the litigation; or
(4) the claimant failed to give his address in the claim form, or gave an incorrect address in that form; or
(5) the claimant is acting as a nominal claimant, other than as a representative claimant under [CPR] Part 19, and there is reason to believe that he will be unable to pay the defendant's costs if ordered to do so; or
(6) the claimant has taken steps in relation to his assets that would make it difficult to enforce an order for costs against him.

*Factors Relevant To The Exercise Of The Discretion To Order Security For Costs*

The case law has identified the following factors which the court should considered when exercising its discretion whether to award security for costs:[110] (1) the action is a sham or is made in good faith; (2) the claimant has a reasonably good prospect of success in the case; (3) there is an admission by the defendant in the statement of case or elsewhere that the money is due or the claim is otherwise sound; (4) there is a substantial payment into court or offer to settle; (5) the application is being used by the defendant to stifle an honest and sound claim; (6) the claimant's lack of funds has been caused by, or aggravated by, the defendant's failure to pay; (7) the application for security for costs has been made late.

*Claimant Resident Outside England and Outside the Territories of the Brussels and Lugano Conventions*

The foreign residence ground (see above) potentially conflicts with Article 14 of the European Convention on Human Rights (now Schedule 1, Human Rights Act 1998) which prohibits direct or indirect discrimination by reference to: 'any ground such as sex, race, colour, language, religion, political or other opinion, national or social origin, association with a national minority, property, birth

---

[110] *Sir Lindsay Parkinson v Triplan Ltd* [1973] QB 609 at 626–7, CA, per Lord Denning MR.

or other status.' Most non-UK residents are likely to be non-UK citizens. And so the foreign residence ground in CPR 25.13, cited above, has the potential to infringe Article 14 (indirect discrimination by reference to nationality).

For this reason the Court of Appeal in *Nasser* v *United Bank of Kuwait* (2002) held that it would be improper for the English courts to 'start with any inflexible presumption that any person not resident in a Brussels or Lugano state should provide security for costs'.[111] Instead, exercise of this discretion should be based on 'objectively justified grounds relating to obstacles to or the burden of enforcement in the context of the particular foreign claimant or country concerned', such as 'substantial obstacles to or a substantial extra burden (e.g., of costs or delay) in enforcing an English judgment ...' In the *Nasser* case, the claimant was resident in the USA. US courts would recognize and enforce the English security for costs order. But this would be more difficult and expensive than if the costs order were to be enforced in a State within the Brussels or Lugano jurisdictional regimes. And so the Court of Appeal found an 'objective' justification on these facts to order security for costs against the American claimant.

*Security for the Costs of Appeal*

In the *Tolstoy* case, the defendant author had lost a libel trial, which had lasted forty days. He appealed. The Court of Appeal held that he must first provide £126,000 as security for the respondent's costs in conducting this appeal. Tolstoy unsuccessfully challenged this security for costs award before the European Court of Human Rights ('ECtHR').[112] The ECtHR attached weight to various features of the English appeal: (1) the security for costs application had been fully considered by the English Court of Appeal; (2) the English courts had considered the general balance of justice and had assessed the effect of the security of costs order against this background (3) the European Human Rights jurisprudence requires that any 'restrictions [on appeal] must pursue a legitimate aim and there must be a reasonable relationship of proportionality between the means employed and the aim sought to be achieved', for example by reference to time, security, or the prospective appeal's merits; (4) but the English award satisfied these criteria.

---

[111] [2002] 1 All ER 401, CA.

[112] *Tolstoy Miloslavsky v UK* (1995) 20 EHRR 442, EctHR.

## 3. Interim Relief

### *Introduction*

Litigation can be very slow. It is, therefore, expedient for the courts to have power to issue provisional or interim relief pending final disposal of the action. Surprisingly perhaps, the courts lacked power to order interim payments until 1969, whereas the equitable jurisdiction to issue interim injunctions is much older.

### *A. Interim Payments*[113]

Interim payments were at first confined to protect plaintiffs in personal injury or fatal accident claims.[114] In 1978 the system of interim payments was expanded to cover all damages or debt claims.[115]

The CPR retains interim payments, which are defined as:

> 'an order (referred to as an order for interim payment) under rule 25.6 for payment of any damages, debt or other sum (except costs) which the court may hold the defendant liable to pay.'[116]

### *General Conditions*

Such an order enables the claimant to recover at least a reasonable proportion of a money claim months or even a year or more before trial. This is fair, provided the claim has been admitted by the defendant or the court can provisionally decide that the claim has real strength on the merits. The rules permit such an order to be made in any of these three situations:[117] (1) the defendant admits liability but there is no immediate settlement of the claim; or (2) the claimant has obtained judgment against the defendant with the amount to be assessed; or (3) the court 'is satisfied' that, if the case went to trial, the claimant would obtain judgment for a 'substantial' monetary award against the defendant, other than costs.

### *The Standard of Proof in Interim Payment Applications*

The word 'satisfied' (see above) was usefully glossed in pre-CPR cases, and this guidance remains helpful. In short, the claimant who wishes to obtain interim

---

[113] CPR 25.6 to 25.9; and PD (25) 'Interim Payments'; Neil Andrews, *English Civil Procedure* (2003) 18–04ff; *Zuckerman on Civil Procedure* (2006) 9–205ff; IS Goldrein (ed), *Commercial Litigation: Pre-emptive Remedies* (2005) 590ff.

[114] S 20, Administration of Justice Act 1969.

[115] Responding to the criticism made in *Associated Bulk Carriers Ltd v Koch Shipping Inc* [1978] 2 All ER 254, CA, of the narrowness of this regime.

[116] CPR 25.1(1)(k).

[117] CPR 25.7.

payment in a context where the underlying claim is contested fully by the defendant will need to share roughly 70 *per cent* probability or more. That is a stiff test.

Thus in one case it was said: 'something more than a *prima facie* case is clearly required; but not proof beyond reasonable doubt. The burden is high. But it is a civil burden on the balance of probabilities, not a criminal burden.'[118] In another case, the court made clear that proof on a 'mere balance of probabilities' is not enough: '[the court must be] satisfied that the [claimant] will succeed and the burden is a high one: it is not enough that the court thinks it likely that the [claimant] will succeed at trial.'[119]

*Amount Awarded*

The sum awarded as interim payment must not be: *more than a reasonable proportion of the likely amount of the final judgment.*[120] Furthermore: *The court must take into account (a) contributory negligence; and (b) any relevant set-off or counterclaim.*[121]

For example, the court might conclude that the claimant is unlikely to obtain any net award at trial because the defendant's counterclaim, which is for a greater amount, is likely to be upheld at trial.[122] Or, where the claim is for £500, 000, but the court is confident that a contributory negligence defence of, say, 50 *per cent*, is likely to succeed at trial, the court would arrive at a provisional award of £250, 000. When deciding, next, how much to award as an interim payment, the court must exercise its discretion and fix a 'reasonable proportion' of that 'likely amount'.

For this purpose the court can take account of the following factors: (1) the strength of the claimant's claim; (2) whether the claim has been admitted; (3) whether the defendant has made a Part 36 settlement offer, and the amount of that offer;[123] (4) the interval which is likely to elapse between the date of the award and the trial or final disposal of the case; (5) whether the defendant can

---

[118] *Shearson Lehman Inc v MacLaine, Watson & Co Ltd* [1987] 1 WLR 480, 489, CA, *per* Lloyd LJ; *Gibbons v Wall The Times* 24 February, 1988, CA, cited *British & Commonwealth Holdings plc v Quadrex Holdings plc* [1989] 1 QB 842, 865, CA.

[119] *British & Commonwealth* case, *ibid*, at 866, CA, *per* Browne-Wilkinson V-C, which was cited by Balcombe LJ in *Andrews v Schooling* [1991] 1 WLR 783, 787, CA; *Crimpfil Ltd v Barclay's Bank plc The Times* 24 February, 1995, CA (held that a court can form impressionistic view of merits of an application even where liability and *quantum* are highly contentious and the issues are complicated).

[120] CPR 25.7(2).

[121] CPR 25.7(3).

[122] Eg *Shanning International Ltd v George Wimpey International Ltd* [1988] 3 All ER 475, CA.

[123] *Fryer v London Transport Executive The Times* 4 December, 1982, CA, supports this aspect of the discretion.

afford to pay;[124] (6) whether the claimant has a pressing need for the money; (7) the likelihood of the defendant's defences of contributory negligence and set-off succeeding in fact at trial; (8) the likely amount of final judgment; (9) the reasons why the claimant believes that the general conditions for awarding an interim payment are satisfied in the present case;[125] (10) details of special damages and past and future loss, in actions for personal injury; (11) in a fatal accidents claim, details of the person(s) on whose behalf the claim is made and the nature of the claim.

*Protection of the Defendant*

A claimant who has received an interim payment cannot discontinue the proceedings unless the defendant consents in writing or the court gives permission.[126] This rule protects the defendant against the risk that if the case had proceeded to trial it might have been shown that the sum was not in fact owed, or at least not in full.

The existence of an interim payment will not be disclosed to the court at trial until all questions concerning liability have been considered, unless 'the court directs', or the defendant agrees otherwise.[127]

*Repayment of Interim Payment*

A claimant might need to repay an interim payment, in whole or in part, in any of these situations: (1) because he has discontinued or settled the claim in circumstances where the interim payment becomes repayable; or (2) he has lost at trial; or (3) or received final judgment for less than the interim payment; or (4) the court has otherwise varied or discharged an interim payment order.

### B. Interim Injunctions

After the procedural amalgamation of the Common Law and Equity courts by the Judicature Acts 1873–5, the injunction became available throughout all three Divisions of the High Court (now Queen's Bench, Chancery, and Family). The court's statutory power to grant injunctions includes the power to issue interlocutory injunctions, that is, preliminary orders given before trial.[128]

---

[124] Eg *Newton Chemical Ltd v Arsenis* [1989] 1 WLR 1297; *British & Commonwealth Holdings plc v Quadrex Holdings plc* [1989] 1 QB 842, CA.

[125] See CPR 25.7.

[126] CPR 38.2(2)(b).

[127] CPR 25.9.

[128] S 37, Supreme Court Act 1981; Neil Andrews, *English Civil Procedure* (2003) 18–41ff; S Gee, *Commercial Injunctions* (2004) ch 2; IS Goldrein (ed), *Commercial Litigation: Pre-emptive Remedies* (2005) pp 1ff; *Zuckerman on Civil Procedure* (2006) 9–5ff; S Gee [2006] LMCLQ 181.

*Classification of Injunctions*

There are many divisions: (1) interim or final; (2) mandatory ('positive') or prohibitory (or 'negative'); (3) 'without notice' or 'with notice' to the defendant (formerly, *ex parte* or *inter partes*);[129] (4) *quia timet* (that is, anticipatory of a legal wrong) or injunctions which apply *ex post facto*; (4) before or after commencement of the main proceedings; (5) before or after judgment.[130] This section concerns interim injunctions, whether mandatory or prohibitory, awarded *inter partes* (with notice). 'Freezing injunctions' and 'search orders' are discussed above: they do not concern the substantive dispute but instead operate in a 'protective' fashion to maintain the monetary or evidential viability of pursuing or enforcing the main claim.

*'Cross-Undertaking' in Favour of Respondents*[131]

An applicant for an interlocutory injunction must give a cross-undertaking to indemnify the respondent (and in some situations non-parties) if the interlocutory order is subsequently held to have been improperly granted. However, an applicant's genuine impecuniosity will not preclude him from obtaining an interlocutory injunction even though his implied undertaking is not likely to be of any real value to the respondent.[132]

*Test for Award of Interim Injunctions Concerning the Substance of a Dispute*

Before 1974, it used to be the practice that an interim injunction would be granted only if the applicant could show a *prima facie* case on the merits.[133] Such decisions became a convenient source of speedy justice.[134] But the House of Lords in *American Cyanamid Ltd* v *Ethicon Ltd* (1974) changed this practice.[135] It held that, in general, the court should not consider a case's merits, especially complicated points of fact. Instead it should strive to balance the hardship to the applicant caused by refusal of relief against the hardship to the other party if he is temporarily bound by an injunction. Only in rare cases would it be necessary

---

[129] CPR 25.3.

[130] CPR 25.2(1), for these last two dichotomies.

[131] *F Hoffmann – La Roche & Co AG v Secretary of State for Trade & Industry* [1975] AC 295, 360–1, HL, *American Cyanamid Co v Ethicon Ltd* [1975] AC 396, 407–9, HL; on enforcement of the cross-undertaking, *Cheltenham & Gloucester Building Society v Ricketts* [1993] 1 WLR 1545, CA, *Goldman Sachs International v Philip Lyons The Times* 28 February, 1995, CA, *Barratt Manchester Ltd v Bolton MBC* [1998] 1 WLR 1003, CA; *Customs & Excise Commissioners v Anchor Foods Ltd* [1999] 1 WLR 1139; cf *Smithkline Beecham plc v Apotex Europe Ltd* [2006] EWCA Civ 658; [2007] Ch 71 at [23] ff.

[132] *Allen v Jambo Holdings Ltd* [1980] 1 WLR 1252, CA; *Re DPR Futures Ltd The Times* 29 November, 1989.

[133] *Hubbard v Vosper* [1972] 2 QB 84, CA; *JT Stratford & Son Ltd v Lindley* [1965] AC 269, 33, HL, *per* Lord Upjohn.

[134] Peter Prescott QC (1975) 91 LQR 168–71.

[135] [1975] AC 396, HL.

to consider the merits. Such consideration would be just and proper only if the court discovered no real difference in weight between the parties' respective potential hardships. Therefore, only in this (rather unusual) situation would consideration of the merits be permitted as a 'tie-breaking' factor.

*The Decision Itself*

The application concerned an alleged patent infringement of a medical substance. This factually complex litigation, requiring extensive expert evidence, would be likely to require a hearing lasting twelve days in the House of Lords. Prudently, Lord Diplock (and his colleagues) decided to eschew three weeks of expert evidence concerning biochemistry.

*The American Cyanamid Principles: Summary*

The elements of this test are as follows:

(1) Has the claimant proved that there is a serious question to be tried?
(2) If damages would not adequately protect a claimant's interests, would the defendant be adequately protected by the indemnification available under the claimant's cross-undertaking if the defendant won the case at trial?
(3) In all the circumstances, would the balance of convenience favour the award or refusal of the interim injunction? Relevant factors, declared the House of Lords, cannot be exhaustively stated, but include: the need to preserve the status quo; the extent of uncompensatable disadvantage to each party if he should succeed at trial having lost at the interim stage; the relevant strength of each party's case on the basis of the documentary material and lawyers' submissions made at the interim hearing.

*Situations Falling Outside the American Cyanamid Guidelines*

Later decisions have identified a network of special contexts where it would be wrong to follow the general *American Cyanamid* embargo upon considering a case's legal and factual merits.

*Where the Injunction Will Dispose Fully of the Litigation.* The court should investigate the merits if the grant or refusal of the interim remedy will dispose finally of the litigation, notably when the delay necessitated by waiting for trial would render the central dispute a 'non-issue' (for example, if a restrictive covenant clause has only three months to run).[136]

*Transparent Cases.* Where the issues are 'plain and uncontroversial' the courts should not hesitate to consider the substantive merits of the case.[137]

[136] *Cayne v Global Natural Resources Ltd* [1984] 1 All ER 225, CA.
[137] *Office Overload Ltd v Gunn* [1977] FSR 39, 44, CA, *per* Bridge LJ.

*Freezing Injunctions and Search Orders.* The court must be assured that the applicant for such an injunction has a *prima facie* case[138] because such relief is draconian and normally granted 'without notice' to the defendant.

*Mandatory Injunction.* A mandatory injunction compels the respondent positively to do something, such as 'thou shall build the wall, as agreed'. This type of order is more intrusive than a negative or prohibitory order (for example, 'do not build the proposed wall'). It would be inconvenient, wasteful and unjust first to make an interim order on tenuous evidence to build and then to require at trial the defendant to demolish. To avoid such inconsistent orders, the decision to make such a positive interim order requires a 'high degree of assurance that the claimant will win at trial.[139]

*Matters of Public Importance.* In some cases, issues of great public importance have been held to justify examining the case's merits at the interim stage.[140]

*Freedom of Expression and the Human Rights Act 1998.* The grant of interim injunctions is now subject to special provisions of the Human Rights Act 1998 which are designed to preserve freedom of expression. Section 12(3) states:[141]

No such relief is to be granted so as to restrain publication before trial unless the court is satisfied that the applicant is likely to establish that publication should not be allowed.

Section 12(4) provides:[142]

The court must have particular regard to the importance of the Convention right to freedom of expression and, where proceedings relate to material which the respondent claims, or which appear to the court, to be journalistic, literary or artistic material (or to conduct connected with such material), to

(a) the extent to which-
  (i) the material has, or is about to, become available to the public; or
  (ii) it is, or would be, in the public interest for the material to be published;
(b) any relevant privacy code.

In *Cream Holdings v Banerjee* the House of Lords held that the word 'likely' in the first of these provisions is intended to accord proper weight to the respond-

---

138 *Polly Peck International plc v Nadir (No 2)* [1992] 4 All ER 769, 786, CA, *per* Lord Donaldson MR.

139 *Shephard Homes Ltd v Sandham* [1971] Ch 340, Megarry J; see also *Locabail v Agroexport ('The Sea Hawk')* [1986] 1 WLR 657, CA affirming this exception to *American Cyanamid.*

140 *Smith v Inner London Education Authority* [1978] 1 All ER 411, CA; *Express Newspapers Ltd v Keys* [1980] IRLR 247; *Thanet DC v Ninedrive Ltd* [1978] 1 All ER 703.

141 S 12(3), Human Rights Act 1998.

142 S 12(4), *ibid*, applicable to interim and final injunctions.

ent's Convention right to 'freedom of expression'.[143] The general approach should be to require a high threshold of proof by the claimant: that he is 'more like than not' to succeed on the merits at trial. But Lord Nicholls, who gave the leading speech, thought this high level of proof should not be applied in all situations. To do so 'would preclude the court from granting an interim injunction is some circumstances where it is plain [that] injunctive relief should be granted as a temporary measure.'[144]

*Defamation: Protection of Freedom of Expression At Common Law.* The Court of Appeal in *Greene v Associated Newspapers Ltd* affirmed that a claimant in a defamation action cannot normally obtain an interim injunction to restrain further publication.[145] The court applied the long-standing 'rule in *Bonnard v Perryman*' (1891).[146] This rule, which is founded on protection of freedom of speech, whether by the media or ordinary citizens, precludes such interim relief unless the claimant can show that it is clear that the defendant (author and/or publisher) has no possible defence of justification (viz that the statement is true and hence not libellous).[147]

The Court of Appeal rejected the argument that the lower threshold of proof provided by section 12(3) of the Human Rights Act 1998 (see above) had replaced in this context the *Bonnard* rule. The court noted that even though the *Bonnard* rule might prevent a claimant from obtaining an interim injunction, his interest in maintaining a good reputation can be eventually vindicated at trial.[148] By contrast, the court noted that a claim for an interim injunction to protect confidentiality concerns a much more fragile interest: like Humpty-Dumpty, rights of confidentiality cannot be put together again by the award of damages at trial; the essence of confidentiality is avoidance of publicity, and so a claimant's failure to obtain interim protection of confidentiality will cause him irreparable harm.

---

[143] [2005] 1 AC 253, HL; noted P Devonshire (1005) 24 CJQ 194.

[144] Ibid at [16],[20].

[145] [2005] QB 972, CA at [57] [60] [77] [78] [81]; [2005] EWCA Civ 1462; noted N Hatzis [2006] CJQ 27.

[146] [1891] 2 Ch 269, CA; a lucid and compelling modern examination of the rule is by Auld LJ, *Holley v Smyth* [1998] QB 726, 743–6, CA, cited with approval by Brooke LJ in the *Greene* case, ibid, at [45].

[147] The claimant might also need to overcome other possible defences, such as fair comment or qualified privilege: see *Holley v Smyth* [1998] QB 726 at 740, citing *Fraser v Evans* [1969] 1 QB 349, 360–1, CA, per Lord Denning MR, and D Price *Defamation: Law, Procedure, and Practice* (3rd edn, 2004) 21–03.

[148] *Greene* case, [2005] QB 972, CA, at [78].

### *Re-assessment of American Cyanamid: The Series 5 Software Case*[149]

Laddie J has attractively suggested that the *American Cyanamid* case's general embargo upon considering the substantive merits of applications for interim injunctions should be 'kept in its place'.[150] He said:

> 'Lord Diplock [in *American Cyanamid*] did not intend ... to exclude consideration of the strength of the cases in most applications for interlocutory relief. It appears to me that what is intended is that the court should not attempt to resolve difficult issues of fact or law on an application for interlocutory relief. If, on the other hand, the court is able to come to a view as to the strength of the parties' cases on the credible evidence, then it can do so. In fact, ... it is frequently the case that it is easy to determine who is (more) likely to win the trial on the basis of the [documentary material].'[151]

However, decisions continue to cite the *American Cyanamid* decision, and it is clear that it has not yet slipped away into the oblivion of procedural history.[152]

### *Conclusion on the American Cyanamid Approach*

With hindsight we can now say, echoing Part 1 of the CPR, that the House of Lords' decision was a rational allocation of the court's resources. It is, however, questionable whether the emphasis on not considering the merits in the run-of-the-mill case is correct. What are the arguments for and against?

General refusal to consider the merits on an interim application for an injunction can be supported on the grounds:

the courts will spare themselves a heavy interlocutory workload and so have more time to devote to hearing trials;[153]

a court cannot safely assess the factual merits until the case has been fully prepared and witnesses have been cross-examined;[154] most applications for interim injunctions precede disclosure of the parties' relevant documents under

---

149 *Series 5 Software Limited v Clarke* [1996] 1 All ER 853; see also Laddie J in *Antec International v Southwestern Chicks (Warren) Ltd* [1997] FSR 278 and in *Direct Line Group Ltd v Direct Line Estate Agency and Others Ltd* [1997] FSR 374, 376.; for comment on *Series 5 Software*, see *Barnsley Brewery Co Ltd v RBNB* [1997] FSR 462, Robert Walker J and *SIG Architectural Products Ltd v Castle House Windows Ltd* (unreported 20 June 1996), Robert Walker J; and see Jacob J in *Cable and Wireless plc v British Telecommunications plc* (unreported, 8 December, 1997).

150 *Series 5 Software* case [1996] 1 All ER 853.

151 Ibid, at 865.

152 Eg *Intelsec Systems Ltd v Grech-Cini* [1999] 4 All ER 11, 25 and *R v Secretary of State for Health, ex p Imperial Tobacco Ltd* [2000] 1 All ER 572, 598, CA, *per* Laws LJ ("*American Cyanamid* is the ordinary rule by which applications for interlocutory injunctions in private law proceedings are decided every day ..."); *R v Secretary of State for Health ex p Imperial Tobacco Ltd* [2001] 1 WLR 127, 131, 135, HL; and *Att-Gen v Punch* [2003] 1 All ER 289, HL, paras 74, 99–100.

153 Eg, comments of Staughton LJ in *Derby & Co Ltd v Weldon (No 6)* [1990] 1 WLR 1139, 1153, CA.

154 *American Cyanamid Ltd v Ethicon Ltd* [1975] AC 396, 406, HL.

CPR Part 31; it would be unfair to consider the merits of the case if one party is likely to be disadvantaged by the fact that disclosure has yet to take place.[155]

However, there are arguments against the *American Cyanamid* doctrine:

the old requirement of a *prima facie* case was satisfactorily applied in many cases;[156] parties often agreed that they would abide by the result of the interlocutory decision on the merits;

the CPR emphasizes the importance of gaining efficient, cheap, expeditious and proportionate resolution of civil disputes;[157] the courts' grant of interim injunctions is a valuable contribution not only to the acceleration of justice, but also to the achievement of swift and informed settlement; but this requires the court to offer its provisional assessment of the merits of each side's case.[158]

Arguably, the general embargo on considering a case's merits when deciding whether to grant an interim injunction, is only appropriate when:

(a) the court cannot reasonably commit substantial judicial time to an interim inquiry into the case's merits, because this would be an unreasonable allocation of the court's resources; or

(b) it would be imprudent for the court to devote substantial time to such an application because the facts will require extensive investigation which should be postponed until much later stage in the litigation.

### C. *Preliminary Issues*

Another relevant technique for accelerating a case is to take a preliminary issue on

a point of pure law or of construction of a document.[159] The court can be asked to pronounce in final form on a preliminary issue, such as a point of general law, or interpretation of a document, before the factual issues have been investigated. A 'preliminary' decision is final. Often the point singled out for accelerated treatment is a 'crux' on which the entire fate of the litigation might depend: points concerning limitation of actions ('prescription');[160] consensual

[155] *Cayne v Global Natural Resources Ltd* [1984] 1 All ER 225, 229, CA.

[156] See comments by an experienced intellectual property and Chancery practitioner: Peter Prescott, (1975) 91 LQR 168–71 (case note); see also the approach of Laddie J in the *Series 5 Software Ltd v Clarke* [1996] 1 All ER 853.

[157] CPR 1.1(2) (the Overriding Objective).

[158] As emphasised by P Prescott (1975) 91 LQR 168–71 (case note).

[159] Neil Andrews, *English Civil Procedure* (2003) 9.33, 9.34, 34.17.

[160] Ibid, at 9.33 n 39; *Haward v Fawcetts* [2006] UKHL 9; [2006] 1 WLR 682, HL (Limitation of Actions Act 1980, s 14A).

time bars;[161] exclusion clauses;[162] disputable duties of care.[163]A decision on a preliminary issue will not necessarily decide the entire dispute. Even so, it might provide the basis for settlement or at least reduce the length of the process.

## 4. Accelerated Forms of Final Judgment

### *A. Summary Judgment*

#### *Outline*

This procedure allows claimants or defendants to gain final judgment if they can show that their opponent's claim or defence lacks a 'real prospect' of success. It is a stream-lined procedure, enabling the applicant to avoid the delay, expense and inconvenience of taking the case to trial. Summary judgment in favour of claimants was introduced in 1855 to provide speedy justice against defendants who dishonour cheques, or fail to make payment under other types of bills of exchange or letters of credit. It has since been greatly expanded.

The claimant cannot seek summary judgment until either the defendant has acknowledged service of the claim form, or he has filed a defence, unless the court or a specific rule otherwise provides.[164] Factual issues are considered on the basis of written evidence in the form of witness statements and statements of truth.[165]

CPR Part 24 makes three main changes to the system of summary judgment:

(1) unlike the former RSC Order 14, CPR Part 24 makes summary procedure available to both claimants and defendants; and so defendants can use this procedure to attempt to dismiss a bad or hopeless claim;
(2) the kernel of the new test in CPR Part 24 is whether the relevant party's claim or defence has a 'real chance of success' at trial; this test allows the court to reject bad claims or defences slightly more readily than under the old RSC Order 14;
(3) the court can now initiate a summary judgment hearing under CPR Part 24, without waiting for a party to make such an application.

---

161 *Senate Electrical Wholesalers Ltd v Alacatel Submarine Networks Ltd* [1999] 2 Lloyd's Rep 243, CA; noted
(1998) 17 CJQ 355; *Laminates Acquisition Co v BTR Australia* [2003] EWHC 2540 (Comm).

162 *Cremdean Properties v Nash* (1977) 244 EG 547, CA.

163 Eg *Customs & Excise v Barclays Bank plc* [2006] UKHL 28: [2007] 1 AC 181; *Deep Vein Thrombosis and Air Travel Group Litigation* [2005] UKHL 72; [2006] 1 AC 495.

164 CPR 24.4(1); A Zuckerman *Civil Procedure* (2006), 8.56, 8.57.

165 CPR 24.5.

*Test for Granting Summary Judgment*

Summary judgment is available both to test the legal (including points of construction of documents) and evidential merits of a claim or defence, or any part thereof.[166] The governing rule in CPR 24.2 states:

The court may give summary judgment against a claimant or defendant on the whole of a claim or on a particular issue if (a) it considers that (i) that claimant has no real prospect of succeeding on the claim or issue; or (ii) that defendant has no real prospect of successfully defending the claim or issue and (b) there is no other reason why the case or issue should be disposed of at a trial.

This formulation is a refashioning and indeed a tightening of the cardinal test which applied under the old 'Order 14'.[167] In essence the change is:

is the defence arguable (giving the defendant a benefit of the doubt) (pre-CPR);

does the defence (or now the claim) have a real chance of succeeding, or is it merely fanciful (less benefit of doubt to defendant/claimant)? (post-CPR)

In *Swain* v *Hillman*, Lord Woolf said that the words 'no real prospect' of success in the new test 'speak for themselves'.[168] This phrase denotes that the claim or defence must have a 'realistic' rather than a 'fanciful' chance of success.[169] He added that the function of CPR Part 24 would be distorted if summary judgment hearings were allowed to become 'mini-trials'. Instead, issues involving detailed factual investigation require the case to progress through disclosure under CPR 31 and preparation of witness statements, perhaps culminating in cross-examination at trial.[170]

*CPR Part 24 and Article 6(1) of the European Convention on Human Rights*

It has been persuasively contended that the CPR Part 24 procedure does not infringe Article 6(1) of the European Convention on Human Rights: sensibly applied, that procedure does not deny a right to a 'fair trial' under that provision.[171]

---

[166] PD (24) 1.2, 1.3.

[167] Under the old law (RSC Ord 14), the test established in *National Westminster Bank plc v Daniel* [1993] 1 WLR 1453, 1457, CA, was "is there a fair or reasonable probability of the defendant having a real or *bona fide* defence?"; for comment on the CPR test, Derek O'Brien, "The New Summary Judgment: Raising the Threshold of Admission" (1999) 18 CJQ 132, esp 137, 145–8.

[168] *Swain v Hillman* [2001] 1 All ER 91, 92, CA; this has not prevented a cascade of case law, mostly unreported, which is collected at *Halsbury's Laws of England* (4th edn, 2001 re-issue), 'Practice and Procedure', vol 37, (by Master John Leslie, QBD), [921] at n 7.

[169] Obfuscatory references to this test in paras 4.1 and 4.2 of PD 24 have been deleted in the later formulation of the rules, as explained in the *Swain* case, ibid, at 93.

[170] For judicial emphasis of this point under the pre-CPR rules, see Neil Andrews, *Principles of Civil Procedure* (1994), 9–024 to 9–026.

[171] L Mulcahy, *Human Rights and Civil Practice* (2001), para 10.52.

*'Safety Valve': Residual Test to Protect Respondents under CPR Part 24*

The court can withhold summary judgment, even though the respondent has failed to present to the court a sufficiently cogent factual or legal response to the application for summary judgment. The court is directed to consider whether 'there is no other compelling reason why the case or issue should be disposed of at a trial.'[172] This gives a respondent a further opportunity to avoid defeat. This ground of possible relief is an example of procedural equity. The same test is also a manifestation of the court's 'Overriding Objective' to ensure that the case is decided justly.[173]

*The Court's Options at a Hearing*

The court's options at the hearing are:

(a) the court can give judgment for the applicant, whether this is the claimant or the defendant, and whether this is on the whole of the claim or merely on a particular issue;[174] [or it can strike out or dismiss the claim or a particular issue];[175]

option (a) involves victory for the summary judgment applicant, whether in respect of the whole or any part of the case; or

(b) the court can dismiss outright the application for summary judgment;[176] option (b) involves defeat for the summary judgment applicant, but not overall defeat in the main action, which survives intact; or

(c) it can grant a conditional order (discussed below) where 'it appears to the court that a claim or defence may succeed but improbable that it will do so'[177] this conditional option is an inconclusive outcome because the court permits

---

172 CPR 24.2(b); and PD (24) 2(3)(b) refers to the applicant's statement of belief that he "knows of no other reason why the disposal of the claim or issue should await trial"; the pre-CPR law was contained in RSC Ord 14, r 3(1), now abolished, on which see Neil Andrews, *Principles of Civil Procedure* (1994), para 9–022; notable pre-CPR decisions concerning this residual test are: *Miles v Bull* [1969] 1 QB 258; *Trafalgar House Construction (Regions) Ltd v General Surety & Guarantee Co Ltd* [1996] AC 199, HL; and *Mount Eden Ltd v Low Profile Fashions Ltd* (unreported,18 September, 1998), noted Scott (1999) 18 CJQ 1.

173 CPR 1.1. and 1.2.

174 CPR 24.1 and 24.2; PD (24) 5.1(1)(2).

175 PD (24) 5.1(2), which should be construed in the light of CPR 24.1 and 24.2 where "claim" is clearly used compendiously to embrace both an active claim and a possible defence to that active claim.

176 PD (24) 5.1(3); in the case of applications by a plaintiff under the old "Order 14", this result was known as 'granting the defendant unconditional leave to defend'.

177 PD (24) 4; this is consistent with the modern practice which was crystallized in *Yorke Motors Ltd v Edwards* [1982] 1 WLR 444, HL (robust attitude to flimsy or shadowy defences; greater resort to conditional leave rather than giving the respondent the benefit of a *scintilla* of doubt); Neil Andrews, *Principles of Civil Procedure* (1994), para 9–028, explains the background to the *Yorke* case; for case law on imposition of conditions under CPR Part 24, see *Halsbury's Laws of England* (4th edn, 2001 re-issue), 'Practice and Procedure', vol 37, (by Master John Leslie, QBD), [921] at n 10.

the respondent to the summary judgment application, whether he is a claimant or defendant, to continue the claim or defence only if he satisfies the relevant condition.

*Conditional Orders*

The test is:[178]

Where it appears to the court that a claim or defence may succeed but improbable that it will do so, the court may make a conditional order.

The possible conditions are: a payment into court or some other 'specified step'.[179] A payment into court will protect the intended beneficiary against the payor's insolvency.[180]

*Modern Attitude to Unrealistic Defences.* In the early 1980s in *Yorke Motors v Edwards*, the House of Lords made clear that a more robust use of conditional leave is justified. This is because many defences are distinctly 'shadowy' and it would be unjust for a claimant to be fobbed off with flimsy defences, often made merely so that judgment can be delayed.[181] Furthermore, allow flimsy defences to proceed to trial would obstruct the flow of other cases.

The *Yorke* case the claim concerned a Rolls-Royce car which the claimant had bought from the defendant, but which had been re-possessed by the true owner. The claimant sued to recover the price, because the defendant had breached its duty to provide good title in the car. The defendant pleaded that he was not in fact the principal in this transaction: and that he had merely acted as agent for a principal, who was in fact abroad. The court in this case described this defence as 'shadowy'.[182]

The House of Lords decided that on these facts it was appropriate to require the defendant to make a payment into court as a condition of his obtaining permission to defend.

The court added that it would be unfair to prescribe that condition if a defendant were unable to find the money. Otherwise, default upon the condition would follow automatically and the claimant could enter judgment without more. That would effectively deprive the defendant of his right to have his case heard.

However, the House observed that courts should take a skeptical view of a defendant's protestation that he lacks funds. The defendant bears the onus of

[178] PD (24) 4 (see also PD (24) 5).

[179] Note to CPR 24.6, cross-referring to CPR 3.1(3); PD (24) 5.2.

[180] *Re Ford* [1900] 2 QB 211.

[181] *Yorke Motors Ltd v Edwards* [1982] 1 WLR 444, HL.

[182] A legal euphemism for 'very dodgy'; the word 'shadowy' was described as a 'not ... unreasonable' description of the defence in a post-CPR case concerning summary judgment: *Foot & Bowden v Anglo Europe Corporation Ltd* (CA, unreported 17 February, 2000, CA), para 6, *per* Henry LJ.

satisfying the court that he cannot be reasonably expected to obtain a loan from a friend, relative or business associate.[183] Perhaps only socially isolated indigents, who lack friends, relatives and business associates, will be likely to convince the court that they lack the means of making a significant payment into court. It would not be enough that a defendant is legally aided (or receiving funding from the Legal Services Commission) or in receipt of social security. Two post-CPR Court of Appeal decisions have endorsed this pragmatic and strict approach.[184]

Of course, it should be noted that the new CPR 24.2 test makes it possible that a court might regard such a suspicious defence as not just 'shadowy' but quite 'unrealistic' and so award unconditional summary judgment in favour of the claimant on such facts.

### *B. Striking out Claims or Defences*

#### *Introduction*

Sometimes a claim or defence can be 'struck out' by the court, often at a very early stage of the proceedings, because the pleading is technically bad or there has been an abuse of procedure, or the claim or issue has already been adjudicated in a binding civil case between the same parties. Under CPR 3.4(2) the court can strike out a pleading (now known as a 'statement of case', whether it is a claim, defence, reply, or counterclaim, or any part of one) on any of these grounds:

(a) the statement of case discloses no reasonable grounds for bringing or defending the claim; or
(b) the statement of case is an abuse of the court's process or is otherwise likely to obstruct the just disposal of the proceedings; or
(c) failure to comply with a rule, practice direction or court order.[185]

Striking out can be exercised whether or not a party makes an application to the court.[186]

---

[183] *Yorke* case, [1982] 1 WLR 444, 449, *per* Lord Diplock, approving Brandon LJ's comment in the CA.

[184] Eg, *Foot & Bowden v Anglo Europe Corporation Ltd* (CA, unreported 17 February, 2000, CA); *Chapple v Williams* (CA, unreported 8 December 1999).

[185] CPR 3.4(2)(a),(b),(c); for case law on striking out, see *Halsbury's Laws of England* (4th edn, 2001 re-issue), 'Practice and Procedure', vol 37, (by Master John Leslie, QBD), [917] at nn 5,6,7.

[186] Similarly, the court at its own initiative can order a *summary judgment* hearing to examine whether a claim or defence should be dismissed because it has 'no real prospect of succeeding': see CPR 24.5(3).

*Overlap Between Striking out Under CPR Part 3 and Summary Judgment under CPR Part 24*

The court's striking out powers overlap with summary judgment under CPR Part 24, notably the power to strike out under CPR 3.4(2)(a) ('*the statement of case discloses no reasonable grounds for bringing or defending the claim*'). These examples of overlap concern the merits of a claim or defence based upon the same suggested legal defect or the factual weakness of the claim or defence.

The Court of Appeal examined this procedural overlap in *S* v *Gloucestershire CC*.[187] This concerned a claim that two local authorities had negligently failed to discharge their statutory responsibility for children's welfare. It was alleged that the authorities had failed to supervise properly its system of foster case and that, as a result, children had suffered sexual abuse by foster-parents.

At first instance the defendant authorities had unsuccessfully attempted to strike out the negligence suits under CPR Part 3 and there had been no consideration of a summary judgment under CPR Part 24.[188] But on appeal, May LJ said that the validity of these claims could also be considered as a concurrent striking out (under CPR Part 3) and summary judgment application (under CPR Part 24, on the basis that the claims should be dismissed as lacking any real prospect of success).[189]

As for striking out, the court said that this is available under CPR 3.4(2)(a)[190] only in 'the clearest case'[191] When considering such an application, the court can receive written evidence when considering a striking out application.[192] As for summary judgment under CPR Part 24, the Court of Appeal said:

> 'For a summary judgment application to succeed in a case such as this where a strike out application would not succeed [because the latter requires proof of the 'clearest case' that the striking out application is justified], the court will first need to be satisfied that all substantial facts relevant to the allegations of negligence, which are reasonably capable of being presented to the court, are indeed before the court; that these facts are undisputed or that there is no real prospect of successfully disputing them; and that there is no real prospect of oral evidence affecting the court's assessment of the facts.'[193]

Unusually, all the relevant evidence in these cases consisted of case-notes made by the defendants' social workers. The court suggested that, provided there are no gaps in the evidence which might still be filled, 'there will ... have been proper judicial scrutiny of the detailed facts of the particular case such as to consti-

---

[187] *S v Gloucestershire CC* [2000] 3 All ER 346, 370–3, CA.
[188] CPR 3.4(2).
[189] *S v Gloucestershire CC*, ibid, at 372.
[190] *"the statement of case discloses no reasonable grounds for bringing or defending the claim"*.
[191] *S v Gloucestershire CC*, ibid, at 373.
[192] Ibid, at 372–3.
[193] Ibid, at 373.

tute a fair hearing in accordance with Article 6 of the [European Convention on Human Rights].'[194] The Court of Appeal then held that one of the claims should be dismissed because it had no 'real prospect of success', but the other should proceed to trial. By contrast, most claims will not involve exclusively documentary evidence. Instead it will be necessary for witnesses to be heard and cross-examined at trial. In these cases, summary judgment under CPR Part 24 would be inappropriate.

### *Overlapping Summary Judgment and Striking Out Applications in Three Rivers DC v Bank of England (No 3)*[195]

The claimants were depositors of the BCCI[196] bank, which collapsed in 1991 because of internal fraud by its senior employees. The claimant sued the Bank of England, which has a statutory duty to supervise banks. The statement of case alleged that the bank had committed the tort of misfeasance in public office, a cause of action which requires an element of dishonesty or recklessness.[197] Trial in this very complex case lasted nearly two years (before Tomlinson J early 2004 to late 2005, when the claimants settled and effectively abandoned their claim).[198]

The 2001 appeal to the House of Lords known as *Three Rivers DC* v *Bank of England (No 3)* concerned an application to strike out the claim on the overlapping basis (1) that it has been improperly pleaded and disclosed no reasonable cause of action or (2) that it was an abuse of process because it had no realistic prospect of success.[199] It was held that the defendant's pre-trial challenge to the validity of the claim could simultaneously be treated as an application by the defendant for summary judgment against the claimant under CPR Part 24.[200] The test applicable to summary judgment is whether the claim has a real prospect of success, and not the severer test whether it is bound to fail.[201]

---

194 Ibid, at 373; May LJ added, at 371 that 'in an appropriate case, a defendant is entitled to a fair summary hearing of a case which, when it is properly investigated, has no real prospect of success.'

195 [2001] 2 All ER 513, HL, notably at [90] ff, and [134] ff.

196 Bank of Credit and Commerce International SA, which is now insolvent and whose financial collapse produced extensive litigation.

197 On the substantive aspect of this case, see M Andenas and D Fairgrieve, 'Misfeasance in Public Office, Governmental Liability, and European Influence, (2002) 51 ICLQ 757–80.

198 *Three Rivers DC v Bank of England* [2006] EWHC 816 (Comm) (12 April 2006), Tomlinson J at [1].

199 Lord Steyn's formulation [2001] 2 All ER 513, HL at [5]; and Lord Hope at [13] referred to CPR 3.4(2)(a) and (b) which permit a statement of case to be struck out if: *(a) the statement of case discloses no reasonable grounds for bringing or defending the claim; or* (b) the statement of case is an abuse of the court's process or is otherwise likely to obstruct the just disposal of the proceedings ...'; see also Lord Hutton at [120] distinguished the 'attack on the pleadings point' and the 'no real prospect of success point'.

200 Ibid, at [13], [88], [120].

201 Ibid at [91], citing *Monsanto plc v Tully The Times* 30 November 1999, CA.

By a majority, the House held that the action should not be struck out, nor should summary judgment be awarded in favour of the defendant.[202] The contrary view had been reached at first instance and by two of the Court of Appeal judges. Five of the nine judges who considered the striking out application thought that the claim was radically defective, but the case proceeded to a two-year trial. The trial did not end in judgment, however, because eventually claimants withdrew their claim because of he weight of evidence supporting the defence.

*Majority Judges: Lords Steyn, Hutton and Hope*

Lords Steyn and Hutton were not convinced that the claimants had no realistic prospect of success, especially because cross-examination and discovery might reveal 'significant materials assisting the claimants'.[203]

Lord Hope noted the extreme complexity of the striking out application: the written cases before the House of Lords ran to over 1000 pages, with supplementary bundles of another 1000 pages.[204] He considered that summary disposal of this complex case by reference to its factual merits is hazardous, that this will produce a mini-trial.[205] He cited with approval Danckwerts LJ's comment in 1965 on the forensic limitations upon striking out hearings:

'This power to strike out [on the ground that the claim is an abuse of process and wholly unmeritorious] was never intended to be exercised by a minute and protracted examination of the documents and facts of the case, in order to see whether the plaintiff really has a cause of action. To do that is to usurp the position of the trial judge and to produce a trial of the case in chambers, on affidavits only, without discovery and without oral evidence tested by cross-examination in the ordinary way. This seems to me to be an abuse of the inherent power of the court.'[206]

*Dissenting Judges: Lords Millett and Hobhouse*

Lord Millett described the claim in the *Three Rivers* case as 'most implausible', 'scarcely credible' and 'extravagant'.[207]

Lord Hobhouse said:

'... it is simplistic to suppose that in complex litigation the exercise should never be attempted. The volume of documentation and the complexity of the issues raised on the pleadings should be the subject of critical scrutiny and should not without more deter

[202] Lords Steyn, Hope and Hutton; Lords Hobhouse and Millett dissented; the majority decision reversed a first instance and Court of Appeal decision to strike out the claim.

[203] Ibid at [7], *per* Lord Steyn; [47] *per* Lord Hutton.

[204] Ibid, [11].

[205] Ibid, [95],[ 98].

[206] *Wenlock v Moloney* [1965] 1 WLR 1238, 1244, CA, *per* Danckwerts LJ.

[207] Ibid, *Three Rivers* case, [180], [181].

the judge from considering whether it is really necessary to commit the parties and court to a lengthy trial and all the preparatory steps which that will involve.'[208]

## C. *Default Judgment*

### *Importance*

Judgment by default is an important means of accelerating the legal process. The CPR defines judgment by default as:

> judgment without trial where a defendant (a) has failed to file an acknowledgment of service; or (b) has failed to file a defence.[209]

A claimant can obtain default judgment if the claim is for: 'a specified amount of money';[210] or 'an amount of money to be decided by the court';[211] or delivery of goods where the claim form gives the defendant the alternative of paying their value.[212] In these situations, subject to some exceptions, the claimant can apply for judgment by administrative process without troubling the judges.[213] If the claimant seeks some other remedy, default judgment must be sought by specific application to the court.[214] Certain classes of claim are not amenable to default judgment.[215]

### *Setting Aside a Default Judgment: Regular and Irregular Judgments*

The CPR preserves this distinction in substance although this familiar terminology is not adopted.[216] A regular judgment is procedurally sound, whereas an irregular judgment is one which has been improperly obtained by misapplication of procedure.

### *Setting Aside On The Substantive Merits Procedurally Regular Judgments*

A judgment by default is rightly regarded as not as strong as a judgment obtained after a full contest between the parties. And so the court has an extensive power to set aside a judgment of default, as was acknowledged by Lord Atkin in a classic statement of principle:

---

[208] Ibid, [156].

[209] CPR 12.1 and 12.3; see also CPR 10.2 and CPR 15.3; generally, Neil Andrews, *English Civil Procedure* (2003) ch 19; IS Goldrein (ed), *Commercial Litigation: Pre-emptive Remedies* (2005) ch 5; *Zuckerman on Civil Procedure* (2006) 8–3 ff.

[210] Formerly known as 'liquidated claims'.

[211] Formerly known as 'unliquidated claims'.

[212] CPR 12.4(1)(a)-(c).

[213] The main exceptions (where judgment must be sought by application to the court) are: claims for costs (other than fixed costs), or service was made out of the jurisdiction without leave under the Civil Jurisdiction and Judgments Act 1982, claims against the Crown, tort claims by a spouse against another, claims against children and patients: CPR 12.9, 12.10, 12.11 for full details.

[214] CPR 12.4(2), 12.10, 12.11.

[215] CPR 12.2; PD (12) 1.2.

[216] CPR 13.2, 13.3; the new language is 'judgment wrongly entered'.

'The principle obviously is that unless and until the court has pronounced a judgment upon the merits or by consent, it is to have the power to revoke the expression of its coercive power where that has been obtained by a failure to follow any of the rules of procedure.'[217]

The court can set aside or vary a regular judgment if 'the defendant has a real prospect of successfully defending the claim' or 'there is some other good reason' why judgment should be set aside or varied.[218] When deciding this discretion, the court will mainly consider whether the defence has objective merits and, secondly, why the defendant failed to acknowledge service or file a defence.[219] When the default judgment was obtained on the question of liability, the power to set aside exists whether or not there was a further failure to contest the quantification of liability.[220]

In 1998 the Court of Appeal held that a court which is asked to set aside a default judgment should not dismiss too peremptorily a defence, even it is has been merely sketched out by the defendant.[221] Ward LJ said:

'... the [defendant's suggested] arguable case must carry some degree of conviction but judges should be very wary of trying issues of fact on evidence where the facts are apparently credible and [those facts] are to be set aside against the facts being advanced [by the claimant]. Choosing between them is the function of the trial judge, not the judge on the interlocutory application, unless there is some inherent improbability in what is being asserted or some extraneous evidence which would contradict it.'[222]

What is the status of a decision which rejects, after consideration of the substantive merits of the dispute, a defendant's attempt to set aside the default judgment? The Court of Appeal in *Clapp v Enron* (2005) held that this confirmatory decision is final and binds the parties.[223] And so the decision cannot be re-opened in another first instance proceeding. It can be attacked only by appeal or (unusually and exceptionally) by a collateral challenge at first instance in which it is shown that the confirmatory decision was obtained by fraud.[224]

---

[217] *Evans v Bartlam* [1937] AC 473, 480, HL.

[218] CPR 13.3.

[219] The leading pre-CPR (but still illuminating) decision is *Alpine Bulk Transport Co Inc v Saudi Eagle Shipping Co Inc (The Saudi Eagle)* [1986] 2 Lloyd's Rep 221, CA; considered in *Allen v Taylor* [1992] 1 Personal Injury and Quantum Reports P 255, CA and *Shocked v Goldschmidt* [1998] 1 All ER 372, 376, CA (the last case in fact concerned with non-appearance at trial).

[220] *Strachan v The Gleaner Co Ltd* [2005] 1 WLR 3204, PC.

[221] *Day v RAC Motoring Services Ltd* [1999] 1 WLR 2150, CA.

[222] Ibid, 2157.

[223] [2005] EWCA Civ 1511 at [36] ff.

[224] Ibid at 36], citing *Odyssey (London) Ltd v OIC Run-off* [2001] Lloyd's Rep (Insurance) 1.

*Conditional Setting Aside*

It appears that the courts can impose a condition upon the setting aside of a regular judgment, for example that the defendant should provide security for the claimant's costs.[225] A more common condition is that the defendant should make a payment into court.[226]

*Setting Aside Procedurally Irregular ('Wrongly Granted') Judgments*

Setting aside proceeds summarily in the following situations: (i) judgment was procedurally premature (it preceded expiry of the time for acknowledging service or filing a defence,[227] or an application for summary judgment was still pending);[228] or (ii) the defendant had fully discharged the claim (including costs);[229] or (iii) the defendant had admitted liability in full and requested more time to pay.[230] Finally, if the defendant satisfies the court that he was unaware of the relevant claim form, the court will 'normally' set aside the default judgment 'unless it is pointless to do so.'[231] There is a cognate power to set aside a judgment where the relevant party fails to attend trial and his claim or defence is struck out.[232] In this situation the court will 'almost always' set aside a judgment if the defendant did not receive notice of the claim form.[233]

---

225 *Burchmore v Hills* (1935) 79 Law Journal Newspaper 30.

226 *City Construction Contracts (London) Ltd v Adam, The Times* 4 January, 1988, CA.

227 CPR 13.2, 12.3(1)(2).

228 CPR 13.2, 12.3(3).

229 CPR 13.2(c) 12.3(3)(b).

230 CPR 13.2, 12.3(3)(c) 14.4, 14.7.

231 *Godwin v Swindon BC* [2001] EWCA Civ 1478; [2002] 1 WLR 997, CA at [49], considering CPR 13.3(1)(b); *Akram v Adam* [2004] EWCA Civ 1601; [2005] 1 WLR 2762, CA at [42], [43] (service technically effective under the deemed service regime even if notice was never received).

232 CPR 39.3(5); which requires, among other things, proof of a 'good reason' for non-attendance at trial; *Estate Acquisition and Development Ltd v Wiltshire* [2006] EWCA Civ 533; [2006] CP Rep 32; for the general common law principles governing this context, *Gaydamak v UBS Bahamas Ltd & Anor (Bahamas)* [2006] UKPC 8; [2006] 1 WLR 1097.

233 *Nelson v Clearsprings (Management) Ltd* [2006] EWCA Civ 1854; [2007] CP Rep 2, at [56].

# Anti-suit Injunctions as a Tool for Governing Private Litigation

*Marco de Cristofaro*

1. Much has been written about the (still) recent judgment of the European Court of Justice *Turner v Grovit*.[1] As everybody knows, in this case proceedings were commenced in England by an employee against his employer; and a spoiling action was then brought against the employee by or on behalf of the employer before the Spanish courts. The behaviour of the employer was specifically aimed at oppressing the impecunious employee. In addition, the English court was undoubtedly seized before the Spanish court. It was the view of the Court of Appeal, in principle shared by the House of Lords in its preliminary reference to the ECJ, that the integrity of the English proceedings needed to be protected by an anti-suit injunction targeting the plaintiff in the Spanish proceedings. The ECJ, however, held that there is no power in the English court within the framework of the Brussels Convention to grant an injunction.

In its decision the ECJ barred the issuance of anti-suit injunctions targeting proceedings in the court of another Member State, but of course could not bring to a complete end the remarkable case-law of the English courts concerning that tool of international litigation. On the one hand the issuance of anti-suit injunctions could not obviously be prohibited as long as they target proceedings in the courts of Non-Member States, and on the other hand it has been considered admissible by the Court of Appeal to issue an anti-suit injunction in order to defend the integrity of an arbitral tribunal sitting in London.[2] The ever growing number of cases in which English courts are requested to issue such restraining orders makes plain that these courts still consider anti-suit injunctions, within

---

[1] Case C-159/02, [2004] ECR I-3565; *Int'l Lis* 2005, 1, 14 (note Merlin).

[2] *Through Transport Mutual Insurance Association (Eurasia) Ltd v New India Assurance Co Ltd*, [2005] 1 Lloyd's Rep 67; see also High Court of Justice, Queen's Bench Division (Colman J.), *West Tankers Inc v Riunione Adriatica di Sicurtà SpA and Generali Assicurazioni SpA ("The Front Comor")*, [2005] EWHC 454 (Comm); see further the preliminary reference of the House of Lords, [2007] UKHL 4, commented by Schlosser, Int'l Lis 2007, 96, and finally the Opinion of Advocate General Kokott, delivered on September 4th, 2008, in Case C-185/07, and the ECJ's judgment, delivered on February 10th, 2009, declaring incompatible with EC Regulation No. 44/2001 the issuance of anti-suit injunctions whenever in support of arbitration agreements.

their proper sphere of application, as entirely acceptable, but also reveals that anti-suit injunctions continue to be regarded by parties involved in international commercial and civil disputes as a fundamental procedural weapon to deal with (actual or prospective) parallel litigation.

This is why it is still worth questioning the rationale of the *Turner* decision, and further investigating whether the answer of the ECJ could or should have been different.

2. Needless to say, *Turner* has been welcomed in civil law systems, where the deployment of anti-suit injunctions has traditionally been considered – loosely characterizing the opinion of continental scholars – as an inadmissible interference in the sovereignty and dignity of the targeted court; on the contrary, the decision has been fiercely criticized by English commentators, one of them observing that the ECJ completed – with *Turner* as well as with its judgments in the cases *Gasser v Misat*[3] and *Owusu v Jackson*[4] – "fifteen months of infamy"[5].

As has been observed, the divide among legal systems over the propriety of international anti-suit injunctions remains a conspicuous one, and emotions over them continue to run high, thus probably preventing the Transnational Principles and Rules of Civil Procedure from even attempting to reconcile the conflicting views surrounding the instrument.[6] This divide essentially depends on the different attitudes that legal systems have regarding international civil litigation: the common law systems considering jurisdiction as being about private law rights and duties, the continental systems on the contrary favouring a public law view of the matter, according to which rules of jurisdiction define a sphere of legal activity in which there is no room for notions of private rights and private wrongs. As often happens, the ECJ has joined the latter view; yet in so doing it not only demonstrated a far too dismissive concern for the interests of litigants, but also chose an approach which is obsolete and even misleading if one considers the fundamentally private nature of interests involved in international commercial and civil disputes.

---

[3] Case C-116/02, [2003] ECR I-14693; *Int'l Lis* 2004, 2, 69 (note Marinelli).

[4] Case C-281/02, [2005] ECR I-1383; *Int'l Lis* 2006, 1, 15 (note Lupoi).

[5] See Briggs, *The Impact of Recent Judgments of the European Court on English Procedural Law and Practice*, *Int'l Lis* 2005, 3, 137, at 140–141; Id., *Anti-suit Injunctions and Utopian Ideals*, 120 *Law Quarterly Review* [2004], 529, at 533: "*but with the anti-European-suit injunction having been destroyed by enemy action or friendly fire, all a litigant can do is salvage what he may from the wreckage, while the rest of us redouble our trust in the legal systems of the other Member States. … It is a state of affairs which makes one rub one's eyes in disbelief. But along with pounds and ounces, there are no anti-suit injunctions in Utopia*".

[6] Bermann, *The Transnational Civil Procedure Rules and Parallel Litigation*, *Int'l Lis* 2006, 1, 27, at 30.

3. In recent decades this latter assumption has determined a major shift in the balance of the respective role of private and public law in most areas of international civil litigation. The dogma of sovereignty drew back as far as service of process is concerned, allowing a greater use of methods of direct service without the need for the cooperation of the officers of the Member State addressed. Especially within the European Union, following EC Regulation No. 1348/2000 and EC Regulation No. 1393/2007[7], direct service by registered mail has become the ordinary method of service, since the Member States may no longer raise an objection to service by post[8] (Article 14); and since the ECJ recognized that the Regulation "does not establish any hierarchy between the method of transmission and service under Articles 4 to 11 thereof [service through the officers of the Member State addressed] and that under Article 14 thereof [also, service by post]".[9]

The same can be said in relation to the field of the taking of evidence abroad. As we will probably see tomorrow, the activity of gathering evidence is no longer seen as a task only the Courts of the Member State requested may be entrusted with, since at least within the European Union, EC Regulation No. 1206/2001[10] admits finally – although upon conditions – the direct taking of evidence by the requesting court (Article 17).[11] And even outside the European Union, in relations with the United States, it is significant that there has not been in recent years any report of attempts to enforce the blocking or claw-back statutes of the late 70s and mid 80s, whose aim at retaliation against the issuance of discovery orders is clearly no longer felt as either useful or sinful.

It is, further, sufficient to mention, in this framework:

– the by now unanimously admitted possibility of arbitration in the field of antitrust private litigation, notwithstanding the strong public interest factor which is involved in such disputes;[12]

– in international insolvency law, the growing importance of cooperation, protocols and agreements between liquidators appointed by Courts of the dif-

---

[7] O.J.E.C., June 30th 2000, L 160, at 37; and O.J.E.C., November 13th 2007, L 324.

[8] A possibility to object that was still provided for within the Hague Convention on the service abroad of judicial and extrajudicial documents in civil or commercial matters, concluded on November 15th 1965.

[9] Case C-473/04, [2006] ECR I-(9th February), *Plumex v Young Sports NV*; Int'l Lis 2006, 129 (note Frigo).

[10] O.J.E.C., June 27th 2001, L 174, at 1.

[11] The Hague Evidence Convention, concluded on March 18th 1970, still requests a specific permission on a case by case basis by the competent authority designated by the State where the evidence is to be taken, or a general declaration by the contracting State, in order to allow the direct taking of evidence in the territory of the State addressed, without compulsion, through commissioners duly appointed in the State of origin of the request.

[12] See, on the one hand, U.S. Supreme Court, *Mitsubishi Motors v Soler Chrysler-Plymouth*, 473 U.S. 614 (1985); on the other hand, ECJ, Case C-126/97, [1999] ECR I-3055, *Eco Swiss China Time Ltd v Benetton International NV.*

ferent States where debtor's assets are situated or where the debtor conducted his business, either on a case by case basis[13] or upon a statutory basis: for example, within the EU insolvency Regulation No. 1346/2000.[14] The latter's "limited universality" approach to the issue of the effects of a main insolvency proceeding[15] admits the opening of secondary proceedings in the Member State within whose territory the debtor possesses an establishment (Article 3, para. 2); but Article 31 ensures the dominant role of the main insolvency proceeding[16], by imposing – among others – the duty for the liquidator in the main proceedings and the liquidators in the secondary proceedings to cooperate and exchange information with each other;[17]

– the decreasing role of public policy[18] as a ground for non-recognition or non-enforcement of foreign judgments, not just because the judgment shall not be recognised only when it is "manifestly" contrary to public policy in the Member State in which recognition is sought, but also since the major field of application of the public policy exception clause consists by now in the violation of one party's procedural right to due process and a fair trial[19] or, more in general, in the violation not of State interests, but of fundamental rights of the individual which form part of the general principles of law enshrined in the European Convention on Human Rights.[20]

---

[13] So the agreements between insolvency courts and liquidators in the *Maxwell* litigation (see Fletcher, *Insolvency in Private International Law*, 2nd ed., Oxford, 2005, 223, No. 3.118; Schlosser, *Jurisdiction and International Judicial and Administrative Cooperation*, 284 *Recueil de Cours* of the Hague Academy of International Law [2000], 262f.): a pragmatic way out from the potential clash of parallel insolvency proceedings (which also prevented a battle of conflicting restraining orders).

[14] O.J.E.C., June 30th 2000, L 160, at 1.

[15] See "Whereas" No. 11: "This Regulation acknowledges the fact that as a result of widely differing substantive laws it is not practical to introduce insolvency proceedings with universal scope in the entire Community [...] This Regulation should take account of this in two different ways. On the one hand, provision should be made for special rules on applicable law in the case of particularly significant rights and legal relationships (e.g. rights *in rem* and contracts of employment). On the other hand, national proceedings covering only assets situated in the State of opening should also be allowed alongside main insolvency proceedings with universal scope".

[16] See "Whereas" No. 12: "To protect the diversity of interests, this Regulation permits secondary proceedings to be opened to run in parallel with the main proceedings [...] Mandatory rules of coordination with the main proceedings satisfy the need for unity in the Community".

[17] See "Whereas" No. 20: "Main insolvency proceedings and secondary proceedings can, however, contribute to the effective realisation of the total assets only if all the concurrent proceedings pending are coordinated. The main condition here is that the various liquidators must cooperate closely, in particular by exchanging a sufficient amount of information".

[18] In the context of Article 34 of EU Regulation No. 44/2001 (O.J.E.C., January 16th 2001, L 12, at 1).

[19] ECJ, case C-7/98, [2000] ECR I-1935, *Krombach v Bamberski*.

[20] See also, in the context of an alleged infringement of "procedural" public policy, the

4. The fading role of the public law factor underlying rules of jurisdiction also becomes apparent in relation to the doctrine of *forum non conveniens*. Yet, in the *Owusu* case the ECJ ruled that, whereas the English court has jurisdiction under Article 2 over a defendant domiciled in the United Kingdom, it has no power to stay proceedings, on the ground of *forum non conveniens*, in favour of the courts of a non-Contracting State. According to the European Court, in the matter of a claim arising from personal injuries sustained by the claimant while on holiday in Jamaica, it was irrelevant that the facts and matters arising for analysis and decision were to be more appropriately tried in Jamaica, which was the place where the facts had occurred and where the evidence was, and where the law to be applied to the claim would be familiar to the court applying it. One of the six defendants was domiciled in England, and that was enough to sustain the jurisdiction of the English courts.

Despite this decision, recent EU legislation shows that the civil law systems are ready to accept that a Court may decline its jurisdiction and transfer the case to the Court of another Member State in so far as it considers that the latter would be better placed to hear the case, or a specific part thereof. A corresponding provision has been enacted within EC Regulation No. 2201/2003[21] and a similar one has been suggested in the context of the Green Papers in divorce and succession matters[22], as a way of going about flexible rules of jurisdiction and as a means to counterbalance the choice – should it eventually be made – to introduce multiple heads of jurisdiction in those matters.

Coming straight to the point: the arguments opposed by civil law scholars and by the ECJ to the *forum non conveniens* doctrine – the need for certainty and foreseeability and the binding nature of the rules of jurisdiction[23] – do not necessarily confer on the plaintiff a vested right to sue before the courts which have jurisdiction under the Brussels Regulations provisions. Certainly, in domestic disputes the State is under the unconditional obligation to open its courts to private litigators and to enforce their right to sue, which is undoubtedly part of the right to due process and to a fair trial, and which is the necessary counterpart to the recognition of substantive rights, according to the ancient saying: *ubi remedium ibi ius*. But in international disputes the right to sue does not prevent the State from declining the exercise of jurisdiction as long as there is

---

opinion of the Advocate General Jacobs in case 341/04, *Eurofood*, and further the ECJ's judgment, [2006] ECR I-3813, para. 62f.

[21] O.J.E.C., December 23rd 2003, L 338, at 1.

[22] See respectively the Commission documents COM(2005) 82, March 14th 2005, at 10–11, and COM(2005) 65, March 1st 2005, at 7.

[23] Gaudemet-Tallon, *Compétence et exécution des jugements en Europe*, 3ème éd., Paris, 2002, 56f.; M.A. Lupoi, *Conflitti transnazionali di giurisdizioni*, Milan, 2002, 326f.; Geimer-Schütze, *Europäisches Zivilverfahrensrecht*, 2. Aufl., München, 2005, 109f.; Marinelli, *La clausola generale dell'art. 100 c.p.c.: origini, metamorfosi e nuovi ruoli*, Trento, 2005, 198f.; Geimer, *Internationales Zivilprozessrecht*, 5. Aufl., Köln, 2005, 362f.

another *forum* where the plaintiff can obtain under equal or comparable conditions the enforcement of his rights.

The cross-border nature of such disputes allows to impose that the plaintiff brings his action in a foreign court, if the denial of the *forum* neither affects nor alters the chances of a fair disposition of his substantive right (which has never been contended, for example, in *Owusu*). Further, the assessment of whether the alternative *forum* is a suitable one will have regard to the plaintiff's interests and therefore will take into consideration especially (or even solely) private law factors, since this is the nature of the interests which are at stake in the exercise of jurisdiction in private disputes. It has long been recognized in English case-law, in contrast with U.S. case-law[24], that in the so-called second limb of the *Spiliada* test the court will concentrate its attention on whether the plaintiff will obtain substantial justice in the foreign jurisdiction[25], and in this context every conceivable obstacle to the possibility of the plaintiff to have his case fairly and justly decided must be taken into account, albeit of apparently minor significance, such as the issues of adequate funding and legal representation.[26]

Therefore the inference that the *forum non conveniens* decision may be tailored to the interests of private litigants, especially of the private plaintiff, is legitimate.

5. A reliable starting-point is also that international commercial and civil litigation is about the assessment of private rights and duties. Therefore, not only must there always be a remedy to enforce such rights and duties, but it must also be clear that any remedy to this end raises questions of merely private law and does not interfere with public law issues. Anti-suit injunctions belong to this class of remedy; they provide injunctive relief and they do not address the foreign court, but they target the applicant party in the foreign proceeding as far as he is amenable to the jurisdiction of the (English) court which is issuing the order.

It is true that the reasoning according to which those injunctions are not concerned with the jurisdiction of the foreign court risks being considered a mere formalism, since it is undeniable that, as a result of a litigant being prohibited, under threat of a penalty, from pursuing an action before a given judicial au-

[24] See House of Lords, *Schalk Willem Burger Lubbe and others v Cape plc*, [2000] 1 WLR 1545, at 1564, per Lord Hope of Craighead – under express disapproval of the U.S. approach in the cases *In Re Union Carbide Corporation Gas Plant Disaster at Bhopal* (1986) 634 F. Supp. 842, and *Piper Aircraft Company v Reyno*, (1981) 454 U.S. 235 –: "the principles on which the doctrine of *forum non conveniens* rests leave no room for considerations of public interest or public policy which cannot be related to the private interests of any of the parties or the ends of justice in the case which is before the court".

[25] *Spiliada Maritime Corporation v Cansulex Ltd* [1987] A.C. 460, at 478; *Connelly v R.T.Z. Corporation Plc* [1998] A.C. 854, at 872; *Schalk Willem Burger Lubbe and others v Cape plc*, [2000] 1 WLR 1545, at 1554–1555.

[26] So a unanimous House of Lords, reversing the dismissal by the Court of Appeal, in *Lubbe*.

thority, the latter will be eventually deprived of jurisdiction to deal with the case.[27] Nonetheless, there is no truth in the further assumption that the result of the restraining order is a direct interference with the "unfettered jurisdictional authority" of the foreign court, nor that it constitutes an interference with the jurisdiction of the foreign court (as such incompatible with the system of the Convention).[28] In fact it is not true that the judgment made as to the abusive nature of the recourse to the jurisdiction of the court of a foreign State implies an assessment of the appropriateness of the proceedings pending before that court.[29]

As long as we keep in mind that in commercial and civil litigation only private interests are at stake, it is clear:

a) that the courts do not have an interest of their own in deciding a specific case, of which they could be deemed to be deprived;

b) that the parties have not a vested right to litigate in whichever court has jurisdiction according to national or conventional or even community rules of law; and therefore

c) that the bringing of an action does not in itself correspond to abusive conduct, but it can admissibly be held as an abuse *in the context of the private relationship*, because – even if there is nothing to "blame" from the point of view of public law – the bringing of an action may give rise to a violation of a contractual right or to oppression or vexation of the aggrieved (counter)party;

d) that in such cases the anti-suit injunctions aim at the pre-emptive protection of the contractual or legal rights and prerogatives of the aggrieved (counter)party, just as well as a claim for damages in contract or in tort would compensate the violation of such rights and prerogatives *ex post facto;*[30]

e) that the bringing of proceedings in the foreign court is not targeted in itself, but only in so far as it is abusive or vexatious, since according to English case-law the mere co-existence of parallel proceedings as such does not mean that the conduct of either action is vexatious or oppressive or an abuse of court, nor justifies the grant of an injunction; and since according to English case-law in any case the injunction should not be issued, and the action should be allowed to proceed in the foreign court, if there is an advantage to the party sought to be restrained in pursuing the foreign proceedings of which she would be deprived of and of which it would be unjust to deprive her;[31]

---

[27] Opinion of the Advocate General Colomer in *Turner*, [2004] ECR I-3565, at para. 34; yet also House of Lords, *Airbus Industrie v Patel and others*, [1998] 2 *All E. R.* 257, at 269.

[28] ECJ, *Turner*, para. 27; opinion of the Advocate General Colomer in *Turner*, para. 34.

[29] So, instead, ECJ, *Turner*, para. 28.

[30] For the assumption that: "If there is a legal right which is in principle sufficient to found the claim for an injunction, that legal right will also found a claim for damages", see Briggs-Rees, *Civil Jurisdiction and Judgments*, 4th ed., London-Singapore, 2005, para. 5.53.

[31] Court of appeal, *Seismic Shipping Inc and Westerngeco Ltd v Total E&P U.K. plc*, [2005] EWCA Civ 985; *Int'l Lis* 2006, 1, 31 (note Bermann); *Société Nationale Industrielle Aerospa-*

f) that the order to discontinue the foreign proceeding targets private conduct, which undoubtedly takes place in front of a court but the abusive, vexatious or oppressive nature of which does not in any event either undermine the authority or dignity of the foreign court, or imply a review or a second-look at the appropriateness of the head of jurisdiction which will be exercised by the foreign court seized;

g) that the injunction aims at protecting the proceeding in front of the English court, not for the sake of the authority of the issuing court, but only in so far as it shelters the domestic applicant and his private right to access to justice from the private wrong of the foreign plaintiff.[32]

6. In fact, the inquiry underlying the issuance of an anti-suit injunction is about circumstances which have nothing or very little to do with questioning the jurisdiction of the foreign court. The pre-requisite that England is the natural *forum* of the dispute, in order to obtain the restraining order, satisfies the need for a sort of subject-matter jurisdiction of the English Courts, which must generally abstain from policing the international observance of jurisdiction agreements or the "morality" of international procedural conduct in cases which have nothing much to do with England.[33] Therefore it does not imply an assessment of the greater convenience of the exercise of jurisdiction by English courts.

The jurisdiction of the foreign court is not otherwise addressed in the analysis underlying the issuance of an anti-suit injunction, because either the presence of a head of jurisdiction is all but questioned, and nonetheless the bringing of proceedings before the foreign court is alleged to be oppressive or vexatious;[34] or the jurisdiction is excluded by a valid and binding forum selection clause for the English courts: and even in such cases the authority of the foreign court should not be impaired by the grant of an injunction to restrain a party from invoking a jurisdiction which she had promised not to invoke and which in

---

*tiale v Lee Kui Jak*, [1987] AC 817, at 894; House of Lords, *British Airways Board v Laker Airways Ltd*, [1984] 3 *All E.R.* 39 (it was not vexatious conduct of Laker to seek, in the U.S., a relief which would not be available anywhere else).

[32] See Briggs-Rees, *Civil Jurisdiction and Judgments*, *supra* note 30, 5.45: "in the decision whether to grant an injunction to restrain a respondent from instituting or continuing with proceedings in a foreign court, the balance of private interests must be undertaken in order to decide whether to make the order"; factors of public interest have to be taken into account, but only to override the private interest case for an injunction.

[33] House of Lords, *Airbus Industrie GIE v Patel and others*, [1999] 1 AC 119, at 138 (per Lord Goff of Chieveley).

[34] So in *Turner*, where proceedings were commenced in England by an employee against his employer, and a spoiling action was then brought against the employee by or on behalf of the employer before the Spanish courts, in seeking to harass and oppress the impecunious employee.

principle it is even the foreign court's duty to decline.[35] In both cases it is the threat of abusive conduct within the context of a private relationship or the breach of a contractual duty which are the target of the restraining order.

On the other hand, the issue of an anti-suit injunction does not assume the inability of the foreign court to detect and sanction the alleged abusive or oppressive or vexatious nature of the conduct of the targeted party. The problem is either that the mere necessity of defending the claim in the foreign proceeding is in itself vexatious and oppressive for the applicant – because he is financially impecunious or because in any event the costs of the defence in the foreign proceeding are not likely to be recovered – and this will prevent him from even taking part in the foreign proceeding and therefore prevent the judge thereof from even having notice of the *lis pendens* (like in *Turner*) or of an arbitration or exclusive jurisdiction agreement; or the problem is that the mere necessity of defending the claim in the foreign proceeding is in itself abusive for the applicant, because the necessity of defending the claim in courts other than the court selected by agreement represents the consequence of a contractual wrong which the party has the right to claim to avoid, without being forced to litigate the issue of jurisdiction except in front of the chosen courts.

As far as the issuance of anti-suit injunctions targets a private wrong or sanctions the breach of a private duty, it does not question the dignity or the jurisdiction of the foreign court and therefore it is not to be deemed incompatible with the system of the Brussels Regulation[36], because the restraining order does not imply any review of the application of the jurisdictional or *lis pendens* rules of the Regulation.[37]An incompatibility may arise though, but only either: if the

[35] *The Angelic Grace*, [1995] 1 *Lloyd's Rep* 87 (CA): order to dismiss a proceeding brought in Italy in breach of a contractual agreement for arbitration in London. In fact it has to be said that the issuance of anti-suit injunctions to protect contractual agreements for arbitration in London spread after the *Marc Rich* case ("*The Atlantic Emperor*"). In *Marc Rich* an Italian court was seized of proceedings for a declaration of non-liability. The English courts proposed to ignore these and appoint an arbitrator, and it was held by the ECJ that they were entitled to do so (Case C-190/89, [1991] ECR I-3855). Yet – without an order to discontinue – in the meantime, the Italian Supreme Court, finding for the plaintiff in Italian proceedings, avoided the arbitration clause and rendered moot the English proceedings by ruling with *res judicata* effects that the exchange of telegrams which took place between the parties did not give rise to an "agreement in writing" according to Article II of the New York 1958 Convention on International Commercial Arbitration (see Italian Corte di cassazione, Plenary session, January 25th 1991, No. 749, *Foro italiano*, 1991, I, 1439).

[36] See also Hartley, *Anti-suit Injunctions and the Brussels Jurisdiction and Judgments Convention*, *ICLQ* [2000], 166, at 168: "the question is, therefore, whether the institutional value of harmony between courts should prevail over the more personal value of justice in the individual case [...] In any event, it would be wrong to grant an injunction simply because, in the opinion of the English court, the foreign court lacks jurisdiction under the Convention. On the other hand, if considerations entirely outside the ambit of the Convention require the granting of an injunction, there is no reason why it should be refused just because another Convention State is involved".

[37] See also Schlosser, *Jurisdiction and International Judicial and Administrative Coopera-*

issuance of an injunction would aim at subverting the "first come, best served" principle underlying the *lis pendens* rule (and there is no evidence in English case-law of such a use of anti-suit injunctions)[38]; or, if the issuance of an injunction would aim at imposing a particular construction of *forum* selection clauses different from the construction which is likely to be reasonably offered by the non-selected court. Even English scholars believe that there is no place for restraining orders if a relevant foreign court, taking a broad and reasonable view of the matter, could be expected to dissent from the view that the bringing of the proceedings by the respondent is a breach of contract.[39] In this context the differences between the traditional broader construction of *forum* selection clauses by English courts, according to which any claim arising from the contractual relationship both in contract and in tort falls within the agreement for the exclusive jurisdiction[40], and the narrower construction of the civil law systems, according to which the claims in tort in principle are not within the range of such an agreement unless expressly specified, have to be resolved not through anti-suit injunctions[41], but through a preliminary reference to the ECJ, whose ruling in this matter is already long overdue, notwithstanding a dozen preliminary rulings in matters of Article 17 of the Brussels Convention.

Therefore, in so far as the alleged correct application of the jurisdictional rules of the Brussels Regulation is not at stake, it is likely that even continental

*tion*, *supra* note 13, 406: "if the interest of justice to be done to individuals requires transborder activity of the court, this is in itself justification to act as long as the court does not act on foreign soil".

[38] To the contrary, in *Molins plc v GD SpA*, [2001] *International Litigation Procedure*, 9 (H.C.; reversed, on other grounds, by the Court of Appeal, [2001] *International Litigation Procedure* 166), Pumfrey J. declined the grant of an anti-suit injunction to protect the English proceedings from an Italian proceedings which was instituted first by means of service of the process by fax, although the service by fax was authorized by the Italian judge upon deceptive information by the Italian plaintiff: "it must be recognised that the jurisdiction (to issue injunctive relief) is directed at preventing abuse of process, not at alleviating inconvenience or assuaging resentment. It is not an abuse of process merely to require a litigant in a tribunal of a Convention country if that tribunal in fact has jurisdiction under the Convention. Nor is it an abuse of process to bring a defendant before a foreign tribunal by a trick when that tribunal has no jurisdiction: it must be assumed that the tribunal will recognise that fact and will deal with the fact that its own jurisdiction has been sought to be invoked by a trick in its own way" (at 26).

[39] Briggs-Rees, *Civil Jurisdiction and Judgments*, *supra* note 30, para. 5.39.

[40] See Briggs-Rees, *Civil Jurisdiction and Judgments*, *supra* note 30, para. 4.24: "When an agreement is governed by, or is construed according to, English domestic law, there is a strong judicial tendency to construe it widely and generously, and not to accede to an argument that (for example) because the claim is framed in tort or in equity, it is not within the scope of a clause which deals with «all disputes arising under this contract», and so forth".

[41] It was the broad construction of a choice of court agreement by the English court that justified the issuance of an anti-suit injunction, against the Greek proceedings instituted in tort, in *Continental Bank NA v Aeakos Compania Naviera SA*, [1994] 1 *W.L.R.* 588: although, even in that case, the Court of Appeal did not rest its judgment on this point, yet issued the injunctive relief "to restrain the appellants' clear breach of contract".

judges can and will feel the urge for devices to prevent private wrongs or breaches of jurisdiction agreements, which resemble very closely the anti-suit injunction. It was surely the need to prevent a private wrong to the abusive benefit of a single creditor and to the detriment of all other creditors, which moved the French *Cour de cassation* in the case *Banque Worms v Brachot* to accept that a French court had the right to order creditors of an insolvent company to discontinue proceedings which they had brought in Spain with the aim of recovering more than the dividend to be expected from the French administration of the whole of the debtor's assets[42]: with an order *in personam* backed by the threat of an *astreinte* which was very like an anti-suit injunction.

It has been said, however, that the exercise of such authoritative discretionary powers – which is perfectly obvious in systems where judges are not thought of as officials, and indeed are supposed to be chosen for their sound discretion – will be accepted with difficulty, should it be entrusted to continental judges, who belong to a bureaucratic selected *milieu.*[43] But, without underestimating the problem, it seems possible to find a solution to this general objection through suitable rules of venue. Civil law systems are, in fact, aware of the need for such rules in so far as pervasive and authoritative powers are at stake, as is shown by the fact that – for example – the issuing of *référé-provisions* is entrusted in France only to the President of the *Tribunal de Grande Instance* (Article 808 of the *nouveau code de procédure civile*).

---

[42] Cour de cassation, Civ. 1ére, Novembre 11th 2002, *Dalloz* 2003, 797 (note Khairallah); *Rev Crit* 2003, 816 (note Muir-Watt); *Intl'l Lis* 2004, 2, 75 (note Montanari).

[43] Consolo, *Int'l Lis* 2005, 3, 137.

# Some Comments on Civil Provisional Measures to Prohibit Specific Actions According to Finnish Law

*Laura Ervo*

## 1. General Remarks[1]

In Finland, preliminary injunctions are in general possible according to Chapter 7, Sections 1–3 of the Procedural Code. In the case, where the judgment has already been given by court, but it is not possible to enforce it straight away, the provisional measure can be exempted by an execution officer according to the Enforcement Act. The enforcement of the provisional measure based on Chapter 7 of the Procedural Code is regulated in Chapter 7 in the Enforcement Act. The system consists of two steps like in other Scandinavian countries and Germany.[2]

In patent, trademark and copyright disputes preliminary injunctions are issued also on the basis of specific statutes in the Law on Securing Evidence in Civil Cases with regard to Industrial or Intellectual Property Rights, in the Patent Act, in the Trademark Act and in the Copyright Act. There are some specific regulations even in the Act on Provision of Information Society Service.

In addition there are possibilities to use coercive measures in the Coercive Measures Act, but I do not cover criminal matters in this article.

All in all, the legislative basis on provisional measures is very complicated in Finland. In order to get the right kind of general review on this topic, it is necessary to study even the specific legislation on this matter.

---

[1] After the presentation there has been some development concerning civil provisional measures in Finland. The new Enforcement Act came into force on 1st Jan. 2008. Because of this, also Chapter 7 of the Procedural Code has been changed. This article was written in 2006 and it is based on the former legislation. The amendments have not been taken into consideration because there were only minor substantive changes on provisional measures and on the proceedings to undertake them. The reform covered mainly other issues. However, the numbering of the sections has been changed and the formulation of the sections has been updated and some minor changes have been made. The main system is, however, still the same.

[2] Lappalainen 1994, p. 274.

## 2. Chapter 7 of the Procedural Code

### *2.1. The requirements*

According to Chapter 7, Section 1 of the Procedural Code it is possible to use provisional measures if the petitioner establishes a probability that he/she holds a debt that may be rendered payable by a decision referred to Chapter 3, Section 1(1) of the Enforcement Act, and that there is a danger that the opposing party hides, destroys or conveys his/her property or takes other action endangering the payment of the debt, the court may order the attachment of the real or movable property of the opposing party to an amount securing the debt.

According to Chapter 7, Section 2 an object or other given property in the possession of the opposing party may be attached also when the petitioner can establish a probability that he/she has a prior right to the object or property in question, enforceable by a decision referred to in Chapter 3, Section 1(1) of the Enforcement Act, and that there is a danger that the opposing party hides, destroys or conveys the said object or property or takes other action endangering the right of the petitioner.

According to Chapter 7, Section 3 of the Procedural Code it is possible to use provisional measures even in such situations where the petitioner can establish a probability that he/she has a right enforceable against the opposing party by a decision and that there is a danger that the opposing party by the deed, action or negligence or in some other manner hinders or undermines the realisation of the right of the petitioner or decreases essentially its value or significance.

In the latter situations, the court may a) prohibit the deed or action of the opposing party, under threat of a fine; b) order the opposing party to do something, under threat of a fine; c) empower the petitioner to do something or to have something done; d) order that property of the opposing party be placed under the administration and care of a trustee; or e) order other measures necessary for securing the right of the petitioner to be undertaken.

When deciding on the issue of a prohibition or this kind of order[3], the court shall see to that the opposing party does not suffer undue inconvenience in comparison with the benefit to be secured.

It is possible to apply Chapter 7, Section 3 even to industrial or intellectual property cases in situations where the special legislation does not give the same possibilities as Chapter 7 does. So, if Chapter 7 gives wider protection, it is applicable.[4]

The provisional measures based on Chapter 7 can be used in situations where the enforcement is not possible because of failing judgment or other grounds for

---

[3] This covers only the situations based on Section 3 in Chapter 7 of the Procedural Code.

[4] Havansi 1993, p. 59–60.

execution, but where there is a danger that the opposing party endangers the right of the petitioner.[5]

## 2.2. *The proceedings*

The decision to undertaking precautionary measures referred above shall be made, on a petition, by a general court of law. The issue of precautionary measures shall be heard by the court where the proceedings on the main claim or right of the petitioner are pending. If the hearing of the main issue has been concluded and the time provided for appeal, the issue of precautionary measures shall be heard by the court that last addressed the main issue. If no proceedings are pending, the competent court shall be determined in accordance with the provisions of normal rules on forums.[6] Even if the main issue is pending or will be pending in the arbitrary court, the general court of law is the only forum, which can make a decision on provisional measures. The arbitrary court cannot even decide the cancellation of the precautionary measures.[7]

However, the cancellation shall be ordered on request of the party. By the court or the other authority referred to above, the cancellation shall be ordered, on request, by the court that has first decided on the precautionary measures.[8] So, even the administrative court may make this kind of decision on the cancellation if the main issue is pending there.[9] In some situations, even the executive officer has the power to cancel the precautionary measure.[10] However, the arbitration court does not have jurisdiction in these situations. If the main case is pending in the arbitration court, the same court has to make the decision on the cancellation, which decided the petition on the precautionary measure.[11]

Also in situations where the foreign forum has the jurisdiction according to Lugano or Brussels conventions, the Finnish court may make a decision on precautionary measures according to Finnish law.[12]

The petition for precautionary measures shall be submitted in writing. If the precautionary measures relate to pending proceedings, the petition may be submitted orally in the hearing where the main issue is addressed with. The petition shall be considered urgently. The petition shall not be granted without reserving the opposing party an opportunity to be heard. However, if the purpose of the precautionary measures can otherwise be compromised, the court may

[5] Lappalainen 2003, p. 1033.
[6] Chapter 7 of the Procedural Code, Section 4.
[7] Havansi 1993, p. 82, 84 and Lappalainen 1994, p. 279.
[8] Chapter 7 of the Procedural Code, Section 8.
[9] Lappalainen 1994, p. 279.
[10] See the Enforcement Act, Chapter 7, Section 13.
[11] Havansi 1993, p. 156.
[12] Article 24 in Lugano convention and article 31 in Brussels convention.

on the request of the petitioner give an interim order on precautionary measures without reserving the opposing party the said opportunity.[13]

In some situations the petition should be decided even on the same day or in every case during the following days. If the vessel is running away for example, the petition should be decided straight away, that is while the petitioner is waiting in the court. The standard of proof is at a low level. The petitioner should proof only that he/she probably has a debt, which means about 50% standard. What the danger is concerned, the standard of proof is even lowered. In most cases it will be enough that the petitioner makes the claim on it.[14] It is also enough to only have a danger of losing the property for some reason. The danger does not have to be based to mala fides of the opposing party. Of course the court may reject the petition in the cases where it seems too surprising and unbelievable for the judge that there would be some danger at all, but in normal situations there is a presumption that the claim is correct.[15]

When the petition has been granted, the petitioner shall within one month of issue of the order bring an action on the main issue before a court or bring the main issue up for consideration in other proceedings that may result in a decision enforceable in accordance with Chapter 3, Section 1(1) of the Enforcement Act.[16]

If the petitioner neglects his/her duty to bring an action on the main issue before a court, the executive officer cancels the precautionary measure at the request of the opposing party.[17]

In the case, where the judgment has already been given by court, but it is not possible to enforce it straight away, the provisional measure mentioned above can be exempted by a execution officer according to the Enforcement Act. In such situations, a provisional measure is in force six months. If there are some special reasons, the execution officer can even exempt the continuation.[18]

### *2.3. Security, damages and costs*

According to Chapter 7, Section 16 in the Enforcement Act the petitioner has to provide the security for the possible damages before the executive officer can enforce the decision. The security can be a pledge or a guarantee and it should be placed at the executive officer. According to Chapter 7 of the Procedural Code, the court may make an exception and release the applicant from providing the security, if the petitioner is found unable to do so and if his/her right is deemed manifestly well-founded.

[13] Chapter 7 of the Procedural Code, Section 5.
[14] Havansi 1993, p. 14–16, 2002, p. 98–99 and 109–110.
[15] Havansi 1993, p. 14, 23–25, 51, 56 and 69.
[16] Chapter 7 of the Procedural Code, Section 6.
[17] Enforcement Act, Chapter 7, Section 13, paragraph 2.
[18] Enforcement Act, Chapter 7, Section 11a, paragraph 1.

The providing of the security then happens at the enforcement level after the court's decision. The petitioner has to place it at the executive officer. However, only the court can release the petitioner from providing the security. Usually, the petitioner does the claim on his/her petition for the provisional measure. The petitioner can ask the court to release him/her even later, if he/she notices this question or if it becomes otherwise current at the enforcement level. In such situations, he/she has to do a new petition on this releasing question.[19]

The releasing happens in very rare situations. It is possible to make an exception and release the petitioner from providing the security if there is nearly full proof on the debt or other kind of substantive or rightful claim. The standard of proof concerning the danger is on the usual level even in these situations, that is the presumption is that there is a danger, if it is not somehow almost notorious that there cannot be any danger.[20]

The expenses incurred by the enforcement of the precautionary measures shall be primarily covered by the petitioner. The issue of the final liability to cover the expenses incurred by the application and enforcement of the precautionary measures shall be decided, on the request of a party, when the main issue is being addressed with.[21] The expenses cover both the costs on the court level and after the decision on the enforcement level.[22]

A petitioner who has unnecessarily resorted to precautionary measures shall be liable to compensate the opposing party to the damage caused by the precautionary measures and their enforcement, and to cover the expenses incurred.[23] The responsibility for the damages is objective.[24] The objective responsibility can be seen as a compensation to the opposing party because of the fact that the standard of proof is at the low level in cases of precautionary measures.[25]

## 3. Law on Securing Evidence in Civil Cases With Regard to Industrial or Intellectual Property Rights

At the beginning of May 2000 came into force the law on securing evidence in civil cases with regard to industrial or intellectual property rights. The idea is to preserve the evidence for trial in special cases, which concern the violation of industrial or intellectual property rights and in some other very special cases.[26]

[19] Havansi 1993, p. 151–152.
[20] Havansi 1993, p. 151 and 155.
[21] Chapter 7 of the Procedural Code, Section 10.
[22] Havansi 1993, p. 179.
[23] Chapter 7 of the Procedural Code, Section 11.
[24] Havansi 1993, p. 190–193, 2002, p. 99 and Lappalainen 2003, p. 1036.
[25] Havansi 1993, p. 190 and 193.
[26] Section1 of the Law on Securing Evidence in Civil Cases with Regard to Industrial or Intellectual Property Rights.

In order to preserve the evidence the court may order that the material which alleged could have significance as a piece of evidence in cases named above, the attachment. The court may even order some other measure, which is less serious than the attachment is. Making the decision the court has to compare the interests between the petitioner and the opposing party. The precautionary measure may, namely, not harm the opposing party in an unreasonable way.[27]

The requirements are that the petitioner can proof that 1) he/she probably has the right mentioned in the legislation concerned and 2) that there is or will immediately be a violation against his/her right and 3) there is a danger that the opposing party or someone, who has the material hides, destroys or conveys the material or takes other action endangering the preservation of that kind of material.[28]

If the purpose of the precautionary measures otherwise be compromised, the court may at the request of the petitioner give an interim order on precautionary measures without reserving the opposing party the opportunity to be heard.[29] It is the duty of the executive officer to enforce the order.[30]

## 4. Sections 60 a and 60 c of the Copyright Act[31]

According to Section 60 a of the Copyright Act the person who has the copyright has the right by a court order to get the contact information of a subscriber from the service provider, who is substantially communicating to the public protected material without the consent. The possible secrecy regulations do not stop this right to information. The petitioner has liability for costs and damages to the intermediary.

According to Section 60 b of the Copyright Act, the assignee has the right to seek an injunction against the alleged infringer. If the case is found for the plaintiff, the court must order that the infringement should be stopped. The court may impose a conditional fine.

When the case is being tried, the court may order an injunction against the intermediary to stop distribution to the public. The request is that the injunction is not prohibitive. In this comparison, the court has to take into consideration the rights of the person who is communicating the material to the public,

---

[27] Section 2 of the Law on Securing Evidence in Civil Cases with Regard to Industrial or Intellectual Property Rights.

[28] Section 3 of the Law on Securing Evidence in Civil Cases with Regard to Industrial or Intellectual Property Rights.

[29] Section 4 of the Law on Securing Evidence in Civil Cases with Regard to Industrial or Intellectual Property Rights.

[30] Section 5 of the Law on Securing Evidence in Civil Cases with Regard to Industrial or Intellectual Property Rights.

[31] See also Sorvari 2005, p. 527–534.

the intermediary and the assignee. In order to make this order effective, the court may impose a conditional fine.[32]

This decision on interruption is possible even before the court proceedings if there is an apparent risk of severe damages to assignees' rights. Even in these situations the court has the duty to hear both, the intermediary and the person who is communicating the material. The petitioner has liability for the costs and damages to the intermediary and to the supposed "infringer".[33]

The provisional measure based on the Section 60 c may not risk the communicative rights of the third party.[34]

These sections came into force on 1st January 2006. However, the parliament has already recently made some reforms on Section 60 c. The amendments have already been passed by parliament, but the president has not yet confirmed them. Therefore even the date when the amendments will come into force is unclear.[35]

According to the new Section, the court may at the request of the petitioner give an interim order on interruption without reserving the "infringer" the right to be heard. The requirement is that the matter is very urgent. Even in these situations the court has to reserve the intermediary the right to be heard. When the court has given the interim order of this kind, it has a duty to reserve the supposed "infringer" the right to be heard as soon as possible. After that the court decides, if the order may be still in force or not. The interim order should be cancelled even if the court cannot reach the "infringer" in reasonable time. The possibility to give an interim order will be very exceptional. It would be possible, 1) when the immediate interruption is very important for the petitioner and 2) when it is impossible to hear the supposed "infringer" urgent enough.[36]

According to the new Section 60 c the petitioner has to provide the security for the possible damages, before the executive officer can enforce the decision. The security should be placed at the executive officer. According to Chapter 7 of the Procedural Code, the court may make even in these cases an exception and release the applicant from providing the security, if the petitioner is found unable to do so and if his/her right is deemed manifestly well-founded.[37]

The order on interruption may become void, if the suit about the main issue is not brought in one month from the date when the court gave the decision on interruption.[38]

---

32 Section 60 c of the Copyright Act.

33 Section 60 c of the Copyright Act.

34 Section 60 c, paragraph 3 of the Copyright Act.

35 The amendments mentioned above came into force on the 1st of September 2006 by the law 678/2006.

36 Amended Section 60 c of the Copyright Act and HE 26/2006, p. 21–22.

37 Amended Section 60 c of the Copyright Act.

38 Amended Section 60 c, paragraph 4 of the Copyright Act.

## 5. Other Special Legislation

### *5.1. Trademark Act*

According to Section 48 of the Trademark Act when an injunction is applied for under this Act, the court may, at the request of the plaintiff, grant an injunction against the defendant either during the proceedings or in its decision, to remain in force until the main action has been settled with legal effect, or until the same or another court has previously ruled otherwise. Before such an injunction is granted, the plaintiff may be ordered to provide reasonable security for any damage that the defendant might suffer from the injunction.

A separate appeal may be made against court ruling handed down during proceedings concerning an injunction or the lifting thereof.[39]

### *5.2. Patent Act*

According to Section 68 of the Patent Act the court may grant at the request of the plaintiff an interlocutory injunction on the use of the patent or may order that the objects of property be provisionally seized for the duration of the proceedings.

Where the court has granted an injunction or ordered seizure mentioned above, the plaintiff may be required to provide such security as the court accepts for any damage of inconvenience that may be suffered by the other party due to the action.[40]

Relief from a decision on the injunction or seizure or the lifting of such measures during the course of the proceedings may be sought by separate appeal.[41]

### *5.3. Amendments*

The amendments in the government bill 26/2006 cover industrial and intellectual rights of all kind and on the basis of it there will be in the nearest future the possibility to make similar decisions on the interruption even on trademark-, patent- and some other industrial and intellectual rights than on the basis of the amended Section 60 c in the Copyright Act. As I have mentioned above, the parliament has recently accepted the amendments and we are still waiting for the president's confirmation.[42]

[39] Section 48 of the Trademark Act.
[40] Section 68 of the Patent Act.
[41] Section 68 of the Patent Act.
[42] The legislation came into force on the 1st of September 2006.

## 6. Act on Provision of Information Society Services[43]

According to Section 16 of the Act of Provision of Information Society Services, the court may order the service provider to disable access to information stored by him/her if the information is clearly such that keeping its content available to the public or its transmission is prescribed punishable or as a basis for civil liability. A public prosecutor, a person in charge of inquiries or a party whose right the matter concerns, may make an application of this kind. The court must urgently process it. The application cannot be approved without reserving for the service provider and the content producer an opportunity to be consulted except if the consultation cannot be arranged as quickly as the urgency of the matter so necessarily requires. A court order must also be made known to the content producer.

An order ceases to be in effect unless charges are raised for an offence based on the content or transmission of information referred to in the order or, when concerning a liability, action is brought within three months of issuing the order. Within the time limit referred above, the court may extend this time limit by a maximum of three months on request by a public prosecutor, by a complainant or by an interested party.[44]

The service provider and the content producer have the right to apply for the reversal of the order in the court where the order was issued. The reversal must be applied for within 14 days of the date when the applicant was notified of the order.[45]

According to this Act it is also possible to prevent the access to material infringing copyright or neighbouring right "voluntarily", that is without the court order. The way is to make a notification to the service provider, who must immediately notify the content producer of prevention of access to the material supplied by him/her. The notification must be done in writing or electronically. If the content producer considers that the prevention is groundless, he/she may get the material returned by delivering to the notifying party a plea in writing or electronically.[46]

---

[43] More information in Sorvari 2005, p. 527–534.

[44] Section 16 of the Act on Provision of Information Society Services.

[45] Section 16 of the Act on Provision of Information Society Services.

[46] See Chapter 5 in the Act on Provision of Information Society Services.

## 7. On Problems and Visions in Precautionary Measures

### 7.1. *A forest of norms*

As you have seen until now the Finnish legislation on precautionary measures is based on one general chapter of our Procedural Code (Chapter 7) and in addition on very many special rules in specific acts. We have also had very many amendments in Finland recently concerning the legislation on interim measures. At the beginning of the 90s the general system (based now on this Chapter 7) was amended in a radical way. However, these amendments concerned mostly the proceedings and not so much precautionary measures itself, that is in their substantive meaning.

Because of the EG-law and very many directives we have got the novelties and amendments especially in legislation on industrial- and intellectual rights.[47] The current situation in this field is that we have a forest of norms, which means that it is very difficult for laymen, even quite difficult for lawyers, to get a general view on this ruling.

The forest of norms may even have some very important effects in practice. The requirements and the standard of proof for instance can become variable in different situations decided by different acts. The possibility of this kind of variation can be unfair for individuals. We can ask if it is fair to get the precautionary measure with the low proof for instance in copyright cases, when at the same time it is possible that the court demands a very high standard of proof for instance in the situations of a debt.[48]

### 7.2. *The principle of legality*

The injunction needs to be interpreted in the light of the principle of legality, which means, for instance, that the injunction must be drafted precisely. That is, vague terms should be avoided.[49]

In my opinion, there is, however, much room for interpretations in every concrete case. The court has to weight the interests and the standard of proof of possible danger for instance in almost every decision. Therefore the decisions on precautionary measures are based in praxis somehow on the "soft law" even if the court has to highly honour the principle of legality, of course.

---

[47] On impact of Community law on provisional judicial protection in Swedish civil and administrative proceedings see Nordback 2005.

[48] These are hypothetic examples – not the reality – made only in order to concretise the possible problems.

[49] Norrgård 2002, p. 334–335.

### 7.3. Requirements

In Finland, the requirements have traditionally been quite high, which has limited the interest for preliminary injunctions in the so-called hard cases where it is difficult to decide whether there is an infringement. The requirements for Chapter 7, Section 3 of the Procedural Code differs from the requirements for specific statutes. However, the differences are in detail and the building blocks are the same in all statutes.[50]

First there is a requirement of infringement, which has a retrospective and a prospective element, both of which must be fulfilled if the court is satisfied that it is likely that there has been an infringement or that there have been some acts which indicate a threat of infringement. The prospective element is fulfilled if there is a danger or risk of infringement in the future. The retrospective element cannot be differentiated from the prospective element if there is no actual infringement, only a threatened one.[51]

After that there is usually a balance of the interests' requirement. It requires the court to take into account, on the one hand, the consequences of a decision of issuing a preliminary injunction and, on the other hand, the consequences of the decision to rejecting the claim for a preliminary injunction.[52]

In most cases, the court has favoured a strict infringement model. That is courts focus on the likelihood of infringement and only rarely take the consequences that are the balance of interests into consideration.[53]

### 7.4. The standard of proof

In Chapter 7 in the Procedural Code, the petitioner must proof that he/she has a debt or other right, which should become protected by a provisional measure. The legislated standard of proof is "likely", which is a vague term. It can be interpreted in several ways. The standard of proof is thus flexible.[54]

The starting point is that the plaintiff must show that it is more likely that he/she has a debt or that there are some kinds of an infringement than that there is no debt or no infringement. However, because of the flexibility of the standard of proof, the outcome of the balancing the interests can and should affect the standard of proof. The greater the interest of the defendant in relation to the plaintiff's interest, the higher the burden of proof and of course, this also works the other way around. The higher the plaintiff's interest in relation to the defendant's, the lower the standard of proof.[55]

---

[50] Norrgård 2002, p. 335–336.
[51] Norrgård 2002, p. 339–341.
[52] Norrgård 2002, p. 341–342.
[53] Norrgård 2002, p. 338.
[54] Norrgård 2002, p. 338–339.
[55] Norrgård 2002, p. 338–339.

*7.5. An adjustment period*

In Finland getting an adjustment period after the issuing of the injunction is not allowed within which the defendant must cease with the infringing activities. However, some researches in Finland have very positive attitudes concerning this kind of "Aufbrauchfrist" and they are arguing that such adjustment period should be allowed.[56]

# Bibliography


| | |
|---|---|
| HE 26/2006 | Hallituksen esitys Eduskunnalle laeiksi teollis- ja tekijänoikeuksia koskevan lainsäädännön muuttamisesta. HE 26/2006 vp. (Governments Bill to the Parliament.) |
| Havansi 1993 | Havansi, Erkki: Uusi turvaamistoimilainsäädäntö selityksineen. Jyväskylä 1993. |
| Havansi 2002 | Havansi, Erkki: Oikeudenkäynti ja pakkotäytäntö. Helsinki 2002. |
| Lappalainen 1994 | Lappalainen, Juha: Alioikeusuudistus 1987–1993. 3.ed. Jyväskylä 1994. |
| Lappalainen 2003 | Lappalainen, Juha: Summaariset prosessit siviiliasioissa. In Prosessioikeus, pp. 1029–1036. Juva 2003. |
| Nordback 2005 | Nordback, Kenneth: Interimistiska åtgärder I EG-rättsliga mål. Om gemenskapsrättens inverkan på det provisoriska rättsskyddet i svensk civil- och förvaltningsprocess. Uppsala 2005. |
| Norrgård 2002 | Norrgård, Marcus: Interimistiska förbud i immaterialrätten. Jyväskylä 2002. |
| Sorvari 2005 | Sorvari, Katariina: Vastuu tekijänoikeuden loukkauksesta erityisesti tietoverkkoympäristössä. Vantaa 2005. |


[56] Norrgård 2002, p. 337.

# Discussion

*Professor Kato:* Presentation and comment time has now concluded. It was a very fruitful international exchange of information. I would like to ask the floor for comments or questions.

*Professor Andrews:* I was particularly interested in the comments of Professor de Cristofaro on the anti-suit injunction saga in Europe, and I was intrigued by his distinction between protection of private rights and the court's interest in protecting the integrity of its process, which is characterized as a public matter. If one considers the facts themselves of *Turner v Grovit*, the question is how does that decision stand in terms of that distinction? In this case, someone alleged before an English tribunal that he had been unfairly dismissed by an employer who was actually employing him in Spain at the relevant time. And what does the employer do? The employer brings a parallel, clearly intimidatory, action in Madrid, which is going to take years to dispose. And what is the motive that the employer has in bringing that claim? Clearly to intimidate, to oppress the employee who is bringing these proceedings in England. If you consider that configuration in light of your distinction, can you not say that the English court in granting the anti-suit injunction against the employer, who was essentially bringing a tit for tat oppressive action in Spain, is not just protecting the private interest of the employee, but is actually protecting its own process? It strikes me, in other words, as a good example of the overlap of private interest and the old-fashioned concept of abuse of process.

*Professor de Cristofaro:* I would say that the English courts are trying to protect their own process and the proceedings that are taking place before them. But their interest is that the English proceedings come to an end against the employer and that it results in an effective remedy for the employee, preventing the employer from having the possibility to say "no, there is another proceeding in Spain and the English judgment is not enforceable against me". The English courts are, though, protecting their process, but they are doing so only to the benefit of the employee complaining with regard to his dismissal. And the labour tribunal in London has no interest in the specific case of Mr. Turner. They have no interest in deciding that matter. They are interested in Mr. Turner being able to achieve an effective remedy within that process, and that he is not oppressed or intimidated by the bringing of a fresh proceedings in Spain. The conduct of the employer is abusive also because, as it was said by the House of Lords, Mr. Turner probably did not have the money to defend himself in Spain and he could not even raise the *lis pendens* objection in Spain, although it was clear that the Spanish proceedings was the subsequent one and the *lis pendens* rule should operate in favour of the English proceedings. And, if he could not participate in the Spanish proceedings and if he could not raise the *lis pendens* objection, maybe the employment tribunal in Spain would go on to find against him and render the full judgment. The essence – or at least the only way to consider anti-suit injunctions admissible within the Brussels system – is to focus only on the interests of the parties, of the plaintiff who asks for an anti-suit injunction. It is not a battle between the courts which have to decide the claim. It should be only a question of abuse of conduct or breach of contract in the case of a choice of court agreement, or arbitration agreement, as in the two cases of 2005, the England – Finland case and the England – Italy case (the latter, in the meanwhile, having led to a fresh preliminary reference to the European Court of Justice, regarding the compatibility with European Union law of anti-suit injunctions in aid of an arbitral proceedings, which for itself falls outside the scope of the Brussels Regulation: case West Tankers vs. R.A.S.).

*Professor Andrews:* I suppose if one tries to put one's finger on the interest that the *Turner* case is seeking to vindicate through use of the anti-suit injunction, for want of a better phrase, I think it is possible to be characterized as 'access to justice'. Would you accept the suggestion that he has, as a private litigant, an interest which is well recognized, of course, in more general terms as access to justice, and that the process should not be stultified as a result of collateral proceedings of an intimidatory nature brought elsewhere in the world by the English defendant?

*Professor de Cristofaro:* Yes, I would accept that, but I would stress again that 'access to justice' is a private factor in this context and it is a fundamental right. It is stated by the European Convention on Human Rights. In the *Turner* case, the access to justice of Mr. Turner has more weight than the right to sue of the employer who was trying to do so, and the European Court of Justice should have allowed the English courts to balance those two conflicting interests, instead of forcing Mr. Turner to defend his case and to raise the *lis pendens* defence within an abusive second proceedings. This was the issue of the *Turner case*, not that of the risk of an "imperialistic" approach on the side of the English Courts.

*Professor Kato:* Before we continue the discussion on this topic, I would like to ask Professor Kawano or another Japanese speaker to briefly explain how this anti-suit injunction is dealt with in Japan.

*Professor Kawano:* In Japan we do not have such a concept. We adopted the provisional remedies system from the German system. In Germany, there is no such way of measures against other court proceedings. It is a very interesting device, but provided mainly in common law systems. In European continental countries there is no tradition of anti-suit injunctions.

*Professor Stürner:* It is correct to say that there is no such tradition. There were some attempts to introduce anti-suit injunctions but, until now, we have had no remarkable cases. The most recent decision of the European Court of Justice stopped any further development even in relation to countries which are not members of the European Union.

*Professor Kawano:* In Japan there is a possibility of such injunctions or provisional remedies, if there is a certain proceeding before the court, especially in arbitration cases, some kind of arbitration clause, though also in these cases there are certain problems so in common law countries sometimes rules against such arbitration clauses. If a party files a lawsuit against an arbitration agreement, the other party could resort to provisional remedies for prohibiting such lawsuit. But such provisional remedies are not regarded to have direct effect on the court proceedings.

*Professor Taniguchi:* When I looked at the program and the title of Professor Kawano's speech for today, I found 'Provisional Measures for Prohibition against Actions'. I thought it meant the injunction against a lawsuit, but the action here seems to have meant something else. I am glad now because our discussion has finally arrived exactly at that point. As Professor Kawano already told us, this issue has not been discussed in Japan very much. I think it raises an interesting question. As Professor Kawano suggested, if a foreign anti-suit injunction is brought to Japan, and if it is provisional in nature, a Japanese court would not recognize and enforce it, because it does not fall under our Code of Civil Procedure Article 118, the provision regarding recognition of a foreign judgment, because such a foreign injunction is not regarded as a final, definitive judgment. But if it is a foreign judgment for a final injunction, then, there is no reason for denying its recognition provided that other requirements for recognition are met. The next hard question is what kind of effect should be given to a recognized foreign injunction.

Under English law, an anti-suit injunction has the so-called *in personam* effect. The respondent who is subject to the jurisdiction of the English court is compelled to comply with the injunction under the threat of contempt. Therefore, he may withdraw or stop prosecuting the litigation in Japan. But what can and should be done by the Japanese court if the injunction judgment is recognized in Japan? I am not sure about it. The so-called Mareva injunction is just a functional equivalent of the provisional attachment, that is, the German *Arrest*. Strangely and unlike the American law, the English law did not have anything equivalent to our provisional attachment. In our system, it has the *in rem* effect, that is, the attached piece of property, whether tangible or intangible, cannot be transferred or relocated. Therefore, it is valid only within the territory of the jurisdiction of the court which issued the order. English court cannot do the same thing in respect of the property in Japan except for the *in personam* effect. Instead, an English court is free to order a person who is subject to the English jurisdiction not to dispose of his property located in Japan. But a transfer of such property in violation of the injunction is perfectly valid under the Japanese law. I think the same is true for the Japanese court when it issues in respect of foreign assets an order of the so-called 'provisional disposition', that is German '*Einstweilige Verfügung*'. It seems theoretically possible to issue such an *in personam* prohibition, which may be only *in personam* effective in a foreign country. But what kind of sanction can be given against a violation of such an *in personam* order? Japanese law does not have the contempt sanction. My guess is that nobody knows the answer yet. Therefore, this is my question to Professor Kawano. What do you think as a matter of interpretation of Japanese law? And also, I would like to address this question to Professor Stürner, because we share a similar system originating in the German legal system. Thank you very much.

*Professor Kawano:* In our globalized society, it is not possible to limit such remedies to our national territories. Sometimes we have to develop a device. One of the very interesting paths of development is to consider such *in personam* matters and to expand beyond national territories. There is no such consideration in Japan at present, but it is one of the new areas we must consider. I am very interested in the movements in European countries. Of course, there are certain problems relating to sanctions against a violation of the order, but at least with regard to preserving the status quo in such cases there must be possibilities to develop such devices.

*Professor Kato:* Thank you very much, Professor Kawano. May I now ask Professor Stürner to answer Professor Taniguchi's question?

*Professor Stürner:* The preliminary attachment has been developed in early Italy. Nearly all countries adopted this institution, and this is also true for England. But England abandoned the preliminary attachment during the nineteenth century. It was Lord Denning who was aware of the urgent necessity for a preliminary protection of claimants, and, as a consequence, he developed the Mareva injunction, for England in this time a revolutionary innovation. The Mareva injunction does not work *in rem*, it works *in personam*. From the point of view of civil law countries, English freezing orders are disproportionate and in many cases superfluous. Regularly, a preliminary attachment will suffice. It has the effects of a charge and works in rem and, consequently, any form of transactions of goods to third persons cannot affect the position of the claimant. Nevertheless, there may be cases of fraud where freezing orders working in personam may have their advantages, especially in cases of worldwide fraud. In international cases where the debtor owns assets all over the world, a sequence of attachments in different countries may be too slow and burdensome. In such exceptional cases, civil law countries may follow the English example and render prohibitive injunctions. But even the U.S. – perhaps Peter Murray could say some words on this problem – are very reluctant to adapt worldwide freezing orders.

Another problem is the execution of worldwide freezing orders in foreign countries. As a judge I had to decide on the execution of English freezing orders in Germany. My court decided only to execute freezing orders against the obligor through contempt measures, not against third persons, because third persons were not parties to litigation and, consequently, the freezing order should not affect the rights of third persons. There were also considerations to enforce a freezing order through replacing the in personam order by preliminary attachments of the obligor's individual assets located in Germany. But this would be not without problems. If the claimant enforcing the freezing order applied for various preliminary attachments for example in France, Italy, and Germany, the judge may ask whether the intention would be to apply for attachments all over the world. In this case, the question of appropriateness will arise again and a civil law court may reject the application for preliminary attachments because of a lack of appropriateness.

*Professor Kato:* Professor Murray, your questions, please.

*Professor Murray:* Thank you very much, Professor Kato. I would like to acknowledge first of all the extremely interesting presentations of Professor Kawano and Professor Andrews, and the delightful discussion. Although most of the discussion has related to the freezing order or the Mareva injunction and the extraterritorial effect of that, I would like to make my own comments.

I first return to Professor Kawano's remarks about the importance of preliminary measures in business litigation. In fact, because I think it is likely to otherwise get lost in the controversy about the Mareva injunction, in our country the so-called 'M&A litigation' which is litigation brought in connection with one company's effort to take over another, or often rival companies bidding to take over other companies, has become an extremely important form of business litigation. And as anyone who has studied that kind of litigation knows, those cases never come to final judgment. It is always a matter of preliminary measures. They are designed as tactical moves, so called, in the litigation. And the issue arises, which has been very thoughtfully discussed by Professor Kawano, as to what kind of process is appropriate in this context where you need fast action, because the businessmen are operating rapidly in their business moves. Yet, at the same time you need the kind of quality of result and due process that you ordinarily associate with completed litigation.

Under the Federal Rules of Civil Procedure, under which we operate in the United States, the provisions authorizing preliminary measures are in two tiers and they are quite similar actually to arrangements in other countries. First, there is the opportunity for a company or a party which is immediately threatened to obtain *ex parte* relief of a very temporary nature basically to preserve the status quo. And then there is a provision for more complete or more long-lasting preliminary relief which requires notice and hearing. And one of the issues often in business litigation is that you have action which must be taken very fast which automatically has final effect, because time goes by and whatever happens becomes a final result. What kind of process is due? Is this a temporary restraining order or is it what we call a preliminary injunction? We don't even get to the process of a final injunction, because that never occurs. The courts in the United States have been troubled by this disconnect between the temporary restraining order and the preliminary injunction and what kind of process is due. There has been a certain amount of judicial improvisation where we now have the temporary restraining order with notice which functions very much like a preliminary injunction and we also have a process whereby courts become quite energetic in advancing the final disposition of the case to a very early stage on the knowledge that that will be decisive anyway. So why not try the whole case out at the time of the preliminary injunction?

I mention these innovations or these dealings in the United States, because I concur very strongly with Professor Kawano's observation that it is very important for us in civil procedure systems in every country to provide methods of adjudication which accord with the needs of business people who pose these very important issues and yet do so on a time schedule which does not comport with traditional judicial processes. And can we adapt our process in a way so as to provide meaningful decisions and to preserve the rule of law in this context? I think that is a very important question that has been posed particularly as it affects international takeovers, international business litigation.

I want also without taking too much time just to give the American response on the worldwide freezing order, to observe that, as Professor Stürner said, even the Americans (which I think means that although we are generally associated with extravagant jurisdiction), in this particular case observe a remarkable degree of restraint compared to our British cousins, and in fact that worldwide freezing orders are not part of the American legal tradition. It is theoretically possible, again as Professor Stürner said, but in fact in American legal tradition it is very unusual to use an *in personam* remedy to secure payment of a money judgment. Only under situations where the plaintiff can show that the defendant actually is fraudulently stealing or secreting assets, is it likely that American courts will enter an *in personam* judgment against the defendant. Now perhaps one exception to that is in divorce cases where frequently an automatic injunction *in personam* is entered against both parties at the commencement of the proceedings so they cannot do anything to secrete their assets. But in the ordinary civil case, unless you can show that the defendant is actually secreting the assets or unless the asset is an unusual thing such as a painting or something otherwise that if secreted would moot the case, we ordinarily function *in rem*, which means we function, as Professor Stürner indicated, locally instead of globally. And so we are very interested in the development of this tension that is created by the use of the worldwide freezing order in Great Britain and how it affects other countries, including the United States. I thank you.

*Professor Andrews:* We are certainly gathering some very interesting and difficult points here. I would like to respond to two of them, if I may. The first one is Professor Murray's suggestion that in litigation which cannot proceed to trial because of the time scale, procedurally we should adapt things so that we recognize the reality of the nature of the dispute. Perhaps we might therefore have a more vigorous review of the merits. Otherwise we are rather like an ostrich ignoring the reality which is that, for the parties, the pre-trial decision is actually going to regulate the entire dispute. I would support that suggestion. I think that this is a problem facing Anglo-American civil procedure. The explanation for this is that in the common law tradition civil procedure has been structured on the assumption that the process is going to end at trial before a jury. The USA still has civil juries, before whom there will be a proper review of all the evidence at trial. So I think there is undoubtedly a difficulty here. We have in common the challenge of adapting our procedures so that we move away from this historical assumption that trial is the only evaluative mechanism for tackling tough points of dispute.

Having said that, there is not much sign in England of a shift in traditional opinion. I mentioned in my presentation that, for example, in summary judgment hearings, the courts consistently say that it is inappropriate to use that procedure to have a full scale factual review of the evidence. What they are prohibiting is oral evidence. It is fine to put in documents, but the pre-trial process bar, the not hearing of experts or lay witnesses and cross-examination, that would be a distortion of the nature of that procedure. So one of our main challenges is whether we can move away from this historical assumption that trial is the only opportunity for reviewing evidence.

The other comment that I would like to make concerns Professor Stürner's very challenging suggestion concerning proportionality. If you recall, Professor Stürner was suggesting that, according to the German tradition, an application for protective relief against the danger of dissipation is conceptualized as an application for attachment and therefore as an *in rem* application. The English *in personam* order, which is of course the essence of the freezing injunction, would from a German perspective be perceived as disproportionate. Can I suggest that actually we view it quite the other way around in England. If one reflects upon this, isn't it rather remarkable to give an unsecured creditor before the full merits have been attained a remedy conferring proprietary priority? Isn't it the more proportionate response in fact, at this pre-trial stage, to order the defendant to stop at any rate dealing with its assets, without of course conferring upon the applicant any proprietary priority? So that is, I think, the mentality which underpins the expansion of the freezing injunction. It also explains why England has actually abandoned a pre-action attachment system. The English are comfortable with that because we take the commercial and common-sense view that the applicant did not himself already take steps to obtain security for the debt. Although he had the opportunity to do that, he failed to do so. That being the case, the best that we can do is to protect that applicant by providing *in personam* relief before trial.

*Professor Stürner:* Mr. Andrews, let me say that I did not describe the German point of view only. It was the point of view of the rest of the world. The freezing order is a special English innovation. It may, however, have its advantages in special cases, but it should not replace the traditional preliminary attachment. You mentioned the priority problem, and indeed, in some legal systems this may be a weak point. But there are many civil law systems where preliminary attachments do not grant any priority to other creditors and protect only against later undue transfer. As a consequence, the argument of disproportionality of freezing orders may be justified if we compare the limited and individualized effects of a preliminary attachment with the broad and unspecified scope of a freezing order. As a result I think that we need both, the attachment and the freezing. But I also think that the freezing order should be the exception for cases of clear fraud and not the rule.

*Professor Trocker:* I am probably not the right person to mediate between England and Germany. This seems to be a 'cultural' conflict. But I am a voice from the 'rest of the world' sustaining very strongly the English innovation as one of the most beneficial of modern times. So, mediation between the two positions is not my task. I simply want to say that the two instruments – attachment and freezing orders – are complementary. They are not interfering with each other. There are different scenarios that we have to consider. In this respect, I would like to go back to one of the early cases decided by Lord Denning when he introduced the Mareva injunction. The following is a scenario that we have frequently in transnational litigation: jurisdiction to adjudicate, because of an exclusive forum selection agreement for country A. The assets to sustain the claim and to satisfy the expected judgment are in country B. There are no assets in the country where the case is tried on the merits. In country B, where the assets are, the courts have no jurisdiction to grant a provisional remedy unless they also have jurisdiction on the merits. So what can they do? The assets are there, but they cannot be attached because the law of that country requires that the courts also have jurisdiction to adjudicate. So what can be done? The scenario in the Siskina case (1977) corresponded exactly to this. And Lord Denning made this highly innovative and fundamental step to allow transnational cases to be examined and decided in an efficient way. We have to step in, he said, and take a protective measure. Although at the time it was not explicitly provided in order to secure justice, this is what the freezing order does; this is its practical usefulness.

My second point: the Mareva injunction is not only an attachment; actually, it is not an attachment order. The Mareva injunction is a very complex instrument. And here I come to the comparison between attachment and the Mareva injunction. The attachment is the old measure of an economy where you knew where the property was and where it was relatively difficult to move property because this property was visible and basically stable in one place, so you could attach it. Today, the assets which are really important in transnational litigation are not particularly visible: we don't know where they are and if we suspect they are in a certain place, in two seconds they will be somewhere else. Now, are we going to ask for attachment all over the world? No, this doesn't work. So the only efficient strategy is to identify the person and order that he/she refrains from dealing with the assets through an order *in personam*. This is the modern instrument that we need in many situations in order to make transnational litigation effective.

*Professor Dogauchi (Waseda University):* I would like to ask one question to Professor Andrews on anti-suit injunctions. As far as I am aware, the means of making such an injunction effective is a contempt of court sanction. However, from the viewpoint of the foreign courts, there would be no contempt towards their courts, even if the party were in violation. So, if you do expect such anti-suit injunctions to be effective in foreign countries, you would have to unilaterally punish the party doing business in the foreign countries. This is why the other countries see such an injunction as very dangerous and also might jeopardize the mutual understanding or the integrity of the judicial system. Do you expect to have the anti-suit injunction enforced in foreign countries?

*Professor Andrews:* It is a very interesting comment. It has never really occurred to me that you would have the desire to enforce the anti-suit injunction in a foreign jurisdiction. Because, of course, its essence, as you rightly observe, is that it is an injunction directed at the defendant who is present within the English jurisdiction. And the sanction applicable, if that injunction is breached, is very much a matter for the domestic application of English contempt of court principles. So, unless you are aware of any development, I think the answer is "yes, that is precisely how we do conceive it". And we don't have a problem with that, because English courts don't actually regard it as an arrogant or an unequal imposition upon the rest of the world. They regard it as a matter of primary justice between the plaintiff and the defendant, both of whom are subject to the English jurisdiction. That is really why the English courts feel comfortable issuing an injunction. Its implementation will be confined within the jurisdiction, although its object is, of course, directed at matters outside of the jurisdiction. It is a strong example of the '*in personam* jurisdiction'.

*Professor Takagi:* I am a bankruptcy specialist. I would like to talk about the anti-suit problem. In a bankruptcy, we have similar problems. Many years ago in Japan, the owner of a golf course located in the State of Colorado was adjudicated as bankrupt in the Tokyo District Court. But the bankrupt, the owner of the golf course, filed under Chapter 11 in the State of Colorado. He wanted to administrate his assets in Colorado using the debtor-in-possession system of Chapter 11. Of course, the Tokyo District Court could order a restraining order not to file the Chapter 11 in the United States but, as Professor Taniguchi said, it may have only *in personam* effect in Japan. Ultimately, in this case, the bankruptcy trustee made an objection to the State of Colorado, or the bankruptcy court, and the bankruptcy judge in Colorado dismissed the Chapter 11 case. But if the Tokyo District Court had issued a restraining order, the bankruptcy judge in Colorado may have respected to some extent the Tokyo District Court order.

I would like to mention another topic. Professor Murray mentioned M&A cases, and Professor Kawano mentioned the *UFJ* case. The *UFJ* case is also an M&A case. A speedy order is necessary in M&A cases. I think the developed countries, or at least many countries, have a very sophisticated statutory regime regarding provisional measures, but the problem is how speedily each court will issue these orders. Regarding the *UFJ* case, the Tokyo District Court issued the order very speedily. This is good. But I was the president or chief judge of a local district court located in the northern part of Japan. Professor Kawano mentioned the 'right to sunlight'. In one case, an injunction was filed to prohibit the construction of a large building which would affect the other neighbours. The judge did not issue the injunction for six months, but he issued the injunction after the completion of the building. It was too late. So the effectiveness of the court system or judge training is important for effective provisional measures. Each country has a sophisticated statutory regime. Even developing countries have sophisticated statutory regimes which are similar to the developed countries, but the problem is the effectiveness of the judicial system. Thank you.

*Professor Murray:* I would just like to respond briefly to these very interesting and helpful comments on the issue of preliminary measures. And I was thinking of an example, because what happens is that if you wait for the full justice system to get a final decision, the decision is often either wasteful, as in the case of tearing down a building, or ineffective. And one thing that has been done by some American judges because, as Professor Andrews suggested, (and I think it is not only true in American justice but in all of the justice systems) there is the idea that the time will come when the process has considered all of the facts properly and that that will be in the later part of the process. Often the '*Beweisaufnahme*', or the taking of evidence, even in civil law countries tends to be put off to the later parts although it can be done at any time in the proceeding. Certainly the Anglo-American trial is an event which happens generally just before judgment and there is a great effort to save the proceedings from doing anything fundamental until the trial is had. What has happened in our country is that, when there are facts in dispute which ultimately are going to decide the judgment, there is a desire to bring up that factual proceeding to a very early stage.

I give you one example: a corporate litigation which I was involved in a few years back. The issue was whether a proxy statement having to do with an annual meeting that was scheduled for a few weeks away was false and misleading. And an action was brought to enjoin the vote at the annual meeting because the proxy statement was false and misleading. The court had two choices. It could either give no preliminary relief, in which case the annual meeting would go ahead. The vote would be had and there would be a good chance that the relief ultimately granted would be ineffective, and this certainly would cause a lot of problems. Or the court could tell the company to postpone the annual meeting for several months to permit the judicial process to run out. In this case, the court did neither. The court said to the plaintiffs whom I was advising, "You have five days in which to put on your complete trial. We will have the trial of the whole business, of the whole case, in five days. No discovery, no preparation. You bring your witnesses; we have the trial in five days. And I will then issue not only a preliminary order, but we will issue a final judgment in five days." Now that is the kind of thing where the courts are trying to solve this problem of getting the process completed and the factual determination done at a time when it can render effective relief. That is only one example about the problems being solved or not solved, because to put on a full case in five days is no fun, but that is one of the ways that the court is trying to solve that problem. It is not easy.

*Professor de Cristofaro:* I just want to join Professor Trocker in backing the Mareva injunctions. Mareva injunctions are a really complex instrument, and they are very effective, because they are backed by disclosure orders. In the modern economy, they are very useful especially for this, because very often you don't even know where the debtor has his assets, and the Mareva injunction forces him or his solicitors, as in the *Duvalier* case, to reveal where the assets are. In the *Duvalier* case, the Republic of Haiti went to England and got the disclosure orders not from the former dictator of Haiti but from his solicitors, and then the Republic of Haiti could know where the assets were, and where it could eventually attach them. Mareva injunctions are also somehow proportionate because normally in the order the debtor is allowed to dispose of his assets at least to pay his lawyers, his solicitors etc., to sustain the costs, and at least to keep on living, keep on eating, while European or civil law attachment does not give the debtor any such flexible possibility to cope with the ordinary needs of life and business.

Last but not least, I just want to remind everyone that the Mareva injunction has been recognized and enforced in recent times in France and in Switzerland. The French Court of Cassassion and the Swiss Federal Supreme Court have acknowledged that the Mareva injunction can be enforced in France and in Switzerland and they enforced them not as an attachment order, but saying that the English *in personam* injunction has to be obeyed by the debtor and backing this order by a penalty of the relevant legal system, also by an '*Ordnungshaft*' or '*Ordnungsgeld*' in Switzerland. And so, they are working in Europe as an *in personam* injunction. They are not to be translated as an attachment order, but they are working as they are, as *in personam* injunctions.

*Chapter 2*

# International Class Actions

# Class Actions in a Global Economy

*Peter L. Murray*[1]

In the modern economy of global mass production and distribution of practically all goods and services, it is not surprising that collective civil litigation has become a topic of such general interest among jurists of all nations.[2]

The age of the mass society is here. Citizens in all countries experience much of their economies as the objects of mass distribution of potentially dangerous products and foods, mass communication of potentially fraudulent or misleading information, mass dissemination of potentially dangerous environmental substances. Crashes of jetliners or collapses of urban buildings can injure hundreds and thousands in a single stroke. More and more citizens, investors, consumers are being affected by "mass defaults" on the part of manufacturers, corporate management, industrial polluters, and governmental organizations.

Mass defaults generally share two characteristics. One is that many individuals are affected by the act or omission and all in the same way. The other is that the mass defaulter is usually a large and sometimes powerful actor. The first of these characteristics suggests that individual suits for redress of damage caused by the mass default tend to be duplicative and wasteful of individual effort and resources. The second characteristic suggests that individual claimants seeking redress face unequal battles against adversaries of many times their economic strength.

## a. Collective Litigation

Under these circumstances, it is not surprising that litigants in virtually all legal systems are considering ways of litigating collectively to adjudicate multiple

---

[1] Robert Braucher Visiting Professor from Practice, Harvard Law School. This paper was delivered at a Symposium on Current Issues in Civil Procedure Law sponsored by the University of Nagoya Institute of International Business Litigation on February 18, 2006. The author thanks Heather Souder, HLS 2007 for research assistance in preparing this article for publication and Professor Rolf Stürner for helpful comments on an earlier draft.

[2] Countries all over the world are considering how mass and collective litigation can be accommodated in their civil procedure codes and legal cultures.

carbon-copy cases or common rights that may have many identical individual consequences. The mechanisms of collective litigation vary a good deal from jurisdiction to jurisdiction and from legal culture to legal culture. At one extreme are those jurisdictions which regard civil litigation as an essentially individual matter, in which named individual parties may assert and vindicate their legal claims against other named individual parties. In such jurisdictions, including Germany and Japan, although free joinder of both plaintiffs and defendants is allowed, mass civil litigation is severely limited.[3] For instance Germany authorizes environmental and consumer interest groups (*Verbände*) to obtain injunctive relief in behalf of their members and others similarly situated against violations of environmental and consumer protective legislation.[4] Very recent amendments to the securities law have authorized some collective action by holders of corporate securities.[5]

Middle positions range from the Greek version of interest group actions, in which a form of damages based on moral outrage can be awarded (payable not to the plaintiff organization, but to the public purse),[6] to the English "group action", in which representative civil parties can bring litigation in behalf of similarly situated quasi parties who consent, or "opt in" to the group complaint against a common defendant.[7] Israel, Australia, Canada and Brazil provide class action remedies somewhat on the American model.[8] The less aggressive utilization of this remedy in those legal cultures may be result of the fact that the role and institution of the "entrepreneurial lawyer" is less developed in those jurisdictions than in the United States.

## b. The American Class Action

The United States enjoys the distinction or notoriety of hosting the currently most extreme development of collective civil litigation in the form of the "opt out" class action. The Federal Rules of Civil Procedure and numerous state counterparts permit representative plaintiffs to bring civil actions in behalf of any number of similarly situated persons or entities so long as "common ques-

---

[3] Peter L. Murray & Rolf Stürner, German Civil Justice 200–205 (Carolina Academic Press) (2004).

[4] Murray & Sturner, *supra* note 3 at 203–204.

[5] Murray & Sturner, *supra* note 3 at 205.

[6] See, *Die Buendlung Gleichgerichteter Interessen im Prozess*, (Jürgen Basedow, et. al. eds., 1999); Harald Koch, "Non-Class Group Litigation under EU and German Law" 11 Duke J. of Comp. & Int'l L. 355.

[7] Neil Andrews, *Multi-Party Proceedings In England: Representative and Group Actions*, 11 Duke J. Comp. & Int'l L. 249 (2001).

[8] See S. Stuart Clark & Christina Harris, *Multi-Plaintiff Litigation in Australia: A Comparative Perspective*, 11 Duke J. Comp. & Int'l L. 289 (2001).; Antonio Gidi, *Class Actions In Brazil–A Model for Civil Law Countries*, 51 Am. J. Comp. L. 311 (2003).

tions of fact and law" predominate and the class action is the best and most economical way to assert the common claims.

The American form of class action has old historical roots. It was exported to the New World in the form of English equity practice which permitted representative proceedings in certain matters affecting numerous potential litigants.[9] Class actions of the "opt in" kind, where each member of the class has to agree to the class representation, were provided for by the 1938 Federal Rules of Civil Procedure. Those Rules were amended in 1966 to greatly strengthen the class action remedy. One of the changes was to make the default class action an "opt out" proceeding. Under this arrangement potential class members would be notified of the action. Those who did not evidence their desire to leave the class would be automatically included and bound by the result.[10]

An essential feature of the American class action is the control by the court over key aspects of the case, notably "class certification" and settlement. If a party or group of parties files a case that purports to be a class action, the court must make an express determination of whether the requirements of Rule 23 are met early in the litigation. Are there common questions of law or fact that apply the same way to all members of the plaintiff class? Do these questions predominate?[11] At one time American courts applied a high threshold to these determinations. Only claims in which all elements, including damages, were virtually identical could satisfy this prerequisite.[12] This excluded most cases of mass tort, in which damages suffered by the injured were deemed too individualized to be susceptible to collective adjudication. More recently, courts have taken a more pragmatic approach and cases have been certified as class actions based on common questions of liability, with the determination of damages to occur individually following decision of the common issues.[13]

Class certification also requires a preliminary determination that the named plaintiffs are in fact fairly representative of the other members of the described class and that they and their counsel are competent to represent the interests of the class.[14] Often a single mass default results in the commencement of several more or less simultaneous class actions. When potential classes overlap the cases are generally consolidated before a single judge for the purpose of class certi-

[9] Charles Alan Wrights & Arthur R. Miller, Federal Practice and Procedure, § 1751 (3d ed. 1998).

[10] See Wright & Miller, § 1753 for a discussion of the 1966 Amendments, how they came to be enacted, and their effect on class action practice.

[11] Fed.R. Civ. P. 23(c)(2)(A)-(B).

[12] See, e.g. *Garfein v. Stiglitz*, 86 S.W.2d 155 (Ky. 1935); *Lile v. Kefauver*, 51 S.W.2d 473 (Ky. 1932).

[13] *In re Estate of Ferdinand E. Marcos, Human Rights Litigation*, 910 F.Supp. 1470 (D. Hawaii 1995). Modern cases construing the complaint to bring class within requirements of Rule 23: *Geraghty v. U.S. Parole Commission*, 719 F.2d 1199 (3d. Cir. 1983); *Farrington v. Adjutant General of State of Michigan*, 492 F.Supp. 1362 (W.D.Mich. 1980).

[14] See Fed. R. Civ. P. 23 (a)(4); Wright & Miller § 1765.

fication and all further proceedings. Counsel for the respective representative plaintiffs vie to be named "lead counsel" for whatever classes will be certified in the consolidated litigation. To the extent that rational case management had previously been hindered by American federalism, which allows class actions to be brought in either state or federal court, a recent statutory amendment has diverted the larger class actions all to federal court where they can be managed in a consistent manner.[15]

Once a class action is certified, all of the potential class members are notified and given the opportunity to opt out of the class should they wish to do so.[16] Notification can be by mail, when practicable, otherwise by publication in mass media, by television, by e-mail and even by web sites on the Internet. Members can opt out by completing and returning a simple form or by otherwise indicating their desire not to be included in the class. If a member opts out, he is not entitled to the benefit of any class settlement but is also not bound by any adverse disposition of the class litigation. If the member fails to opt out within the time specified in the notice, he is automatically included in the class and entitled to the benefit and bound by the burden of any judgment or settlement obtained by the class action.[17]

American civil litigation is characterized by the high percentage of cases which settle before trial – easily over 90%. The proportion of class actions which are resolved by settlement is even higher. In fact trial and judgment in a class action is very much the rare exception rather than the rule. The process of settlement of a class action once again involves the participation of the court. No class action can be settled unless the settlement is examined and approved by the court as fair and equitable to all members of the class.

Although the representative parties are nominally responsible for direction of class litigation undertaken in their name for the benefit of themselves and their fellow class members, as a practical matter the lawyers representing the class have the deciding voice. Typically class actions are taken on contingency fees. The representative plaintiffs have no downside risk. They are not asked to bear the considerable expenses of getting a class action certified and the members duly notified. The class lawyers, on the other hand, invest huge amounts of professional effort and make substantial out of pocket disbursements in getting the class certified and in prosecuting the action to settlement or judgment. This inversion in the amount at risk between lawyer and client means that the lawyer-client relationship is also inverted. The lawyer makes

---

[15] Class Action Fairness Act of 2005, Pub. L. No. 109–2, § 5 (2005).

[16] Fed.R. Civ. P 23 (c)(2)(B).

[17] This is the key characteristic of the opt-in class action. See Fed. R. Civ. P. 23(c)(2); *Matsushita Elec. Indus. v. Epstein*, 516 U.S. 367 (1996).

decisions for the class with little regard for the views of the nominal plaintiff he represents.[18]

The recent history of American class action litigation has included several developments that are regarded as greater or lesser abuses by all but the most dedicated class action aficionado. Entrepreneurial lawyers organize class actions to vindicate rights of which the class members were not even aware, and then settle those class actions on terms which concretely benefit the lawyers, but which provide little measurable benefit to the class represented. Defendants have incentives to collude with plaintiffs' lawyers to generate class action settlements that will provide universal absolution against potential liability. Plaintiff's lawyers utilize the leverage of class actions to increase the stakes to such a level that all but the most hardy defendants will settle almost any claim for something in order to avoid the risk of a horrendous jury verdict.[19]

These abuses have been and continue to be met with corrective legislation. The Private Securities Litigation Reform Act of 1995 set higher thresholds for class action pleadings to screen out securities class actions of little merit.[20] The Class Action Fairness Act of 2005 addresses some of the abuses perpetrated by a handful of class-action-friendly state courts by permitting removal of all but the most insignificant class actions from state to federal court based on a relaxed standard of diversity of citizenship.[21] Additional legislative measures are currently under consideration.[22]

## c. The "International" Class Action

In a global economy, mass defaults are frequently not constrained by national boundaries. An airplane that crashes may kill citizens of many countries. Investment securities today are marketed world wide. Environmental pollution knows no national barriers. Products and drugs are marketed to worldwide consumer markets.

When mass defaults cross national lines can one invoke a collective litigation process of one nation in behalf of all the claimants regardless their respective

[18] See Deborah R. Hensler, et. al., "Class Action Dilemmas: Pursuing Public Goals for Private Gain," (RAND Institute for Civil Justice 2000).

[19] James M. Underwood, *Rationality, Multiplicity & Legitimacy: Federalization of the Interstate Class Action*, 46 S. Tex. L. Rev. 391 (2003); Milton Handler, *The Shift from Substantive Procedural Innovations in Antitrust Suits*, 71 Colum. L. Rev. 1, 9 (1971); John Beisner, Matthew Shors, and Jessica Miller, *Class Action "Cops": Public Servants or Private Entrepreneurs?*, 57 Stan. L. Rev. 1441 (2005).

[20] *Private Securities Litigation Reform Act*, Pub. L. no 104–67, 109 Stat. 737 (1995).

[21] *Id.*

[22] David Rosenberg and Randy J. Kozel, *Solving The Nuisance-Value Settlement Problem: Mandatory Summary Judgment*, 90 Va. L. Rev. 1849. (2004); American Law Institute, *Principles of the Law of Aggregate Litigation (Discussion Draft)* (2006).

nationality or legal culture? Can one certify an American class that includes securities holders in Germany and Japan in a class action for fraud on the marketplace? Will a judgment in a US class action brought in behalf of users of a certain drug world wide be enforceable against the defendant in Germany or Japan? By the same token, will a judgment or settlement bind class members in Germany or Japan so that they cannot thereafter start their own cases in their own jurisdictions?

Under the current state of the law, there is serious doubt about whether an American class action can include class members from countries other than the United States without problems and complications.[23] Considerations of national legal culture as well as requirements of personal notice and right to be heard mean that a US class action settlement or judgment might well not be binding on European and Japanese class members who have failed to opt out even after receiving actual notice of the proceeding. Such class members would be entirely free to commence their own cases in their own countries based on the same mass default. This circumstance has been utilized to prevent certification of classes that include such un-bound members and limitation of the class to members from the US and other countries, such as Canada, that seem to recognize the binding effect of US class action judgments. The result is that some of the victims of a mass default may have the option of class litigation to redress their wrong, while others may not, depending on where they live.

One can regard this difference in options with a degree of equanimity, depending somewhat on the individual circumstances of the case. After all, victims of a mass default who live in those lands that are less friendly to American class litigation have their own civil remedies, which are frequently complemented by programs of social insurance that might outweigh the dubious benefits of class litigation. On the other hand, would German and Japanese shareholders of an international company that had misstated its earnings, thus fraudulently inflating the markets for its shares, have access to a mechanism for redress of their economic damages as powerful and effective as class action civil litigation? Does it make overall sense in a global economy to subject the defendant to a variety of justice regimes for the redress of a single mass default? Is it sensible to ask private individual litigants to take on an international mass defaulter on an individual basis?

[23] Peter Murray & Detlev Vagts, *Litigating the Nazi Labor Claims: The Path Not Taken"*, 43 Harv. Int'l L.J. 503 (2002); John Haberstroh, *In Re World War II Era Japanese Forced Labor Litigation and Obstacles to International Human Rights Claims in U.S. Courts*, 10 Asian L.J. 253 (2003); Kevin R. Johnson, *International Human Rights Class Actions: New Frontiers For Group Litigation*, 2004 Mich. St. L. Rev 643 (2004).

## d. The *Royal Ahold* Case

An example of the workings of American class action litigation on the global marketplace is the *Royal Ahold* class action litigation. On February 24, 2003 Royal Ahold, a multinational grocery and food service enterprise organized under Dutch law and headquartered in the Netherlands announced a $500 Million restatement of earnings for the two previous fiscal years. The investigations which followed uncovered evidence of significant inflation of reported earnings, largely relating to Ahold's US operations. These developments spawned a flurry of U.S. class action lawsuits in behalf of purchasers of Ahold securities, both U.S. residents and foreigners. [24]

The litigation was consolidated in the U.S. District Court for the District of Maryland.[25] The consolidation raised the issue of who would be the "lead plaintiff" entitled to steer the plaintiffs' side of the litigation. One potential lead plaintiff group included a party who had bought a large volume of Ahold securities on foreign exchanges in behalf of foreign customers. Although the putative class included many foreign purchasers of Ahold securities, the defendants early on had raised doubts about a class that included foreign members based on the likely unenforceability of a judgment or settlement against plaintiff class members in many foreign jurisdictions, among them Germany.[26] Under these circumstances the choice of a representative of these fragile putative class members as a lead plaintiff seemed imprudent to the court. The lead plaintiffs ultimately designated were all Americans.

Ahold and the individuals named as co-defendants vigorously contested both jurisdiction and the legal sufficiency of the claim asserted in behalf of the yet uncertified class. The docket of the case discloses a veritable snowstorm of procedural and preliminary motions filed by every party. Surely there was a lot of work for all of the many lawyers involved.

The key issues were raised by motions to dismiss filed by Ahold and all of the other defendants.[27] These motions were decided on December 21,

---

[24] See, e.g. *F. Richard Manson v. Koninklijke Ahold N. V., et al.*, C.A. No. 1:03–1243; *Lillian Kleinman v. Koninklijke Ahold N. V., et al.*, C.A. No. 1:03–1251; *John Li v. Koninklijke Ahold N. V., et al.*, C.A. No. 1:03–1257; *Franklin Wilson v. Royal Ahold N. V., et al.*, C.A. No. 1:03–216; *U-2 Club v. Royal Ahold N. V., et al.*, C.A. No. 1:03–222; *Ralph P. Sbraccia v. Royal Ahold N. V., et al.*, C.A. No. 1:03–223.

[25] *In re Royal Ahold N. V. Securities, "ERISA" Litigation*, 269 F.Supp.2d 1362 (Jud.Pan. Mult.Lit.,2003).

[26] *In re Royal Ahold N. V. Securities & ERISA Litigation*, 219 F.R.D. 343 (D.Md.,2003).

[27] Reply Memorandum of Law of Royal Ahold N.V., U.S. Foodservice, Inc., Ahold U.S.A., Inc. and Ahold U.S.A. Holdings, Inc. in Further Support of Their Motion to Dismiss Certain Defendants and Counts and to Strike Certain Allegations of the Complaint (Aug. 27, 2004) 2004 WL 2359081; Defendants James Miller, Michael Resnick and David Abramson's Reply Memorandum in Support of Their Motion to Dismiss Plaintiffs' Amended and Consolidated Complaint for Violation of Erisa (2003) 2003 WL 24256347; Defendant Robert G.

2004.[28] Most of them, include the motions of Ahold and its chief officers, were denied. Ahold's substantial American operations, which were directly involved in much of the alleged fraud, supported both subject matter and personal (international) jurisdiction. The court ruled that the plaintiffs' core allegations against Ahold and several of its key officers stated valid claims under the United States' securities laws, which could support private rights of action by securities holders damaged by such misconduct. International jurisdiction over Ahold's officers was upheld or denied depending on the nature and extent of their activities in the U.S. or affecting any alleged fraud perpetrated in U.S. filings or statements.

Following this key court ruling, the parties commenced both discovery activity and negotiations aimed at reaching a comprehensive settlement. The lead plaintiffs filed an amended complaint refining and particularizing their allegations against some of the defendants. Discovery skirmishes ensued over access to written memoranda of witness interviews prepared by Ahold counsel in connection with the earnings restatement. Defendants ran up huge bills for legal representation, which they paid. Plaintiffs' counsel, working on contingency fee arrangements, increased their already immense investment of time, energy and their own funds in hopes of a resolution that would shower them with money.

Following the path of almost all class action cases, the Royal Ahold litigation was ultimately settled. Ahold had to consider the risk of a potentially staggering award to a class of thousands or tens of thousands of claimants. The lead plaintiffs and their counsel were willing to accept a small percentage of what they might have recovered by jury verdict in settlement at an early stage of the litigation. After all, they also had born the risk of losing their already substantial investment of time and money if they were come up with a zero verdict after trial.

At this point the issue of potential unenforceability of a class action judgment in foreign countries took on an entirely new and different significance. Royal Ahold, had raised such unenforceability as a barrier to class certification and to disqualify a potential lead plaintiff. At the settlement stage, however, Ahold wanted the pact to be as binding as possible, world-wide. Yet it was confronted

Tobin's Reply Memorandum in Further Support of His Motion to Dismiss (Mar. 2, 2005) 2005 WL 3741551 ; Reply Memorandum of Law in Further Support of Defendant Cees Van Der Hoeven's Motion to Dismiss the Consolidated Amended Securities Class Action Complaint (Aug. 31, 2004) 2004 WL 2359086; Reply Memorandum of Law in Further Support of Motion by Defendant Henny De Ruiter to Dismiss the Consolidated Amended Securities Class Action Complaint (Aug. 31, 2004) 2004 WL 2359089; Reply Memorandum in Further Support of Defendant Roland Fahlin's and Jan Andreae's Motion to Dismiss the Consolidated Amended Securities Class Action Complaint (Aug. 31, 2004) 2004 WL 2359092.

[28] *In re Royal Ahold N.V. Securities & ERISA Litigation*, 351 F. Supp.2d 334 (D. Md. 2004).

by the possibility that it would be funding a comprehensive settlement but it might yet be faced with new claims from class members resident in many foreign countries.

As is usually the case, the settlement was concluded despite uncertainty about its status in many lands. Ahold must have figured that the likelihood of post settlement individual claims was small. Very likely statutes of limitations would have made such claims easy to defend. At any rate Ahold's former objections to including foreign claimants in the class were quietly dropped and a comprehensive settlement was reached. Royal Ahold agreed to pay a total of $1.1 Billion to pay claims of class members and attorneys fees and expenses in return for a complete release of all claims against Ahold and all the remaining defendants plus some other persons and entities who could conceivably become defendants in future litigation.[29] According to contemporary press accounts, the settlement payment was expected to yield $1.00 – $1.30 per share to Ahold's shareholders as the time of the fraud. While this amount is not immense, to a holder of several hundred or several thousand shares, $1 or more per share could be a significant recovery.[30]

The class was duly certified and the settlement approved by order entered on January 6, 2006.[31] The order approving the settlement sets forth formulae for allocating the settlement proceeds among class members who shall submit claims. Class members either in the US or abroad have the right to opt out of the class and the settlement in favor of litigating their own claims. Attorney's fees payable from the settlement fund will be determined and reviewed by the court at a later date.

From one perspective, the *Ahold* case has settled in a manner presumably satisfactory to all concerned. On the other hand, although the settlement purports to include them, the current lack of legal clarity over the status of foreign class members and the enforceability of any judgment or settlement against them meant much ultimately unnecessary legal disputation prior to settlement and leaves a shadow on the settlement itself that is likely more disquieting to Ahold than its former adversaries.[32]

---

[29] *In re Royal Ahold N. V. Securities & Erisa Litigation*, 2006 WL 132080 (D.Md. 2006).

[30] Andrea K. Walker. "Judge Gives Preliminary Approval to Royal Ahold Settlement." *Baltimore Sun* January 6, 2006; Reuters. "World Business Briefing Europe: Netherlands: Ahold Settlement Advances." The New York Times. January 10, 2006; "Local Briefing" The Washington Post. January 10, 2006; "Global Business Briefs" The Wall Street Journal. January 9, 2006; Ylan Mui. "Royal Ahold Lowers Sales Forecast for Giant." The Washington Post. March 30, 2006; Conrad Raj. "Singapore shareholders of Ahold can claim payout." The Business Times Singapore. March 15, 2006; Simon Bain. "Royal Ahold investors stand to share 1.1 billion dollar pay out." The Herald (Glasgow) February 16, 2006.

[31] *In re Royal Ahold N. V. Securities & ERISA Litigation*, 2006 U.S. Dist. LEXIS 1928 (D. Md. 2006).

[32] For commentary on problems with international class litigation in the securities area and possible reforms see, Jeffrey Cook, *Redrafting the Jurisdictional Framework for Private*

## e. Some Simple Proposals

Is there some way that American class action litigation seeking economic redress based on international mass defaults can be coordinated to benefit all potential victims and provide a degree of certainty and finality for the defendant? Without trying to sell either Europe or East Asia on the benefits of "entrepreneurial lawyering" and the extreme features of the American class action as currently maintained, is there a middle ground on which we can meet in collectively litigated matters involving citizens of different nations and legal cultures?

The short answer, of course is "No", or ""Not now!". However maybe we should think back on the recently adopted Transnational Principles of Civil Procedure as an example of the process by which jurists from different cultures can find common ground in policy and shared underlying values. At the outset the Americans somewhat naively proposed Rules of Transnational Civil Procedure that bore a suspicious resemblance to the Federal Rules of Civil Procedure.[33] Many Europeans reacted, "No" or "Not now" or even "Never!" But over a period of some three or four years of mutually respectful academic dialogue the original American-inspired Rules were transmuted to general Principles which resonated on both sides of the Atlantic.[34] Identification of underlying policy values and compromise as to procedural form produced a body of procedural principles that may well guide the process of convergence in international civil procedure as the world shrinks and the global economy becomes ever more independent of national boundaries.

The primary objection of European and East Asian jurists to American international class actions seems to be to the notion that persons can be included in a plaintiff class without actual notice and assent.[35] Other international concerns about proper steering of the class action are shared by Americans as well as jurists from other nations, although perhaps not to the same degree. These concerns can be addressed in various ways.

One possible solution would be to create a special procedure for collective litigation when a putative plaintiff class includes citizens of more than one state. A judgment arising from such litigation would only be enforceable against citizens of a state other than the state in which it was brought if the case was regis-

*Rights of Action Under the Federal Securities Laws*, 55 Am. U.L. Rev. 621. (2006); Michael Mann and William Barry, *Developments in the Internationalization of Securities Enforcement*, 39 Int'l Law. 937 (2005).

[33] See American Law Institute, Transnational Rules of Civil Procedure, Tentative Draft #1 (1997).

[34] Compare American Law Institute, Transnational Principles of Civil Procedure, Final Council Draft (2004).

[35] See, e.g. Richard Cappalli and Claudio Consolo, *Class Actions for Continental Europe? A Preliminary Inquiry*, 6 Temp. Int'l & Comp. L.J. 217 (1992).

tered at the outset in a designated court of the foreign state. At the time of registration the foreign court could specify the kind of notice that would be required in order to bind residents of that state in the class. Possibilities would include personal service, mail, publication, and web based notice, based on the circumstances. Translation of the notice and relevant papers into the national language could be required. The registration court could even take a second look at the appropriateness of the class from the standpoint of the foreign members and the adequacy of the representation. Finally, the registration court could assess the reasonableness of the class settlement from the standpoint of its own nationals. Failure to register and follow any requirements of the registration could jeopardize enforcement of the judgment or settlement against the class members of the registration court's jurisdiction .

A simpler measure, that would not require an additional judicial function would be to agree that in foreign jurisdictions which do not recognize class action judgments all collective litigation is "opt in". Thus only persons who actually sign up for the class action would be covered. Potential class members would be given the opportunity to opt in at the time the class is certified. For cases certified at time of settlement, people would be entitled to "opt in" at the time of settlement. Widespread notice to the potential class members of the class action and the settlement should result in a fair number of opt in class members. An opt in class would at least offer mass default victims an opportunity to participate in the class action.

A third course of action would be for nations such as Japan and Germany to simply decide to recognize judgments and settlements in American-style class litigation provided that certain specified thresholds of jurisdiction and notice to class members are achieved. This is the approach of some countries which do not themselves have collective litigation on the class action model.

A fourth course of action is to do nothing. Despite the caveats and disparagements of foreign scholars and judges, classes which include citizens of countries which are skeptical about recognizing class actions are being proposed and certified, at least for settlement purposes. So citizens of Germany and Japan are included in settlements class and have the opportunity to receive proceeds of the class settlements regardless of whether or not Germany and Japan would enforce a class action judgment against the defendant or would recognize the settlement as a bar to a future claim by a member of the class. All members of the class who file claims and receive payments are required to sign releases. The risk that other German and Japanese class members who do not file claims and receive payments will bring their own claims in the courts of their native lands is a risk that the settling parties are willing to bear.

American style class actions can bring great benefits to victims of international mass defaults who are citizens of countries other than the United States. As currently practiced, it is an imperfect remedy. There are clearly weaknesses, problems and abuses arising out of the inverted lawyer-client relationship in many such cases. We must continue to reform this remedy. Examples from abroad, such as the interest group actions in the EU Member States, can be helpful in this process.[36]

On the other hand it makes little sense for us to close our eyes to the reality of international mass defaults. A class action that can array all of the victims of the default against the defaulter, and can obtain reimbursement for all of the victims in a single proceeding is a remedy that cannot be ignored. Can we work together to make participation of class members from all countries in international class actions a legal as well as a practical reality?

[36] See Directive 98/27 of the European Parliament and of the Council for the protection of consumers' interests of May 19, 1998, L166/51; but see, Daniel J. Schwartz, "*Loose Teeth in European Union Consumer Protection Policy: The Injunction Directive and the Mass Default Scenario*", 28 Ga. J. Int'l and Comp. L. 527; Michele Taruffo, "*Some Remarks on Group Litigation in Comparative Prospective*", 11 Duke J. Comp. & Int'l L. 405 (2001)

# International Class Actions From a German Point of View

*Rolf Stürner*

## I. Introduction

Class actions are the sharp weapon of consumers, shareholders, copyright owners, or the victims of mass accidents against big corporations or mighty firms mostly acting as global players. American class actions have special attractiveness towards foreign claimants: first, the law of torts of many or most American individual states and some statutory federal laws provide for punitive or multiple damages, a worldwide more or less unique institution and unknown in nearly all other countries which could be a competent forum for the claimants' case; second, American lawyers take good cases of plaintiffs on speculation without any prepayment or retainer and bear the risk of a lost case, while the clients owe a contingency fee when they are the winner. Especially for lawyers big classes may have the advantage of a high contingency fee resulting in a good business. U.S.-American law firms are therefore fishing for claimants all over the world with the intention to represent a worldwide international class in American courts. Big global players are not afraid of administrative governmental measures of individual states but the fear class actions which put them under the threat of high punitive damages or treble damages awards with disadvantageous consequences for their public image and goodwill. This paper is designed to discuss problems of international class actions not from the point of view of the plaintiffs but from the standpoint of the defendant.

## II. Involvement of European Firms

At present, many European firms are or have been involved in U.S.-American international class action litigations. The internationalization of the shareholders of big corporations is the basis of international classes in securities litigations like Daimler-Chrysler, Deutsche Telekom, Ahold (Netherlands), or Parmalat (Italy). Copyright owners have lodged an international class action (17 billion dollars) against Bertelsmann, a big German publisher and global player, arguing that Bertelsmann as the purchaser of Napster may be liable for all past infringements of copyrights by Napster.

## III. Attacking the Certification of the International Class

It must be the tactics of the defendant to convince the American judge not to certificate the international class and thus to split the international dispute into various litigations before different national courts. Daimler-Chrysler was successful in doing so, settled the case of the remaining smaller American class under good conditions and won the case against its now more or less isolated former big shareholder Kerkorian. With the decrease of the number of class members the plaintiffs' lawyer's interest to go on litigating diminishes because of the decrease of the contingency fee, while his readiness to settle will grow. Consequently the decisive question for a defendant's lawyer is how to attack the certification of an international class. An American judge will not certificate an international class when there is no good chance that foreign courts will recognise the effects of a contested class action judgment or a judgment based on a settlement as binding. It is important to know that the recognition of the positive effects of the American judgment, especially enforceability in the foreign country and in Europe, are not so important because enforcement in the U.S. itself will nearly always be possible when the defendant is a global player owning assets in the U.S. More important and decisive for the rendition of the certification order is the recognition of negative preclusive effects preventing class members from lodging a second action against the defendant in foreign courts when they are not content with the result of the U.S. judgment, especially in case of a settlement based consent judgment. Because under U.S.-American understanding a class litigation makes little sense when the final decision does not really and reliably end the dispute with all class members which did not opt out.

## IV. Grounds for Non-recognition of Negative Preclusive Effects of Class Action Decisions

European continental or continental influenced legal cultures like Japan may have mainly two grounds not to recognize the negative preclusive effects of U.S.-American class action judgments. These grounds for non-recognition shall now be discussed under the provisions of German law, and because of many similarities between the German and Japanese situation this discussion may be of some interest for our Japanese hosts and visitors of this symposium.

The first ground for non-recognition is a lack of due notice in a manner that strictly complies with the requirements of the Hague Service Convention. The second ground is a lack of personal jurisdiction of American courts over class members.

## V. No Preclusive Effect without Due Notice

### *1. The Constitutional Right to be Heard and the Limited Scope of Representative Actions under German Law*

a) It is a well-settled principle of German law that judgments may not confer a negative preclusive effect on third persons when these third persons were not parties to litigation, had no fair opportunity to actively participate in the proceeding, or did not receive procedurally compliant service of process. This principle is based on the rationale that a third person's constitutional right to be heard[1] is infringed by a detrimental judgment resulting from a procedure where the third person was not a party to the litigation. According to these principles, German law does not grant final preclusive effect to judgments rendered in actions where an individual's right to be heard has been seriously compromised by a lack of "correct representation".[2] The eminent significance of the right to be heard has important consequences for the requirements for recognition and enforcement of foreign judgments. Germany does not recognize foreign judgments rendered in actions where an individual's right to be heard has been infringed by a lack of "correct representation"[3] or by improper service of process.[4]

b) German law makes no general provisions for a class action or any variation thereof as it exists in the United States. The legislature created few forms of representative actions that apply for discrete circumstances such as actions filed by a court-appointed representative of shareholders or creditors of companies under very special circumstances[5] or by the representative of bondholders who has been elected by the bondholders' assembly.[6] The mechanism of these rules

---

[1] German Constitution Art. 103[1].

[2] German Constitutional Court, 51 Neue Juristische Wochenschrift 745 [1998]; see also German Code of Civil Procedure §§ 321a, 579[1][4].

[3] German Federal Supreme Court, 144 BGHZ 390, 393 [2000]; European Court of Justice, Krombach v. Bamberski 2000 ECR 1935 sub. Nô 44.

[4] German Code of Civil Procedure § 328 Nô 2 and 4.

[5] German Law on Special Corporation Procedures of June 12, 2003, Bundesgesetzblatt I, 838, §§ 1 and 6: compensation for shareholders in case of various forms of transformation or for a minority of shareholders of a controlled corporation, etc.; §§ 26, 206 German Law Regulating the Transformation of Companies: compensation for members or creditors of a corporation or a company in case of incorrect transformation.

[6] § 14 German Law on the Common Rights of Bondholders.

applies only in very rare cases when the complicated and very special requirements of these provisions are strictly met. A broad application of this or a similar mechanism in other cases by courts without specific authorization of the parliamentary legislature would be considered a serious infringement of the constitutional right to be heard.[7] Even then, the parliamentary legislature could act only in a manner reconcilable with the German Constitution. Moreover, at the present time, according to prevailing opinion in Germany, the need for group actions does not justify any limitation of the right to be heard. Class actions for consumers, shareholders or bondholders have been and are being discussed again and again in Germany. But, at the present time, the infringement of the constitutional right to be heard by negative preclusive effects of judgments or settlements against group members is one of the most important grounds why Germany has not adopted American-style class action proceedings.

c) A somewhat comparable form of representative action that may be brought in Germany is an action filed by a consumer protection association seeking a prohibitory injunction. The policy of vindicating collective rights of consumers is supported by the European Directive on Injunctions for the Protection of Consumers' Interests.[8] Implementing this directive, German statutory law does not grant a judgment rendered in an injunction action any negative preclusive effect against individual consumers.[9] This narrow construction of the preclusive effect of a judgment on collective consumer rights is the consequence of the aforementioned German understanding of the constitutional right to be heard.

d) The German legislature recently enacted a form of test procedure to simplify mass securities litigation.[10] In a mass securities litigation a state district court hearing the multiple claims may certify a factual or legal issue material to the outcome of all pending cases to the state court of appeals for authoritative resolution.[11] The court of first instance must order the stay of all the other actions pending certification procedure with the appellate court.[12] Parties to this test procedure before the state court of appeals are the claimant and defendant of the individual case chosen by the district court for the test procedure; but the court will require notice to the parties of all the other pending actions inviting intervention.[13] The appellate court's decision will be given preclusive effect only

[7] *See* German Constitutional Court, 59 BVerfGE 330, 333–334 [1982].

[8] *See* European Parliament and Council Directive 98/27/EC of May 19, 1998 on Injunctions for the Protection of Consumers' Interests, 1998 O.J. (L 166) 51 ("Injunction Directive").

[9] Injunction Actions Law of August 27, 2002, Bundesgesetzblatt I 3422, § 11.

[10] Law on Test Procedures in Securities Litigation of August 16, 2005, Bundesgesetzblatt I 2437.

[11] Test Procedure Law §§ 1, 4.

[12] Test Procedure Law, § 7.

[13] Test Procedure Law, § 8.

against parties of other pending cases which were correctly invited to intervene.[14] Like decisions in the aforementioned injunction actions test procedure decisions do not prejudice or alter the rights of third persons who have not commenced their own action and therefore are not a party to the certification procedure after due notice.

## 2. *Service Requirements Necessary to Obtain Preclusive Effects*

a) Recognition of preclusive effects of American judgments against German domiciliaries requires correct individual service of process as an indispensable prerequisite.[15] With respect to service of German nationals by American claimants, Germany requires strict compliance with the provisions of the Hague Service Convention when the German nationals have their domicile or residence in Germany.[16] Service under the Hague Convention is only permitted in cooperation with German authorities. According to the German understanding of the service of process as a public act of state, service without consent or judicial assistance of the state where the addressee has her domicile or residence is considered an infringement of foreign sovereignty and international law.[17] Germany has objected to the use of methods of transmission pursuant to Art. 10 of the Hague Service Convention which permits service by registered mail solely with the consent of the state of destination. Only within the European Union direct service of translated documents by registered mail is permitted.[18]

b) Under the Hague Service Convention as applied in Germany, the Ministry of Justice in each of the sixteen German states ("Bundesländer") – in a few individual states the administrative branch of a state court – is designated as the Central Authority for receipt of requests for service of process.[19] An applicant seeking to serve a German national must therefore first determine in which state that German national resides, and then direct the request for service to that state's Ministry of Justice. The applicant must send to the Ministry of Justice a request for service of process accompanied by the documents to be served, a summary of those documents and a certificate form for the requested foreign authority.[20] The Ministry of Justice will then consider whether the request con-

---

[14] Test Procedure Law, § 16.

[15] § 328 Nô 2 German Code of Civil Procedure.

[16] German Federal Supreme Court 120 BGHZ 305, 309–313 [1992]; 141 BGHZ 286, 302–304 [1999].

[17] German Federal Supreme Court 120 BGHZ 305, 310–313 [1992]; 141 BGHZ 286, 302–304 [1999]; *see also* German Code of Civil Procedure § 183[1] as revised 2002 which provides direct service by registered mail only with the consent of the foreign state.

[18] Council Regulation on the Service of Process in Civil and Commercial Matters Nô 1348/2000 of May 29, 2000, 2000 O.J. [L 160] 37, Art. 14; *see also* German Code of Civil Procedure § 1068 as enacted 2003.

[19] *See* Hague Service Convention, at annex n.7a.

[20] *See* Hague Service Convention, art. 3, 5 and annex "Forms".

forms to the requirements of the Hague Service Convention, and, if the request is deemed defective, the Ministry of Justice is required to inform the applicant and specify its objections.[21] If the Ministry of Justice determines that the request complies with the applicable requirements of the Hague Service Convention, it will normally forward the request to a local court ("Amtsgericht") in the district in which documents are to be served.[22] The local court will invite the individual who is to be served to come to the court in order to accept the documents. The Central Authority (§ 4[1] German Implementation Law) or the local court may also serve the documents by registered mail, although they will not send by registered mail documents that are not accompanied by a German translation. In addition, if an individual refuses to accept service of an English-only document, he or she has the right to receive a translated version.[23]

c) The Hague Service Convention "does not apply where the address of the person to be served with the document is not known".[24] Nevertheless, the Hague Service Convention may apply in a matter in dispute where it seems to be difficult and burdensome but not really impossible to identify the address of each individual bondholder. As a consequence, the American applicant may request service or notice by publication[25] on all German shareholders together to avoid the described burdensome procedure of individual service. Germany may refuse to comply with this request when the particular method requested is incompatible with German law. German law permits service and notice by publication only under very limited circumstances. According to the German Code of Civil Procedure sections 185–188, service by publication is permitted when the address of the person to be served is unknown. But the applicant has to give strong evidence of reasonable efforts to discover the address of the person to be served. In case of judicial assistance for actions in foreign courts it would be for the competent local courts of each German state to decide on the permissibility of service by publication. An application for service by publication must contain the name of the person to be served and his or her last known residence. German law does not generally provide for notice by publication to a large group of creditors. In rare and exceptional cases, as in proceedings for the appointment or election of representatives of shareholders or bondholders, German law permits notice by publication.[26] But without a special formal legal authorization by the legislature, service or notice by publication is not permitted

---

21 *See id.*, art. 4.

22 German Law on the Implementation of the Hague Convention on Service Abroad and the Taking of Evidence Abroad of December 22, 1977, Bundesgesetzblatt I, 3105, § 4[2].

23 Hague Service Convention Art. 5[3] and German Implementation Law § 3.

24 Hague Service Convention art. 1[2].

25 Hague Service Convention art. 5[1][b].

26 E.g. § 6[1], [4] and [5] German Law On Special Corporation Procedures; §§ 26[3], 206 German Law Regulating the Transformation of Companies; § 6 German Law on the Common Rights of Bondholders.

and would be considered a serious infringement of the constitutional right to be heard.

d) As to personal notice, in the context of a damages class action suit involving large numbers of potential class members, parties seeking to serve notice upon members of the class located throughout Germany would essentially have to secure the cooperation of 16 Ministries of Justice or of numerous local courts. The right of individuals to refuse documents that are not accompanied by a German translation would further delay this process. All in all it is not very probable that the plaintiffs of a class action will be able to serve process on all or even the majority of all class members under the provisions of German law. As a consequence, the certification of an international class with German class members would not be recommendable in the eyes of an American judge.

### 3. *Present Atmosphere not Favourable for Service of Process from the U.S.*

Finally, it should be mentioned that the atmosphere within the German judicial branch and judicial establishment is at present not as favorable for service of process from the U.S. as it was some years ago.[27] Initially, the German Constitutional Court showed a clear tendency to determine issues of service of foreign process in favor of generous cooperation. According to this policy of the Constitutional Court, German authorities granted judicial aid for service of process from the U.S. on German citizens or corporations even in cases where the claimant applied for punitive and exemplary damages,[28] although German courts decline, in principle, recognition and enforcement of punitive damages awards[29] because of their incompatibility with German public policy and fundamental principles of German law (compensation only for damages, as a principle of the German law of liability, principle of proportionality, strict separation between criminal law and civil liability, etc.). Most recently, the German Constitutional Court granted a prohibitive interim injunction,[30] which blocked the assistance of German authorities for service of process from the U.S. in a case, where the claiming class demanded seventeen billion dollars from the German defendant. The Constitutional Court argued that assistance for service of process from the U.S. may be declined under the Hague Service Convention, art. 13 (1), if the claiming class abuses the American action by putting public pressure and the threat of a lost big case on the German defendant with the clear intention to make him bend to the plaintiff's will on the basis of a case without convincing substance.[31] As a consequence of this interim decision, German judicial assistance for service of process from the U.S. is now more restrictive and

[27] *See*, e.g., State Court of Appeal [Oberlandesgericht] Frankfurt, 1991 OLGZ 89, 94.
[28] *See* German Constitutional Court, 91, BVerfGE 335 et seq. [1994].
[29] *See* German Federal Supreme Court, 118 BGHZ 312, 334 et seq. [1992].
[30] 108 BVerfGE 238 et seq. [2003].
[31] 108 BVerfGE 238, 248 [2003]; for the voluntary termination of the case see 26 ZIP 2128

time consuming than it was before.[32] It should be noted that this case was disposed of by voluntary termination before a final judgment could be reached that would clarify the Constitutional Court's future policy. As a consequence, American courts should be aware of a changed atmosphere in matters of foreign service in Germany when determining the certification of a class with German members. Assistance for service of process from the U.S. is in Germany no longer the judicial routine only, strict and intensive control by the various state authorities and state courts may result from the Constitutional Court's new critical approach.

## VI. No Preclusive Effect without U.S. Personal Jurisdiction under the Provisions of German Law

### *1. Personal Jurisdiction over German Group Members as a Prerequisite of Acknowledgement*

Even if all the German shareholders received notice complying with the requirements of German law, recognition of a negative preclusive effect of a U.S. judgment or consent judgment based on a settlement by German courts will not be granted without personal jurisdiction over the group members under the provisions of German law. U.S. judgments are only recognized when U.S. courts have personal jurisdiction over a party to litigation under the provisions of German law.[33] When service of process on a person in Germany as a possible class member is performed or notice is given to the German group member, it may happen that the German group member remains completely passive, neither opting out nor taking any affirmative steps which could be interpreted as an implied consent to U.S. personal jurisdiction under the provisions of German law.[34] In this case, a lack of jurisdiction over the group member would be a ground for non-recognition. As a consequence, the U.S. judgment would not prevent a passive German group member from bringing a new action before German courts. Thus in a decision of the State District Court of Stuttgart the court stated:

> "A judgment ... entered in a class action without active participation of the [German] claimant ... could not be recognized. There are ... no good arguments that U.S. courts would have personal jurisdiction ... under the provisions of German law...."[35]

---

(2005) and *Stürner* 61 JZ 60–68 (2006); without clear policy BVerfG 62 JZ 1046 (2007) with comment *Stadler*.

[32] *See* the report of *Juergen Hess*, 58 JZ 923, 926 [2003]; critically *Stürner* 61 JZ 60–68 (2006).

[33] German Civil Procedure Code, § 328 Nô 1; "mirror image principle".

[34] German Code of Civil Procedure, § 39.

[35] *See* State District Court [Landgericht] Stuttgart 2001 IPrax 240, 241.

### 2. *Personal Jurisdiction for Negative Declaratory Judgments of American Courts*

The procedural configuration as produced through a completely or partially adverse judgment entered against the class in a class action is similar to the case that an American court, on the defendant's motion, renders a negative declaratory judgment against German group members. It is clear and not questionable that German courts will only recognize effects of such a judgment against individual group members if provisions of German law justify jurisdiction of U.S. courts over the individual German group member.[36] Only under very special circumstances this may be the case, but this will very often be a rare exception to the rule. Under German law grounds for jurisdiction are domicile or residence;[37] main place of activity or statutory seat of entities;[38] branch or agency for claims which arise out of the branch's or agency's activity;[39] location of assets within a foreign jurisdiction;[40] location of an immovable in dispute;[41] place of performance of a contract when a claim arises out of this contract;[42] in tort cases the place where the harm occurred;[43] various forms of consent of the parties to litigation[44]; etc.[45] It is unlikely that German group members will always have sufficient contacts with U.S. to meet the requirements of these grounds to support U.S. jurisdiction under German law.

### 3. *Exclusive Personal Jurisdiction of German Courts under the New Law on Test Procedures in Securities Litigations*

In fall 2005, the German legislator enacted a new ground for non-recognition of U.S. class action judgments in securities litigations, when German issuers of bonds or certificates, German brokers or German corporations are involved. The German Law on Test Procedures provides exclusive jurisdiction of the German court where the obligor has its main place of administration or seat.[46] At first glance this new provision is a venue rule only, but, in general, all provisions of the German Civil Procedure Code specifying venue for civil actions within Germany also describe the extent to which German courts claim jurisdiction to adjudicate in international matters.[47] It is therefore very convincing

[36] German Code of Civil Procedure, § 328 [1][1].
[37] German Code of Civil Procedure, §§ 12, 13, 20.
[38] German Code of Civil Procedure, § 17.
[39] German Code of Civil Procedure, § 21.
[40] German Code of Civil Procedure, § 23.
[41] Exclusive in rem jurisdiction, German Code of Civil Procedure, §§ 24 et seq.
[42] German Code of Civil Procedure, § 29.
[43] German Code of Civil Procedure, § 32.
[44] German Code of Civil Procedure, §§ 38, 39.
[45] For a complete analysis *see Murray/Stürner*, German Civil Justice, 2004, Ch. 12 [B].
[46] § 32b German Civil Procedure Code 2005.
[47] *Murray/Stürner*, German Civil Justice, 2004, Ch. 12(B), p. 504.

to argue that this new rule does not only establish an exclusive venue for domestic cases but introduces exclusive international or personal jurisdiction of German courts in foreign cases where a German issuer, broker, or corporation is a party to litigation.[48] As a consequence, German courts will no longer recognize U.S. class action judgments against obligors located in Germany, even if a German class member takes actively part in the American procedure and submits expressly to American jurisdiction or if the claimed harm occurred totally or in part in the U.S. or if the German obligor has a branch in the U.S. German obligors may argue on a more and more clear legal basis that international classes should not be allowed in securities litigations against German obligors because of a lack of recognition of negative preclusive effects in Germany. This lack of recognition may cause the real danger of a second procedure against the obligor and hinder the function of a class action procedure to cope with the whole case once and for all.

### *4. No Significance of Personal Jurisdiction under European Law*

A common concept of European law under which a U.S. court would have the authority to bind European members of a class does not exist. It is true that the European Regulation on Jurisdiction and Enforcement[49] provides for forms of ancillary personal jurisdiction in case of connected claims against various defendants with domiciles in different Member States (Art. 6 No 1) or in case of a claim against a third party with a domicile in a Member State but outside the forum seized of the original proceedings (Art. 6 No 2). But, as already explained, a strictly passive class member has the position of a defendant in a case where the obligor applies for a negative declaratory judgment. The aforementioned European provisions do not apply if a defendant added to the proceeding is not domiciled in a Member State of the European Community. In this case, personal jurisdiction of a Member State's court is determined by the law of that Member State (Art. 4[1]). German law does not provide for ancillary personal jurisdiction. As a consequence, German courts will not permit ancillary personal jurisdiction of U.S. courts over German parties when determining recognition and enforcement of U.S. judgments. Any statement based on alleged common principles of Continental Codes of Civil Procedure seems to be too general, far too broad and even misleading, because it is mainly the law of the individual European state which governs recognition and enforcement of U.S. judgments. Careful and detailed analysis of the law of the various European states is absolutely necessary when prospects of recognition of an U.S. judgment in European countries are in dispute. General European principles may be a desirable future ideal, but until now they are not reality.

[48] *Haß/Zerr* 51 RIW 721–727 (2005); *Stein/Jonas/Roth*, ZPO 22nd ed. 2006, § 328 mn. 75.

[49] Council Regulation [EC] No 44/2001 of 22 December 2000, 2000 O.J. [L 12] 1 et seq.

## VII. Conclusion

Let me end with two final conclusions. Effectuating proper notice to residents of Germany who may be included in a U.S. class presents considerable logistical, practical and legal difficulties. But a German court will not recognize negative effects of a class action judgment or court confirmed settlement in any subsequent actions against the obligor absent the provision of notice to German group members that complies strictly with the Hague Service Convention. Even where service has been properly effected under the Hague Convention, German courts will not grant a preclusive effect to an American judgment against completely passive German group members because of a likely lack of American personal jurisdiction over the individual group members under the provisions of German law. Thus, there are very strong arguments of German and European obligors against the judicial certification of an international class with German members. They may convince a judge not to certify an international class as it was the case in Daimler Chrysler or they may motivate the claiming group to settle the case under conditions favourable to the obligor.

Class actions are no effective remedy to change the social reality. The increase of class actions in the U.S. is the consequence of the ongoing deregulation especially of the capital markets combined with the outsourcing of risks to normal citizens. Banks and other intermediaries do not protect individuals from risks and losses any longer. Collective actions are the response of the individuals who cannot balance and manage these risks efficiently. But the procedural approach is cost intensive and its results are all in all not very convincing. Only the legislature is able to improve regulation and to hinder undue risk shifting by preventive measures. The future of class actions depends on the development of the society's structure as a whole.

# Class Actions – Scandinavian Novelties

*Laura Ervo*

## 1. Sweden

In Sweden, there has been the system of class actions in force since 2003 on.[1] The possibility of class actions covers civil cases, which belong to the competence of general courts as well as the cases concerning environmental damages in environmental courts.[2] According to the Class Actions Act the class action is a suit, where the plaintiff acts for many persons in order to get legal effects for them, without them as parties in the case.[3] During the first three years there have been only six class suits in Sweden and some of them have been cancelled, so the experiences are rather petty yet.[4]

There has been a class suit against a travel agency in order to get compensation on the journeys, which have not come true, against a building company in order to finish the building of a boat harbour, against a life insurance company in order to get compensation on the unauthorized distribution of profits, against a guarding company in order to get compensation on illegal person register, against an electricity company in order to get compensation on the estopped selling of electricity and against the afternoon paper in order to get compensation in the play on the internet, which did not work.[5]

One of these, namely the suit against the electricity company is a public suit, sued by the consumer ombudsman, whereas the others are individual suits. The action concerned the play on the internet was dismissed and the suit against the guarding company was not accepted for class action. It will be tried as a normal civil case. The suit against the insurance company was cancelled, because the

[1] Lindblom has commented the earlier Swedish proposals, see Lindblom 1997, p. 15–21.

[2] Class Action Act, Section 2 and Code of Environmental matters, Chapter 32, Section 13.

[3] Class Action Act, Section 1, paragraph 1.

[4] Lindblom has examined the convenience of the class action system into Sweden already much before the system came into force. See Lindblom 1989, p. 638–707. Until 2008 there have been 12 class actions. See Lindblom 2008, pp. 209–234.

[5] OMM 2006:4, p. 25.

insurance company and the parent company decided to deal with the issue of the distribution of profits in the arbitration court.[6]

The possible class actions in Sweden can be individual group actions, governmental (public) class actions as well as suits by organizations.[7] The system is based on the opt-in-method.[8] One individual, who is a member in the group concerned, can bring a suit against a defendant in the case of individual group action. The individual group action can be sued by physical or legal persons.[9] In suits by organizations, the plaintiff is a non-profit-making-association by consumers or employees.[10] In environmental cases, the non-profit associations can bring class actions if they work for the interests of nature- or environmental conservation. Also the associations for fishermen, farmers, reindeer management and forest societies can bring the organizational suit in the environmental issues.[11] The public class action is possible in the cases, where a suit was not brought as an individual class action nor by the organization named above.[12] The possible authorities, who can bring the public suit, are a consumer ombudsman and conservancy authorities in environmental cases.[13]

The proceedings are the same as in usual (that is individual) suits. Of course, there are also specific paragraphs on class actions (which focus for instance on the right to plead, party succession and situations of a kind, which differ from individual suits), but otherwise and mostly the proceedings are the same.[14]

The attorney proceeds the action in individual and organizational class actions. If there are some special reasons, the court may decide that the action can be proceeded without the attorney or by a trustee, who is not an attorney.[15]

On the contrary to the class action system in the United States, the court does not decide separately if the suit is admissible as a class action or not. The court only examines that the absolute requirements for an admissible action exist. After that the party has the right to make a plea that the requirements for the class action don't exist.[16]

The costs are covered by the party who has lost the case. The members of the group are not responsible for the costs. Only the representative of the group is. The member is, however, responsible for the costs, which he/she has incurred to the opposite party with his/her negligence.

---

[6] OMM 2006:4, p. 25.

[7] Class Action Act, Sections 1, 4, 5 and 6.

[8] Class Action Act, Section 14.

[9] Class Action Act, Section 4.

[10] Class Action Act, Section 5.

[11] Code of Environmental matters, Chapter 32, Sections 13 and 14.

[12] RP 2001/02:107, p. 54.

[13] Class Action Act, Section 6 and decisions 1995:868 and 2001:1096 of the Council of State.

[14] See Class Action Act and Code of Judicial Procedure.

[15] Class Action Act, Section 11.

[16] Code of Judicial Procedure, Chapter 34.

The attorney's fee is possible to agree to be conditional. In such situations, the fee depends on the result of the case. The members of the group are responsible for the conditional fee for the won amount.[17]

The appeal is possible by usual measures.[18]

## 2. Finland[19]

In Finland, a system of class actions is in planning. The Ministry of Justice named a working group in the beginning of August 2005 for writing a proposal for government bill on class actions and the group left its proposal on the 16 March 2006.[20] The pre-working group left its report on March 2005.[21]

However, both of these working groups have been rather disunited and therefore it is quite impossible to estimate when the system of class actions will be in force in Finland, but I believe that it is coming in the nearest future in some form in any case.

The Swedish model and Swedish experiences have had an important primus motor -effect in Finland. Because Sweden has now adopted the system, it is only a matter of time when it will be in force in Finland as well, which is quite an interesting phenomenon in jurisprudence. The pilot model in some quite similar legal order is often the better method in order to organize reforms than plan-

[17] Class Action Act, Sections 30–41.

[18] Class Action Act, Sections 42–48.

[19] The development concerning class actions has been rapid since this presentation. The government bill was given on the 26th of September 2006 (see the Government bill 154/2006) and the President of the Republic ratified the Act on Class Actions on the 13th of April (see the act 444/2007). The Act came into force on the 1st of October 2007. So, even the parliament accepted the government bill rapidly and without any important amendments. The development was much quicker than I could imagine during my presentation in 2006. One reason for that was that the government bill was very careful and only the very first step was taken with it. Namely, class actions will be possible only in disputes between consumers and entrepreneurs. The new act has been criticized because of its name compared with the contents. The fact is that the new act covers only consumer suits and with it came no common class action system to Finland. The other critical point has put on the fact that the new act does not cover disputes relating to environmental damage. This is the most important difference between the new act / the government bill and the earlier proposals made by working groups.

Participation in a class action requires registration as a member of the class. The Consumer Ombudsman will bring the class action and act as the representative of the class, thereby ensuring that an action cannot be brought for malicious purposes. A class action will be possible for example in disputes relating to defects in consumer goods or the interpretation of contract terms. Also disputes between consumers and entrepreneurs regarding investment products and insurances, for example pension insurances, savings life insurances and the sale and marketing of corresponding investment products, will fall within the scope of application of the Act.

[20] OMM 2006:4.

[21] OMM 2005:3.

ning groups and wide clarifications. The legislation on class actions has been accepted in Norway as well and a new chapter of the Danish Civil Procedural Code on group proceedings came into force in January 2008. I suppose that the other Nordic countries will follow the Swedish and Norwegian models, at least if they do not get very dramatic and negative experiences in these countries, where they already have this system in force or will have in the near future.

Namely we have had in Finland a lot of plans even before, but none of them have led to reforms. The basic clarification was made already in 1992.[22] This clarification was made as official duties by the Ministry of Justice because the Nordic Council had made the proposal for legislation on class actions in Nordic countries. After this basic clarification the first working group began its work in this field and left its report in the form of a Government bill at the end of 1994.[23] This proposal did not lead to legislative measures and one reason for this was that the opinions in statements on this proposal were very disunited and the system of class actions was found to be a strange institution in the Finnish legal order. According to negative opinions there was no need for class actions in Finland and the effects and alternatives of class actions had not been clarified well enough.

In 1996, the Ministry of Justice appointed a new working group with the same task to plan a proposal for legislation on class actions in the form of the government bill. Again this proposal[24] did not lead to legislative measures because of the same reasons. That is the opinions in statements on this proposal were again very disunited. The concrete effects were instead that the field of legal aid became wider and the consumer ombudsman got wider possibilities in order to proceed an action.

So, we have just now the third bid in order to get class actions to Finland. This time it will come, I suppose. At least the government will probably give the bill, but the other question will be what does the parliament say? In any case it will still take a lot of time until the law will be in force in some form or another. There will probably be the need for compromises as well, before the parliament can accept the new legislation.

The proposal is to make a class action possible in consumer disputes and disputes relating to environmental damage. A class action means an action initiated on behalf of a group in a dispute to be handled by a general court of law. The Working Group proposes that the scope of application of the Act be limited to matters in which the need for a class action is the strongest. These include consumer disputes affecting a large group of parties and disputes relating to exten-

[22] OLJ 3/1992.
[23] OLJ 1/1995.
[24] OLJ 3/1997. For the end of the legislative history see note 19.

sive environmental damage. In these issues, a class action would be a new alternative to the procedures in force at present.[25]

The reform would bring to the legal system enforceable claims, which are affecting a large group, which, at present, either due to the costs or lack of information and skills, are not taken to court. For example, in a matter where the maximum claim is EUR 1,500, it is at present not sensible to go to court. In the case of a class action, a class member would not be responsible for the litigation costs; instead, they would be paid by the plaintiff or the defendant. A possibility for a class action could also be preventive and thus enhance compliance with the laws.[26]

The handling of a matter as a class action would require several people with a claim against the same defendant based on the same or similar facts. In addition, it should be appropriate to handle the dispute in a form of a class action and the class should be sufficiently well defined. Participation in a class action would require an express joining of the class. So, the system would be based on opting in -method. The Act would not set a minimum or maximum limit to the size of the class.[27]

In class action issues, the plaintiff and representative of the class would be an authority. This would ensure that no one could bring a class action for the purpose of harming another. In disputes between a consumer and an entrepreneur, the action would be brought by the Consumer Ombudsman. A class action would be possible for example in disputes relating to a defect in consumer goods or the interpretation of contract terms. Also disputes between a consumer and an entrepreneur relating to investment products or insurance would belong to the scope of application of the Act.[28]

In disputes relating to environmental damage the class action would be brought by the West Finland Regional Environment Centre, which is the largest of the regional environment centres. Environmental damage may be the result for example of the pollution of water, air, soil or noise.[29]

An association has a secondary right of action in cases of environmental damage. If the Environment Centre did not bring a class action in a matter meeting certain requirements, the secondary right of action would lie with a registered association or foundation, the purpose of which is to promote pleasant sur-

---

[25] http://www.om.fi/tulostus/35312.htm, date of visiting this page 13 June 2006, OMM 2006:4, p. 48, 53 and 61–65.

[26] http://www.om.fi/tulostus/35312.htm, date of visiting this page 13 June 2006. OMM 2006:4, p. 48, 58 and 71–72.

[27] http://www.om.fi/tulostus/35312.htm, date of visiting this page 13 June 2006, OMM 2006:4, p. 51 and 68–69.

[28] http://www.om.fi/tulostus/35312.htm, date of visiting this page 13 June 2006 and OMM 2006:4, p. 62.

[29] http://www.om.fi/tulostus/35312.htm, date of visiting this page 13 June 2006 and OMM 2006:4, p. 62–64.

roundings, nature protection, fishing, agriculture, reindeer husbandry or forestry. An association representing part of a town for example could act as a plaintiff in an issue relating to aviation noise or an odour nuisance. The initiation of a class action by an association would require that the association has the financial and other prerequisites to act as a plaintiff in the matter. On the demand of the defendant, the association would have to set security for the compensation of the litigation costs.[30]

A class action could be used to demand monetary compensation from the defendant or to demand that the defendant does not undertake certain action or allow certain action. The claims for the damages of the injured parties could vary in amount. It would also be possible to handle qualitatively different demands, such as a price reduction and the cancellation of a purchase, as a class action. The claims would, however, have to be based on the same or similar facts and the proof to be presented in favour of the claims could not be very different in the case of the different class members.[31]

A plaintiff representing the class could notify the people of a class action in a newspaper or in the internet and for example a form could be used to join the class. The procedure to be used would primarily correspond to the ordinary legal procedure in a civil case. The members of the class would not be parties to the litigation nor would they have the rights of a party; these rights would be used by the plaintiff.[32]

The judgment to be given to the basis of a class action would be binding on the plaintiff, the members who have joined the class and the defendant. A class member would, for his part, have the right to appeal the judgment only if the plaintiff does not appeal it.[33]

With the introduction of a class action liability for a violation of one's rights would be realized more often than at present. This would enhance legal protection and the equal treatment of the citizens. It would also be good for companies that no one could gain an advantage vis-à-vis other companies through illegal action.[34]

The Working Group estimates that few class actions would be brought. Sweden has had a similar type of procedure since 2003. It has not been noticed that

---

[30] http://www.om.fi/tulostus/35312.htm, date of visiting this page 13 June 2006 and OMM 2006:4, p. 65–67.

[31] http://www.om.fi/tulostus/35312.htm, date of visiting this page 13 June 2006 and OMM 2006:4, p. 57–61.

[32] http://www.om.fi/tulostus/35312.htm, date of visiting this page 13 June 2006 and OMM 2006:4, p. 68–69.

[33] http://www.om.fi/tulostus/35312.htm, date of visiting this page 13 June 2006 and OMM 2006:4, p. 71–72.

[34] http://www.om.fi/tulostus/35312.htm, date of visiting this page 13 June 2006.

the entry into force of the Act would have had an effect on the national economy or on the establishment of undertakings in Sweden.[35]

The Memorandum relating to the class action includes five dissenting opinions. They oppose the introduction of the class action in general or its introduction in cases of environmental damage. The doubts and reasons for dissenting opinions are for instance if there is a real need for class actions, how it would work in practice, poor foreign experiences,[36] need of extra economical resources and the competitiveness of Finland in international markets.[37]

It is proposed that a class complaint, which is lighter than a class action, be introduced in the Consumer Complaint Board. The class complaint would be cost-free for the parties and procedurally simpler than a class action tried in a court. The decisions of the Board in class complaints would be recommendations just like in other issues handled by the Board. The Consumer Complaint Board handles disputes between consumers and businesses relating inter alia to defects in goods or services.[38]

## 3. Norway

In Norway, the parliament adopted the new legislation on class actions in June 2005. The statutes should come into force on 1 July 2007.[39] The field of class actions is open.[40] In spite of this very open statute, the typical cases will be for instance consumer- and environmental cases even in Norway, I suppose.

According to the Code, the class action is a suit where the plaintiff or the defendant is a group which has the same or similar basis and which the court has accepted admissible as a class action. So, according to the law the group can act even as a defendant.[41]

The suit is admissible as a class action, if there are demands or obligations, which have the same or similar ground. In addition the court has to be compe-

---

[35] http://www.om.fi/tulostus/35312.htm, date of visiting this page the 13th June 2006.

[36] The very common argument has been that the system is not suitable for the Finnish or Scandinavian legal system. Lindblom has examined the class action system from the European point of view. See for example Lindblom 1997, p. 14. He has been very positive for the system and seen it suitable first for Sweden and after some years of experiences for Finland as well. About the Scandinavian discussion see the proceedings on the Nordic symposium on class actions held in Oslo 2002 (http://www.norden.org/pub/ebook/2003–528.pdf).

[37] http://www.om.fi/tulostus/35312.htm, date of visiting this page the 13th June 2006 and OMM 2006:4, p. 142–159. On the positive sides and drawbacks of the class action system, see Lindblom 1989, p. 435–484.

[38] http://www.om.fi/tulostus/35312.htm, date of visiting this page the 13th June 2006, OMM 2006:4, p. 88 and OMM 2006:1, p. 9–10.

[39] OMM 2006:4, p. 25.

[40] Code of Judicial Procedure in Civil Cases, Chapter 35, Section 2.

[41] Code of Judicial Procedure in Civil Cases, Chapter 35, Section 1.

tent in the same composition and according to the mainly same procedural norms. The class action has to be the most reasonable way of proceedings for this case and the court has to be able to order the competent representative for the group. If the case fulfills these requirements, the court can decide it admissible as a class action.[42] On contrary to Sweden, the court decides separately in Norway if the case is admissible as a class action or not.

The possible class actions can be individual group actions, governmental (public) class actions as well as suits by organizations or funds.[43] The system is based normally on opt-in -system. Even opt-out -system is possible in some situations.[44]

The representative of the group is responsible for the costs. He/she has even the right for the fee for his/her work and costs. If the group loses the case, the fee for the attorney will be covered with the amount, which the group has accounted for it. After that the costs of the opposite party will be covered. If there still is some money left after these costs, the fee for the representative, that is plaintiff, will be covered.[45]

## 4. Denmark

Even in Denmark a system of class actions is in planning. The working group has left its preliminary report in December 2005. The proposal is very similar to the Norwegian model. However, it would be possible for the group to act as a plaintiff only. The field of class actions would be open.[46]

The suit could be admissible as a class action if there are similar demands in different fields. Individual, organizational and governmental (public) class actions would be possible. It is suggested in the report that the consumer ombudsman for instance should have the right to sue the class action.[47]

In order to try the class action the court should have international jurisdiction in the case. The court would be nationally competent if it had the competence in one of these suits.[48] The court would make a separate decision if the case was admissible as a class action or not. In this decision, the court would order the representative, that is the plaintiff, for the group. The representative of the group would be a party in the case.[49]

---

[42] Code of Judicial Procedure in Civil Cases, Chapter 35, Section 2.

[43] Code of Judicial Procedure in Civil Cases, Chapter 35, Section 3.

[44] Code of Judicial Procedure in Civil Cases, Chapter 35, Section 6 and 7.

[45] Code of Judicial Procedure in Civil Cases, Chapter 35, Section 12, 13 and 14.

[46] Retsplejerådet 2005, p. 243–244. The new legislation on class actions came into force after the presentation of this paper on January 1[rst] 2008.

[47] Retsplejerådet 2005, p. 249.

[48] Retsplejerådet 2005, p. 246–247.

[49] Retsplejerådet 2005, p. 247–248.

The systems of opt in and opt out would be possible. However, the opt out -system would be possible only in class actions proceeded by an authority. The other requirement for the opt out -system is that there are very small interests in different claims, which would be otherwise too small for proceedings.[50] In the opt in -system, the court could even order that the member of the court has to place the security for the costs before the court can accept the registration. The form for registration is in planning as well. Even in the opt out -system, the members would be partly liable for the costs in some situations.[51]

## Bibliography

http://www.norden.org/pub/ebook/2003–528.pdf , date of visiting this page was 13 June 2006.

http://www.om.fi/tulostus/35312.htm , date of visiting this page was 13 June 2006.

| | |
|---|---|
| OLJ 3/1992 | Ryhmäkanne. Perusselvitys ryhmäkanteen käyttömahdollisuuksista Suomen oikeusjärjestelmässä. Oikeusministeriön lainvalmisteluosaston julkaisu 3/1992. Oikeusministeriö, Helsinki 1992. |
| OLJ 1/1995 | Ryhmäkannetyöryhmän 1992 mietintö. Oikeusministeriön lainvalmisteluosaston julkaisu 1/1995. Oikeusministeriö, Helsinki 1995. |
| OLJ 3/1997 | Ryhmäkannelaki: Työryhmän 1996 mietintö. 1997/3. Oikeusministeriön lainvalmisteluosaston julkaisu 3/1997. Oikeusministeriö, Helsinki 1997. |
| OMM 2005:3 | Selvitys ryhmäkanteesta. Työryhmämietintö. Oikeusministeriö, Helsinki 2005. |
| OMM 2006:1 | Kuluttajavalituslautakunnan kehittämistyöryhmän mietintö. Oikeusministeriö, Helsinki 2006. |
| OMM 2006:4 | Ehdotus laiksi ryhmäkanteesta. Työryhmämietintö. Oikeusministeriö, Helsinki 2006. |
| Lindblom 1989 | Lindblom, Per Henrik: Grupptalan. Det anglo-amerikanska class actioninstitutet ur svenskt perspektiv. Göteborg 1989. |
| Lindblom 1997 | Lindblom Per Henrik: Group Actions and the Role of the Courts – A European perspective. Forum internationale, No. 23, May 1996. |
| Lindblom 2008 | Lindblom, Per Henrik: Grupptalan in Sverige. Vällingborg 2008. |
| RP 2001/02:107 | Regeringens proposition 2001/02:107. |
| Retsplejerådet 2005 | Reform av den sivile retspleje IV, Gruppesögsmål mv., betänkning nr. 468/2005. |


[50] Retsplejerådet 2005, p. 244–246.
[51] Retsplejerådet 2005, p. 259–262.

# Discussion

*Professor Kato:* We would like to begin our discussion now. First, Professor Yoshimura, with a comment on the situation in Japan.

*Professor Yoshimura:* I was very interested in Professor Murray's and Professor Stürner's presentations on class actions, which are based on quite different, quite opposite opinions on this problem. I will take the liberty of giving a very brief introduction to the system in Japan.

In Professor Murray's presentation, the class action system under the principle of equity in the United States was discussed. The opt-in system switched over to the opt-out system. For the first time, I was able to get an understanding of the history behind this transition. Given this, I would like to first touch upon unilateral responses in Japan to a mass dispute or default. First of all in Japan, there was the equivalent of a class action by shareholders and that would normally be interpreted as a class action whenever it had something to do with litigation by the shareholders. The other form is the selection of one representative among the people who have a common interest. The selected elite, therefore, would be the person who makes the claim on behalf of the other people with a common interest. There was a very significant revision of the civil law in Japan some years ago. However, after due consideration of the class action at that time, the adoption of the class action per se was not realized. Nevertheless, the selected claimant system does incorporate the opt-in-system. Anybody with the same interest can raise his/her hand to become a claimant as well. This is a new system, which I believe resembles an opt-in-method of the class action in Japan. Also, in 2002, there was a council for judicial reform and proposals were made at that time. Included in those was a review of the two systems of the class action and the German '*Verbandsklage*'. However, this did not lead to an adoption of the class action per se. Nevertheless, when it comes to a collective suit, particularly by consumers, special consideration is given to trying to protect or guarantee their rights. With regard to the mass dispute or default, consumer harm and environmental damage, how to handle the suits in those two particular areas, how to respond to class actions in Japan, and whether we should side with an American perspective or a Japanese perspective are questions that remain unresolved.

As you know, our judicial system is very close to the German system in principle, and therefore what Professor Dr. Stürner reported is actually quite similar to what we have in Japan. But, as Professor Murray pointed out, with globalization nowadays, matters such as how to cope with international disputes in the context of class actions are something that we need to take up sooner or later. One possible solution that I would like to suggest is that in the case of an opt-in-system, the method I mentioned before shows the right tendency. However, regarding the opt-out class action, we need to consider how far we can realize this method in Japan. For that purpose notice has to be given for enforceability. Therefore, notice has to be adequate so that the opportunity for class members to join in the suit is guaranteed. The importance of that is shared by Japan as well. And, therefore, the composition of the class members and identification of possible victims, and at which point and by what methodology we are to grasp that situation correctly, are essential aspects. With an understanding of that, the class members may thus identify how to give notification, how to give service, and how to give notice. In this way we are able to realize class actions. That is my brief comment on the situation in Japan. Thank you.

*Professor Kato:* Thank you very much.

Well, Japan now has a Consumer Contract Act and this year it will be revised. And some new type of injunction by consumer interest groups will be introduced. But only consumer interest groups are covered, not environmental groups.

Now we would like to ask the floor to make comments or ask questions to the speakers.

*Professor Taniguchi:* I would like to ask a technical question to Professor Murray. As Professor Yoshimura just mentioned, there are two basic problems when we consider possibilities for class actions in Japan, I think. One is a basic policy question. And the other is a more technical. I was very interested and enthusiastic about the adoption of class action in the 1980s. I wrote some articles on the issue at that time. But today I regret to say that there is any possibility of adopting the American type of class action in Japan. I think this is a political question rather than a legal question, so I am not going to say much about that. I would like to ask you a more technical question about American class action. You emphasized that certain American lawyers are eager to bring a class action on the contingent fee basis. I perfectly understand that. But a class action can be brought for an injunction rather than for money. Now you said that as a matter of general principle you can opt out. And when you opt out, even if this class action is lost, a possible member of the class who opted out can sue again for the same cause. Now I wonder if this kind of technique can be used or has been used for strategic purposes. In a money recovery class action, of course, if you opted out you may be able to sue separately, but your class is now very small, so it may not mean much. But for injunctive class actions, even if the number of class members is small, the effect remains the same. Therefore, the mechanism of opting out can be utilized strategically in order to perpetuate a viable cause of action. Has this kind of strategy been used in the United States?

*Professor Murray:* Thank you very much, Professor Taniguchi. Speaking first to your technical question, you are absolutely right that the injunctive class action, which occasionally does occur, is problematical from the standpoint of the method of compensation of the plaintiff's lawyer, because of the absence of an immediately identified pool of money from which to pay the plaintiff's lawyer. And the way those class actions usually take place is either of two ways. Some kinds of cases, such as discrimination cases are brought as class actions and result in injunctive remedies, "You shall not discriminate any more," for instance. And in those cases there are frequently in the United States statutory attorneys fees, so that the person who brings the successful discrimination case in behalf of a large class of individuals who may be discriminated against because of their age or their sex or their race, even though there is no money recovery, can get reimbursement of attorneys fees from the defendant by statute. That is one class of injunctive class actions which are commonly brought and in those cases I am not aware particularly of any strategic dividing of the class in the way you suggested to have a opt-out member sue, who would have what we would call a second bite at the apple as it is called. I am not aware of that as being a conscious strategic gamble.

There is another area of injunctive class actions and those are in the areas where there are no attorneys fees provided for. Those class actions are only brought where the plaintiff's lawyer is able to make the argument that the injunction has brought economic benefit to the members of the class and therefore has created a pool of money that is usually contributed, in the case of a settlement, by the defendant that will pay the attorneys fees. The plaintiff class members are scarcely ever, if ever, able to pay anything by way of attorneys fees and so the lawyer has to be able to show that the injunction brought an economic benefit and therefore that there is an economic value created, so that the injunction consists of an injunction and an additional payment that funds the attorney's fees. Again I have never run into the situation where there has been a conscious two-bite-at-the-apple philosophy.

I was just discussing with Professor Stürner, however, a phenomenon which has occurred among some very savvy American shareholders and activist shareholders. And that is that when a class action, particularly a securities class action such as this Royal Ahold class action, is brought and if these members own securities in the group, then it is very common for them to opt out, let the class action be settled, then start their own carbon copy case based on the same claims.

They have the benefit of all of the pleadings, everything that has been filed in the class action. So they can carbon copy it and the company that has just settled the class action often will pay a lot more per capita to get rid of the nuisance of this carbon copy action than the shareholders would have got had they have stayed in the class action. So this activity of opting out and then bringing carbon copy actions actually is having the effect of undermining the class action as an effective remedy, because if the person who settles the class action is faced with a whole bunch of carbon copy actions which come later that require him to pay more money, then the value of the settlement is compromised.

Of course that is somewhat the theory that Professor Stürner was advancing about there being the risk that after settling a US class action the German, Japanese and other members of the class would bring their own actions in their own countries. This particular phenomenon has up until now not occurred in any great numbers, but what has occurred is the carbon copy class action in the American courts by persons who have opted out intentionally, so they can bring the carbon copy actions. That has resulted in, as they say, settlements which per share or per unit have been sometimes as much as a hundred or a thousand times as much as the class action settlement have been per unit, so that there is a little bit of that process. It has not been so much in the injunctive actions, it has been more in the actions for money.

*Professor Andrews:* Could I please ask a question about the process of judicial ratification of settlements under U.S. class action procedure? In your opinion, how satisfactory is that process of ratification?

The second question is whether there is any experience in the U.S. class action litigation of the conjoining of that style of litigation with ADR techniques, mediation and perhaps exploration of types of settlement other than purely monetary awards?

*Professor Murray:* Professor Andrews, I thank you for those two questions. The judicial ratification of settlements has not worked well. The American system presupposes that judges function as arbiters in a sense between two vigorously contesting parties and that the judge will have the benefit of two opposing presentations from directly opposing interests to make a choice and that, in theory, the truth somehow emerges from that collision. The settlement process is not that kind of a process. Everyone is basically taking the same position to the judge, namely that the settlement should be ratified. There is no opposing side, so to speak. And the judges, by the way that they are staffed, by the way they are trained, by the way they are supported in terms of the facilities available to them, are not in a good position to make an independent analysis of the settlement. There has been talk about, and indeed some judges have talked about, experimenting with appointing various kinds of guardians *ad litem* or other figures to represent and create an artificial adversity for the purpose of addressing the fairness of class action settlements. But that remains a very serious problem. And many writers have contented themselves with general suggestions that judges should do more, but without equipping our judges with how to do this different role, they are not going to be able to do it.

The second question was about conjoining class action litigation with various ADR. Of course, once a class action is put together by what we call an entrepreneurial law firm, and that is truly a law firm that has the economic muscle to be able to raise the money necessary to finance the class action and the necessary strength in order to oppose the often very large and financially powerful adversary, then it is very important that the class action be terminated in a way that has money available for the lawyer, so that forms of ADR which do not include the payment of money to the lawyer are of course not attractive to the class action litigant. By the same token, for the defendant in this problem, suppose we are talking about not a class action, but a problem involving, say, the fact that Ahold had perhaps inflated the earnings and therefore caused the stock to go up artificially and then it fell, people lost money, that is the problem. One way to solve that problem is by the class action, but the defendant wants to have the problem solved as far as they are concerned and the only way for them to get what looks like any form of wide ranging release or settlement that will bind large numbers of people is to get the people under the umbrella of a class action and then settle the class action. Otherwise to go around and get individual releases would be incredibly burdensome and very difficult. So that that is why the defendants have an interest in having these resolved under the class action remedy, because they have the benefit of this class action settlement rule that binds so many people. So those are my responses. However, within the class action framework, that is in settling the class actions, all forms of ADR are being used in terms of negotiation techniques and mediation to resolve class actions. Big mediators are getting involved in these. And interestingly enough, the firms are now experimenting with arbitration in class actions and so there are truly class action arbitrations, which are now being experimented with.

*Professor Kawano:* My interest relates to international class actions, especially if the defendants are foreigners, such as most of the examples given by Professor Stürner. In these cases, there are very difficult questions. First of all, there are jurisdiction problems: how to deal with the international jurisdiction, and what establishes the American authority to deal with the case. And more interestingly, most cases are settled by settlement. Sometimes the parties do not want a judgment, rather a very good settlement. There may be some special problems involved. But typically in the settlement procedure of international class actions, there are certain difficult situations of multi-party settlement. Are there any special solutions?

*Professor Murray:* I would just make the comment that Professor Stürner and I, although we look at class actions perhaps from different national perspectives, are in substantial agreement as far as the actual issues of international legal jurisdiction and international notice to the parties and so forth concerned. So I can concur pretty much with Professor Stürner's excellent analysis of the problems of jurisdiction and problems of notice that he outlined in his remarks. I think those exist and that any thoughtful lawyer will agree that the American class action without some form of special adoption or adaptation will not strictly speaking satisfy the requirements of notice for many other foreign countries outside of those countries, such as Canada for instance, which have become more friendly to American class actions.

That having been said, we are operating now in a world where we have arguments being made from Germany or other countries such as in the Royal Ahold case, "these are not going to bind our residents." But then guess what happens? The settlement occurs and the settlement says 'Oh yes, everybody is at least in the settlement. They all get the money of the settlement and if they are going to accept the cheque from the settlement, they have to sign the release.' So that it seems clear from that that there is a very strong policy reason to have some form of comprehensive class litigation. And the question is how can we do that having due regard for the notice and jurisdiction elements that apply in many other countries other than the United States.

I suggested four possible approaches at the end of my paper. One is to have the American class action go through a supplementary judicial process in either a foreign country or group of foreign countries such as the EU to have it then examined by a judge of that culture and who would then determine what additional or special arrangements as far as notice, opt-in, whatever should be made to have the class action be accepted in that country. Another would be to have the foreign countries adopt regulations that are directed to class actions establishing a threshold which would say what has to be done. To say right now that you have to give notice according to the Hague Convention is simply impractical if you want to have a comprehensive remedy. Now, if you want to say, if you want to acknowledge that there are many other things that could be done that would give better notice than most class actions give, that perhaps could be required by different foreign countries. The third would be a rule that you can have an international class action, but that citizens in countries other than the home country of the class action would be on an opt-in basis only. In America you can have opt-out, but if it covers anybody in any other country they are opt-in. And I think an opt-in arrangement is much more consistent with European notions both of jurisdiction as well as notice; that is, if the person had to have actual notice and actually sign up to become a plaintiff, then it is pretty hard to say that there was no jurisdiction and no proper notice.

Those are three possibilities of ways to try to reconcile this and still maintain a meaningful, comprehensive class action type of approach for those jurisdictions such as the United States which are willing to sponsor that kind of litigation. And this of course would not stop any other country in the world from sponsoring class action litigation for defendants within their borders. Certainly the EU and Japan, having many big companies that are within their jurisdiction, would be certainly appropriate sponsors of class action litigation which could cover international class actions but, for reasons of their own legal cultures, if they choose not to do it that is certainly understandable.

I am going to take one moment to reiterate the very wise words that were stated by Professor Stürner at the end of his remarks with which I completely agree. And it says, I believe, that the class action movement is – and the need for collective litigation which I hear all over the room, for every country is considering some way in which consumers or individuals or holders of securities who have been damaged can respond collectively – that this is in part, and maybe the biggest part, the result of a combination of deregulation and outsourcing of the risk. So when indeed the risk of loss in terms of either deregulation of regulation that would stop the risk from the beginning, or in terms of channelling that risk into big players – such as outsourcing of risk on securities instead of the securities being held by banks and then the banks giving interest to the account holders so that the securities are passed down to the individuals – whenever that happens, there are losses which occur. And, in fact, the only way that these individuals can respond to those losses is to collectivize, because they are individuals facing very big players. If the government has abandoned them through deregulation and the banks have abandoned them through outsourcing of securities risk, then the individuals have to respond in some way collectively because no individual can take on Royal Ahold or Daimler Benz or some of these other big players. So if the direction of the world is in the favour of more privatization and less regulation, then I think class actions or some form of collective response is going to be necessary for our legal culture to provide remedies for people who are injured. If on the other hand we go to a culture in which government will take a bigger responsibility for regulation and that banks and other regulators will protect individuals *ab initio* from risk and loss in terms of these economic transactions, then the need for collective litigation will diminish.

*Professor Stürner:* I agree completely with my dear colleague Peter Murray. Let me make an additional remark. Continental legal cultures or continentally influenced legal cultures should understand that class actions without punitive damages make no real sense. The purpose of class actions is compensation and deterrence. Big firms can calculate the result of proceedings which grant compensation only. Deterrence is mainly a consequence of the threat of punitive damages awards which cannot be calculated. The adoptions of class actions by continental legal cultures must be combined with a change of substantive law and especially the law of compensation. Without the adoption of forms of exemplary or punitive damages private law enforcement will not really work well. Even in case of an adoption of these sanctions the effects of deterrence are questionable. The number of fraudulent transactions in the U.S. is really not lower than on the Continent. Class actions should not be discussed as a form of procedural techniques only. It is necessary to consider the whole system of law, substantive law included, and the economic and political structure of a society.

*Professor Murray:* Well, we don't want to dominate this discussion, but because Professor Stürner says so many interesting things, I feel compelled to just add, in large agreement I can say, two points. One is that I think his point about the damages structure, namely that you need damages that will produce enough money to make it worthwhile for the law firms to produce the action, is probably true. I am not sure that punitive damages are always a necessity, because many of these cases are brought without punitive damages. But you need a damages structure that probably is more generous in terms of general damages, pain and suffering, other forms of damages which are available in the United States, but which are not always as available as generously to provide the kind of monetary cushion.

And that brings me to another point, which is Professor Stürner's suggestion. I don't think that there is anybody who maintains that the class action system is either effective or cheap. It is neither. It is a very expensive way to do regulation, it is *ex post facto*, it is extremely expensive. The amount of the money that is used for the lawyers on both sides compared to the amount that gets to the injured party, most of the money goes for the systematic costs, very little for reimbursement of the injured parties, is such that the actual results in class actions do not always follow the public interest very well, so that as a method of regulation it is very expensive and it is not particularly effective. The theory that its proponents say is that this is part of deregulation and that by deregulating, that is taking the government out, you get so much more economic activity that you can tolerate the high costs and the somewhat erratic results of a class action system. Now that is their position. I happen to be personally more close to Professor Stürner's view of the matter that deregulation has so many unseen costs that the touted increased economic vitality is perhaps not that great in comparison. But I merely point out what the proponents of this deregulated and free wheeling class action system are saying to justify these high costs of the class action.

*Professor Trocker:* In Italy we had a big financial scandal about a year ago and all of a sudden we 'discovered' that our civil justice system did not offer proper instruments to handle multi-party cases. I refer to the Parmalat case. And we were also confronted with the fact that at the same time a class action was started in the United States, brought into effect immediately, and people from outside tried to opt in because in their country they had no effective way of handling this kind of matter or case. Our alternative today is to rely on criminal enforcement, but then we discovered that our public prosecutors are not in any condition to handle the matter efficiently and so the cases will probably be pending for years and years. Now, I agree with Professor Stürner and other remarks that have been made. We cannot even think of importing this instrument – the class action – without accepting, apart from punitive damages, the contingency fee, the organized lawyer structure, and so on. But the question remains. We should be critical, we should be negative about certain aspects, but the potential that this instrument has should be seriously considered. So my main question is to my friend Professor Stürner, what alternatives do we have on the continent? I mean, you know the European Union is pushing in a certain direction – there are all these consumer protection plans. Have you seen anything concrete in terms of effect, in terms of going beyond the promised remedies? I think that we should still analyze very carefully the potential of the American approach without having any sort of prejudice towards the negative implications. Thank you.

*Professor Stürner:* It is true that all European countries have more and more problems with mass damages. But, Professor Trocker, nevertheless it remains questionable to seek the solution through the adoption of American style class actions. Private law enforcement and class actions are a necessary counterweight to deregulation and the outsourcing of risks. And the Europeans and the European-influenced cultures have to decide whether to take the American way to deregulate and to outsource risks or not. If they decide to do this, there may be no alternative to private law enforcement and class actions. But they should be aware of the fact that the success of the American economic culture is the result of the last two decades. The time before, in the 80s, 70s, 60s, this form of rather deregulated economic culture was not so successful compared with continental European or continental European-influenced economic cultures. My answer is that we should not be too hasty. At present, Europeans are very quick in imitating American patterns. Perhaps it is good to wait some years and to observe the American development very carefully. I think that exaggerated outsourcing of risks, to make each citizen a shareholder, is perhaps the wrong way. And if the degree of deregulation diminishes and outsourcing of risks does not go on, the problem of private law enforcement will not be so urgent in Europe. But if Europe and European-influenced cultures don't find their own way of balancing neo-capitalism and socialism and follow the present American example, we will have private law enforcement and class actions. Therefore, let me say again that it is not possible to discuss the problems of class actions on a merely technical basis. We have only these two alternatives: deregulation with an increase of class actions or prevention by regulation with class actions as a supplementary remedy.

*Professor Trocker:* I think there could be a combination of different solutions. On the one hand, we could take the idea of collective enforcement efforts and, on the other hand, we could take the Scandinavian example as a possible integration of a model that can work with some sort of public figure like the ombudsman. I mean, what is the alternative to private? Stick with public enforcement? Didn't work, won't work. Therefore, we have to find a combination of the basic private enforcement idea with an attempt to rationalize the elements that we cannot produce immediately in terms of organization of lawyers, in terms of contingency fees. Therefore, let's look to the Scandinavian model, I think that is something that we should consider carefully.

*Professor Stürner:* The Scandinavian models will not be the near common future. The high end level of lawyers in Europe is more and more dominated by Anglo-American law firms. Take Germany: we have about two or three big German law firms, all the other prominent firms are under Anglo-American control. The Anglo-American firms bring their legal institutions and legal instrumentalities to the continent. I think the possibility of developing special European legal techniques is the past. These big Anglo-American firms are very powerful and they have much influence, the Japanese situation may be different from the continental one. Take the case, for example, that the European Union considers to introduce private law enforcement in anti-trust cases. If you organize congresses or symposiums on this topic, these symposiums are also dominated and frequently visited by members of Anglo-American firms. Under their lobbying and law marketing the public opinion changes. It is my impression that the coming decades Europe will more and more adapt to Anglo-American patterns. For the next five or ten years the idea of a special European way seems to be strange. It is my impression that Italy is also under increasing American influence. There are many Anglo-American firms now dominating the high end level of lawyers. Only if the Anglo-American legal hegemony will become weaker there is a real chance for change and a chance for a phase of new continental creativity.

*Professor Trocker:* I don't think that Italy will introduce the class action because there is an awareness that it would not work. But we are faced with the need to consider situations, i.e. cases that we have not been able to handle so we are thinking seriously about being selective, but at the same time not preclusive.

*Professor Stürner:* Let me give a prognosis of the result of the present prominent securities litigations in the U.S. They will be settled and they will not be more successful than *Ahold*. And what is the result? Does it really change the reality? Class actions are a business, yes, but the social reality will be the same afterwards. The expectation that a class action could change and improve the social reality is very questionable or even erraneous. I don't think so.

*Professor Takagi:* I would like to comment on two points. One is again from the point of view of a bankruptcy specialist. The success of the American class action system is related to the entire American legal culture, I think. For example, our Italian colleague mentioned the *Parmalat* case. American corporations have strong weapons to resolve big damages claims. For example, take the many asbestos chapter 11 cases: the asbestos chapter 11 cases were filed to resolve the tremendous amounts involved in the mass tort litigation lawsuits. In Japan, the restructuring or reorganization culture is now changing Japan. But it is very notorious to file corporate reorganization proceedings in Japan. It is not like chapter 11. Filing a petition for corporate reorganization might cause severe damage to the business's reputation.

But there have been changes. Now, more troubled corporate organizations are going to file for reorganization at an earlier stage, but still they are rare. The Japanese culture is changing in many aspects. For example, we are now experiencing an accounting fraud case, a big case. We have the *Horiemon* case, the *Livedoor* case. Many individual personal investors are buying stocks using personal computers every day so now the environment in Japan is changing. Still, the Japanese business community is maybe very hostile to representative litigations, which claim damages against defendant corporate officers. The business corporations try again and again to force delays onto the representative litigations. As Japan is changing, for example, the number of private lawyers is increasing and many law firms are now becoming bigger and bigger, so in the future – not the very near future, but in the future – Japan may have more and more lawyers who handle business related cases, but not like the United States.

So I would like to ask Professor Murray to recommend American lawyers to suggest very good cases for class actions. For example, the defendant should be an American company doing business in the United States, and there may be many alleged victims who are potential plaintiffs, both in the United States and Japan. And American lawyers could cooperate with Japanese lawyers to effect notice to Japanese consumers, for example using mass media, the Internet and such. If American lawyers demonstrate good prospects for class actions in Japan, of course the litigation will be made in the United States, but many Japanese consumers could benefit from that in the future. Class actions still don't have such a good reputation in Japan, but please recommend American lawyers to show good examples even in Japan.

*Professor Murray:* I think that is a very constructive and very interesting observation. And the points that I tried to make in my little presentation were designed to try to build that bridge, so that we could provide for an international class action culture in this particular mass society that we live in, that would be satisfactory to and would be thought of as a positive development by the Japanese, European and other legal cultures. Even though perhaps those cultures would not by themselves want to sponsor class actions, nonetheless it would make it possible for the class action where it was properly grounded in the United States, to be recognized in these other legal cultures and to have citizens of these other cultures participate in the class action, whether it would be Parmalat or whether it would be some of these other corporations where there is clearly jurisdiction in the United States, but a wide participation by people in other countries.

And I have two observations to make. One is that the point we can all see is that there is, with these developments in the world – deregulation, outsourcing of risk or whatever – a tendency all over the world for people to think of collective measures to deal with these problems. What is interesting to me is that in the United States we have generalized it in our Civil Procedure Code whereas in many other systems which are considering collectivization it is embedded in specific laws such as the environmental laws or the consumer laws or most recently the securities laws. And, as our speaker just said, as you find individuals buying securities with their computers on the Internet or other ways, the need to find ways in which they can be protected is very important. And if the government is not going to protect them by regulation, they can't protect themselves individually so there is a very strong pressure to provide for some way for them to have some kind of collective measure. Even in Germany there are efforts to think about very limited methods for security holders to act together kind of thing. So I think that this pressure is there.

Now to make the US class action at least palatable, I think there are two things we need to do. One is to address the notice and jurisdiction issues raised by Professor Stürner. I have suggested some ways to do that. I think we also have to improve the remedy, because it is so problematical now because of the steering problem or the inversion problem as I have mentioned it. The fact that there is no real client to tell the lawyers what to do and so that the conflict of interest is so pervasive. Some of these European measures, whether you talk about the ombudsman measure or you talk about the representative client measure or interest group proceedings, provide at least a better client model than we have in the entrepreneurial lawyer and I think that we should look to these and see if there is some way we can restore some kind of a proxy for a real client as would be the case for instance if Deutsche Bank owned 10,000 shares of Ahold and were suing Ahold or suing the management because its shares had been devalued. You can bet that Deutsche Bank would be telling its lawyers what to do in the ordinary client way instead of having the lawyers telling the class what to do. We need to reform that part of the class action to make it into something that is reputable either in the United States or anywhere else.

And so I think we need to do two things. One is to deal with the notice problems to make it palatable for people in other countries to participate, but second to deal with the core remedy in a way that it will be a remedy that is positively regarded rather than negatively. I agree totally with Professor Stürner that as long as we are in this deregulated environment we are going to have a strong need for a collective remedy and it would be great if it could be one that could function well on an international basis and provide as good a remedy as possible under the circumstances.

*Professor Andrews:* A couple more questions, if I may. Under the US class action, the remuneration of counsel, the attorney, can be extremely lavish. I don't have a problem with that, because the politics of envy is I think disreputable. What I do have a problem with is the fact that the remuneration of counsel is a slice taken from the victorious plaintiff class's damages. It has always struck me as very difficult to defend lawyers enjoying a significant percentage of plaintiffs' recovery. What the class action clearly presupposes is a large financial incentive for the plaintiff class's lawyer, hence the terminology of 'the entrepreneurial lawyer'. Can you not contemplate in the United States a system where a plaintiff's lawyer receives a financial incentive, but it does not take the form of slicing off some of the damages recovered by the victorious class; instead, the victorious plaintiff's legal costs will be payable by the defeated defendant, and the plaintiff's attorney's 'bonus' will not be expressed as a percentage of the plaintiff's damages, but instead as a percentage of the ordinary fee that the lawyer would expect for undertaking that type of work. So you would have the economic incentive, you would have the contingent element, but you would have sidestepped what I regard as objectionable, which is really a conspiracy to conceal the fact that actually a large portion of the plaintiff class's recovery under the US class action is transparently very sizeable remuneration for entrepreneurial lawyers.

*Professor Murray:* Yes, I think your comment is very well taken and that is another one of the problems with the remedy. I have a couple of responses to it. First of all, the fee shifting with uplift does occur in some kinds of class actions in the United States, traditionally in the employment discrimination class actions. There are a handful of others where there is an uplift. One of the interesting hybrids is antitrust. Though that is not a class action usually, there is a fee shifting operation that is sometimes combined with a contingency fee. But certainly in the class actions the fee shifting occurs and there is an uplift in the way it is computed. Now the second question is if we switch to this would this do away with the abuse in the settlement? And my own feeling is that it would not, because what I would expect, is that unless we had better oversight of the settlement, the defendant in negotiating the settlement would be thinking in terms of its total exposure, that is fees plus payment to the class members, and whether he was paying the fees in terms of a percentage of the payment to the class member or in terms of a fee shifting plus uplift, those would be counted as dollars that he would take into account and determine how much by way of settlement he would pay the class members. So I suspect that in cases of class actions which are settled, which is in our case more than 90% of them, that changing to a fee shifting by itself would not seriously improve the situation. If it were combined with stronger oversight over the class action to protect the class members, it might help.

*Professor Andrews:* On another point, on page 4 of your excellent paper, at the end of the first paragraph there is a sentence which greatly intrigues me and I think would intrigue all English lawyers, which is the statement: "More recently, (obviously US) courts have taken a more pragmatic approach and cases have been certified as class actions based on common questions of liability, with the determination of damages to occur individually following decision of the common issues." Now, as you probably know, that type of arrangement represents an English equivalent to the class action. In other words, we in England are capable of issuing a representative judgment based on the question of liability with a sequel being individual partitions for the quantification of damages. My question is how common is that, and in your view is it a satisfactory arrangement?

*Professor Murray:* The answer is that the number of cases which have actually been tried to verdict on this kind of arrangement is very small to vanishing. The only one that comes to mind is the *Marcos* case, the Ferdinand Marcos case, which did actually go to verdict. It was partly uncontested, so it is not a very good example, but Marcos was a human rights class action that was combined as to liability and then there was quasi-individual determination of damages thereafter. There are a number of class actions that have been brought under this kind of arrangement with a claim for punitive damages and those cases are settled based upon a leap-frogging of the actual damages whereby the punitive damages claim and liability are settled. The class members are then given a piece of punitive damages and then they are invited if they wish to proceed on their own on the individual compensation that is basically set adrift at that point. But the punitive damages provide enough money to give some kind of a benefit to them and to provide the lawyers fees. Again the number of those is very small, but that is one way they try to get around that individualized determination to reach a settlement with a monetary payout that will short-circuit the million individualized cases.

*Professor Kato:* Thank you. Lastly, I would like to make a comment.

The US has a very good history of using class actions, but the European and Japanese speakers show some kind of negative attitude or at least hesitation against the introduction of the class action. It seems to me that this is influenced by the people's notion or image of a nation as a whole. Well, European countries, especially Germany and Japan, have a very strong power of administration and the people tend to think that the enforcement of the law is monopolized by the administration. This was a different image from the US and they did not have such enforcement of the law by the private sector, though it seems to me that the class action has been a very pragmatic way to protect individual citizens. But European people and Japanese people feel some kind of hesitation towards enforcement by the private sector with monetary incentives. This is the basic difference, it seems to me.

Anyway, we enjoyed the lively discussion today. Thank you very much to the speakers and the commentators.

*Chapter 3*

# Taking Evidence Abroad

# Transnational Litigation, Access to Evidence and U.S. Discovery: Learning from American 'Exceptionalism'?

*Nicolò Trocker*

*Content*


1. Introduction: a first glimpse at American "exceptionalism" . . . . . . . . . . 146
2. Differences between procedural systems as a source of conflict over "extraterritorial" discovery . . . . . . . . . . . . . . . . . . . . . . . . . 149
   2.1. Fact pleading *versus* notice pleading . . . . . . . . . . . . . . . . . . . . . 150
   2.2. Evidence *versus* discovery: the relevancy standard . . . . . . . . . . . . 152
   2.3. The scope of evidentiary obligations: the obligation to produce documents . . . . . . . . . . . . . . . . . . . . . . . . . . . . . . . . . . 155
   2.4. The limit of confidentiality . . . . . . . . . . . . . . . . . . . . . . . . 158
   2.5. Discovery and American litigation culture . . . . . . . . . . . . . . . . 158
3. The Hague Evidence Convention as a means for bridging differences and managing conflicts . . . . . . . . . . . . . . . . . . . . . . . . . . . 161
   3.1. The procedural framework of the Convention . . . . . . . . . . . . . . 161
   3.2. The Convention and U.S. discovery: the ambiguities of a commitment. The background of Article 23 . . . . . . . . . . . . . . . . . . . . . . . 164
   3.3. Exclusivity of the Convention? The U.S. Supreme Court's response in "Aérospatiale" . . . . . . . . . . . . . . . . . . . . . . . . . . . . . 167
   3.4. The impact of "Aerospatiale" on American discovery: a policy of self-restraint? . . . . . . . . . . . . . . . . . . . . . . . . . . . . . . . 170
   3.5. U.S. discovery requests before English courts: Lord Denning's "Blue Pencil" . . . . . . . . . . . . . . . . . . . . . . . . . . . . . . . . 172
   3.6. U.S. discovery requests before German courts: substituting document production with oral depositions . . . . . . . . . . . . . . . . 175
   3.7. U.S. discovery requests and nondisclosure (or "blocking") statutes . . 178
4. New perspectives for the taking of evidence abroad: learning from American "exceptionalism" . . . . . . . . . . . . . . . . . . . . . . . . . 180
   4.1. Obtaining evidence in the United States for use abroad: foreign litigants are discovering U.S. discovery . . . . . . . . . . . . . . . . . 182
   4.2. Evidence obtained in the U.S. and its use in foreign courts: a welcomed benefit? . . . . . . . . . . . . . . . . . . . . . . . . . . . . . . 184
   4.3. When procedural systems converge: "discovery" prior to the commencement of proceedings . . . . . . . . . . . . . . . . . . . . . . . . . 185

4.4. Pre-action disclosure and the Hague Evidence Convention: a new field of judicial cooperation? . . . . . . . . . . . . . . . . . . . . . 190
4.5. Direct access to pre-action disclosure in support of foreign proceedings? . . . . . . . . . . . . . . . . . . . . . . . . . . . . . . . 193
4.6. New standards for access to information and evidence: the "Principles of Transnational Civil Procedure". . . . . . . . . . . . . . . . . . . . . . 196

## 1. Introduction: a first glimpse at "American exceptionalism"[1]

"No aspect of the extension of the American legal system beyond the territorial frontier of the United States has given rise to so much friction as the application of U.S. discovery rules to the taking of evidentiary material located in foreign countries for investigation and litigation in the United States".[2]

Moreover, unlike many other focal points of controversy, the controversy over discovery is not one opposing the common law to the civil law, but rather one putting the United States against the rest of the world.

A basic premise of U.S. civil litigation is that fair and effective dispute resolution requires giving litigants the legal power to obtain largely unhindered access to all information that could be relevant to the resolution of their dispute. In the words of the U.S. Supreme Court:

"Mutual knowledge of all relevant facts gathered by both parties is essential to proper litigation. To that end either party may compel the other to disgorge whatever facts he has in his possession".[3]

Foreign persons engaged in litigation in the U.S. often perceive this system as strange, and indeed, oppressive upon defendants and resist in general requests for disclosure of material located outside the forum state. American lawyers instead tend to consider this attitude as a sort of conspiracy to conceal and are distrustful of the efficiency of the taking of evidence in foreign countries.

There are various ingredients in this *Justizkonflikt* (conflict about justice) between the United States and other countries involved in transnational litigation[4]. Often the conflict about discovery reflects a more general discontent among foreign parties with some of the typical features of the American legal

[1] The expression American "exceptionalism" is used here to describe the distinctive aspects of the American system of litigation. For an insightful discussion see *O. Chase*, American "Exceptionalism" and Comparative Procedure, 50 Am. J. Comp. Law (2002) 277.

[2] See Restatement (Third) of the Foreign Relations Law of the United States, § 442, Reporters Note 1 (1987).

[3] *Hickman v. Taylor*, 329 US 495 (1947).

[4] See *A. F. Lowenfeld*, International Litigation and the Quest for Reasonableness, General Course on Private International Law, 245 Recueil des Cours, Collected Courses of the Hague Academy of International Law, 1995, 191 ff. On the Justizkonflikt or conflict about justice between The United States and Europe see *P. Schlosser*, Der Justizkonflikt zwischen den USA und Europa, 1985. For a Japanese perspective see *Y. Taniguchi*, The Japanese in American

system: aggressive lawyering, jury trials, punitive damages and the overall American approach to civil litigation.

Lord Denning, the great English judge, captured vividly this widespread feeling towards some of the characteristics of American style – disputing in *Smith Kline & French Laboratories Ltd. and others v. Bloch.*

"As a moth is drawn to the light, so is a litigant drawn to the United States. If he can only get his case into their courts, he stands to win a fortune. At no cost to himself, and at no risk of having to pay anything to the other side. The lawyers there will conduct the case 'on spec' as we say, or on a 'contingency fee' as they will take 40% of the damages, if they win the case in court, or out of court on a settlement. If they lose, the litigant will have nothing to pay to the other side. The courts in the United States have no such costs deterrent as we have. There is also in the United States a right to trial by jury. These are prone to award fabulous damages. They are notoriously sympathetic and know that lawyers will take their 40% before the plaintiff gets anything. All this means that the defendant can be readily forced into a settlement. The plaintiff holds all the cards"[5].

These features should be contrasted with the approach to civil litigation elsewhere. Without the support of contingency-fee agreements which most legal systems consider illegal – on the grounds that if the lawyer had a financial stake in the outcome of the case, he might be encouraged to act dishonestly – and faced with the risk, in case of non success, of having to pay both his own attorney's fees and also those of his opponent – a party, outside the U.S., is hardly encouraged to start a lawsuit, unless he/she has some confidence of success[6].

Moreover, there are technical constraints to bring a lawsuit outside the U.S. It is, in fact, a fairly general policy, that a party should not embark on litigation unless he/she already has a clear concept of his/her cause of action. There is strong disapproval of so-called "fishing expeditions", that is the practice of using discovery for the purpose of finding out whether a cause of action exists.

---

Litigations. Problems of Procedural Conflict, in Der Justizkonflikt mit den Vereinigten Staaten, *W. Habscheid ed.*, 1986, p. 93ff.

[5] [1983] 2 All England Law Reports 72 (C.A.)

In England, lawyers are now allowed to represent clients on the basis of a conditional fee agreement. The system of conditional fees provided by sec. 58 of the "Courts and Legal Services Act 1990" has been amended by sec. 27 of the "Access to Justice Act 1999". The "Conditional Fee Agreements Order 2000", provides that agreements may be used in all litigation except in criminal and certain family matters and fixes the amount of the maximum uplift of the success fee. On the recoverability of success fees, see the House of Lords decision *Campbell v. MGN Ltd. (2005) U.K.H.L. 61.*

[6] For more details see the discussion in *G. C. Hazard – M. Taruffo*, American Civil Procedure, An Introduction, Yale Univ. Press., 1993, 96ff. For an interesting comparative analysis see *M. Zander*, Will the Revolution in the Funding of Civil Litigation in England Eventually Lead to Contingency Fees?, 52 De Paul L. Rev. (2002) 256ff. For an extensive discussion of the modern litigation-funding arrangements that have been introduced in England, see *A. Zuckerman*, Zuckerman on Civil Procedure. Principles of Practice, London, 2006. Also on the Continent there is now a trend to repeal provisions prohibiting the stipulation of success or contingency fee agreements. For Italy, see, art. 2 of the Law of August 4, 2006, n. 248.

There are exceptions to this rule, but these exceptions are not intended, at least in principle, merely to allow a party to "fish out" his/her case[7].

Not only are the risks of, and the disincentives to, litigation greater outside the U.S.; the rewards are considerably less significant. Jury trials in civil cases have been virtually eliminated everywhere – England maintains exceptions for libel and slander – and punitive damages are very rare. The function of awarding damages is essentially limited to compensate actual damages. In such circumstances, a party will hardly venture in the gamble of bringing an action for damages on what appears from the outset as a doubtful case[8].

All these differences add themselves up to a more general difference in the view regarding the function of civil litigation.

In the U.S., civil actions serve important public functions, for example, promoting products safety and maintaining an effective system of competition between business enterprises. Treble damage awards in antitrust suits, and punitive damages in product-liability cases, are justified on these grounds. Elsewhere, "public interest litigation" in the ordinary courts is the exception rather than the rule. Law enforcement actions going beyond the purpose of enforcing private legal rights and punishing the wrong-doers are left to criminal law enforcement and administrative regulation[9].

In view of these differences, it is hardly surprising that foreign lawyers and parties find some aspects of American civil procedure hardly acceptable; and that foreign governments seek to protect their own interests and concepts of justice by limiting (or refusing to provide) judicial assistance in civil matters to the U.S., while American parties and lawyers operating on the basis of their domestic concept of civil justice are likely to consider that this is nothing out of the ordinary and feel justified in applying American discovery rules in order to seek evidence located outside the United States.

But there are also other ingredients in the mentioned *Justizkonflikt*.

Some of the controversies over fact or information gathering across national frontiers are affected by the underlying substantive claims for which discovery is sought. Indeed, some of the adverse reactions to American discovery are aimed against what are perceived as too far extended concepts of jurisdiction to prescribe and excessive practices of jurisdiction to adjudicate.

In the field of antitrust and securities litigation, for example, it is the American practice of applying U.S. laws to foreign conduct and interests – a practice

---

[7] For a more detailed treatment of this theme see *infra* text n. 2.1 and 4.3.

[8] See *J. Y. Gotanda*, Punitive Damages: A Comparative Analysis, 42 Col. J. Trans'l Law (2004) 391. On U.S. developments in this field see *A. M. Welker – S. Wilske*, Keine Entwarnung bei Punitive Damages, Recht der internationalen Wirtschaft (RIW), 2004, 439ff; the U.S. Supreme Court decision in *State Farm v. Campbell*, 123 SCt., 1513 and the Oregon Supreme Court decision of February 2, 2006, *Philip Morris v. Williams*.

[9] For an analysis of the different purposes and roles of civil justice in Germany and the United States, see *P. L. Murray – R. Stürner*, German Civil Justice, 2004, 575.

based on the so called "effects" doctrine – that provokes reactions and criticism abroad[10], while in connection with product liability suits it is the assumption of *in personam* jurisdiction on the basis of "minimum contacts" that is frequently being questioned because of its outcome; outcomes that foreign observers regard as unacceptable and are likely to describe as contrary to the principles of international law, whether it be territorial sovereignty or a reasonably close linkage requirement[11]. And so the conflict over what is regarded in foreign countries as an excess of jurisdiction can lead to a conflict over the application of American discovery rules to evidence located outside the United States, with foreign countries using blocking statutes in order to prohibit compliance with U.S. discovery orders in so far as they involve disclosure of information (of an economic, commercial, industrial, financial or technical nature) to be used as evidence in U.S. judicial or administrative proceedings.

Because each of these themes deserves further consideration, they are hereunder discussed separately before turning to the specific problems of evidence gathering in transnational litigation with U.S. courts or agencies.

## 2. Differences between procedural systems as a source of conflict over "extraterritorial" discovery

The first part of our analysis will focus on the differences between the U.S. procedural system and the procedural systems of other countries involved in transnational litigation, that have traditionally been a primary source of conflicts in the area of taking evidence across state boundaries. The differences to

[10] For the first time the effects-doctrine has been adopted in the famous *Alcoa* case in the United States, and it has been confirmed in various decisions by the United States Supreme Court. In *Hartford Fire Insurance Co. v. California*, 509 U.S. 764, 796 (1993) the Court held it to be "well established by now that the Sherman Act applies to foreign conduct that was meant to produce and did in fact produce some substantial effect in the United States". For a comparative analysis of this topic see *J. Basedow*, International Antitrust: From Extraterritorial Application to Harmonization, 60 Lousiana L. Rev. (2000) 1037. For the notion of "independent foreign harm", see the recent Supreme Court decision in *Hoffmann – La Roche Ltd. v . Empagran S.A. et al.* 124 S.Ct. 2359 (2004). For comments, see *P. Hay – T. Krätschmar*, RIW 2004, 667 ff.; *S.F. Halabi*, 46 Harv. Int'l L.J. (2005) 279.

[11] See *F.A. Mann*, The Doctrine of International Jurisdiction Revisited After Twenty Years, 184 Recueil des Cours, (1984), III, 69–71; *L. Silberman*, The Impact of Jurisdictional Rules and Recognition Practice on International Business Transactions: The U.S. Regime, Rivista di diritto internazionale privato e processuale, 2004, 707 ss. A recent example of jurisdiction based on "minimal contacts" is *In re Ski Train Fire in Kaprun, Austria*, 230 F. Supp. 2d 376 (S.D.N.Y. 2002) finding that German corporation, Siemens AG, conducted sufficient activities to constitute "doing business" jurisdiction under New York law and was subject to suit by U.S. plaintiffs with respect to a ski train accident in Austria. For a critical appraisal, *H. Schack*, Unglücke in Europa – Klagen in den USA, in Festschrift für P. Schlosser, Tübingen, 2005, 839–850.

be considered in this context can be grouped into four categories: (a) fact pleading versus notice pleading; (b) evidence versus discovery; (c) the scope of evidentiary obligations; (d) the confidentiality limits.

### *2.1 Fact-pleading v. notice pleading*

In procedural systems of civil law tradition strict requirements limit the scope of the fact-finding process at a relatively early stage of the dispute. Civil procedure codes of continental Europe generally require the assertion of detailed facts and the proffer of specified means of evidence during the pleading phase of the proceedings. To mention just a few examples: under sections 130 and 253 of the German ZPO, the complaint must contain definite and particularized claims for the relief as well as a definite statement of the factual subject matter of the proceeding. Article 163 of the Italian Code of Civil Procedure requires that the first pleading (citazione), in order to be validly introduced, contain the definition of the subject matter of the claim; the statement of facts and law sustaining the case together with the relief sought; the identification of evidence and produced documents. In Japan, the new Code of Civil Procedure requires that the plaintiff's complaint be specific about the underlying facts and that the evidence be itemized and written out to each point to be proved[12]. In England, traditionally, a party is expected not to embark on litigation unless he/she has already a clear concept of his/her cause of action. Under the new Civil Procedural Rules, a party has to assert sufficiently detailed facts in the statement of the case capable of disclosing reasonable grounds for bringing a case.[13]

In contrast, American civil procedure at the federal level does not require the assertion of detailed facts and the presentation of individualized means of evidence during the pleading phase. The action may be drawn up in very general terms. Notice pleading – which is common practice in the federal courts – means that "a plaintiff need only make a short plain statement of claim rather than the statement of facts setting forth a cause of action"[14].

[12] *T. Kojima*, Japanese Civil Procedure in Comparative Law Perspective, 46 U. Kan. L. Rev., (1998), 687, 694.

[13] See *L. Collins*, Opportunities for and Obstacles to Obtaining Evidence in England for Use in Litigation in the United States, 13 Int'l Lawyer (1979) 27: "English pleadings (...) have a far greater particularity than their American counterparts, the length of which is sometimes, if not always, matched by their vagueness". As to the "statement of case", the new term for a pleading, under the Civil Procedure Rules see *N. Andrews*, English Civil Procedure: Fundamentals of the New Civil Justice System, Oxford, 2003, 10.60, 10.70. General guidance as to the function of statements of case, "critical to identify the issues and the extent of the dispute between the parties", was given by Lord Woolf in *Mc Philemy v. Times Newspaper Ltd.*, [1999] 3 All ER 775. See also *Loveridge v. Healey* [2004] EWCA Civ. 173.

[14] See e.g. the introduction by *J.H. Friedenthal – M.K. Kane – A.R. Miller*, Civil Procedure, 2nd ed., 1993, Ch. 5, 237ff. For another overview, see Outline of a Lawsuit, in *L. Silberman – A. Stein – T. Wolff*, Civil Procedure: Theory and Practice, 2nd ed., 2006, pp. 1–12. For recent trends in specific fields see, *D. Moos*, Pleading Around the Private Securities Litigation

In a famous House of Lords decision – *British Airways Board v. Laker Airways Ltd. a.o.* (1984) – Lord Diplock pointed to this prominent feature of American procedure not without critical tones:

"one of the characteristics of the rules of civil procedure in the federal courts of the United States (as well as in most state courts), which seems to any English lawyer strange and, indeed, oppressive on defendants, is that a 'complaint', the document by which an action is begun, while it alleges that the complainant has a cause of action against the defendant or defendants, does not disclose, or discloses only in a most exiguous form, the facts which the plaintiff will eventually rely on at the trial as giving rise to that cause of action. Instead, the complaint is accompanied, or immediately followed, by a request to the defendants for pre-trial discovery which bears little resemblance to the kind of discovery that is available in English civil actions. Its breadth, the variety of methods, oral and written, that it makes available for a wide-roving search for any information that might be helpful to the case of the party seeking discovery, the enormous expense, irrecoverable in any award of costs to a successful defendant, in which it may involve parties from whom discovery is sought, and its potentiality for oppressive use by plaintiff, received sufficient mention in the various speeches in this House"[15].

Moreover – one should add –, it is the parties and their attorneys that dominate the discovery scene. In most other legal systems, judicial control of litigation is the principal instrument for accommodating law enforcement with the objective of justice on the merits[16]. Therefore, not only are the requirements as to the content of complaints considerably more rigorous, but it is the court that plays a significant role in the actual shaping of the case. From the very inception of the procedure, it is the court that discusses with the parties' attorneys the potential lines of argument and attempts to narrow the issues to those which are likely to be dispositive of the case. The result is that the process of evidence-taking can be focused on these specific issues which have been identified as potentially dispositive.

Reform: Reevaluating the Requirements for Market Manipulation Claims, 78 Southern Cal. L. Rev. (2005) 763 ff. Not all individual American States have followed the notice-pleading system developed in federal civil procedure. Some States practice fact-pleading.

[15] [1984] 3 WLR 419.

[16] In comparative perspective, *Murray – Stürner, supra*, note 9, at 595. For the recent development in England *A. Zuckerman*, Court Control and Party Compliance. The Quest for Effective Litigation Management, in The Reforms of Civil Procedure in Comparative Perspective, *N. Trocker – V. Varano eds.*, Torino, 2005, 144. In his Access to Justice Report Lord Woolf concluded that to avoid the excesses of the past "there is now no alternative to a fundamental shift in the responsibility for management of civil litigation from litigants and their advisers to the courts".

Case management has become an element of procedural reform also in the United States. See *S. Burbank – L. Silberman*, Civil Procedure Reform in Comparative Perspective: The United States of America" 45 Am. J. Comp. Law (1997), 675, 678–683. But it can hardly be considered as one of the significant features of American civil litigation.

## 2.2. *Evidence v. discovery: the relevancy standard*[17]

When a *notice pleading rule* applies, as it is in the United States, much work has to be done by the parties and their lawyers after the filing the claim, in order to determine whether or not there are facts sufficient to support the claim. Since American lawyers are not expected to have particularly comprehensive command on the relevant facts at the time they file suit, the investigation and uncovering of facts and information potentially relevant to the adjudication of the case takes place between the completion of the pleadings – i.e. the submission of complaint and answer or counterclaim – and the beginning of trial: this is the period of *pre trial discovery*. During this stage, lawyers dispose of powerful tools of discovery to require the opposing party and third parties to provide potentially relevant information about the facts of the case in the form of documents and things, interrogatory answers and deposition testimony. The paradigm provision is *Rule 26 (b) (1) of the Federal Rules of Civil Procedure* which now reads:

"Parties may obtain discovery regarding any matters which is relevant to the claim or defence of any party seeking discovery, including the existence, description, nature, custody, condition and location of any books, documents or other tangible things and the identity and location of persons having knowledge of any discoverable matter. It is not ground for objection that the information sought will be inadmissible at the trial if the information sought appears reasonably calculated to lead to the discovery of admissible evidence".

The standard of relevance required under this provision for discovery is much broader and more flexible than the one which applies to evidence. Only if the material sought bears no conceivable relationship to the subject matter of the litigation does the concept of relevancy limit the scope of the discovery process.

This remains true despite the scope-narrowing provision which has been embodied in Rule 26(b)(1) by the 2000 Amendments of the Federal Rules of Civil Procedure. The move from the pre-amendment standard which had permitted discovery of "any matter not privileged which is relevant *to the subject matter* involved in the pending action" (at least from 1970) to the 2000 version of Rule 26(b)(1) which allows discovery of any non-privileged matter "that is relevant *to the claim or defence* of any party", does not seem to have brought about any significant restriction on the scope of discovery.

To some extent it was clear from the beginning that "the dividing line between information relevant to the claims and defences and that relevant only to

[17] For an in-depth analysis of the various aspects, *D.J. Gerber*, Extraterritorial Discovery and the Conflict of Procedural Systems: Germany and the United States, 34 Am. J. Comp. Law, (1986) 745, 761–764; more recently, Id, Comparing Procedural Systems: Toward an Analytical Framework, Law and Justice in a Multistate World, Essays in Honor of Arthur T. von Mehren, 2002, 665ff.

the subject matter of the action could not be defined with precision. And so it does not come to any surprise that the concern (or, from a different point of view, the expectation) that the new rule could (or would) serve as a significant barrier to the receipt of discovery finds little, if any, support in the cases"[18]. There are strong indicators that the "new burden" is nominal, or in effect non-existent.

To mention just one illustrative post-amendment case, in *Sheldon v. Vermonty* an individual plaintiff sought discovery from the broker defendant in a securities fraud suit seeking proceeds data for a five years period. The defendant, however, contended the only relevant time period was during the one-year period over which plaintiff contemplated and purchased the stock. Granting the plaintiff's request, the court announced its understanding of the scope of discovery in light of the new standard stating [r]elevancy is broadly construed, and a request for discovery should be considered relevant if there is any possibility that the information sought may be relevant to the claim or defence of any party... [D]iscovery should be allowed unless *it is clear* that the information sought can have *no possible bearing* on the claim or defense of a party.[19]

Discovery can be used to investigate, ascertain and expose potentially relevant facts to a great level of detail with relatively little interference from the court. For the lawyers "fuelled by contingency fee agreements with plaintiffs and hourly rates paid by defendants"[20] there are incentives to acquire as much information as possible in order to support any legal argument which may turn out to be "relevant" to the issues which will eventually be identified as dispositive of the case. And the State makes them available the legal tools necessary to ensure compliance with their demands for information.

Despite recent efforts and attempts to curb and control discovery or excesses thereof through active case management[21], the judge's presence during the pre-trial stage of the proceedings remains substantially limited[22]. The court may

---

[18] See *Ch. Frost*, The Sound and the Fury or the Sound of Silence?: Evaluating the Pre-amendment Predictions and Post-Amendment Effects of the Scope-Narrowing Language in the 2000 Amendments to the Federal Rule of Civil Procedure 26 (b) (1), 37 Georgia L. Rev. (2003) 1038ff. For the notion of documents, see the 2006 version of Federal Rule of Civil Procedure 34 (a).

[19] 204 F.R.D. 69 (D. Kan. 2001).

[20] *Murray – Stürner, supra* note 9, at 594.

[21] For a description of the discovery amendments through 1998 and their background, see *R. L. Marcus*, Discovery Containment Redux, 39 Boston College L. Rev. (1998) 747. See also, *C. Tobias*, Congress and the 2000 Federal Civil Rules Amendments, 22 Cardozo L. Rev. (2000) 75. For an excellent survey of discovery practice reforms in the State courts, see *S. Moskowitz*, Rediscovering Discovery: State Procedural Rules and the Level Playing Field, 54 Rutgers L. Rev. (2002) 595. On the changing role of the judge in the United States, *Murray-Stürner, supra* note 9, 636–639.

[22] Also because "the relative proportion of lawyers and judges helps dictate American discovery practices. There are approximately a million lawyers in the United States. In 1998 there were 9065 state judges of courts of general jurisdiction. At the federal district courts

issue protective orders restricting discovery, but the grounds for issuing such orders are limited and not clearly defined and the party seeking any such protective order bears the burden of persuading the judge that it should be issued.

In clear contrast, where a strict *fact pleading rule* is applied, once the case is started, there is little need or room for the parties to go around searching ("fishing") for facts and information; there is need for evidence. Parties and their lawyers are expected to have developed their relevant factual assertions, by the time they commence suit. They are also expected to be in a position to point to potential sources of proof for these factual assertions. Complaints are tested for sufficiency not only on their factual allegations, but also for the required reference to the sources of evidence relevant in relation thereto.

*Evidence* is probative material that supports, contradicts or weakens a fact at issue in the proceedings. The standard for admission of evidence is *relevancy.* The logical relevancy of an item of evidence is usually determined on the basis of the capacity of that evidence to produce useful knowledge concerning a fact. Under a fact-pleading system, the concept of relevancy of evidence refers to the statements of facts that are alleged in the pleadings as a basis for claims or defences[23]. Its standard is substantially higher and significantly stricter than that of Rule 26(b)(1) of the Federal Rules of Civil Procedure, according to which discovery may be sought whenever the "information sought appears reasonably calculated to lead to the discovery of admissible evidence". Mere speculation of a party that a witness or documents may say something relevant to the litigation process is not enough to trigger the use of state power. A court will not admit evidence merely because it might lead to, or in the direction of, relevant information, as it is the case in the U.S. Evidence will only be admitted if it affects the determination as to whether an asserted fact is true or not. The requirement of substantiation, i.e. the requirement that the relief sought and the subject matter of the suit are specifically spelled out, is designed to assure that evidence is actually taken only where the party nominating the evidence can show that it is likely to yield information useful to the court. And the court will order testimony or the production of documents only where a party can describe the facts that the evidence is intended to prove. If a party nominates evidence to support an assertion of fact, the court will receive the evidence by ordering the designated persons to testify or to produce the designated document insofar as a

level, there were 642 authorized life tenured judgeships and 436 magistrate judges. In addition, there were 337 senior status district judges. This means we have approximately one hundred lawyers for each judge who presides over a court of general jurisdiction. Also, judges are increasingly preoccupied with criminal matters. Whether it is a good idea or not, the judiciary does not have the personnel to replace lawyers as having the primary responsibility for pretrial discovery. Nor is it likely that state or federal legislators will soon drastically increase the funding for the judiciary". *S. Subrin*, Discovery in Global Perspective. Are We Nuts?, 52 De Paul L. Rev. (2002) 299, 310.

[23] See *M. Taruffo*, Rethinking the Standards of Proof, 51 Am. J. Comp. L. (2003) 675.

material fact – a fact which is itself an element of a litigation claim or defence – is at issue and the nominated evidence is material to the proof of such fact[24].

In view of these differences, it is hardly surprising that the "relevancy issue" plays a particularly important role in the controversies over the taking of evidence abroad. One source of potential conflict (and confusion) lies, however, in a far too common lack of clarity about discovery's dual purpose: the ordinary purpose to allow the gathering of extensive amounts of unspecified and detailed *information*, but also the purpose of making it possible to obtain *evidence* in a technical sense, which will then be used at trial. Since information sought in the discovery stage may not be tendered at the trial, not every United States discovery request can be qualified as a request for *evidence* to be taken in or from a foreign country.

### 2.3. *The scope of evidentiary obligations: the obligation to produce documents*

Related to the differences in the treatment of fact or information gathering are the differences between American procedure and the procedure of most (if not all) other countries involved in transnational litigation as to the scope of the obligations to provide "information", particularly in relation to the production of documents. In the U.S., the obligation of a party to provide information pursuant to the discovery process is extremely broad. A party may be deposed, and he/she may also be compelled to answer interrogatories and to produce documents. Federal Rule of Civil Procedure 34 authorizes litigants in a civil action to request the other parties to the action to produce all documents within their "possession, custody or control" that are relevant to the action, whether or not the documents are within the territorial jurisdiction of the court. Information may be requested even if the party making the request does not know that the information exists or cannot describe it with specificity. Thus, for instance, a request for all correspondence or memoranda of meetings between the defendant and X in a given time period would ordinarily not be regarded as too broad under American civil procedure.

Furthermore, discovery is not limited to the parties. Anyone with discoverable information can be requested and if necessary, required, to make it available, either by way of an oral deposition under oath or by the production of documents or other evidence. Non-parties who do not voluntarily comply, may be subpoenaed and there are direct sanctions for non-compliance. The success of the system does not depend on the parties and non-parties spontaneous cooperation.

Things are significantly different elsewhere.

Until recently, Continental European procedure has shown a "considerable degree of tolerance – almost insouciance – for the incompleteness of evidentiary

[24] *Gerber, supra* note 17, 757 ff.

material". The codes of civil procedure of the 19th century strictly adhered to the principle *nemo tenetur edere contra se*, i.e. the principle that no party has to help her opponent in his/her inquiry into the facts. The litigation process maintained the primitive nature of a legalised fight where each litigant strove to defeat his/her opponent leaving no room for cooperation between the parties. This concept had (and to a significant extent still has) a strong impact on the parties' access to documentary evidence. Public policy reasons, such as the interest of justice or disposing fairly of the process, could only be applied, according to the traditional construction, to order the production of documents in the possession of third parties on the same theoretical basis on which a general duty of testimony was disposed. A procedural obligation of the parties to the dispute to produce a document could exist as far as it was the projection of substantive property rights of the opponent in the document.

More recently, however, the idea has gained ground, gradually and not without difficulty, that if the proceeding is to get as close as possible to the truth concerning the litigated issues, it must rely on techniques through which each party can have access to items of evidence not in its possession[25].

In France, art.10 of the Code Civil, as amended in 1972, introduced a general duty of procedural discovery, by providing that "each party must bring her contribution to the administration of justice in view of the ascertainment of truth", and that the party who breaches this duty once she has been formally requested to comply with it, without any justification, can be subject to the imposition of an *astreinte*, without prejudice of damages. Art. 11 of the "dispositions liminaires" of the new Code of civil procedure reaffirms the obligation of the parties to contribute in the taking of the evidence, and specifies that, as far as the disclosure of documents is concerned, this obligation is qualified by the power of the judge to impose the payment of an *astreinte*[26].

The French lead has been followed to some extent by the German *Zivilprozessnovelle* of 2002, which provides for the power of the judge to order parties or third parties to disclose documents in their possession on the simple basis that they may be useful to the ascertainment of the facts of the case. Commentators do not hesitate to define the new wording of §§ 142 and 144 of the ZPO as a meaningful innovation of the recent reform[27].

---

[25] For a brief comparative survey see *N. Trocker – V. Varano*, Concluding remarks, in The Reforms, *supra* note 16, 256–258.

[26] See *J. J. Daigre*, La production forcée de pieces dans le procès civil, Paris 1979 ; *L. Cadiet – E. Jeuland*, Droit judiciaire privé, 4th ed., Paris, 2004, 425 ; *J. Héron – Th. Le Bars*, Droit Judiciaire Privé, 3rd ed., Montchrestien, 2006, 824.

[27] This "although the reform failed to introduce a duty to give disclosure of all relevant [evidence] to the opposing party without a court's order: there remains therefore no automatic disclosure rule in German civil procedure". *P. Gottwald*, Civil Procedure Reform in Germany after the Reform Act of 2001, 23 Civil J. Quarterly (2004) 341.

The new Japanese Code of Civil Procedure includes Art. 163 which allows litigants to serve written requests for information on other parties. Thus a duty of disclosure is imposed on the parties in litigation. In addition, the new Code expanded the scope of the court's power to order the production of documents[28].

These are important developments towards greater cooperation between the parties; that is, greater exchange of pertinent information. However, the basic obligations to provide "information" for use in litigation remain, in general, significantly more limited than they are in the U.S., due to the *relevance* and *specificity* standards required for the taking of evidence. Courts operating within the continental tradition are reluctant to order the production of a class of documents or to order the taking of evidence without detailed factual or evidentiary contentions. Under French law, for example, a party can apply to the court for an order requiring the opponent or a non-party to produce documents, but the application will be granted only if the documents are identified with precision[29]. In Germany, there is comparable authority for civil litigation whereby a non-party can be required to produce documents.

In England, pre-trial requests for documents have been traditionally limited to those concerning facts alleged by the pleadings; recent reforms of English procedure have limited document requests even further, by introducing the parties' duty to regulate their behaviour to conform to the "overriding objective" of the CPR Rules directed at the achievement of efficiency, speediness and proportionality[30]. English law – Professor Zuckerman notes – has always set its face against so-called "fishing expeditions"[31]. And a recent decision of the Court of Appeals reemphasises the traditional hesitation to allow the court's machinery

[28] See *Kojima*, *supra* note 12, at 701–702; in addition see *T. M. Mochizuki*, Baby Step or Giant Leap?: Parties Expanded Access to Documentary Evidence under the New Japanese Code of Civil Procedure, 40 Harv. Int'l L. J., (1999) 285.

[29] *H. Solus – R. Perrot*, Droit judiciaire privé, Tome III, Paris, 1991, 560; *Héron – Le Bars*, *supra*, note 26, 825: "la demand doit indiquer de façon précise les pièces dont la production est demandée. Une partie ne saurait obtenir du juge un droit d'examen général de l'ensamble des papiers de son adversaire."

[30] "English discovery [traditionally] is limited largely to the discovery of relevant documents (...) relating to the issues". "The differences between English and American discovery (...) lie at the heart of the obstacles to obtaining evidence in the United Kingdom for the purpose of American proceedings". *Collins*, *supra* note 13, 27, 29. As to disclosure (standard disclosure and orders for specific disclosure) under the new system of procedure see *N. Andrews*, The Pursuit of Truth in Modern English Civil Proceedings, Zeitschrift für Zivilprozess International, 2003, 71, 75, 84. The author reminds us that "in England there is no deposition system allowing a party to conduct pre-trial oral examination, including cross-examination, of an opposing party or of a non party. Such a system is a prominent feature of American procedure". See also *Ch. Hollander*, Documentary Disclosure: Lessons from the English Experience, in *M. Adenas – N. Andrews – R. Nazzini*, The Future of Transnational Litigation, 2003, 151 ff., 153: "the emphasis of the new Rules is on less disclosure".

[31] Civil Procedure, London, 2003, 490; Id. Zuckerman on Civil Procedure, *supra* note 6, 570.

to support "wide roving inquisitions" for any information that might be helpful[32]. "Liberal" discovery remains a prominent feature of American procedure.

*2.4. The confidentiality limits.*

Legal systems generally provide confidentiality protection. There are no striking differences between the various systems as far as privileges based on confidential professional relationships – such as doctor-patient and attorney-client – are concerned.

Confidentiality restrictions on the scope of information which can be subjected to the litigation process are a source of conflicts mainly in the area of business related information. An example is the difference between the protection of "trade secrets" under Rule 26 (c) of the Federal Rules of Civil Procedure and the protection of the *Betriebs-* and *Gewerbegeheimnis* pursuant to sections 383 and 384 of the German ZPO where basically any information which is not public and which an enterprise has a legitimate interest in protecting (product information, information on marketing, enterprise strategy and the like) is included. The latter protection – explain commentators – responds to a perceived need to prevent firms from utilizing the litigation process to gain access to business secrets[33].

In the context of transnational litigation where foreign business information is sought, the relatively weak protection of business secrets under U.S. law can become a source of conflict or provoke negative reaction by parties (or governments) who find American discovery requests inappropriately intrusive in that they allow a party to rummage through the files of an adversary simply because they are involved in a litigation.

In view of these divergences among the procedural systems as to the scope of the obligation to produce information and the treatment of personal and organizational "private spheres", it should not be a surprise that in foreign eyes the American, rather than the systems of other countries of the civil as well as of the common law world, appears to be the *inquisitorial* system of litigation.

*2.5. Discovery and American litigation culture.*

As we have already noted, another difference which is constantly pointed at by those comparing American discovery to that of other countries is that the latter avoid and condemn discovery "fishing expeditions". American discovery is criticized because it is expensive and time consuming for both private individu-

---

[32] *Black v. Sumitomo* [2002] 1 WLR 1562, CA.

[33] For more details see *Gerber, supra* note 17, 764–767; and *A. Stadler*, Der Schutz des Unternehmensgeheimnisses im deutschen und U.S. – amerikanischen Zivilprozess und im Rechtshilfeverfahren, 1989; *L. Rosenberg – K.H. Schwab – P. Gottwald*, Zivilprozessrecht, 16th ed., München, 2004, 828ff.

als and the court system; it is invasive of privacy and unfair in forcing defendants to expend resources when plaintiffs do not have advance information on liability.

However, as it has been rightly pointed out, to label the U.S. system as one that wrongly permits "fishing expeditions" is to present a rather partial picture[34]. A number of qualifications have to be made.

Broad discovery is not a typical feature of every American litigation. Extensive empirical research shows that in the vast bulk of "ordinary" American civil cases – automobile accidents suits, landlord-and-tenants disputes; divorce and other family legal problems – there is no discovery at all or remarkably little discovery. A 1997 survey by the Federal Judicial Center concluded that "the typical case has relatively little discovery, conducted at costs that are proportionate to the stakes of litigation, and ... discovery generally – but with notable exceptions – yields information that aids in the just disposition of cases"[35].

This does not mean that there are no discovery abuses and discovery excesses; there are such abuses and excesses, as empirical data and vivid descriptions in numerous works show. Almost all amendments to the federal discovery rules during the last twenty-five years have been in the direction of restraining discovery: discovery and pre-trial conferences, judges and lawyers encouraged to view discovery in terms of "proportionality" of stakes involved, limitations of the number and length of dispositions and interrogatories and sanctions for obstructive behaviour[36].

Yet, "liberal discovery is a way of life in American litigation"[37]. This statement of the author of a recent evaluation of "The Pre-amendments Predictions and Post-amendments Effects of the discovery-scope narrowing language in the 2000 amendments to Federal Rule of civil procedure 26 (b)" (1) – the paradigm provision in the American legal system providing access to information, which in its pre-amendment standard permitted discovery of "any matter not privileged, which is relevant to the *subject matter* involved in the pending action" and in the 2000 version allows discovery of any non-privileged matter "that is relevant to the *claim or defence* of any party" – shows how strongly engendered in the U.S. litigation culture is the belief in the necessity of maximum access to facts and information. After more than fifty years that statement echoes the words of the U.S. Supreme Court in *Hickman v. Taylor* (1947): "Mutual knowledge of all the relevant facts gathered by both parties is essential to proper litigation. To that end, either party may compel the other to disgorge whatever facts she has in her possession". The desire for information in connec-

---

34 *Subrin*, *supra* note 22, 309.

35 *T.E. Willing et al.*, An Empirical Study of Discovery and Disclosure Practice Under the 1993 Federal Rule Amendments, 39 Boston College L. Rev., (1998), 525, 527.

36 *Subrin*, *supra*, note 22, at 313.

37 *Frost*, *supra* note 18, at 1087.

tion with the resolution of civil disputes remains nearly universal. No one seems to advocate the elimination of requiring full discovery of relevant information.

This has to be put in a larger perspective; a perspective that includes "the nature of [American] government, the composition of the bench and bar, the constitutional right to a jury, methods of lawyer compensation, ideology and beliefs about power, the degree of safety provided by the welfare state, attitudes about government regulation, and the place of discovery in the overall procedural scheme"[38]. The U.S. discovery mechanism is not so irrational when seen in the context of *a specific category of* American litigation and the role this kind of civil litigation plays in the governmental and societal structure of the United States.

Alexis de Tocqueville, the great nineteenth century French observer of the American scene, noted that "there is hardly a political question in the United States which does not sooner or later turn into a judicial one". These questions and issues are frequently, if not usually, raised by private litigants in civil litigation. More recently Professors Murray and Stürner, comparing the purposes and roles of civil justice in Germany and the United States, rightly emphasized that while "in Germany litigation in the ordinary courts is generally not considered as a substitute or even a supplement for public regulation of economic and social actions", in the United States "the system of private civil justice is seen as an important element in effective regulation of social and economic actors such as manufacturers of products, public officials, issuers of securities, environmental polluters, and the like. Class actions and jury trials have been seen as important tools by which private litigants keep such actors "in line" with the public interest and public priorities"[39].

Broad discovery seems critical in many situations in which private individuals use civil litigation to enforce civil rights, products liability rules, securities and antitrust regulations. In such instances, evidence to make a *prima facie* case frequently resides in the files and minds of the defendants. In these lawsuits it would often be very difficult, if not impossible, for the plaintiff to plead her facts or evidence with particularity in the complaint, as is required in the pleading rules of most countries outside the U.S. The lack of precise pleading means that the defendant also frequently needs extensive discovery.

Professor Subrin reminds us that it took years of litigation and discovery to uncover concealed information in the asbestos and tobacco cases. In such cases, at least the plaintiffs perceive that expansive discovery is critical to the ultimate outcome. "These are situations – he concludes – when discovery restraint will not make sense".[40]

---

[38] *Subrin, supra* note 22, at 309; *Chase, supra* note 1, 280, 293–295.

[39] *Murray – Stürner, supra* note 9, 575–576.

[40] *Subrin, supra* note 22, 317–318.

So we are confronted with some challenging questions: is it the pejorative cast of the term "fishing expedition" with more than a hint that it means "excessive" if not "abusive" search, or is it a widespread misunderstanding of the American approach to civil litigation that creates so much friction when it comes to the taking of evidence located in foreign countries for investigations and litigation in the United States? Is U.S. style discovery really unsuitable for a dialogue to be channelled through mechanism and procedures of judicial cooperation on a multilateral level? In order to answer these questions our attention must now be directed to the most important contemporary instrument in the field: the *Hague Evidence Convention*.

## 3. Bridging differences and managing conflicts: The Hague Evidence Convention

It might be of some interest to note that it was on the initiative of the United States, which had submitted to the Hague Conference concerns about a number of limitations of the existing system of rogatory letters[41], that the Hague Conference on Private International Law negotiated and drafted between 1968 and 1970 the *Hague Convention on the Taking of Evidence Abroad in Civil or Commercial matters*, while the 1905 Hague Convention on Civil Procedure (followed by the 1954 Hague Convention on Civil Procedure) already provided for transborder judicial cooperation in this field among civil law countries.

According to the preamble, the new agreement was designed "to improve mutual judicial cooperation in civil and commercial matters"; but the negotiating history tells us that the drafters of the Convention also intended to pursue the more ambitious objective to provide "methods to reconcile the different legal philosophies of the Civil Law, the Common law and other systems".

How are these goals achieved under the Convention?

### *3.1. The procedural framework of the Convention*

Broadly speaking, the Convention's drafters sought to accomplish these goals by establishing a relatively simple and uniform system for obtaining evidence abroad pursuant to letters of request through the judicial authorities of the contracting States as well as by streamlining the various procedures for obtaining evidence through diplomatic and consular officials and commissioners.

#### *a) Letters of request*

An important feature of the Hague Convention is that it requires each of the contracting States to designate a *Central Authority* for the purpose of receiving

[41] See Report of U.S. Delegation, Int'l Legal Materials, 1969, 785, 820.

incoming letters of request from abroad and transmitting them to the authorities competent to put them into effect.

Requests for assistance have to be made by "judicial" authorities and may under Article 1 (2) be used "to obtain *evidence*" which is intended for use in judicial proceedings, commenced or contemplated.

Art. 3 of the Convention sets forth a number of requirements concerning the information to be included in the request. In order to simplify the drafting of the request, a model form of letter of request, in revised version, was recommended by the Special Commission of the Hague Conference in May 1985.

Letters of request can be in English or French, unless the Contracting state to whom the letter is addressed has made an appropriate reservation. As to the execution of the request, Article 9 (1) establishes the general principle that "the judicial authority that executes a letter of request shall apply *its own law* as to the methods and procedures to be followed", but in order to secure evidence in a foreign country in a form and by a method which will make it of effective use in the court where the action is pending, Article 9 (2) sets out an obligation for the receiving State to follow the "special method of procedure" (for example verbatim transcripts of witnesses' testimony, cross-examination and the like), indicated by the requesting State unless it is entirely impracticable or "incompatible" with the internal law of the state of execution.

The Explanatory Report on the Hague Convention stresses the narrowness of the grounds on which the requested authorities can refuse to follow the special procedure indicated by the requesting State. According to the report, "to be 'incompatible' with the internal law of the State of execution does not mean 'different' from the internal law. That means that there must be some constitutional inhibition or some absolute statutory prohibition. Similarly, the use of the words 'impossible or performance' rather than 'impracticable' was deliberate with the view to maximising international cooperation. As the Explanatory Report further notes, "It is not sufficient for the foreign practice to be 'difficult' to administer or 'inconvenient'; compliance must be truly 'impossible'"[42].

An important aspect of the Convention concerns the right of the parties and the representatives of the requesting court to be present at the taking of evidence in the foreign country. Article 7 provides that the requesting authority shall, if it so desires, be informed of the time when, and the place where, the proceedings will take place, so that the parties concerned and their representatives may be present. Article 8 extends the same possibility to be present at the execution of the letter of request to representatives of the requesting authority.

Article 10 governs the use of compulsion against those who refuse to provide the evidence sought through a letter of request. In these circumstances, the re-

[42] References in *S. O' Malley – A. Layton*, European Civil Practice, London, 1989, 193.

quested States are under an obligation to use coercive process to obtain the evidence sought.

As to the delicate issue of privileges and immunities, the Convention adopts a "cumulative solution": parties and non-parties may claim the privileges provided for under the law of both the requested and the requesting State (Art. 11). A witness may thus refuse to answer a question on the ground of a privilege or a duty not to do so under the law of either the State of execution or the State from where the request is issued.

The only grounds on which the execution of a letter of request which is consistent with the requirements of the Convention may be refused are that its execution does not fall within the functions of the judiciary according to the law of the requested State or that this State considers that its sovereignty or security will be prejudiced thereby (Art. 12). Once a letter of request has been executed, the deposition or other evidence taken is transmitted back to the sending authority by the same channel which was used for the transmittal of the letter of request.

The only costs which the state of execution may generally recover from the requesting state are the fees paid to experts and interpreters, or the cost occasioned by the use of any special procedure requested in the letters of request.

*b) Evidence taken by consuls and commissioners*

The Convention in its Chapter 2 includes provisions permitting specific alternative methods for the taking of evidence which go beyond the basic Central Authority mechanism: the taking of evidence by *diplomatic officer* or *consular agent* for use in proceedings which have been commenced in the State which they represent, and the taking of evidence by *commissioners* appointed by a court in other contracting states for the purpose of taking evidence for such proceedings. Unlike the Central Authority mechanism, however, these alternatives cannot be used without the approval or acquiescence of the receiving state and they do not ordinarily permit the use of compulsion to obtain evidence.

Unless the State in which the evidence is to be taken (the host state) declares that its prior permission is required, a consul may take the evidence of a person who has the nationality of the state which he represents. He may also take the evidence of nationals of the host state or of a third state, if the competent authority has given its permission in general or in relation to the particular case, and if he complies with any condition specified in the permission (artt. 15–16). These latter provisions also apply to a commissioner appointed for the purpose of taking evidence, whatever the nationality of the witness (art. 17).

A witness may not be compelled to give evidence by the consul or commissioner but, if the state so declares, the consul or commissioner may apply to the competent authority of that state for appropriate assistance to obtain the evidence by such measures of compulsion as are available under its law (art. 18).

The consul or commissioner may, subject to terms of any permission by the authorities of the host state, take all kinds of evidence which are not incompatible with the law of the state and administer an oath (art. 21 (a)). Similarly, the evidence may be taken in the manner provided for under the law of the country in which the action is pending, provided that such manner is not forbidden by the law of the State where the evidence is taken. A witness may invoke a privilege to the same extent as if he/she were giving evidence pursuant to a letter of request (art. 21(d)) and may be legally represented (art. 20).

### *3.2 The Hague Evidence Convention and U.S. discovery: the ambiguities of a commitment*

According to the opening statement of Article 1 (1), the Hague Convention is applicable to the taking of *evidence* abroad in civil and commercial matters; pursuant to Article 1 (2) requests for assistance may be used to obtain *evidence* which is intended for use in judicial proceedings, commenced or contemplated. The term "evidence", one is inclined to argue, has to be read in its strict sense of material to prove or disprove the facts in issue, and cannot be extended to encompass material which may lead to the discovery of evidence. Thus, the Convention does not include a system of broad discovery as it is practiced in the United States.

Article 3 sets forth a number of requirements for specifications of requests. In particular, Article 3 (f) and Article 3 (g) provide that the letter of request shall specify, in the case of oral evidence, "the question to be put to persons to be examined or a statement of the subject matter about which they are to be examined" and, in the case of production of documents "the documents ... to be inspected". These requirements are likely to put U.S. courts operating in a notice pleading system in a position not familiar to them, in so far as they have to specify the necessary "evidence" at a very early stage of the proceedings. Yet, according to Article 5, the requested State may object to letters of request that fail to satisfy the specification requirements of Article 3.

And then there is Article 23, which provides that

> "A Contracting State may at the time of signature, ratification or accession, declare that it will not execute Letters of Request issued for the purpose of obtaining pre-trial discovery of documents as known in Common Law countries".

More than any other provision, Article 23 reflects the ambiguity of the commitments the States parties to the Convention were willing to assume with regard to American style discovery.

The preparatory works show, quite surprisingly, that the United States delegation did not, in the proceedings in 1968, which led to the Convention, suggest that the United States was primarily concerned with the conduct of discovery abroad. As already mentioned, the United States – the prime mover of the Convention – sought improvement in the system of letters rogatory in order to eliminate "formal and technical obstacles to securing evidence abroad in a form that is usable in the court where the action is pending". It was the British delegation that insisted on a provision to be inserted in the Convention which afterwards became Article 23[43]. The reasons for this insistence are clear.

At the time the Convention was drafted, the United Kingdom was the only country which had some experience with American style discovery.

In two important decisions before the 1968 Hague Conference, involving United States litigation, it was held that English courts would not allow foreign letters rogatory to be used to obtain discovery, i.e. material which may lead to the discovery of evidence, either by way of documents or oral depositions, from third parties.

In *Radio Corporation of America v. Rauland Corporation [1956]*[44], a case out of an action instituted in the U.S. in which RCA claimed infringement of patents, the defendant obtained from the U.S. court letters rogatory addressed to the judicial authorities in England seeking evidence from two English companies, third-parties to the litigation. The application was made under the [English] *Foreign Tribunals Evidence Act 1856* and asked the English courts to order the officers of the English companies to produce documents and answer oral interrogatories. It was held that – without any convention or treaty to the contrary –, where the order related to oral testimony or documents, all that could be obtained under the Act was *direct material* immediately relevant to the issue in dispute and such as might be used at the trial and not *indirect material* by way of discovery and testimony for that purpose.

Lord Goddard thought that the application was "merely an attempt to get evidence in the course of discovery proceedings which are known to the American courts (...). It is an endeavour to get in evidence by examining people who may be able to put the parties in the way of getting evidence. That is mainly what we should call a *"fishing" proceeding which is never allowed in the English courts*"[45].

In *American Express Warehouse Co. v. Doe*[46], an action pending in New York against a number of Lloyd's underwriters arising out of a claim by the plaintiff for indemnity under policies alleged to cover a series of frauds, the warehouse company wished to seek/obtain evidence in England under the Foreign Tribunals Evidence Act 1856 from Lloyd's brokers, who were not parties to the American action, as to similar insurance placed with Lloyd's underwriters. It was held that the application related to evidence, and not to discovery, and was therefore

---

[43] See *L. Collins*, The Hague Evidence Convention and Discovery: A Serious Misunderstanding?, 35 Int'l. & Comp. L.Q. (1986) 765, 773.

[44] [1956] 1 A.B. 618.

[45] Id. at. 649.

[46] [1967] 1 Lloyd's Rep. 222, CA.

admissible. Lord Denning MR indicated that where documents were *sufficiently specified*, there was no objection to an order being made to give testimony and produce supporting documents ancillary to the testimony. It was not a mere application for discovery and the documents were sufficiently specified.[47]

During the negotiations that led to the Hague Convention, the United Kingdom delegation raised the issue that the possibility of expanding the expression "evidence" in Article 1 of the draft Convention would entail the risk that the Convention might be used to obtain discovery of documents and that foreign courts were not properly equipped to execute letters rogatory requesting discovery of documents. What ultimately emerged from these discussions – which saw the United States delegation conspicuously silent – was Article 23 as proposed by the United Kingdom delegation and adopted in October 1968.

Mr. Amram's final report on the Convention – Mr. Amram of the United States acted as chairman of the Special Commission of Experts – presents Article 23 as the provision that

> "... refers to a procedure by which one of the Parties to an action may obtain access, before trial, to documents in the possession of his adversary, to aid him in the preparation of his pleadings or in preparation for the trial. The procedure varies widely among the various States and is not even uniform in all Common Law jurisdictions. Accordingly, some States may be quite prepared to accept Letters for this purpose while other States may refuse them. Art. 23 provides the machinery for the exercise of this option".[48]

The original ratifying States which made a reservation under Article 23 (Denmark, Finland, France, Norway, Portugal and Sweden) flatly declared that they would not execute letters of request for the purpose of obtaining pre-trial discovery of documents as known in common law countries. The United Kingdom, on the contrary, in ratifying the Convention (in 1976) decided to make a more limited reservation by declaring that it would not execute requests for evidence which lack specificity; i.e. requests that do not describe precisely enough the documents do be obtained or examined.

In the following period, in part as a result of the discussion in the Special Commission on the Convention in 1978, in part as a result of the campaign of the United States to have reservations under Article 23 withdrawn or modified in order not to turn the Convention into a "one way street" as far as the United States are concerned, a substantial number of parties to the Convention have brought their declarations into line with that of the United Kingdom.

In joining the Convention in recent years – a sign that contrary to some predictions and some perceptions, the Hague Evidence Convention is alive and well – major actors in transnational litigation (South Africa, Switzerland, China) have followed the same path and framed their declarations along the lines of

---

[47] Id. at. 225.

[48] Reference in *Collins*, *supra* note 43, 776.

the reservation formulated by the United Kingdom. Today, the majority of States parties, while still affirming the necessity of a reservation in order to prevent abuses which would otherwise arise in connection with U.S. requests of pre-trial discovery of documents, recognize that an unqualified reservation as permitted by Article 23 is excessive and detrimental to the proper operation of the Convention. It would seem therefore that the United States, which was silent about its use for discovery purposes before the conclusion of the Convention in 1970, has since 1978 onwards, been at least partially successful to encourage the use of the Convention for discovery purposes. Does this mean that the ambiguity of the commitment assumed by the contracting parties with regard to American style discovery is resolved and that the Convention which was intended primarily to apply to "evidence" in the sense of material required to prove or disprove facts in issue can be successfully used to channel also "reasonable" requests for discovery, that it allows the search for material which might lead to the discovery of admissible evidence? A brief survey of what has been achieved through the Convention practice will give us some insights to answer the question.

### *3.3. Exclusivity of the Convention? The U.S. Supreme Court's response in "Aérospatiale"*

The Evidence Convention provides for various procedures for the taking of evidence *abroad*, but does not specify whether these procedures are designed for the taking of evidence *in* a foreign country as well as for the taking of evidence *from* a foreign country or whether the procedures apply only when evidence has to be taken on foreign soil, while no procedures for taking evidence *from* a state are provided under the Convention. Yet the question soon came up whether the availability of Convention procedures was in any way limiting access to domestic procedures for taking evidence *from* a foreign country and whether Convention procedures, if available, should be used instead of having recourse to domestic procedures for the *transfer* of evidence located in a foreign State (documents located in this state, witness residing there) to the forum State. In other words the questions were: how do Convention procedures relate to domestic procedures? Is the Convention exclusively applicable whenever its procedures are available? Does the Convention offer an option in addition to the availability of domestic procedures? Or does the Convention constitute the primary way of taking the evidence necessary in a particular law suit?

The Convention's text does not side with any of the above, nor any additional alternatives. Article 27 simply says that contracting states are not prevented from being more generous than provided under the Convention by permitting through internal law or practice additional methods of taking evidence.

The response of the U.S. Supreme Court came with the decision in *Société Nationale Industrielle Aérospatiale v. U.S. District Court (1987)*[49].

In a product liability suit based on the crash of an aircraft manufactured by two French corporations (Societé Nationale Industrielle Aérospatiale and one of its subsidiaries) initial discovery was conducted by both sides pursuant to the Federal Rules of Civil Procedure without objection. The problems arose when plaintiff served on the defendants a second request for the production of documents pursuant to Rule 34 asking the defendants to produce "*all of the design specifications, line drawings and engineering plans and all engineering change orders and plans and all drawings concerning the leading edge slots for the Rallye type aircraft manufactured by the defendants*". The defendants objected and filed a motion for a protective order alleging that because "the discovery sought can only be found in a foreign state namely France" the Hague Convention dictated the exclusive procedure that must be followed for pre-trial discovery. The motion was denied in the District court and in the Court of Appeals. The Supreme Court granted certiorari.

In its decision, the Supreme Court rejected the "extreme position" of considering the Hague Convention procedures "the exclusive and mandatory procedure for obtaining documents and information located within the territory of a foreign signatory". In the opinion of the Court the Convention did not deprive the District court of the jurisdiction it otherwise possessed to order a foreign national party before it to produce evidence physically located within a signatory nation. According to the Justices, when information is to be produced "from" (but not "in") a Convention signatory by a party over whom the court has personal jurisdiction, two alternative discovery procedures are available: direct discovery under the Federal Rules of Civil Procedure or a Letter of Request through the Convention. The choice between these two alternatives must be informed by principles of "international comity" rather than dictated by the Convention.

At the meeting in April 1989 of a Special Commission consisting of representatives of the signatories of the Hague Convention, convened by the Secretary General of the Hague Conference on Private International Law, there was extended discussion of *Aérospatiale*. Many delegates expressed the view that the decision was wrong and its concentration on U.S. sources was parochial[50]. Severe criticism also came from American authors[51].

---

[49] 482 U.S. 522 (1987). For an excellent discussion of its background, reasoning and impact see *G. Born*, The Hague Evidence Convention Revisited: Reflections on its Role in U.S. Civil Procedure, 57 Law & Cont. Problems (1994) 77ff.

[50] See the Report published by the Permanent Bureau of the Conference, 28 Int'l Legal Materials (1989) 1556.

[51] See, e.g., *C.E. Woodward*, Note, Discovery: Application of the Hague Convention in United States Courts, 29 Harv. Int'l. L.J. (1998) 160, 168.

In the view of the U.S. Supreme Court, the Convention was not intended to shield foreign litigants from the normal burdens of litigation in American courts, and, in particular, from pre-trial discovery even where the documents or information sought are physically located in the territory of a foreign State.

One might argue that the purpose and objective of the Convention would have been better served if the Court had adopted a rule of "first resort" to the Convention as suggested by the (in part concurring and in part dissenting) minority opinion in *Aérospatiale*. However, *Aérospatiale* can hardly be criticized for rejecting the view – taken for some time by the government and attorneys acting on its behalf to support German corporations which were sued in American courts – that American courts are not permitted to order the production of documents or other evidentiary material not located on American soil because this would infringe the sovereignty of the State where materials are located.

Strict "territorialization" of evidence-gathering would complicate or frustrate the administration of justice in many cases. In Professor Schlosser's words:

> "International judicial cooperation in this field means: not to interfere with foreign proceedings by artificially erecting "Chinese walls" against the normal conduct of civil proceedings just because the information needed is located beyond the jurisdiction's territory"[52].

It is a well settled practice (principle) in many countries outside the U.S. that the provision of specific information may be ordered from a foreign defendant in the same way as from a domestic defendant. The foreign defendant cannot be privileged as compared to a domestic defendant. Any defendant must comply with the "rules of the game". When under the domestic law of the court where proceedings are pending the defendant is bound to disclose the information available to him/her, in particular to produce a document or to make a deposition, it does not make any difference whether the defendant resides within the jurisdiction of the court or abroad.

Courts in civil law jurisdictions do not hesitate to use their power to require parties to a local proceeding to produce documents in their possession, even though the documents may be located abroad. A party with access to evidence located abroad may be placed under an obligation to provide the evidence under threat of sanctions or of an adverse decision in the matter at issue.

The principle that Convention procedures are not the exclusive way to obtain evidence abroad applies also to the *E.C. Regulation on Cooperation between the Courts of the Member States in the Taking of Evidence in Civil and Commercial Matters* which became effective on January 2004. Article 1 of the Regulation states that "this Regulation shall apply in civil or commercial matters

[52] *P. Schlosser*, Jurisdiction and International Judicial and Administrative Co-operation, 284 Recueil des Cours (2000) 118.

where the court of a Member State, *in accordance with the provisions of that State*, requests the competent court of another Member State to take evidence".

This means that the Brussels Evidence Regulation is designed to provide procedures by which a court in one Member State may seek the aid of a corresponding court in another Member State to obtain evidence from persons or things within its territorial jurisdiction for use in the requesting state. It does not mean that the procedures set forth in the Regulation for obtaining evidence located in another Member State are exclusive. There is no requirement of mandatory use of these procedures unless the domestic law of the court, where proceedings are pending, so provides[53].

### *3.4. The impact of "Aérospatiale" on American discovery: a policy of self-restraint?*

The existence of the power to order a thing done does not resolve the question of the *propriety of exercising* that power, particularly in the international context. For analytical purposes it matters little whether we regard the issue of the proper exercise of power as jurisdictional or discretionary. The absence of outside control necessitates a *policy of self-restraint*.

In order to moderate "global" discovery when information is to be produced by a party over whom the court has personal jurisdiction, the Supreme Court in *Aérospatiale* formulated "guidelines" designed to give content to the principle of reasonableness in the formulation of requests for foreign discovery.

"American courts – the Supreme Court said – in supervising pre-trial proceedings, should exercise special vigilance to protect foreign litigants from the danger that unnecessary, or unduly burdensome, discovery may place them in a disadvantageous position. Judicial supervision of discovery should always seek to minimize its costs and inconvenience and to prevent improper uses of discovery requests. When it is necessary to seek evidence abroad (...), the District Court must supervise pre-trial proceedings particularly closely to prevent discovery abuses. For example, the additional cost of transportation of documents or witnesses from foreign location may increase the danger that discovery may be sought for the improper purpose of motivating settlement, rather than finding relevant and probative elements. Objections to "abusive" discovery that foreign litigants advance should therefore receive the most careful consideration".[54]

---

[53] As to the German practice, *Murry-Stürner*, *supra* note 9, 558. On the European Regulation see *A. Müller*, Grenzüberschreitende Beweisaufnahme im Europäischen Justizraum, Tübingen, 2004.

[54] 107 Supreme Court Reporter (1987) at 2557.

Similar indications – on which the Court, actually, seemed to rely – are contained in section 442 of the Restatement (Third) Foreign Relations Law (1987) which reads as follows:

"(1) (c) [a court or agency in the United States], in deciding whether to issue an order directing production of information located abroad, and in framing such an order should take into account the importance to the investigation or litigation of the documents or other information requested; the degree of specificity of the request; whether the information originated in the United States; the availability of alternative means of securing the information; and the extent to which non-compliance with the request would undermine important interests of the State where the information is located".

The comments of § 442 state that as a rule, extraterritorial discovery should be ordered in relation to materials that are "necessary to the action – typically, evidence not otherwise readily obtainable – and directly relevant and material". This standard is considerably more rigorous than the one which usually applies to discoverable material under U.S. domestic law.

The question thus became: how have state and federal trial courts interpreted their responsibility for judicial restraint?

In the absence of clear empirical evidence, we are confronted with conflicting appraisal and statements. Critics note that U.S. courts are strongly inclined to resort to the Federal Rules invoking reasons of efficiency and show little sensitivity in their evaluation of foreign interests to international system values[55]. The minority opinion of a recent Third Circuit Court of Appeals decision goes even further and argues that *Aérospatiale* needs to be "revisited because many of our courts have not exercised the special vigilance to protect foreign litigants that the Supreme Court anticipated"[56].

Radically different the assessment of a highly respected American scholar. "What has happened – notes Professor Nafziger – is that nearly one hundred reported cases after *Aérospatiale* have considered the applicability of the Evidence Convention "and there is a substantial commitment to a form of particularized analysis that balances competing claims and interests, as set forth in the Third Restatement and more or less prescribed by *Aérospatiale*, in the interest of comity".[57] Moreover, the courts of two States – New Jersey and Oregon – have applied the first-resort rule advocated by Justice Blackmun's dissent in *Aérospatiale*. As a result, the case law since *Aérospatiale* allays the anxiety ex-

---

[55] *H. L. Buxbaum*, Assessing Sovereign Interests in Cross-Border Discovery Disputes: Lessons from Aérospatiale, 38 Texas Int'l L.J. (2003) 96ff.

[56] In Re: Automotive Refinishing Paint Antitrust Litigation, February 13, 2004, 358 Federal Reporter 3d, 2004, 288, 306.

[57] *J. A. R. Nafziger*, Another Look at the Hague Evidence Convention after Aérospatiale, 38 Texas Int'l. L.J. (2003), 114–115.

pressed years ago that the Supreme Court's decision had virtually nullified the Convention.

"What remains in the West Reporters are typically the tough cases involving diehard – though presumably good faith – efforts to avoid what are seen to be restrictions, delays and other complications of the procedures prescribed by the Evidence Convention. Unfortunately, a few of these cases did not give adequate attention to the *Aérospatiale* dicta designed to discourage legal tourism by lending content to the principles of reasonableness and comity. It is certainly disappointing to find conclusory opinions that a defendant has failed to carry the burden of proving the applicability of the Convention, even though the plaintiff's request for discovery abroad is vague or unparticularized. These opinions are particularly discouraging when one considers that the Federal Rules themselves require reasonable particularity in the formulation of requests for some types of discovery".

The overall picture leads the author to the conclusion that:

"the case law may be less determinate and more unilateralist than many would like, but reports of the death of guidance about discovery appear to be exaggerated"[58].

### *3.5. U.S. discovery requests before English courts: Lord Denning's "Blue Pencil"*

In the view of *Aérospatiale* the focus of the Hague Convention is on "information" under control of third parties who are not subject to the *in personam* jurisdiction of the United States court: information and persons that cannot be "domesticated" for discovery purposes. This does not mean that the Convention has no role to play in the production of evidence by the parties.

There are situations in which evidence located abroad can only be reached through the mechanism of judicial cooperation even though personal jurisdiction may be present, e.g. when a sanction cannot be enforced for lack of property located within the State attempting to take evidence, or when the foreign co-defendant does not appear, and its evidence turns out to be necessary to prove a case against another co-defendant. There may be also cases where, for other reasons, it is essential that evidentiary steps be taken in a foreign country: one could think of an order for on-site inspection of the defendant's plant abroad or a search in a large quantity of documents or electronically stored information present therein.

A different question is what is the role of the Convention in practice and what results are achieved through its procedures and mechanisms when U.S. discovery requests are presented to foreign courts or authorities.

As already pointed out, on its accession to the Hague Evidence Convention, the United Kingdom made a *limited* reservation in relation to Article 23 of the Convention. The reservation reads as follows:

---

[58] Id. at 114.

"In accordance with Article 23 Her Majesty's Government declare that the United Kingdom will not execute Letters of Request issued for the purpose of obtaining pre-trial discovery of documents. Her Majesty's Government further declare that Her Majesty's Government understand "Letters of request" issued for the purpose of obtaining pre-trial discovery of documents" for the purposes of the foregoing declaration as including any letter of request which requires a person:

a) to state what documents relevant to the proceedings to which the letter of requests relates are, or have been, in his possession, custody or power; or

b) to produce any documents other than particular documents specified in the Letter of Request, as being documents appearing to the requesting court to be, or to be likely to be, in his possession, custody or power"

The reservation is incorporated in the domestic law under the *Evidence (Procedure in Other Jurisdictions) Act 1975.* Section 2(3) of the Act provides that an order giving effect to a request for evidence by a foreign court for the purpose of civil proceedings which have been instituted or are about to be instituted should not "require any particular steps to be taken unless they are steps which can be required to be taken by way of obtaining evidence for the purposes of civil proceedings in the court making the order"[59]. This rather obscure phrase has been interpreted in the sense that English courts should refuse to make an order in aid of foreign requests for evidence if it appears that evidence is not requested for the purpose of the trial, where it is admissible and relevant to the issues in those proceedings, but it is instead requested for the purpose of discovery, something in the nature of the inquiry in which the party is attempting to "fish out" some material which might lead to obtaining admissible evidence at the trial.

In the *Westinghouse* case, an American court submitted to the English authorities a request for the production of a multitude of documents drawn up in 73 categories. One single document read as follows:

"Copies of all contracts, letters of intent, enquiries and quotations together with invoices of actual deliveries of uranium, thorium and their ores and compounds provided by members of the organization and organizations known variously as the 'uranium marketing research organization' the 'uranium producers club' the 'secretariate' and the 'société d'études et des recherches d'uranium'."

The Court of Appeal (Lord Denning) decided to modify the request (using a "blue pencil") so as to allow discovery of only those documents which were specified with such distinctiveness as it would be sufficient for a *subpoena duces tecum*. However, these documents did not have to be ancillary to oral testimony.

[59] *K. Lipstein*, The Evidence (Proceedings in Other Jurisdictions) Act 1975: An Interpretation, 39 Int'l & Comp. L.Q. (1990) 121.

"The description of the documents – Lord Denning stated – should be sufficiently specific to enable the person to put his hand on the documents or the file without himself having to make a random research – in short, to specifically know what to look for"[60].

*In re Asbestos Insurance*, in giving effect to a request for discovery of documents and oral depositions made during the pre-trial phase of a civil proceeding pending in the U.S. between a group of American corporations who manufactured asbestos and insurers with whom they had a large number of insurance policies to cover asbestos related claims, the House of Lords emphasized first, that "mere fishing expeditions" would not be permitted; and second, that only "separately described" documents could be obtained: "an order for production of the respondent's monthly bank statement for the year 1984 to his current account" with the named bank could satisfy the requirement. But a general request for "all the respondent's bank statements for 1984 would (...) refer to a class of documents and would not be admissible". Third, the documents requested "must be actual documents about which there is evidence which has satisfied the judge that they exist, or at least that they did exist"[61].

As to oral testimony, it was immaterial for the court to determine whether or not the request had a fishing character.

The prerequisite of *specificity* has been upheld also in *The State of Minnesota a.o. v. Philip Morris Inc. a.o. (1997)* – one of the big lawsuits against the American tobacco companies – which included a letter of request aimed at deposition of former officers of one of the defendants residing in England. In that case, the following statement was made: "American discovery (...) is not within the scope of the 1975 Evidence Act".[62] Under this term, the judge understood only discov-

[60] See *Rio Tinto Zinc v.Westinghouse*, [1978] 1 All ER, 443. For a detailed description of the Westinghouse case, *R.J.Augustine*, Obtainig International Judicial Assisstance under the Federal Rules and the Hague Convention on the Taking of Evidence Abroad in Civil and Commercial Matters: An Exposition of the Procedures and a Practical Example: In Re Westinghouse Uranium Contract Litigation, 10 Georgia J. Int'l & Comp. L. (1980), 101.

[61] [1985] 1 W.L.R. 331.

[62] International Litigation Procedure, 1997, 170, see also *First American Corporation v. Zayed* [1999] 1 WLR 1154 CA: where the Court noted that: "under the United States rules, the questioning of the intended witnesses can cover both the eliciting of admissible evidence and an investigatory search for information leading to a train of inquiry. The latter type of questioning would not be permitted in this country save in a Norwich Pharmacal type of action".

A remarkable cooperative attitude has been shown by the Cour d'Appel de Paris in its decision of September 18, 2003. Ruling on a U.S. pre-trial discovery request for the production of classes of documents – formulated in terms of "all ...documents" over a certain period of time – the Court held that it was admissible since the French declaration to Article 23 of the Hague Convention: "ne s'applique pas lorsque les documents demandés sont limitativement énumérés dans la commision rogatoire et ont un lien direct et précis avec le litige",

"Une description exacte de la pièce reclamée ne peut être exigée [...]".

"[...] au sens de la réserve française, l'énumération des documents est limitative dès lors que ces derniers sont identifiés avec un degré raisonnable de spécificité en fonction d'un certain nombre de critères tels que leur date, leur nature ou leur auteur". For a favorable comment see

ery aimed at information not as such admissible at trial, but not every request made during the discovery phase of the proceedings.

This means that American discovery is not excluded from all forms of judicial assistance. An American request made during the pre-trial stage of the proceedings can be successfully channelled through the Convention procedures, unless it is overly broad and unspecific. The crucial point is to determine whether the intention underlying the request is one of obtaining evidence for use at trial or whether the request is grounded on some other investigatory, and therefore impermissible, intention.

In controlling the sufficient "specificity" requirement, however, the requested court will not undertake a minute examination of whether the material is required as evidence *stricto sensu*. As Lord Fraser said in the *In re Asbestos Insurance*: "It would be quite inappropriate, even if it were possible, for any English court to determine in advance the matters relevant to the issues before the requesting (foreign) court". "The court of request should not be astute to examine the issues in the action and the circumstances of the case with excessive particularity for the purpose of determining in advance whether the evidence (...) will be relevant and admissible"[63].

### *3.6. U.S. discovery requests before German courts: substituting document production with oral depositions*

In *Aérospatiale* the U.S. Supreme Court expressed the view that through Article 23 reservations signatories to the Convention "could unilaterally abrogate the Convention's procedures"[64]. This is clearly a misunderstanding. There is no support whatsoever for a similar construction in either the language or the application of Article 23.

As English judicial practice shows, a reservation to Article 23 – and today the majority of States limit their reservations along the lines of the reservation formulated by the United Kingdom – is not a significant obstacle to discovery under the Convention as the broad wording of Article 23 might suggest. Reasonable requests for the production of documents will be executed by the foreign state. The Convention is available for discovery requests that are judicially supervised and scrutinized in accordance with the "special vigilance" standard suggested by the U.S. Supreme Court. Evidence which is directly relevant and material is readily obtainable. Moreover, the requested court – as Lord Fraser

*M.J. Reufels – M. Scherer*, Pre-Trial Discovery nach dem Haager Beweisübereinkommen, IPRax, 2005, 465.

[63] [1985] 1 All ER, 722–723. For a general overview see *C. Mc Lachlan*, Obtaining Evidence in England in Aid of a U.S. proceeding, International Litigation Practice, New York, 1998, 188ff.

[64] 482 U.S. 536.

pointed out – will not undertake a minute examination of whether the material is required as evidence *stricto sensu*.

In addition, another important point to be made is that even an unqualified Article 23 declaration does not significantly deprive U.S. litigants of all means for obtaining evidence located in a foreign country through the Convention's letter of request procedure. The German experience illustrates this point.

On its accession to the Hague Convention Germany made it clear, by way of a reservation to Article 23, that it would not execute letters of request issued for the purpose of obtaining pre-trial discovery of document as defined in Article 23 of the Convention. The Federal Minister of Justice was authorized to adopt, with the consent of the Federal Council, a regulation providing for the execution of such requests to the extent that "they do not violate basic principles of German procedural law, and that the legal interests of the individuals involved are taken into account". Such a regulation has never been adopted. Experience shows that the exclusion of the possibility to channel through the Convention procedures requests issued for the purpose of obtaining pre-trial discovery of documents, does not make judicial assistance through the Hague Convention meaningless. The production of documents can be requested later at the trial stage of the proceedings and, more importantly, for practical purposes, such requests can be substituted with a request for depositions to be taken at the pre-trial stage. In fact, substituting documentary evidence with depositions during the pre-trial stage has stood the test of German – U.S. practice. A good example is the *Siemens case* (1980)[65].

In a lawsuit pending in the U.S. between the American company Corning Glass Works and the American company ITT (International Telephone and Telegraph Company) over alleged infringement of U.S. patents held by the plaintiff for optical moveguide fibres and counterclaim for damages alleging the misuse of patents by entering into restrictive agreements with dominant telecommunication companies throughout the world, including Siemens AG of the Federal Republic of Germany, the American Court issued a letter of request pursuant to the Hague Evidence Convention. The request sought the production of numerous documents as well as the examination as witnesses of leading managers of Siemens and two of its subsidiaries. In order to give an idea of how broadly the request for oral deposition was formulated, it is worth mentioning that areas of examinations included:

"(1) The educational and professional background and job responsibilities of each of the witnesses, with particular emphasis on their involvement in . . . their contacts with [defendant] and their responsibilities with respect to [German and US subsidiaries of Siemens], the [defendant's] joint ventures in Germany and the United States respectively.

---

[65] See the English translation, in 20 Int'l Legal Materials, 1981, 1025.

(2) A description of the business and operations of [Siemens] in general with particular emphasis on [i] the extent of [Siemens] activities in the United States and [ii] the nature and extent of its operations in various fields of (...) including the extent of its research and development activities, past and present, and its marketing and sales activities.

(3) The nature and extent of the relationship between [defendant and Siemens] in the field of (...) with emphasis on the terms and conditions, intent and implementation of various agreements, between [defendant and Siemens] (...)

The witnesses are to be asked whether there are any other agreements, written or unwritten, between [defendant] and [Siemens] in the field of ... and to what extent [defendant and Siemens] have cooperated and/or coordinated their research and development, marketing and pricing activities in ..."

In that case, the Bavarian Minister of Justice (Germany's Central Authority for the region) decided, on the one hand, to decline the request for the production of documents and, on the other hand, to grant the request for depositions. The decision of the Minister of Justice was confirmed on both counts by the courts. In its decision, the Munich Court of Appeals pointed out that American "pre-trial" discovery is in principle not incompatible with German public policy nor incompatible with German law and therefore under Article 9, par. 2, of the Convention, the German parties should execute the request and a special method or procedure should be followed.

Depositions were consequently taken with respect to the material listed in the request for the production of documents, even if this request had been denied.

Counsel for the American party seeking evidence in Germany later reported: "To the credit of the presiding German Judge, once the initial procedural hurdles were overcome the depositions were conducted in a remarkable orderly and efficient fashion (...). The German Judge proceeded to conduct an extensive examination of each witness in the first instance, after which he allowed us to examine the witness at length. Wide latitude was allowed in this follow up examination. We were not limited to filling in the details of the judge's interrogation, but we were permitted to question on relevant areas not covered in the judge's initial examination. Six witnesses were examined on complex antitrust issues over the course of four weeks (...). A verbatim transcript was taken, rather than the judge's minutes as in the usual practice. All things considered, the German depositions in the end worked out rather well and were a significant factor in the resolution of the action and were well worth the effort"[66].

The Permanent Bureau to the Hague Conference on Private International Law stated in its 1985 Report on the operation of the Convention: "The decision of the Higher Regional Court Munich of 27 November 1980 ... illustrates that even where the requested state, as in case of the Federal Republic of Germany,

[66] *Ch. Platto*, 16 Int'l Lawyer, (1982) 575.

has made an absolute reservation under Article 23, it may be possible to obtain information or documents which themselves could not be surrendered or produced, by way of the compulsory examination of third persons as witnesses concerning the contents of those documents"[67]. With a liberal approach to judicial cooperation, the distinction between discovery of documents and other ways to obtain information becomes rather insignificant.

### *3.7. U.S. discovery requests and nondisclosure ("blocking") statutes*

In transnational cases where strong and competing governmental interests or policies are at stake – typically in antitrust cases – States are more reluctant to cooperate in the taking of evidentiary material located within their territory. A telling example is the *Westinghouse Uranium Antitrust Litigation.*

The litigation arose from long-term contracts between Westinghouse, on the one hand, and numerous electrical utilities, on the other. Under the contracts, Westinghouse was under an obligation to sell uranium to the utilities at fixed prices for specified terms. When world uranium prices dramatically escalated in the 1970s, Westinghouse refused to fulfil its agreements. In addition to claims that its obligations to utilities were excused by commercial impracticability, Westinghouse filed an antitrust suit against a number of uranium producers, alleging that they had unlawfully conspired to monopolize the market for uranium. In order to support its claims, Westinghouse sought discovery of many documents in the possession of foreign uranium producers. Most foreign uranium producers refused to comply with Westinghouse's document requests and a number of States (e.g. Canada, South Africa) enacted statutes to prohibit disclosure of information regarding uranium production.

The English House of Lords, in rejecting a request for documents submitted by Westinghouse under the Hague Convention, stated the principle that where it appears that a Minister or Department of another State has intervened in the letters rogatory proceedings in order to exercise extraterritorial jurisdiction in matters which prejudice U.K. sovereignty, the court will refuse to give effect to the letters rogatory. Following this decision, the U.K. Parliament enacted a blocking statute, the *Protection of Trading Interests Act 1980.* Section 4 of the Act provides that a court shall not give effect to a foreign letter of request "if it is shown that the request infringes the jurisdiction of United Kingdom or is otherwise prejudicial to the sovereignty of the United Kingdom". The Act also provides that the Secretary of State may issue certificates and directions in relation to such requests[68].

---

[67] *Supra* note 50.

[68] *Lowe*, Blocking Extraterritorial Jurisdiction: The British Protection of Trading Interests Act 1980, 75 Am. J. Int'l L., 1981, 257. See also *F.A. Mann*, Foreign Affairs in English Courts, 1986, 134.

Similarly, French Penal Code Law N° 80–538 was adopted to protect French interests from abusive foreign discovery procedures and excessive assertion of extraterritorial jurisdiction. Article 1 A of the law provides:

"Subject to treaties or international agreements and applicable laws and regulations, it is prohibited for any person to request, to investigate or to disclose, in writing, orally or by any other means, economic, commercial, industrial, financial or technical matters leading to the constitution of evidence with a view to foreign judicial or administrative proceedings or as a part of such proceedings...

2. The parties mentioned in (Article 1 A) shall forthwith inform the competent minister if they receive any request concerning such disclosure".

A number of countries have similar "blocking" statutes granting discretionary authority to particular governmental agencies to prevent compliance with specific foreign discovery orders or requests. There is a long history of such statutes enacted in response to major U.S. antitrust investigations in the field of various economic activities[69].

The phenomenon of blocking statutes is sometimes presented as a reaction against American discovery.

"In response to what they perceive as unilateral, extraterritorial, invasive, and privatised discovery – all in violation of their sovereign prerogatives – some countries have adopted blocking statutes or non-disclosure laws – which specifically prohibit compliance within the foreign state territory".

This is the explanation given in one of the recent American casebooks on transnational litigation[70].

But what appears to be a conflict about discovery is in reality a surrogate conflict reflecting a different discontent among foreign parties coming into contact with the American legal system. Blocking statutes or non-disclosure laws are instruments to react to what is regarded by a foreign country as an excess of jurisdiction of the forum state by excess of *regulatory jurisdiction*. Such excess is perceived particularly when – as it happens in the field of antitrust law – the forum state's jurisdiction is based on the *effects* principle, i.e. where the connecting factor for the application of a statute is not the territorial link with the act or the event, but only the effects which are felt within the forum state. It is well established by now – as it was affirmed by the United States Supreme Court in *Hartford Fire Insurance Company v. California [1993]* – "that the Sherman Act applies to foreign conduct that was meant to produce and did in fact pro-

[69] For example, investigations in the paper industry, investigations of anticompetitive practices in the shipping industry. For further indications and a discussion of the various non-disclosure statutes see *G. Born*, International Civil Litigation in United States Courts, 1996, 850–855.

[70] *R. G. Steinhardt*, International Civil Litigation: Cases and Materials on the Rise of Intermestic Law, Lexis Nexis, 2002, 297.

duce some substantial effect in the United States"[71]. Where the effects doctrine is rigorously applied, foreign countries react by resorting to blocking statutes in order to protect their spheres of sovereignty[72].

Also the assumption of *in personam* jurisdiction on the basis of "minimum contacts", perceived abroad as *minimal* contacts – such as jurisdiction based on corporate affiliations or agency relationships, "alter ego" status or "doing business" – when its assertion is coupled with the exercise of enforcement jurisdiction to compel the production of material abroad, can also lead to similar reactions[73].

In these cases, the conflicts with foreign jurisdictions are not caused by the discovery obligations of foreign parties, but by the consequences of the assumption of wide rules of regulatory or adjudicatory jurisdiction. The solution to these problems does not lie in the Hague Evidence Convention. The dilemma caused by a blocking statute is not sorted out by the parties resorting to the Hague Convention. The Hague Evidence Convention cannot provide an answer to the underlying problems of regulatory jurisdiction or *in personam* jurisdiction and – some may regret it – of sovereign wills and hegemony[74].

## 4. New perspectives for the taking of evidence across state boundaries: learning from American "exceptionalism"?

Differences in procedure have been a major source of conflicts in the gathering of evidence abroad. Criticism of discovery "fishing expeditions" has been a constant theme for those dealing with American pre-trial discovery. The fear that a State could be required to offer judicial assistance to execute U.S. style discovery requests led to the efforts to limit the use of the Hague Evidence Convention for that purpose. Although Article 23 reservation has not turned out the

[71] 509 U.S. 764, 798–799 (1993).

[72] See *P. C. Pettit – C. J. D. Styles*, The International Response to the Extraterritorial Application of United States Antitrust Laws, 37 Bus. Law. (1982) 697. In particular, the United Kingdom repeatedly expressed the view that the pure effects doctrine has no basis recognized in international law.

[73] See *B. H. Oxman*, The Choice Between Direct Discovery and Other Means of Obtaining Evidence Abroad: The Impact of the Hague Evidence Convention, 37 Univ. Miami L. Rev., (1983) 740–742.

[74] As to the instruments or tools to manage or prevent conflicts of jurisdiction to prescribe – bilateral treaties, "positive-comity" previsions, harmonization of competition laws – see *Basedow*, *supra* note 10, 1042 ff.

As to personal jurisdiction, unfortunately the Hague negotiations on world-wide acceptable grounds for international jurisdiction have not been successful; the plan proved to be too ambitious. However a significant result has been achieved: the recently (30 June 2005) adopted Convention on choice of court agreements. For an illustration of the work that has led to the convention, see *L. E. Teitz*, The Hague Choice of Court Convention: Validating Party Autonomy and Providing an Alternative to Arbitration, 53 Am. J. Comp. Law (2005) 543.

significant obstacle to discovery under the Convention that the broad wording of Article 23 could suggest, the dominant view is that the focus of the Hague Convention is on evidence, that is on materials required to prove or disprove the facts at issue and not on materials which may eventually lead to the discovery of evidence. This view is apparently shared by those States which ratified the Hague Convention in recent years – and several of them are major actors in transnational litigation – since in acceding to the Convention they wanted to make clear that in accordance with Article 23 of the Convention concerning letters of request issued for the purpose of obtaining pre-trial discovery of documents as known in common law countries, they will execute "only the requests for obtaining discovery of the documents clearly enumerated in the letters of request and of direct and close connection with the subject matter of the litigation"[75].

Things are however changing. Recent trends and developments in procedure as well as in attitude to litigation, on a worldwide scale, are shading a different light on American style discovery and are opening interesting perspectives for the taking of evidence across national frontiers. Two developments are of particular interest.

First, persons and entities involved or interested in transnational litigation resort to U.S. discovery with increasing frequency in order to get access to facts and information necessary to successfully vindicate substantive rights, taking advantage of United States liberalism in providing assistance to foreign courts as well as to litigants (prospective or actual) in foreign proceedings in the gathering of evidence located on U.S. soil. Foreigners are thus discovering the valuable aspects of American discovery.

Second, legal systems traditionally aimed at discouraging litigation through strict fact pleading requirements and severe relevancy standards for probative material to be admitted in court, are revisiting their attitudes and policies in this field. In a substantial number of countries, there is a significant trend to admit or impose forms of pre-action disclosure; to admit or impose exchange of information before commencement of proceedings, to adopt mechanisms and procedures suitable to promote greater openness between the parties as well as between prospective litigants, which in their structure and underlying purposes are not very different from the frequently condemned U.S. pre-trial devices.

These trends and developments – and their (potential) impact on a new, less confrontational approach to the taking of evidence across state boundaries – deserve some closer illustration.

[75] Text of China's declaration to Article 23 of the Convention.

### *4.1. Obtaining evidence in the United States for use abroad: foreign litigants are discovering U.S. discovery*

More than forty years ago Congress amended Title 28, § 1782 of the United States Code in order to make assistance available to foreign proceedings, actual or contemplated, on the most comprehensive basis. For a long time neglected, but recently resorted to with increasing frequency, § 1782 is a provision of great liberalism, the final outcome of which is to make American-style discovery available to proceedings abroad, even if the rules applicable to them do not provide for comparable methods of information gathering. The provision, in its section (a), reads as follows:

> "(a) the district court of the district in which a person resides or is found may order him to give his testimony or statement or to produce a document or other thing for use in a proceeding in a foreign or international tribunal. The order may be made ... upon the application of any interested person and may direct that the testimony or statement be given, or the document or other things be produced, before a person appointed by the court. By virtue of this appointment, the person appointed has power to administer any necessary oath and take the testimony or statement. The order may describe the practice and procedure, which may be in whole or part the practice and procedure of the foreign country or the international tribunal, for taking the testimony or statement or producing the document or other things ..."[76]

U.S. courts have repeatedly held that § 1782 imposes no requirement of reciprocity in order to have access to the taking of evidence on U.S. territory for use in foreign judicial proceedings.

Different approaches have been taken by the courts on the issue as to whether a § 1782 order requires that the information sought be "discoverable" under the law of the state where the main proceedings are conducted or contemplated to be conducted, and in particular, whether or not the relevancy standards of the foreign State control. For the courts who apply the provision following a liberal approach, obtaining information under Title 28 § 1782 is not subject to "any implicit requirement that any evidence sought in the United States be discoverable under the laws of the foreign country"[77]. In the words of Judge Cala-

---

[76] For valuable insights and explanations on the history, the background and the scope of the prevision, see *H. Smit*, The Supreme Court Rules on the Proper Interpretation of Section 1782: Its Potential Significance for International Arbitration, 14 Am. Rev. Int'l Arbitration (2003) 295ff.; see also *W. B. Stahr*, Discovery Under 28 U.S.C. § 1782 for Foreign and International Proceedings, 30 Virg. J. Int.'l Law (1990), 597ff.

The provision reveals also some questionable aspects where it is applied to "temporary visitors". See the Tattinger and Sasaki cases discussed in *R. W. Scott*, Minimum Contacts, No Dog: Evaluating Personal Jurisdiction for Nonparty Discovery, 88 Minnesota L. Rev. (2004), 968.

[77] Detailed references in *Smit*, *supra* note 76, 315ff. See also *Born*, *supra* note 69, 921, 932ff.

bresi of the Second Circuit's Court of Appeals *In the Matter of the Application of Euromepa* (1995)[78],

"examination of foreign law regarding the existence and extent of discovery in the forum country in order to ascertain the attitudes of foreign nations to outside discovery assistance, is not desirable. A request for cooperation should not turn into an unduly expensive and time-consuming fight about foreign law. That would be quite contrary to what the drafters of the provision sought to be achieved: providing wide assistance to tribunals and litigants involved in litigation with international aspects. An enquiry into the discoverability of requested materials should consider only authoritative prove – such as an authoritative statement of legislative or judicial character – that information obtained with the aid of § 1782 – will not be taken into consideration in the court where proceedings for the substance of the matter are pending or are contemplated to be instituted."

By a similar reasoning courts following a liberal interpretation of the provision at hand refused to read into § 1782 a "quasi-exhaustion requirement" that would force litigants to seek "information through the foreign or international tribunal before requesting discovery from the U.S. court".

Relying on the plain language of the statute and its legislative history, the U.S. Supreme Court in its recent decision *Intel Corporation v. Advanced Micro Devices*[79] approved this liberal approach, virtually ruling out the limitations that lower courts had read into Section (a) of § 1782.

The Court ruled that:

first, § 1782 does make discovery on U.S. soil available not only to those who have the status of actual litigants before foreign or international tribunals but also to "any person who possesses a reasonable interest in obtaining the assistance";

second, the "proceeding for which discovery is sought under § 1782 must be in reasonable contemplation, but need not be "pending" or "imminent";"

third, the term "tribunal" (...) includes investigating magistrates, administrative and arbitral tribunals, and quasi-judicial agencies, as well as conventional civil, commercial, criminal, and administrative Courts";

fourth, § 1782 contains no threshold requirement that evidence sought from a federal district court will be discoverable under the law governing the foreign proceeding.

The Court also emphasized the obvious point that § 1782 (a) merely authorizes, but does not mandate, the requested court to order a person "residing" or "found" in the district to give testimony or produce documents for use in a proceeding abroad and indicated as a possible and plausible ground for refusing

---

[78] 51 Federal Reporter 3rd 1095 (2nd Circ. 1995).

[79] 124 S. Ct. 2446 (2004). For an analysis and comment from a European perspective see *O. Rieckers*, Europäische Wettbewerbsverfahren und US-amerikanische Discovery, Recht der internationalen Wirtschaft, 2005, 19ff.; and *D. Eschenfelder*, Möglichkeiten deutscher Unternehmen, US-amerikanische Discovery auch vor deutschen Gerichten zu nutzen, in IPRax, 2006, 89ff.

in whole or in part a discovery order, the attempt to use a § 1782 request to circumvent foreign proof-gathering restrictions or other policies of a foreign country or the United States, or the "unduly intrusive or burdensome" nature of the request[80]. A clear message to avoid any categorical limitations and to preserve § 1782's great liberalism in affording efficient means of assistance to participants in transnational litigation.

How is this attitude being received by foreign courts and authorities?

### *4.2. Evidence obtained in the U.S. and its use in foreign courts: a welcomed benefit?*

There is relatively little evidence available as to how the courts in other countries react to "evidence" produced after having been obtained in the United States under the provision of Title 28 § 1782 U.S.C.

In *South Carolina Ins. Co. v. Assurantie Maatschapii "De Zeven Proincien" N. V.* (1996) the House of Lords vacated an injunction issued by a trial judge and affirmed by the intermediate appellate court enjoining a party to a British litigation from seeking third-party discovery under § 1782 in the United States, on the grounds that pre-trial discovery of this sort was not permitted under English procedures and that "the English court should retain control of its own procedure, and the proceedings that are before it". The House of Lords rejected the lower courts' reasoning and held that the contested discovery was not "conduct which is oppressive or vexatious or which interferes with the due process of the [British] court" and those did not "amount to unconscionable conduct warranting an injunction"[81]. With this decision it has become clear that evidence obtained in, or from sources uncovered in, the United States may well be used in English courts[82].

A Dutch judgement rendered in 1996 by the District Court of Utrecht on a preliminary relief petition by an American corporation for the issuance of an order to enjoin parallel Section 1782 proceedings against it before the Fifth Circuit on the basis of their inconsistency with fundamental principles of Dutch procedural law, confirmed that "the mere fact that Dutch civil law has no procedure which corresponds with pre-trial procedure does not mean that such

[80] Id. at 2483. On the factors that bear consideration in ruling on a § 1782 request see In re Application of the Procter & Gamble Co., 2004 U.S. Dist. Lexis 18290. (E.D. Wisconsin, September 1, 2004). The decision applies rather generously the standards indicated by the Supreme Court. See also, In re Application of Imanagement Services Ltd., 2005 WL 1959702 (E.D.N.Y., August 16, 2005).

[81] [1996] 3 WLR 398.

[82] *Andrews, supra* note 38, 83 Fn. 108: "it is not *necessarily* improper to obtain by foreign process disclosure of documents or other information for use in pending English proceedings". The argument that England would not oppose the granting of assistance under § 1782 was used in the recent case In re Application of Jonathan Guy Phillips 2004 U.S. Dist. Lexis 16426, 6–7 (S.D.N.Y. August 18, 2004).

proceeding would be in conflict with fundamental rules of Dutch procedural law"; and that the absence of contempt of court proceedings in the Netherlands "is insufficient to justify a general prohibition [to seek discovery under Section 1782 in the U.S.]". Affirming that judgement, the Amsterdam Court of Appeals added that the Dutch reservation to the Hague Evidence Convention that it would not execute letters of request aimed at "discovery" cannot be traced back to any principle objections against this legal concept itself, but to arguments which are more practical in nature"[83].

Regrettably different the reaction of the E.U. Commission. In its *amicus curiae brief* presented in the above mentioned case (*Intel Corp. v. AMD*) decided by the U.S. Supreme Court, the Commission opposed the granting of assistance under Section 1782, surprisingly arguing that it did not qualify as a foreign international tribunal within the meaning of Section 1782; a highly questionable judgement.

There appears to be no good reason for precluding recourse to Section 1782 in all proceedings before the Commission, which is exactly what the Commission sought to achieve. The Supreme Court, quite appropriately, rejected the Commission's argument and thus preserved for litigation before the Commission a benefit that the Commission was ready to forego.

### *4.3. Discovery prior to commencement of proceedings: the convergence of procedural systems*

"Before discovery has unearthed relevant facts it may be difficult to define the precise formulation of the required prima facie case", says the U.S. Supreme Court in *Swierkiewicz v. Sorema*[84], drawing a connection between notice pleading and liberal discovery and emphasizing the latter's function to enable parties not only to gather evidence to prove or disprove facts recited in the complaint or statement of claim but also to provide access to facts that enable parties to establish claims that they could not establish without disclosure of information in control of defendants.

In systems that apply the fact-pleading rule, there seems to be a growing awareness that some sort of preliminary discovery has to be allowed in order to prepare certain legal disputes and calculate their risk, and to prepare the presen-

---

[83] See *Smit*, *supra* note 76, 326 Fn. 65.

A similar position had been taken by the German Federal Court (BGH) in its decision of June 4, 1992 (in International Legal Materials 1993, 1327) where the Court stated that summoning the defendant to a "pre-trial discovery" does not violate order public as defined by § 328 of the German Code of Civil Procedure (ZPO). However, objections to the granting of assistance under § 1782 came recently from a German public prosecutor, fearing that the U.S. discovery could interfere with the criminal investigation pending in Germany. See *Schmitz et al. v. Bernstein Liebhard Lifshitz*, 376 Federal Reporter 3d 79, 84 (2nd Cir. 2004).

[84] 122 S. Ct. 992, 997–998 (2002).

tation of the relevant facts in reasonable detail and a description of the available evidence with sufficient specification during the pleading phase.

Interestingly, recent developments in a number of countries are moving in this direction. In France, for example, courts have interpreted Article 145 of the Code of Civil Procedure (*mesures d'instruction à future*) so as to facilitate access to documents (and other evidentiary material) from an opponent or third parties before, and independently from litigation on the merits, even beyond the requirement of there being a reason to preserve evidence upon which a solution of the dispute may depend. In this way, prospective litigants are able to obtain "information" prior to the institution of proceedings on the subject of the matter, before coming to them, whether to initiate a suit and against whom, or to look for a determination as to extrajudicial settlement of the dispute[85]. These seem to be strikingly similar goals as those pursued by the American pre-trial discovery when it is used in view of clarifying the controversy[86]. The information that is made available through Article 145 goes beyond a strict notion of evidence. Also classes of documents may be disclosed and subjected to inspection, as it is shown in the following order made by the Paris Cour d'appel :

"enjoint la société Delaroche et ... de communiquer, dans le trois jours suivant la signification du présent arret, l'ensemble des actes intervenues entre eux y compris les bordereaux de transfert d'actions, les comptes de valeurs nominatives, les extraits des registres mentionnant le transfert des titres y compris les procès verbaux d'assemblées générales et des conseils d'administration"[87].

Professor Taniguchi in a recent contribution informs that Japan, after having adopted in 1996 a new device called "interparty inquiry", which allows a party to ask for relevant information from the adversary, and expanded the scope of the document production order[88], has introduced a further amendment in the same direction (in force from April 2004) "which enables the parties to collect information and evidence from the prospective adversary or from a third party even before instituting the action". Professor Taniguchi explains that the reason

[85] The French *Cour de Cassation* held that "le caractère légitime de la demande se dèduit du constat que les allégations de son auteur n'étaient pas imaginaires et qu'elles présentaient un certain intéret". Cass. com. November 5, 1985, Bull.civ., 1985, 4, n. 260. For a description of the mentioned development see *J. Desprès*, Les mesures d'instruction in futurum, Paris, 2004; for details on the conditions that need to be satisfied in order to obtain a disclosure measure and on the relevant case-law, see *L. Cadiet*, Code de procedure civile, Paris, 2006, 141 ff.

[86] See for a similar remark *Le Berre*, in Vers un procès civil universel? Les regles transnationales de procèdure civile de l'American Law Institute, Paris, 2001, 129.

[87] Gaz. Pal., 1986, 163.

[88] *Y. Taniguchi*, Japan's Recent Civil Procedure Reform : Its Seeming Success and Left Problems, in Reforms *supra* note 16, 101: "the experience for some five years under the new Code has shown that the interparty inquiry is not effective because of lack of sanction for non-compliance. But the expanded document production order has been working relatively satisfactorily".

for this amendment is that "it is sometimes necessary to have sufficient information in order to formulate a complaint", in order, in other words, to better define the scope of the controversy and to better prepare for it[89].

The German Code of Civil Procedure has a specific provision dealing with the "independent taking of evidence" (*selbständiges Beweisverfahren*), pursuant to which an expert may be appointed to inspect documents or other things and make a report of these findings, independently from the institution of a lawsuit[90].

In the Netherlands, Article 186 of the Code of Civil Procedure deals with "preliminary hearing of witnesses prior to the bringing of proceedings". This provision – explains the Amsterdam Court of Appeal ... "is not only intended to enable material evidence to be taken from witnesses shortly after the facts in dispute and to prevent evidence from being lost but also, and in particular, to provide an opportunity for persons involved in an action subsequently brought before the civil courts – those considering bringing such an action, those who anticipate that the action will be brought against them, or third parties otherwise concerned by such an action – to obtain advanced clarification of the facts (with which they are perhaps not entirely familiar), so as to enable them better to assess their position, particularly with regard to the issue of identification of the party against whom proceedings must be instituted"[91].

---

[89] Id. at 107–108. For more details see *M. Yoshida*, Die Beweisbeschaffung vor Klageeinreichung nach der japanischen Zivilprozessordnung, ZZP Int., 2004, 293ff.

[90] See *Schlosser, supra* note 52, 151–152. In addition it has to be pointed out that there are a number of important provisions of substantive law which create a "right of information", in the context of specific legal relationships. A good example is section 810 of the German Civil Code. Such substantive legal rights can be enforced judicially, and are functional to gain factual information from private parties or from the administration in order eventually to start a proceeding. The phenomenon has no close analogue in the United States system and, therefore, its potential role in securing information generally goes unnoticed in the American literature.

The German Federal Court rightly argued in its decision of June 4, 1993 "it is not just the principles of German procedural law which must be considered...; the legal system as a whole, including the duties of disclosure under German substantive law, which could supersede foreign procedural regulations which have a comparable effect, also have to be taken into account".

[91] See the referral for a preliminary ruling on the question whether the provision at hand constitutes a measure within the meaning of Article 24 of the Brussels Convention on Jurisdiction and the Recognition of Judgements in Civil and Commercial Matters and the decision of the European Court of Justice, *St. Paul Dairy Industries NV v. Unibel Exser BVBA*, April 28, 2005, International Litigation Procedure, 2005, 416, 419. The Court held that Article 24 of the Brussels Convention on Jurisdiction and Enforcement of Judgments in Civil and Commercial Matters "must be interpreted as meaning that a measure ordering the hearing of a witness for the purpose of enabling the applicant to decide whether to bring a case, determine whether it would be well founded and assess the relevance of evidence which might be adduced in that regard is not covered by the notion of 'provisional, including protective, measures'". For critical comment, see *P. Mankowski*, Selbständige Beweisverfahren und einstweiliger Rechtsschutz in Europa, in Juristenzeitung, 2005, 1144.

Of the utmost interest are two innovations under English law: the *pre-action protocols* introduced by the new Rules of Civil Procedure (CPR 26.4) and the system of *pre-action disclosure* established under the same Rules. Their stated purposes are: (1) to encourage the exchange of early and full information about the prospective legal claim; (2) to enable parties to avoid litigation by agreeing a settlement of the claim before the commencement of proceedings; (3) to support the efficient management of proceedings where litigation cannot be avoided.

English procedure traditionally provided no facilities for enabling parties to a dispute to obtain documents from each other prior to the commencement of proceedings. In order to overcome the considerable hardship arising therefrom where the victim of an alleged wrong is unable to ascertain whether he has a cause of action against another person without access to that person's documents, the Administration of Justice Act 1969, section 21 (1) empowered the courts to order pre-action disclosure at the request of a person who appears likely to be a party to subsequent proceedings in respect of personal injuries (for example, injuries sustained as a result of hospital treatment). The power to order pre-action disclosure in personal injuries claims was intended to assist potential claimants who could not otherwise establish whether they had grounds for action, as well as those who required support for a case they could already plead[92].

Matters have been taken much further with the coming into force of the new Civil Procedure Rules. Pursuant to Rule 31.16, an application for disclosure may be filed with a court before the commencement of the proceedings. The applicant must satisfy the court that he/she and the respondent "may well be parties to proceedings if such proceedings were to take place", indicate as clearly as possible the causes of action that are likely to be put forward and identify, as far as practicable, the documents sought and their possible bearing on the issues that are likely to arise. As Rix LJ observed in *Black v. Sumitomo* "if the case is a personal injury claim and the request is for medical records, it is easy to conclude that pre-action disclosure ought to be made; but if the action is a speculative commercial action and the disclosure sought is broad, *a fortiori* if it is ill-defined it might be much harder"[93]. This observation reflects the main issue with which the court is confronted.

"As a matter of principle, explains Zuckerman, orders of disclosure are intended to assist parties to establish a case they already have, not to find out whether they have a case. English law has always set its face against so-called "fishing expeditions". However, he also recognizes that "in certain situations, allowing a person to embark on, what might otherwise be regarded as, fishing

[92] See *Zuckerman*, *supra* note 31, 485–486; Id. Zuckerman on Civil Procedure, *supra* note 6, 564.

[93] [2002] 1 WLR 1562, at 83.

expeditions is dictated by considerations of justice"[94]. This suggests that the English pre-action disclosure, at least in some cases, may be comparable to a (judicially supervised) American-style pre-trial discovery.

Modern English law also provides for early disclosure orders against non-parties. A witness summons was traditionally limited to securing production of documents at the trial. Pursuant to Part 34 of the new Civil Procedure Rules, the court may issue a witness summons directing a person to produce documents either on a day fixed for a hearing or in advance of a hearing so that the parties may study it before the hearing. Although it is said that the availability of such summons is "limited to specific identified documents" and that a witness summons "cannot be used to require a non-party to search for documents of a general description"[95], it remains unclear what distinguishes the device at hand from American depositions given in the context of discovery, since the Civil Procedure Rules do not give any indication that the third party must be informed, in the written summons, on the precise issue of his duty to disclose.

Then there are the *Norwich Pharmacal orders*: a judge made category of disclosure orders whereby a non-party may come under an obligation to provide information in advance of proceedings[96]. Anyone against whom the plaintiff has a cause of action out of the same wrong is bound to disclose the identities of other wrongdoers, even if the (prospective) plaintiff contemplates only to bring proceedings against (one of) the unidentified wrongdoer(s). An application under the *Norwich Pharmacal* rule will normally be made "where it is clear that the applicant suffered a wrong – the wrong may take the form of a tort, breach of contract, or some other civil or criminal wrongful act- but it is not known who perpetrated it. But an order of disclosure may also be made where information is required so as to determine whether a wrong has been committed against the person seeking disclosure"[97]. Doesn't this amount to a "fishing expedition"?

---

[94] *Zuckerman, supra* note 31, 490; Id. *supra* note 6, 570.

[95] *Zuckerman, supra* note 31, 493; Id., *supra* note 6, 571. As to the scope of documents that a non-party may be required to disclose in response to an order under CPR 31.17, see *Three Rivers District Council v. Bank of England* (Disclosure) (No. 4) (2002) EWCA Civ. 1182.

[96] In *Norwich Pharmacal v. Customs and Excise Commissioners* the House of Lords held: "if through no fault of his own a person gets mixed up in the tortious acts of others so as to facilitate their wrongdoing he may incur no personal liability but he comes under a duty to assist the person who has been wronged by giving him full information and disclosing the identity of the wrongdoers". [1973] 2 All ER 943.

[97] *Zuckerman, supra* note 31, at 499; Id., *supra* note 6, 581. *Andrews, supra* note 30, at 88–89. For the re-statement of this jurisdiction see House of Lords, *Ashworth Hospital Authority v. MGN Ltd.* [2002] 1 WLR 2003. Access to information can also be obtained through disclosure orders in "freezing injunctions" (formerly *Mareva* injunctions) and search orders (formerly *Anton Piller* orders). It is usual to seek freezing relief including disclosure orders in anticipation of civil proceedings and in support of civil proceedings which are pending outside England, or indeed are merely contemplated. The English courts are generous in their

### *4.4. Disclosure before the commencement of proceedings and the Hague Evidence Convention*

It is clear that behind the pre-action disclosure devices introduced in various countries lies the idea that, at least in some situations, disclosure from prospective opponents or from third parties is necessary in order to enable a person to know where she stands so that she can make informed decisions about the prospects and the conduct of her case; in short, to enable a person to vindicate his/her rights. A sense of injustice would ensue if the courts did not come to his/her assistance and order disclosure. But what about the availability of these devices in cases of transnational litigation? Are the instruments of pre-action disclosure and the other facilities to obtain "evidentiary information" in advance of proceedings available to prospective (or actual) litigants where main proceedings are conducted or intended to be conducted before a foreign court? Could the procedures provided for in the Hague Convention be used to obtain access to pre-action discovery? Do the mentioned facilities qualify as means of "pre-trial discovery" within the meaning of Article 23 of the Hague Convention with the result that pre-action disclosure requests or relating to the production of documents by third parties will not be executed in a State having made a declaration under Article 23?

There are solid arguments to answer the first two questions in the affirmative, while the third question suggests a "new" reading of Article 23 of the Hague Convention.

In order to resort to the Convention mechanism and request a contracting State judicial assistance, proceedings in civil or commercial matters do not need to be already pending. Article 1 (2) explicitly sets out that letters of requests may be used to obtain evidence located abroad for existing proceedings as well as for *contemplated proceedings*. Thus, judicially directed pre-action disclosure is to be included within the Convention's scope of application.

The more difficult problem stems from the fact that the Convention's emphasis appears to be on the taking of *evidence*, evidence in the technical sense of materials to prove or disprove the facts at issue. Therefore it could be argued that procedures designed to enable parties to collect information and evidence from prospective adversaries or third parties before an action is instituted are within the Convention's scope only if the request is for the *preservation* of evidence which will not be available during the course of the action. Yet, a closer look at the Convention's language and purpose shows that it is not so clear that the Convention does not include the gathering of "information" in a broader sense, that is information which is intended to enable a prospective litigant to verify whether she has a claim against somebody for which legal proceedings

approach to this "supportive jurisdiction". For a detailed account, see Zuckerman on Civil Procedure, 349ff., 367f.

could be instituted before a court or to identify the person against whom proceedings should be instituted.

Article 1 of the Hague Convention, in its official French text, says that assistance to foreign proceedings is to be given for the performance of an *acte d'instruction*. The expression like that of *mesure d'instruction* used in Article 145 of the French Code of Civil Procedure – which has been interpreted by the French courts so as to include access to evidentiary material, in particular documents, from an opponent or third parties before, and independently from litigation on the merits, even beyond the requirement of there being a reason to preserve evidence upon which a solution of the dispute may depend – appears to be broad enough to support the proposition that the Convention scheme is not restricted to the taking of evidence *stricto sensu*. The argument put forward in the past that it "is unlikely" that the expression in the French text, *acte d'instruction*, was intended to comprehend discovery, since it is not known in any civil law or French-speaking countries[98], has lost most of its force since forms of pre-action disclosure in view of clarifying the terms of prospective claims with strikingly similar goals to those pursued by the American pre-trial discovery have been adopted in various countries of civil law tradition. Equally debatable appears today the observation that representatives of the United Kingdom could not have intended "evidence" to include discovery since it was well established in the English case law that "evidence" is material in the nature of proof for trial[99]. Present-day English pre-action disclosure and the various judge made disclosure orders – Norwich Pharmacal orders, Mareva injunctions (now freezing injunctions), Anton Piller orders (now search orders) – put the traditional dichotomy evidence/discovery into a different light. Besides that, it must be stressed that the legislative history of the Convention and the Conference reports invoked by the author of the mentioned objections, certainly provide important clues and insides as to the background of the Hague agreement, but do not have any conclusive weight as to the interpretation and actual meaning of its provisions.

There is an additional reason which supports the proposition that the Convention does not necessarily refer only to evidence in the strict sense but includes the taking of "evidentiary materials" necessary to enable the parties to establish a claim that they could not establish without access to information in control of prospective defendants or third parties; "evidentiary material" relevant to issues likely to arise in the projected claim.

The avowed objective of the Hague Convention, according to its preamble, is to "improve mutual cooperation in civil and commercial matters"; mutual cooperation directed at the achievement of justice in the resolution of cross-border

---

98 *Collins*, *supra* note 43, at 776–777.

99 *Collins*, *supra* note 43, at 777.

disputes. It would be a mistake to read in this reference a merely, more or less, rhetorical statement, devoid of relevance for those interpreting the Convention. As stated in Article 31 (2) of the Vienna Convention on the Law of Treaties, the preamble to a treaty forms an integral part of the context and it is thus useful for the determination of the object and purpose of the instrument to be construed.

It would be hard to conceive that the Convention regulates in detail the procedural framework to obtain judicial assistance not only when lawsuits are pending but also where lawsuits are *contemplated* without first providing for that which alone makes in fact valuable the benefit of cross-border cooperation: that is access to information needed for the institution of proceedings. The facility to resort to the mechanisms of judicial assistance (through letters of requests) where proceedings are contemplated would be of little value if not combined with the possibility to require the execution of requests for information (located abroad) crucially relevant to a party's prospective litigation, i.e. to a party's legitimate interest to vindicate his/her rights.

As to article 23 of the Convention, neither its wording – today more than ever "Delphic in its text"[100] – nor its asserted purpose conjure seriously against the proposed construction. In a strict formal sense the new pre-action disclosure devices introduced in various countries do not qualify as means of "pre-trial discovery" within the meaning of that Article, with the result that the part of pre-action requests relating to the production of documents by prospective opponents or third parties could not be executed in a state having made a declaration under Article 23. More importantly, it is the changed reality that suggests a different reading of that provision.

The way in which modern procedural systems have developed moving from what once might have been considered an evil to what is now perceived as a good and needed complement to strict fact pleading rules and severe claim substantiation requirements, shows that there is a practical necessity – if one is serious about justice- to permit discovery to some extent and at least in some cases. Using the words of the U.S. Supreme Court one could say: "no longer can the time-honored cry of fishing expeditions serve to preclude a party from inquiring into the facts underlying the opponent's case"[101]. Exchange of information and access to facts are crucial in situations in which "evidentiary material" to make an arguable case is within the sphere of potential defendants or third parties. Examples are medical malpractice and product liability actions, actions for commercial fraud, unfair competition, insider trading and other securities related cases. To extent the scope of judicial cooperation to the gathering of evidentiary material from future opponents or third parties in such cases where no lawsuit on the substance of the matter is pending, does not mean that the Con-

---

[100] According to Professor Lowenfeld, Article 23 is "not only Delphic in its text, it is unsound in concept". *Supra* note 4, at 198.

[101] *Hickman v. Taylor*, 329 U.S. 495 (1947), at 507.

vention mechanisms can be used to support wide-roving searches or inquisitions. Judicial supervision and the jurisdictional conditions set up in the various legal systems for obtaining disclosure before the commencement of proceedings are suitable constraints to prevent the abuses and excesses that Article 23 ultimately was and is intended to prevent.

Like other statutory instruments which adopt broad and flexible terms or expressions in order to determine their scope and coverage, the Hague Convention leaves room to consider new situations where it is appropriate for its mechanisms to be used where they have not previously been used. The limits which constrained the Convention's use in the past as a consequence of the legitimate concern that courts of various countries, due to normative constraints and concepts of procedural justice, were not properly equipped to execute letters rogatory requesting pre-trial discovery of documents should not be allowed to frustrate its application now that reality has changed and courts in an increasing number of States parties are empowered to order the uncovering of information to assist actual or potential claimants who could not otherwise establish whether they have good grounds for vindicating their rights through the judicial process.

### *4.5 Direct access to pre-action disclosure in support of foreign proceedings?*

A different question arises as to whether the facilities that exist in various countries enabling prospective litigants to obtain information, particularly evidence, prior to the institution of proceedings on the subject matter, may be used by persons contemplating litigation on the substance of the matter to be instituted elsewhere. In other words, is it conceivable that a person seizes the domestic judge for the sole purpose of obtaining through the latter's authority access to information located within the judge's jurisdiction or should access to information only be available if there is an official request of a foreign court (channelled through the procedures of a convention)?

As noted above, Title 28, § 1782 of the United States Code makes assistance to foreign proceedings, actual or contemplated, available upon the application not only of "foreign sovereigns and the designated agents of those sovereigns" but also of "interested person", persons, in the words of the U.S. Supreme Court, who "possess a reasonable interest in obtaining the assistance".

When Congress in 1964 deliberately redrafted § 1782 in broad terms to encourage courts to be as liberal and flexible as possible, the hope was "that the initiative taken by the United States in improving its procedures would invite foreign countries similarly to adjust their procedures"[102]. So far foreign states have not granted reciprocal treatment. Procedures established for the specific

[102] As to "the twin aims of [the revised § 1782] to provide efficient means of assistance to participants in international litigation" and "to encourage foreign countries ... to provide

purpose of giving *direct assistance* to foreign litigants do not exist outside the United States.

In the last 25–30 years, courts, and to some degree legislators, have developed various devices of mutual assistance between judges or courts by adapting remedies available in the context of interim measures of protection to the needs of cooperation. Forms of transborder cooperation have been achieved through means of interim measures of protection by empowering the courts in one state to issue, upon the application of "interested persons", any of the measures available to it for the purpose of facilitating the enforcement of a judgment expected to be rendered abroad even where the court was lacking personal jurisdiction for the matter[103]. In some cases, the necessity of international cooperation was taken as sufficient ground by the courts to grant interim measures of protection in favour of litigants involved in foreign proceedings[104].

From April 1997 the English High Court's jurisdiction to grant interim relief under the 1982 Civil Jurisdiction and Judgments Act was extended to include non-Convention and non-Member States and to apply to civil proceedings outside the scope of Article 1 of the Brussels Convention and its successor (Jurisdiction Regulation EC 44/2001). This interim relief jurisdiction offers an important route also to obtaining information. Freezing injunctions, for example, including disclosure orders, can be obtained in support of civil proceedings which are pending outside England or are merely contemplated. And the English courts are generous in their approach to this "supportive jurisdiction"[105].

---

similar means of assistance", see In re Ishihara Chemical Co., 251, Federal Reporter, 3rd, 120, 124 (2nd Circ. 2001).

[103] For an excellent discussion see *Schlosser, supra* note 52, 156ff.

[104] See Lord Denning's recourse to comity in The Siskina, [1977] 3 All ER at 813. See also *Credit Suisse Fides Trust SA v. Cuoghi* [1997] 3 All. ER 724, where the English Court of Appeal emphasized the importance of granting freezing injunctions to assist other jurisdictions: "... commercial necessity has encouraged national courts to provide assistance to each other without waiting for such cooperation to be sanctioned by international convention ... Comity between the courts of different countries requires mutual respect for the territorial integrity of each other's jurisdiction but this should not inhibit a court in one jurisdiction from rendering whatever assistance it properly can provide to a court in another in respect of assets located or persons resident within the territory of the former".

[105] See *S. Gee*, Commercial injunctions, London, 2004; Zuckerman on Civil Procedure, *supra* note 6, 349ff. Article 24 of the Brussels Convention (now Article 31 of Regulation 44/2001) authorizes a court of a Contracting State to rule on application for a provisional or a protective measure even though it does not have jurisdiction to hear the substance of the case. Unfortunately the European Court of Justice in Van Uden (E.C.R. 1998, I 7091, 7122) held that: "The granting of provisional or protective measures on the basis of Article 24 of the Convention of 27 September 1968 is conditional on, *inter alia*, the existence of a real connecting link between the subject-matter of the measures sought and the territorial jurisdiction of the Contracting State of the court before which those measures are sought".

In civil law countries interim relief in aid of foreign proceedings has never been a problem. In some instances interim measures of protection have also been used to empower a party to obtain the information sought. See *Schlosser, supra* note 52, 166ff., 184ff.

It appears desirable that a similar attitude develops, beyond the interim relief jurisdiction, among the courts empowered to dispose disclosure prior to the commencement of proceedings in order to provide direct assistance to interested parties in their effort to pursue their rights even where the main proceedings are conducted or intended to be conducted abroad; i.e. when foreign courts are vested with jurisdiction of the matter[106].

However, at least in civil law countries, absent a specific legal provision, courts do not have jurisdiction to render direct assistance to prospective litigants in the gathering of information located in their territory unless they are vested with jurisdiction for the substance of the matter[107]. In this respect, the lack in civil law countries of anything closely corresponding to the concept of a court's natural "personal jurisdiction over persons" is decisive[108]. In civil law countries, courts only have competence in matters, whether litigation or others, conferred upon them by an act of legislation[109]. In cases of concurrent jurisdiction of more than one State, however, nothing seems to prevent a court vested with jurisdiction to grant access to evidentiary material to a person who then decides to bring proceedings on the substance of the matter into a foreign court[110].

---

[106] The English Norwich Pharmacal jurisdiction, which allows to extract information from non-parties for the purpose of sustaining a claim and the vindication of the claimant's rights is exercisable in support of foreign proceedings. *Equatorial Guinea v. Bank of Scotland International*, (Guernsey) [2006] UKPC 7.

For the restrictive attitude of German courts, see the decision of the Hamburg Court of Appeal, September 29, 1999, in IPRax, 2000, 530f. For critical comments, see *A. Stadler*, Grenzüberschreitende Beweisaufnahmen in der Europäischen Union – die Zukunft der Rechtshilfe in Beweissachen, in Festschrift R. Geimer, München, 2002, 1281, 1302ff.; *Mankowski*, *supra* note 91, 1149f.

[107] On the topic see, *H.J. Ahrens*, Grenzüberschreitende selbständige Beweisverfahren – eine Skizze, in Festschrift für R.A. Schütze, München, 1999, 1–15.

[108] See the statements of the Court of Appeal in Credit Suisse, *supra* note 104, at 729–730: "It is, of course, the case that, statute and convention apart, the jurisdiction of the English court does not depend on domicile but on service. Proceedings may be served on persons temporarily present within the jurisdiction, or, with leave (...) on persons outside the jurisdiction. (...) Where the defendant is domiciled within the jurisdiction, such an order cannot be regarded as exorbitant or as going beyond what is internationally acceptable. To treat it as such merely because the substantive proceedings are pending in another country would be contrary to the policy which informs both art. 24 [of the Brussels Convention] and s. 25 [of the 1982 Civil Jurisdiction and Judgments Act]".

[109] *Schlosser*, *supra* note 52 at 155. An example of specific legislative provision is Article 187 of the Netherlands Code of Civil Procedure, according to which "the court in whose jurisdiction the person who is to give evidence is domiciled or resident has territorial jurisdiction to order the preliminary examination of that witness" (i.e. the examination of that witness prior to commencement of proceedings), even if a foreign court is vested with jurisdiction for the substance of the matter.

On the uneasy relationship between the courts personal jurisdiction over persons (applied to the "temporary visitors") and non-party discovery, see *Scott*, *supra* note 76, 968ff.

[110] Id. at 153.

### *4.6 New standards for access to information and evidence: the Principles of Transnational Civil Procedure*

The Principles of Transnational Civil Procedure which in Spring 2004 were accepted with unanimous approval by the Governing Council of Unidroit and by the members of The American Law Institute – two highly respected institutions – share with the Hague Convention the objective to "reconcile the different legal philosophies of the common law, civil law and other systems", but move an important step further[111]. Designed to contribute to a world wide harmonization of civil procedure, they offer a detailed and well-balanced set of fundamental standards for the conduct and adjudication of transnational civil disputes which countries could adopt replacing domestic procedural rules. In combining the most attractive attributes of the various national systems, their effort is to breach the differences in civil litigation which are particularly relevant to controversies with international aspects and are a frequent source of conflicts, most dramatically between the United States and the rest of the world. The reduction of these differences – differences, as we have seen, in the structure of the litigation process as well as in the approach to civil litigation – is crucial to improve efficiency and achieve more fairness and predictability in international litigation. In the context of the present analysis, the standards established for the pre-trial (or preparatory) stage of the proceedings and those suggested for the access to information and evidence or of specific interest.

The Principles express a clear preference for the practice of fact pleading common to all civil procedure codes of continental tradition as well as to modern English law. They require the assertion of detailed facts and the presentation of individualized means of evidence during the pleading phase. But well aware of the substantial burden that the fact pleading rules place on a party seeking to use the judicial machinery to pursue his/her rights and conscious that there are situations in which it is very difficult, if not impossible, for the plaintiff to plead his/her facts or evidence with particularity in the complaint because the information or evidence necessary to make an arguable case resides in the files and minds of the defendant or third persons the Principles also permit more general factual assertions and a more general description of a class of documents needed to be produced by the opponent or third persons. The carefully drafted Principle 11.3 after stating that

[111] For an excellent illustration of the Principles, see *R. Stürner*, The Principles of Transnational Civil Procedure. An Introduction to Their Basic Conceptions, in 69 Rabels Z (2005), 201–254. The focus of the Principles is on harmonization as opposed to unification. In fact, not only would it be unrealistic to standardize procedural law worldwide; it would not even be desirable to have only one uniform law of procedure. Plurality of procedure – within the framework of general normative standards – encourages experimentation and promotes evolutionary progress.

"in the pleading phase the parties must present in reasonable detail the relevant facts, their contentions of law, and the relief requested, and describe with sufficient specification the available evidence to be offered in support of their allegations"

adds that,

"when a party shows good cause for inability to provide reasonable details of relevant facts or sufficient specification of evidence, the court should give due regard to the possibility that necessary facts and evidence will develop later in the course of the proceeding".

The solution reasonably combines elements of the main conflicting procedural systems, thereby avoiding both the excesses of the American Procedure where notice pleading encourages overbroad discovery requests – which lead to resistance and are difficult to channel through the mechanisms of international judicial cooperation – and the shortcomings of the procedures of other countries where strict substantiation requirements at the pleading stage create the danger of a too early termination of the fact finding process[112]. At the same time, the proposed solution offers the basis for a compromise on extraterritorial discovery in that it requires both the United States and its trading partners involved in transnational litigation to moderate their positions on the acceptable scope of discovery, thereby creating the condition for better worldwide procedural cooperation[113].

Section 16 of the Principles deals with "Access to information and evidence" and (in the relevant parts) reads as follows:

"16.1 Generally, the court and each party should have access to relevant and non-privileged evidence, including testimony of parties and witnesses, expert testimony, documents, and evidence derived from inspection of things, entry upon land, or, under appropriate circumstances from physical or mental examination of a person. The parties should have the right to submit statements that are accorded evidentiary effect.

16.2 Upon timely request of a party, the court should order disclosure of relevant non-privileged, and reasonably identified evidence in the possession or control of another party or, if necessary and on just terms, of a non-party. It is not a basis of objection to such disclosure that the evidence may be adverse to the party or person making the disclosure.

16.3 To facilitate access to information, a lawyer for a party may conduct a voluntary interview with a potential non-party witness".

The adoption of the fundamental rule that the court and the parties to litigation should generally have access to all relevant evidence implies that all the parties are under the obligation to disclose to the other parties and to the court all the relevant evidence that is in their possession or control. This will certainly require several legal systems to abandon their restrictive tradition of disclosure;

[112] *Stürner*, at 237.

[113] For an earlier proposal in a similar direction see *Born*, *supra* note 49, 96ff.

and changes in attitude and perception of ethics are also needed in order to accommodate the suggested principle of allowing preliminary (i.e. prior to commencement of proceedings) contacts between lawyers and potential witnesses. But, as Professor Stürner, the General Reporter for the Principles rightly points out the concern that the improvement of the access to means of evidence under the opponent's or third parties' control could lead to the adoption of American style discovery has no justification. The introduction of more generous rules of access to information and evidence, a trend – as we have seen – present in modern procedural cultures does not imply that the judicial process is open to roving inquisitions. Fundamental and decisive for a reasonable limitation of discovery and evidence-taking is not the limitation of access to means of evidence, it is the sufficient specification and individualization of facts and means of evidence as a pre-condition for commencing fact-finding procedures[114]. Once clear claim or pleading substantiation requirements are introduced, disclosure can only be obtained on the basis of a relevance standard that is stricter as the one used for American style discovery. Thus Principle 16.2 says that the court should order disclosure of *relevant and reasonably identified* evidence in the possession of a party or a non-party. Relevance is to be determined by reference to the facts in issue that should have been specified in the pleading and the reasonable identification of evidence is aimed at preventing the party from sifting the records of the other party in the hope of finding out something useful. Therefore the model of "disclosure" – a term not so intimidating as "discovery" – adopted by the Principles is less broad than the discovery existing in the American system, known for being possibly abused and therefore criticized and rejected in the transnational context. This should allow to overcome the frequent discussions over the appropriate latitude of discovery between the United States and the rest of the world when the courts avail themselves of the mechanism of the Hague Convention.

Parties to international litigation are increasingly seeking a "level-playing field" rather than the variances of the procedural law of domestic legal systems. Sceptics of the Principles' goal to contribute to a world wide harmonization of civil procedure in order to meet a need which manifests itself very clearly where different legal and procedural cultures are clashing in transnational proceedings, might observe that differences in procedure are so deeply embedded in the legal culture that the goal of profiting from one another's experience is beyond our reach and might also object that in procedure everything is so related that if one makes a change, one ought to consider the effects on all other aspects of the system. There may well be considerable forces in this contention. However, I believe that the remarkable trends of convergence that we see today between the various systems and cultures (not only on the issue of access to information and

[114] *Stürner*, at 234.

evidence) show that elements of procedure are "portable" and that it is possible to adopt elements of procedure from several sources and emerge with a result – like the Principles of Transnational Civil Procedure – that is superior to each of its ancestors.

# Taking Evidence Abroad – Understanding American Exceptionalism

*Peter L. Murray**

For some time now there has existed an issue of disagreement between American courts and litigants on the one hand and the civil justice regimes of most European and East Asian nations on the other regarding the correct process for obtaining of discovery and evidence abroad for use in American civil proceedings. American litigants sometimes utilize American discovery mechanisms to get access to documents and oral testimony from foreign nationals abroad.[1] Many jurists outside the United States view this activity as a circumvention of the requirements of the Hague Convention on Taking Evidence Abroad and a disrespect for the processes of local law.[2] This dispute has burdened international cooperation in facilitation of judicial proceedings for more than 20 years. An understanding of the peculiar evidentiary needs of American civil litigation may help illuminate a way toward resolution of the current misunderstanding.

---

* Robert Braucher Visiting Professor from Practice, Harvard Law School. This paper was delivered at a Symposium on Current Issues in Civil Procedure Law sponsored by the University of Nagoya Institute of International Business Litigation on February 19, 2006. The author thanks Benjamin Barron, HLS 2007 for research assistance in preparing this article for publication and Professor Rolf Stürner for helpful comments on an earlier draft.

[1] *See* Joseph P. Griffin & Mark N. Bravin, *Beyond* Aérospatiale*: A Commentary on Foreign Discovery Provisions of the Restatement (Third) and the Proposed Amendments to the Federal Rules of Civil Procedure*, 25 INT'L L. 331, 334-40 (1991); Robert B. von Mehren, *Discovery Abroad: The Perspective of the U.S. Private Practitioner*, 16 NYU J. INT'L L. & POL'Y. 985, 985–87 (1984); Thomas J. Tallerica & Jan L. Herrick, *Discovery of Witnesses and Documents Located Abroad*, 69 MICH. B.J. 664 (1990).

[2] *See* PETER MURRAY & ROLF STÜRNER, GERMAN CIVIL JUSTICE 567–68 (2004); Paul A. Batista, *Confronting Foreign "Blocking" Legislation: A Guide to Securing Disclosure from Non-resident Parties to American Litigation*, 17 INT'L L. 61, 62–70 (1983); James S. McLean, *The Hague Evidence Convention: Its Impact on American Civil Procedure*, 9 LOY. L.A. INT'L & COMPT. L. REV. 17 (1986–1987); Vincent Mercier & Drake D. McKenney, *Obtaining Evidence in France for Use in United States Litigation*, 2 TUL. J. INT'L & COMPT. L. 91 (1994); *see also* von Mehren, *supra* note 1.

## 1. The Hague Convention on Taking Evidence Abroad

The Hague Convention on Taking Evidence Abroad of 1970 (hereinafter referred to as the Hague Convention)[3] and the Brussels Regulation on Cooperation among the Courts of the Member States (hereafter referred to as the Brussels Evidence Regulation)[4] have memorialized and regularized procedures for obtaining judicial assistance in obtaining evidence abroad. The idea under both of these is that when a court in one jurisdiction needs particularly designated evidence or testimony that is to be found in another jurisdiction, that court can request judicial assistance in obtaining that evidence through the justice establishment of the other nation. The Brussels Evidence Regulation streamlines the process by authorizing direct communication between the requesting court of a Member State and a designated "requested court" of another Member State in which the sought testimony or evidence is located.[5]

Under these regulations the requesting court formulates the subject matter of the testimony or evidence to be obtained, including, in some cases, the questions to be posed by a judge of the requested court to a designated witness.[6] The requested court then uses its process to obtain attendance of the designated witness or production of the designated evidence.[7] In most civil law jurisdictions a judge of the requested court generally questions the witness although in some jurisdictions (such as Japan) the attorneys for the parties may conduct the examination.[8] The witness's responses are recorded in minutes made by the judge or other court personnel.[9] Upon request the testimony can be recorded verba-

---

[3] Hague Convention on the Taking of Evidence Abroad in Civil or Commercial Matters, Mar. 18, 1970, 23 U.S.T. 2555, 847 U.N.T.S. 231 [hereinafter Hague Convention]. The Hague Convention was promulgated at the impetus of the United States in the hope of facilitating discovery requests between common law and civil law nations. ANDREAS LOWENFELD, INTERNATIONAL LITIGATION AND THE QUEST FOR REASONABLENESS: ESSAYS IN PRIVATE INTERNATIONAL LAW 180–81 (1996). The Hague Convention now has 49 signatory nations, including the United States, Germany, France, the United Kingdom and China.

[4] Council Regulation 1206/2001 of 28 May 2001 on Cooperation Between the Courts of the Member States in the Taking of Evidence in Civil or Commercial Matters, 2001 O.J. (L 174) 1 (EC) [hereinafter Brussels Evidence Regulation]. The Brussels Evidence Regulation went into effect on January 1, 2004, superseding the Hague Convention among signatory nations. The Hague Convention, however, remains intact for any signatory nation that is not a member of the European Union.

[5] *Id.* at art. 2(1)-(2).

[6] *Id.* at arts. 4(1), 17(1)-(4).

[7] *Id.* at art. 10(1).

[8] *See* JOHN HENRY MERRYMAN, The Civil Law Tradition 114–116 (2d ed. 1985); Craig P. Wagnild, *Civil Law Discovery in Japan: A Comparison of Japanese and U.S. Methods of Evidence Collection in Civil Litigation*, 3 ASIAN-PAC. L. & POL'Y J. 1, 20 (2002).

[9] In most civil law jurisdictions a court clerk or the judge makes a summary protocol of the witness's testimony.

tim.[10] The minutes, transcript or evidence thus obtained are then forwarded to the requesting court for use in its proceeding.[11]

Both the Hague Convention and the Brussels Evidence Regulation contemplate that the parties may have counsel present at the evidence-taking by the requested court and that such counsel can participate according to the procedure and practice of the requested court.[12] In most civil law countries such participation consists of suggesting supplemental questions to the court or possibly posing such questions themselves after the court's initial questioning.[13] In most jurisdictions there is no opportunity for wide-ranging questioning of witnesses for discovery purposes. Nor is there any opportunity for counsel to perform a presentational direct examination or a suggestive cross examination using hard leading questions of American trial advocacy.

The Hague Convention and the Brussels Evidence Regulation work smoothly when both the requesting and the requested courts follow procedures in which evidence is generally received directly by the judge who will decide the matter. Under such procedures the parties designate witnesses and evidence to support their fact contentions, often with some particularity. But in most cases it is up to the judge to elicit the expected proof from the designated sources. There is no "presentation" of the proof by the lawyers as is the case at American trials. The lawyers' supplementary questions are designed to make sure that the judge does not miss something, but can scarcely be characterized as an evidentiary presentation.[14]

---

[10] Both the Hague Convention and Brussels Evidence Regulation allow requesting courts to specify the methods by which the evidence is taken, so long as those methods are practicable and comply with the procedural requirements of the requested court. Hague Convention, *supra* note 3, art. 9(2); Brussels Evidence Regulation, *supra* note 4, art. 10(1)-(2).

[11] Hague Convention, *supra* note 3, art. 13; Brussels Evidence Regulation, *supra* note 4, art. 16.

[12] Hague Convention, *supra* note 3, arts. 8–9; Brussels Evidence Regulation, *supra* note 4, arts. 11, 17; *see also* Darrell Prescott & Edwin R. Alley, *Effective Evidence-Taking Under the Hague Convention*, 22 INT'L LAW. 939, 952-54 (1988). *Cf.* Hague Convention, *supra* note 3, arts. 15–19 (authorizing a contracting state's diplomatic officers to take evidence within the territory of another contracting state).

[13] For instance in Germany counsel for the parties are generally permitted to question live witnesses after the court has performed the initial questioning. MURRAY & STÜRNER, *supra* note 2, at 15. In France, counsel cannot question witnesses except in rare circumstances when permission is granted from the trial judge. However, counsel are permitted to draft questions for witnesses and propose them to the judge. Jacques Borel & Stephen M. Boyd, *Opportunities for and Obstacles to Obtaining Evidence in France for Use in the United States*, 13 INT'L LAW. 35, 36–37 (1979). In Japan, on the other hand, it is customary for counsel to question the witnesses, although the style of such questioning reflects the reality of an active engaged judge rather than a passive jury. Takeshi Kojima, *Japanese Civil Procedure in Comparative Law Perspective*, 46 U. KANS. L. REV. 687, 706 (1998).

[14] For an examination of the divergences of litigation styles in civil and common law jurisdictions, see John H. Langbein, *The German Advantage in Civil Procedure*, 52 U. CHI. L. REV. 823 (1985). *See also* Javier H. Rubinstein, *International Commercial Arbitration: Reflec-*

## 2. The Hague Convention and American Needs for Discovery and Evidence for Trial

The procedures of the Hague Convention can be of very limited assistance to American lawyers preparing and presenting evidence in jury and non-jury trials when the evidence is sought in a civil law jurisdiction such as Germany. The process available under the Convention can fail to meet the needs of American litigants in two separate respects. The first of these is the need of American litigants for pretrial discovery in order to prepare for fact presentation at trial. The second is the need of the American trial process for the facts to be presented by the respective parties to a passive judge and jury rather than elicited by the fact-finder, or a proxy, directly from the sources of proof. Even in Japan, where attorney examination may be permitted, the absence of an opportunity to prepare for the examination in advance by some sort of discovery hampers the lawyers who are presenting the witness whose testimony is being taken.[15]

The American trial process places a huge burden on the litigants and their lawyers not only to designate the sources of potential proof of their claims, but also to present that proof in a concentrated "trial" to a totally passive audience of either jury or judge.[16] The lawyers must determine with some precision the available facts and how they can be effectively presented in advance. There is no opportunity for discovery and development of proof at the trial itself. The various tools of American discovery proceedings are designed to enable the lawyers to perform their task of preparing in advance for the demanding task of trial presentation.[17]

Any foreign lawyer who has participated in American discovery and then trial proceedings can immediately understand how painstaking must be the pretrial preparation in order to enable a lawyer to make an effective fact presentation in the intensity of a civil jury or non jury trial. It is not enough for the lawyer to have an idea of what might be in a document. The document must be examined and then fit into the mosaic of the lawyer's core theory of the fact

*tions at the Crossroads of the Common Law and Civil Law Traditions* 5 CHI. J. INT'L L. 303, 307-10 (2004).

[15] It should be noted that Japan is not a signatory to the Hague Convention and is not subject to the Brussels Regulation, which is only binding within the EU.

[16] RONALD L. CARLSON & EDWARD J. IMWINKELRIED, DYNAMICS OF TRIAL PRACTICE: PROBLEMS AND MATERIALS 1-6 (1989); GEOFFREY C. HAZARD, JR. & MICHELE TARUFFO, AMERICAN CIVIL PROCEDURE: AN INTRODUCTION 86–150 (1993); PETER MURRAY, BASIC TRIAL ADVOCACY 7–19 (1995); *see generally* ALBERT J. MOORE, Trial Advocacy: Inferences, Arguments and Techniques 10–64 (1996).

[17] THEODORE Y. BLUMOFF et al., Pretrial Discovery: The Development of Professional Judgment 9–32 (1993); Richard D. Freer, Introduction to Civil Procedure 347–49 (2006); EDWARD IMWINKELRIED & THEODORE Y. BLUMOFF, PRETRIAL DISCOVERY: STRATEGY AND TACTICS § 1:1 (Rev. ed., 2005); *see also* ROBERT G. BONE, Civil Procedure: The Economics of Civil Procedure 200–24 (2003).

presentation. A lawyer who calls a potential witness at trial without having interviewed or deposed the witness beforehand will be taking a great risk with his client's fortunes. Without a highly accurate idea of the witness's perspective and potential testimony the lawyer will not be able to present that perspective and testimony to the best advantage of his client's case.[18]

It has been observed that the effect of privatizing the presentation of evidence in this manner means that the evidence must be received twice in American proceedings, once when the lawyers elicit the evidence in discovery and witness preparation, and then all over again when the evidence is presented by one party or the other to the court.[19] This is indeed true, and accounts for a large part of the very high cost of litigating disputed facts in the United States. Our retention of a passive fact finder and our privatization of the process of fact development and presentation have a heavy price.[20]

One can criticize these features of the American trial process as hostile to the impartial determination of the truth by the fact finder. Why not take the witness's testimony as it comes, untrammeled and uninfluenced by prior contact with friendly or hostile lawyers? Why not figure out the significance of a document when it is produced in court? While this approach may be ultimately preferable in environments with active judges and serial proceedings, the American model of the passive fact-finder and a concentrated and dramatic trial is based on and requires competitive party presentations of a very high quality.[21] The clash of such presentations is supposed to illuminate the truth.[22] Until and unless American procedure approaches the civil law procedures of Germany and most of the nations of the EU the burden will remain on the lawyers to prepare and present the facts.

The Hague Convention does not address American lawyers' very real need for pretrial discovery in order to prepare to present the facts at trial. The Convention itself refers to the reception of "evidence" and, outside of Article 23, makes no reference at all to discovery. Early on some authors advocated use of the Hague Convention to secure the testimony of potential witnesses abroad

---

[18] *See* V. HALE STARR, WITNESS PREPARATION § 1 (1998); Patricia J. Kerrigan, *Witness Preparation*, 30 TEX. TECH L. REV. 1367, 1367–69 (1999).

[19] MURRAY & STÜRNER, *supra* note 2, at 603.

[20] *See* John H. Langbein, *Mixed Court and Jury Court: Could the Continental Alternative Fill the American Need?*, 1981 AM. B. FOUND. RES. J. 195, 201 (1981); *see also* Jeffrey S. Wolfe & Lisa B. Proszek, *Interaction Dynamics in Federal Administrative Decision Making: The Role of the Inquisitorial Judge and the Adversarial Lawyer*, 33 Tulsa L.J. 293 (1997).

[21] *See* ELLEN E. SWARD, THE DECLINE OF THE CIVIL JURY, 115–119 (2001); Stephan Landsman, *The Decline of the Adversary System: How the Rhetoric of Swift and Certain Justice has Affected Adjudication in American Courts* 29 BUFF. L. REV. 487, 495–496 (1980).

[22] *See* DEBORAH L. RHODE, IN THE INTERESTS OF JUSTICE: REFORMING THE LEGAL PROFESSION 15, 81–82 (2000); Sharon Dolovich, *Ethical Lawyering and the Possibility of Integrity*, 70 FORDHAM L. REV. 1269, 1634 (2002); Carrie Menkel-Meadow, *The Limits of Adversarial Ethics*, *in* ETHICS IN PRACTICE 123 (Deborah L. Rhode ed., 2000).

before the start of the American trial on the theory that the parties could decide whether the resulting evidence should be presented to the court or jury or not.[23] In this sense evidence secured in advance of trial would provide some discovery. The evidence obtained could be used at trial as well by either party. On the other hand, foreign courts have not been hospitable to requests which have had any flavor of party discovery, and as discussed below,[24] the usual form of testimony obtained via the Hague procedure has not been well adapted for use in an American trial presentation.

The Convention does expressly address the issue of pretrial discovery of documents in Article 23, where it offers any signatory country an opportunity to deny use of the Convention "for the purpose of obtaining pretrial discovery of documents as known in Common Law countries." [25] Many signatories of the Hague Convention, including both Germany and France, have made declarations under Article 23. American litigants are thus expressly forbidden from using the Hague Convention from obtaining pretrial access to documents in many countries in preparation for presentation of cases in American courts.[26]

The second sense in which the Hague Convention does not fit perfectly with American trial process relates to the form in which the foreign evidence is generally obtained, preserved, and above all, presented to the American judge or jury at trial.

As indicated above, the Hague Convention contemplates a judge-to-judge process for requesting and receiving foreign evidence. This accords well with civil law methods for adducing proof. However in the American trial process the control and the responsibility for the presentation of the evidence is left with the parties. The parties "examine" friendly witnesses with prepared series of "questions" which are really cues to guide the witnesses through their stories in a coherent and persuasive way. On cross examination the opposing lawyers are given a good deal of leeway to ask strongly suggestive questions in an effort to develop facts that detract from the opponent's overall picture, that positively

---

[23] *See, e.g.*, Nicholas C. Ulmer, Note, *Obtaining Testimony Outside the United States: Problem for the California Practitioner*, 29 HASTINGS L.J. 1237, 1253–56 (1978).

[24] Rio Tinto Zinc Corp. v. Westinghouse Elec. Corp. (1978) 1 All E.R. 434 (H.L.) (U.K.); Oberlandesgericht [OLG] [Higher Regional Court] Nov. 27, 1980, 1981 JZ 538 (F.R.G.); Corning Glass Works v. International Telephone and Telegraph Corp, Oberlandesgericht München [OLG] [Higher Regional Court] Oct 31, 1980 (F.R.G.), 1981 Juristenzeitung 538, *reproduced in English in* 20 INT'L LEG. MAT. 1049.

[25] Hague Convention, *supra* note 3, art. 23.

[26] Whether this exclusion of document discovery was also intended to cover oral depositions for discovery has been debated. *See* LOWENFELD, *supra* note 3, at 183; *see also* LAWRENCE COLLINS, *The Hague Evidence Convention and Discovery: A Serious Misunderstanding?*, *in* ESSAYS IN INTERNATIONAL LITIGATION AND THE CONFLICTS OF LAWS 301–04 (1994); Bernard H. Oxman, *The choice Between Direct Discovery and Other Means of Obtaining Evidence Abroad: The Impact of the Hague Evidence Convention*, 37 U. MIAMI L. REV. 733, 771–79 (1983).

contribute to the fact picture asserted by the cross-examiner, or which undercut the credibility of the witness or her testimony.

The special nature of trial questioning is so important to presentation of evidence at trial that when American lawyers are required to record and present testimony of witnesses far from the trial site, whether within the United States or abroad, they frequently will schedule two oral depositions of each witness.[27] Sometimes these are scheduled morning and afternoon of the same day. The lawyers' questioning at the first deposition is aimed at discovering what information the witness has that may be relevant to the case, favorable or not. It should come as no surprise to experienced German and Japanese judges that the questioning technique generally used in this kind of deposition is the so-called "funnel technique". The lawyer starts with broad questions that allow the witness to tell the story in her own words, and then increasingly narrows in on facts and distinctions important to the lawyer's theories in the case.[28] Such discovery depositions can be rambling and time-consuming as both lawyers explore all potentially relevant facts and their ramifications.

Following the discovery deposition the lawyers will conduct the "trial deposition" of the same witness. These trial depositions are now frequently videotaped. Using the information learned during discovery, the lawyers prepare questions to cue the witness to present the information as effectively as possible to the absent judge or jury. The witness is asked to "Tell the jury (the camera) about a particular key fact," The witness' testimony is presented rather than elicited.

The lawyer generally presents to the jury only a small portion of the information unearthed during the discovery session. Usually much of what is learned during a discovery deposition is relatively useless. The idea is to package the most useful information in the most persuasive form and present it in a way that will give it the most impact in the trial process.

Under the Hague procedure the American judge collects from the American lawyers (who generally do not know exactly what the foreign witness will say) some questions that the lawyers hope will generate evidence that might be helpful to them.[29] These questions are then transmitted via a sometimes roundabout

[27] For instance, in *Pharmacia, AB v. Ventrex Laboratories, Inc.*, U.S. Dist. Ct. (D. Me. 1985) the plaintiff took the discovery deposition of Robin Coombs in Cambridge, U.K. the day before the defendant took Dr. Coombs' deposition on videotape for the purpose of preserving and presenting his testimony at trial.

[28] *See* David M. Malone & Peter T. Hoffman, The Effective Deposition: Techniques and Strategies that Work § 9.2 (Rev. 2d ed. 2001); Chris Martiniak, How to Take and Defend Depositions § 4.01 (3d ed. 2002).

[29] For an explanation of American practice under the Hague Convention, see Prescott & Alley, *supra* note 12. *See also* Jennifer S. Bales, *Initiating and Responding to Discovery in Transnational Litigation: Procedures and Challenges*, 66 Tenn. L. Rev. 765 (1999); Kenneth C. Miller & Nancy Pionk *The Practical Aspects of Litigating Against Foreign Corporations*, 54 J. Air L. & Com. 123, 141–53 (1988).

channel to a judicial colleague abroad. The foreign judge then poses the questions to the witness, sometimes without really appreciating the importance of nuances of answers, and records the answers. It is no wonder that this process does not produce either a direct of a cross examination of the finely honed quality that American trial lawyers can obtain by first obtaining discovery from a witness and then preparing and posing their own questions in the classical manner.

To be sure, the Hague Convention envisions that parties will be notified of the time and place the requested court is planning to take the requested evidence in case they wish to be present.[30] Lawyers may be permitted to pose supplementary questions. However these opportunities fall far short of the creative and directive role afforded lawyers in American litigation and do not suffice to allow them to perform it. American lawyers seeking to obtain evidence in Japan must use the pre-Hague "letters rogatory"' technique, which makes the entire process longer and less likely to fit in with the needs of trial presentation.[31]

It cannot be denied that the Hague Convention has been an improvement over previously existing mechanisms for obtaining evidence abroad. In many cases, American lawyers are glad to use it. After all, evidence or testimony of almost any kind is usually better than no evidence at all.

## 3. American Discovery Rules in Cases with Foreign Parties

The Federal Rules of Civil Procedure and their many state counterparts envision that lawyers will conduct pretrial discovery and gives them the tools to

[30] Hague Convention, *supra* note 3, art. 19.

[31] A letter rogatory (also called a letter of request) is a formal letter issued from the court of one nation to the courts of other nations requesting the performance of judicial acts. The requested court arranges for service of the intended person and prepares a return of service, or it summons the intended person for interrogation or production of documents and then forwards the record of examination to the requesting court. The execution of letters rogatory varies depending on agreements between nations. In some instances, there is no obligation to execute the request and no timetable for the execution. Additionally, the intended targets of discovery may find it easy to throw obstacles in the way of the request and delay it. ANDREAS F. LOWENFELD, INTERNATIONAL LITIGATION AND ARBITRATION 809 (1993). A sample letter rogatory is reproduced on page B-35 of ROGER S. HAYDOCK & DAVID F. HERR, DISCOVERY PRACTICE (4th ed., 2005). Letters rogatory sent to Japan must include the names of the parties to the litigation; the manner in which the evidence is to be taken; the name, nationality and residence of the person to be examined; a statement of the essential facts of the case; and the matters to be investigated. Yoshio Ohara, *Judicial Assistance to be Afforded by Japan for Proceedings in the United States*, 23 INT'L LAW. 10, 18 (1989). Unlike the requirements set forth in Article Nine of the Hague Convention, Japanese courts are not required to comply with the Federal Rules of Civil Procedure in executing a letter rogatory. Thus, much of the evidence taken in Japan through letters rogatory are not admissible in American courts. Wagnild, *supra* note 8, at 20–21.

perform it. The discovery system is largely run by the parties, with only mediate court oversight. Parties and even third parties can be required to produce documents at the behest of another party. Parties and witnesses can be compelled to submit to pretrial depositions. Parties can be compelled to answer detailed interrogatories about the nature of their case and the evidence that will support it.[32]

As long as only American parties are involved, the playing field is more or less level and there is no special reason to complain. The problem arises, however, in cases in which foreigners are parties, either as plaintiff or defendants. Can the foreign parties be required to provide discovery and access to witnesses to the same extent as if they were Americans? Subject to special considerations related to language and distance, most American courts have ruled that American procedural rules apply to all parties who find themselves before American courts, regardless of whether similar rules apply in the foreign parties' own jurisdictions.[33] Thus foreign litigants are expected to open their company files for document discovery to the same extent as do American litigants, despite differing rules favoring confidentiality of business records or other papers.[34] Foreign parties are sometimes required to produce for deposition employees and other persons whom they would not be expected to produce for trial in their own countries.[35] Sometimes foreign parties are required to participate in unpleasant deposition hearings held in their own countries before stenographic reporters and video cameras flown in from abroad in order to generate testimony in the proper form for an American trial.[36]

---

[32] *See* Fed. R. Civ. P. 26–37; Jay E. Grenig & Jeffrey S. Kinsler, Handbook of Discovery and Disclosure (2d ed. 2002); Imwinkelried & Blumoff, *supra* note 17; Haydock & Herr, *supra* note 31.

[33] *See In re* Auto. Refinishing Paint Antitrust Litig., 358 F.3d 288 (3d Cir. 2003); *In re* Anschuetz & Co., 754 F.2d 602, 615 (5th Cir. 1985); Del Ditrich v. Bauer, No. 95 Civ. 7051, 2000 U.S. Dist. LEXIS 11729 (S.D.N.Y. Aug. 9, 2000); Minpeco, S.A. v. Conticommodity Servs., Inc., 116 F.R.D. 517, 529 (S.D.N.Y. 1987); Work v. Bier, 106 F.R.D. 45, 55–6 (D.D.C. 1985).

[34] *See In re* Matter of Grand Jury Subpoena Duces Tecum Addressed to First National City Bank, 396 F.2d 897 (2d Cir. 1968); Fundacion Museo de Arte Contemporaneo de Caracas v. CBI-TDB Union Bancaire Privee, No. 93 Civ. 6870, 1996 U.S. Dist. LEXIS 1482 (S.D.N.Y. Feb. 9, 1996); Compagnie Francaise D'Assurance Pour Le Commerce Exterieur v. Phillips Petroleum Co., 105 F.R.D. 16 (S.D.N.Y. 1984).

[35] *See In re* Vitamin Antitrust Litig., No. 99–197, 2001 U.S. Dist. LEXIS 25070 (D.D.C. September 10, 2001); *In re* Application of Asta Med. for an Order to Take Discovery of David W. Moriarty, Jr., 794 F. Supp. 442 (D. Me. 1992), *rev'd* 981 F.2d 1 (1st Cir. 1992) (finding that requests for discovery in foreign nations must be discoverable therein), *overruled in part by* Intel Corp. v. Advanced Micro Devices, Inc. 542 U.S. 241 (2004) (holding that discovery conducted in a foreign nation for use in American courts under 28 U.S.C. § 1782 does not require discoverability under the foreign nation's laws); *Work*, 106 F.R.D. at 18.

[36] *See* Tailift USA, Inc. v. Tailift Co., Ltd., No. 3:03-CV-0196-M, 2004 U.S. Dist. LEXIS 28648 (N.D. Tex. March 26, 2004); Int'l Ins. Co. v. Caja Nacional de Ahorro y Seguro, No. 00C6703, 2004 U.S. Dist. LEXIS 4280 (N.D. Ill. March 17, 2004) (holding that deposi-

This application of American discovery rules to foreign parties is often perceived by those parties as unfairly onerous.[37] This is particularly true of foreign defendants who wind up before American courts by virtue of what some consider an exorbitant American international civil jurisdiction.[38] The reach of American discovery abroad gives an impression of extraterritoriality and evokes comment on "American hegemony".[39] Even knowledgeable European and East Asian jurists who understand the *lex loci* theory on which the American position is based argue that Americans should first resort to international agreements before unilaterally extending their judicial power to persons and things abroad.[40]

## 4. Societe Nationale Industrielle Aerospatiale v. U.S. District Court

The tension between the application of American discovery rules to foreign litigants and the Hague Convention was considered by the United States Supreme Court in *Societe Nationale Industrielle Aerospatiale v. U.S. District*

---

tions taken abroad may comply with the Federal Rules of Civil Procedure rather than foreign procedural rules); Generale Bank Nederland N.V. v. First Sterling Bank, No. 97–2273, 1997 U.S. Dist. LEXIS 20040 (E.D. Penn. Dec. 17, 1997); Oxford Indus., Inc. v. Luminco, Inc., No. 86–6417, 1990 U.S. Dist. LEXIS 15685 (E.D. Penn. Nov. 19, 1990).

37 *See* Murray & Stürner, *supra* note 2, at 566–68; Andrew N. Vollmer, *Revive the Hague Evidence Convention*, 4 ILSA J. Int'l & Comp. L. 475, 476 (1998).

38 This perceived unfairness has let to the enactment by some countries of "blocking statutes" that forbid their nationals from participating in American discovery in their own territory. *See* Foreign Proceedings (Prohibition of Certain Evidence) Act, 1976 Austl. Acts P. 1125, as amended by Foreign Judgments Act, No. 112 (1991) (Austl.); Foreign Extraterritorial Measures Act, R.S.C., ch. F-29 (1984), *amended by* Department of External Affairs Act, S.C., ch. 5 (1995) (Can.); Law No. 85–538 Pertaining to the Disclosure of Documents and Information of an Economic, Commercial, Industrial, Financial or Technical Nature to Foreign Natural or Juristic Persons, Journal Officiel de la République Française [J.O.] [Official Gazette of France], July 16, 1980 (Fr.); Protection of Business Act, no. 99 (1978), *as amended by* Protection of Business Act Amendment, no. 114 (1979), *and* Protection of Business Act Amendment, no. 71 (1984), *and* Protection of Business Act Amendment, no. 87 (1987) (S. Afr.); Protection of Trading Interests Act, 1980, c. 11, *amended by* Civil Jurisdiction and Judgments Act, 1982, ch. 27 and Statute Law (Repeals) Act, 1993, ch. 50 (U.K.).

39 *See* Rolf Stürner, *Der Justizkonflikt zwischen U.S.A. und Europa*, *in* Der Justizkonflikt mit den Vereinigten Staaten von Amerika 35 (Walther J. Habscheid ed., 1986).

40 The "first resort" argument was put forward by the governments of France, Germany, Switzerland and the United Kingdom in their amicus briefs to the Supreme Court in *Societe Nationale Industrielle Aerospatiale v. U.S. District Court for the Southern District of Iowa*, 482 U.S. 522 (1987), discussed *infra*. The briefs are reproduced in 25 Int'l Leg. Mat. 1475, 1519 (Fr.), 25 Int'l Leg. Mat. 1475, 1539 (Ger.), 25 Int'l Leg. Mat. 1475, 1549 (Switz.), and 25 Int'l Leg. Mat. 1475, 1557 (U.K.). *See also* Fang Shen, *Comment: Are you Prepared for this Legal Maze? How to Serve Legal Documents, Obtain Evidence, and Enforce Judgments in China*, 72 U.M.K.C.L. Rev. 215, n.25 (2003) (stating that Chinese jurists deem the Hague Evidence Convention the mandatory and exclusive means of obtaining evidence abroad).

*Court for the Southern District of Iowa*[41]. In that case a French litigant argued that the Hague Convention provided the *exclusive* method by which American litigants could gain access to evidence abroad. The United States Supreme Court ruled, however, that the Hague Convention was intended to supplement other available means to obtain evidence abroad and would not preclude American litigants from lawful and appropriate use of American discovery rules to achieve the same purpose.

Although the *Aerospatiale* case has been greeted with consternation by some foreign commentators, it is hard to imagine how the court could have decided differently.[42] The Hague Convention was designed to provide member nations with a new means for obtaining evidence abroad, not to supplant or replace all pre-existing or subsequently developed processes that might also result in foreign proof in some form abroad. No country maintains that the Hague Convention is the only way that evidence can be obtained by its litigants abroad or by litigants in other lands from its own nationals.[43] Perhaps the adverse reaction of some foreign jurists to *Aerospatiale* was mainly disappointment that the US Supreme Court did not use the case to resolve what had become perceived in many quarters as an annoying collision between American and foreign litigation policy.

## 5. Finding a Solution

What are the real interests underlying the debate over American exceptionalism in taking evidence abroad? As indicated above, American litigants find that the Hague-type procedures for taking evidence abroad do not meet the needs of American litigation, particularly if there is an alternative available through the American discovery rules. On the other hand, foreign litigants and their legal cultures are affronted by a privatized procedure that allows American litigants to export intrusive and burdensome American discovery into other nations without any local judicial control or oversight. This ennui is fully understandable. While American courts may be within their rights to insist that foreign litigants must play by the same discovery rules as American litigants, surely the resulting impact on foreign civil justice systems and legal cultures calls for both consideration and comity.[44] The picture of American justice is not enhanced if

---

41 482 U.S. 522 (1987).

42 *See, e.g.*, J. Albert Garcia, *A Look Behind the Aerospatiale Curtain, or Why the Hague Evidence Convention had to be Effectively Nullified*, 23 Tex. Int'l L.J. 269 (1988); *see also* Lowenfeld, *supra* note 25, at 189–90.

43 *See* Murray & Stürner, *supra* note 2, at 568–69.

44 For a discussion of cases that followed *Aéropostale*, see James Chalmers, *The Hague Evidence Convention and Discovery Inter Partes: Trial Court Decisions Post-Aérospatiale*, 8 Tul. J. Int'l & Comp. L. 189 (2000).

it appears abroad as an overbearing and intrusive expression of hated American hegemony.

There must be a middle ground. Can there be a way by which American litigants can obtain reasonable discovery from their foreign opponents and access to trial proof abroad in a form that is suited to the unique American trial presentation process? By understanding the needs of American litigants and exercising thoughtful respect for the legal culture and institutions of foreign states can we devise a system better than the Hague Convention to resolve this dispute?

The fate of the recently proposed Hague Convention on Jurisdiction and the Recognition and Enforcement of Foreign Judgments[45] certainly is not encouraging. On the other hand, that bad experience has caused many jurists on both sides of the Atlantic to question whether both sides were too unyielding in those negotiations. There is a general feeling that an opportunity was lost.[46]

Certainly there are many signs of greater international understanding in civil justice matters and some real convergence in institutions of civil justice and procedure. American discovery, long an expensive battleground for unsupervised private litigants and their lawyers, is being reined in. "Judicial management" is becoming accepted terminology in the United States and there is hope that it may be ever more reality. On the other hand some civil law countries are cautiously extending access to proof, encouraging lawyers to take larger roles in litigation, and even considering various forms of collective litigation. The success of the joint UNIDROIT/ American Law Institute *Principles of Transnational Litigation* shows that jurists from many legal cultures can come together and agree on what really matters in the prosecution of a civil lawsuit.

## 6. A Proposal

Here is a first effort at a proposal for a new convention on taking evidence abroad. It is designed to make it possible for common law (American) litigants to obtain evidence abroad in the form and manner in which they need it under the control and oversight of the justice systems of the foreign sovereigns.

---

[45] *See* Kevin Clermont, *Jurisdictional Salvation and the Hague Treaty*, 85 CORNELL L. REV. 89 (1999); Jenny S. Martinez, *Towards an International Judicial System*, 56 STAN. L. REV. 429, 442 (2003); Arthur T. von Mehren, *Drafting a Convention on International Jurisdiction and the Effects of Foreign Judgments Acceptable World-wide: Can the Hague Conference Project Succeed?*, 49 AM. J. COMP. L. 191 (2001); Linda J. Silberman & Andreas F. Lowenfeld, *A Different Challenge for the ALI: Herein of Foreign Country Judgments, an International Treaty, and an American Statute*, 75 IND. L.J. 635 (2000).

[46] *See, e.g.*, von Mehren, *Drafting a Convention on International Jurisdiction and the Effects of Foreign Judgments Acceptable World-wide: Can the Hague Conference Project Succeed?*, *supra* note 45.

First of all, the convention should govern all efforts to obtain evidence from persons or institutions domiciled or located in nations other than the nation of the forum of the proceeding. The convention would thus partly overrule *Aerospatiale* and provide a comprehensive regulation of the process of obtaining evidence abroad. Of course parties would be free to agree on other methods to obtain evidence from each other, but any process to *compel* production of evidence abroad, either directly or indirectly, would be governed by the convention. This puts everyone on a level playing field regardless of differing discovery rules and roles of lawyers and judges.

Second, requests for evidence abroad could be made by either litigants or judges. Requests by litigants would be submitted through the judges handling their cases, who would rule on objections to requests based on procedural regulations or law of the forum states.

Third, requests for evidence abroad could include documents and witness examination for purposes of discovery, subject to a threshold of likely relevance to the subject matter of the proceeding. The requesting judge would initially rule on issues of relevance in formulating and issuing the request. All documents would be produced to the requested court, which would rule on local objections to production based on local laws, including privileges and laws respecting confidentiality.

Fourth, any oral testimony would be taken under the mediate or (at the request of either party) immediate supervision of the requested court. Questioning of witnesses would be conducted in a manner consistent with the procedure of the requesting court. If the requesting court were American, British, Australian, Canadian, etc. the witness would presumably be examined and cross-examined by counsel for the parties. On the other hand, if the requesting court followed the civil law tradition, the examination of the witness would likely be conducted by a judge of the requested court. In any event, the requested court would be available to rule on issues of local privilege or confidentiality and to protect the witness from undue burden or harassment. The testimony would be recorded in the form (including videotape) specified by the requesting court.

The proposed procedure would provide American litigants some controlled access to discovery abroad. American litigants would be able to obtain trial evidence abroad in a form appropriate for American trial presentations. On the other hand all such discovery and proof taking would be subject to immediate judicial oversight in the jurisdiction in which the discovery or evidence is sought. Local law and policies of confidentiality or privilege could be effectively maintained and enforced. American discovery and any proof faking incident to such discovery would be restricted to the procedures of the convention.

This does not mean that foreign litigants could use their more expansive foreign privileges and confidentiality rules to frustrate discovery or production of evidence with impunity in American civil proceedings. Invocation of a local privilege or confidentiality rule to block production of relevant evidence can be used to support a negative inference against the party which invokes the privilege in both civil law and common law legal cultures.[47] Such inferences are specifically approved in the Principles of Transnational Civil Procedure.[48] The thoughtful use of such inferences can go some way to counteract the temptation to withhold relevant information sought in discovery.

"Fishing expeditions" without a reasonably particular description of potentially relevant evidence would find little support under this arrangement. A standard of likely relevance would be required to trigger a request under this proposal.

The foregoing is just a bare-bones outline that would have to be fleshed out with some more detailed provisions to make it work. Issues such as how requests should be routed, language and translations, timing and costs would have to be raised and resolved, hopefully in favor of practical simplicity, expedition and economy. Experience under the Brussels Evidence Regulation may suggest some places to start.

## 7. Conclusion

An international arrangement under which American litigants would have access to discovery abroad under judicial supervision in both nations and the ability to obtain evidence abroad in a form suitable for American trial presentation should address all identified interests at stake. Would a proposal of this kind find support among jurists in both civil law and common law nations? Is the current political climate conducive to international cooperation in civil justice matters? Is a proposal such as this really practical?

Of course one can easily think of objections. Foreign courts do not want to be burdened by American procedures that they consider wasteful and duplicative. Americans may feel unreasonably constricted by arrangements that give foreign parties in American law suits special protection from having to produce evidence usually called for by American procedural rules. Does this procedure adequately recognize and protect the sovereignty of all national participants?

It is hard to answer these questions. All one can do is put the idea forward and see how responsible jurists evaluate it. International discussion and dialogue is the first step to solving problems by international reform.

---

[47] *See* ROGER S. HAYDOCK & DAVID F. HERR, *supra* note 32, at § 15.02; MURRAY & STÜRNER, *supra* note 2, at 305–06.

[48] ALI/UNIDROIT PRINCIPLES OF TRANSNATIONAL CIVIL PROCEDURE §§ 17.3, 18.2 (2004), *available at* http://www.unidroit.org/english/principles/civilprocedure/ali-unidroitprinciples-e.pdf.

# Taking Evidence Abroad – Hungarian Aspects

*Miklós Kengyel*

## Introduction

Taking evidence abroad raises mainly technical difficulties, although problems of conflicting legislation may also arise during the application of the rules. The law of evidence is closely connected with substantial law, which also raises the question of the application of the foreign lex causae. The existing most detailed study of taking evidence abroad can be found in Coester-Waltjen's excellent book.[1] The lecturer's task is to give an account of the fact to what extent Hungary has managed to facilitate the taking of evidence abroad within the fifteen years that have passed after the change in the political system.

## 1. Internal Legal Norms

The *Hungarian Code of Civil Procedure of 1952* also contains special rules concerning the taking of evidence abroad. However, the three provisions laid down in Section 204 can only be considered the "top of the iceberg". According to Subsection (1),

*if evidence must be taken in another country with which an international convention concluded by the Hungarian State or reciprocity exists with regard to the fulfilment of petitions, measures shall be taken for taking evidence accordingly.*

According to Subsection (2),

*in lack of an international convention concluded by the Hungarian State or of reciprocity, the court may fix a time limit for a party – at his request – to present a public document on taking evidence which is in conformity with the legal rules of the other country and is legalized if necessary.*

With regard to the validity of taking evidence abroad, the Hungarian Code of Civil Procedure contains a special provision. In general, it lays down the princi-

[1] Dagmar Coester-Waltjen: *Internationales Beweisrecht. Das auf den Beweis anwendbare Recht in Rechtsstreitigkeiten mit Auslandsbezug.* Ebelsbach 1983, Verlag Gremer.

ple of *lex fori*, that is *the law of the country of the taking of evidence must be applied* with regard to the validity of evidence. An exception to this rule is made in favour of *lex patriae*, namely, if evidence is considered invalid under lex fori but valid under the Hungarian Code of Civil Procedure, it shall be deemed valid.

## 2. International Legal Assistance

Petitions concerning the taking of evidence are usually fulfilled within the framework of *international legal assistance.* General principles and rules are contained in *Legislative Decree No. 13 of 1979 on Private International Law.* Due to the nature of international legal assistance, the detailed rules concerning legal assistance to be provided for the courts and authorities of the individual states may be found in bilateral or multilateral international agreements.

If the taking of evidence is to be performed in a country outside the territory of the European Union, first of all, it shall be examined if there is a bilateral or multilateral international agreement or practice of reciprocity in existence between the given state and Hungary which also covers the fulfilment of petitions concerning the taking of evidence. Such international agreements include *agreements for mutual legal assistance*, which, besides regulating issues of jurisdiction, service of process, the recognition and enforcement of the judgement in civil and family litigation, also cover the taking of evidence.[2]

In legal assistance matters, *Hungarian courts* contact foreign courts and other authorities via the Minister of Justice, while other authorities contact them via the Minister of Foreign Affairs through the interposition of the minister exercising supervisory authority. *Bilateral agreements on legal assistance* almost wholly coincide in the specification of the range of acts of procedure to be mutually performed. In civil and family law matters, legal assistance covers the service of documents and the execution of acts of taking evidence – the examination of witnesses, hearing of an expert, conducting an inspection etc.

## 3. Taking Evidence Based on The Hague Convention of 1954

Out of the multilateral international agreements, it is *the International Convention signed in The Hague on 1 March 1954 concerning Civil Procedure* that regulates requests concerning the taking of evidence. According to the Conven-

[2] Miklós Kengyel: Anerkennung und Vollstreckung der gerichtlichen Entscheidungen außerhalb des Geltungsbereichs der Brüsseler und Lugano-Übereinkommen, in Gerhard Walter – Samuel P. Baumgartner: *Recognition and Enforcement of Foreign Judgements Outside the Scope of the Brussels and Lugano Convention.* The Hague 2000, Kluwer.

tion still in force today, in civil or commercial cases, the judicial authority of one Contracting State may – in accordance with her own regulations – *send* a request to the competent authority of another Contracting State, requesting the performance of an act of procedure or other judicial acts. The request, which are usually aimed at taking evidence, are transmitted to an authority designated by the requested State via the *consul* of the requesting state. The requested judicial authority is obligated to execute the request and for this purpose it may also apply measures of compulsion. The judicial authority executing the request applies *the laws of its own country* with regard to the procedure. One may derogate from the principle of *lex fori* only if the requesting authority *requests so in a separate petition* and the rules to be applied are not incompatible with the laws applied by the requested authority.

Hungary acts upon this Convention exclusively in relation to Argentina, Denmark, Japan, Kyrgyzstan, Lebanon, Macao, Morocco, Moldavia, Norway, Armenia, Surinam, Switzerland and the Vatican. Out of these countries, in respect of Argentina, Denmark, Macao, Norway and Switzerland, the Hague Convention dated 17 March 1970 shall be applied beginning from the date when the given State files a declaration on and recognizes Hungary's accession to this latter Convention.

## 4. Taking Evidence Based on The Hague Convention of 1970

Hungary accessed to the Convention on the taking of evidence abroad in civil and commercial cases signed in The Hague on 18 March 1970 *more than thirty years later.*

Article 2 of the Convention provides that each Contracting State shall designate a Central Authority for receiving request. (*Hungary* designated the Ministry of Justice to undertake this task.) Requests concerning legal assistance shall be written *in the language of the requested authority* or accompanied by a translation into that language (Article 4). Hungary – similarly to the overriding majority of the States participating in the treaty – excluded the possibility of also accepting requests written in the English or French languages, and it did not specify any further languages with regard to requests concerning legal assistance.

The idea reflected in this provision of the law is different from the Government Decree 1147/2002. (IX. 4.), according to which, when applying Council Regulation 1206/2001/EC, Hungary may accept requests concerning the taking of evidence *in the English language* as well.

When executing the request – performing the act of taking evidence requested in it – the requested judicial authority shall apply *the laws of procedure of its own state*, including measures of compulsion as well. Similarly to the Hague

Convention of 1954, it is possible for the requested judicial authority to apply other rules of procedure – at the special request of the requesting authority – unless they are incompatible with the internal laws of the State of execution or are impossible of performance by reason of its internal practice (Article 9).

A request concerning legal assistance may only be *rejected* if execution does not fall within the functions of the judiciary or it would be incompatible with the public order of the State addressed. Requests may not be rejected on the basis that the procedure requested by the requesting authority is unheard of in the internal law of the State addressed (Article 12).

The Convention also enables a diplomatic officer or consular agent of a Contracting State to take evidence in the territory of another Contracting State in aid of proceedings commenced in the courts of the State represented by him. The act of taking evidence may only concern citizens of the State represented by him, and measures of compulsion may not be taken (Article 15). Hungary also filed the required declaration to this effect.

The Convention – with the approval of the Contracting States – also allows direct taking of evidence. According to the legal institution adopted from common law legal systems, an appointed person (commissioner) may take evidence in the territory of a Contracting State in aid of proceedings commenced in the territory of that State (Article 17). It means most often the examination of witnesses. Although this institution is unknown in continental legal systems, the majority of the Member States (including Hungary) accepted Section 17 without reservation, that is they principally enable a representative appointed by the judicial authority of another State (e.g. the United States, Great-Britain) to perform acts of taking evidence in their territory.

The Convention of 1970 – in lack of an agreement to the contrary – *replaced* The Hague Convention of 1954 (Article 29). At present this Convention is to be applied solely with regard to *Israel.* It shall also be applied concerning Argentina, Denmark, Macao, Hong Kong, Norway and Switzerland from the date when the given State declares her acceptance of Hungary's accession to this latter Convention.

## 5. Reciprocity

In lack of bilateral or multilateral international agreements, requests concerning the taking of evidence may be executed on the basis of *reciprocity.* Reciprocity may not be presumed, a declaration by the Minister of Justice is required on its existence, which is binding on the courts. Failing reciprocity, decision about the execution of the request is made by the Minister of Justice – in concert with the Minister of Foreign Affairs and the minister competent in the subject-matter.

## 6. Community Law Regulation

Council Regulation 1206/2001/EC on co-operation between the courts of the Member States in the taking of evidence in civil and commercial matters entered into force on Hungary's accession to the European Union. The Regulation and, related to it, the Amendment of the Legislative Decree of 1979 on International Private Law came into force on 1 May 2004.

The Regulation is a *norm directly applicable* in the Member States, thus there is no need to adopt separate rules. Member States are only obligated to create the legal framework required for the implementation of the Regulation, that is they shall appoint the trial courts and the so-called Central Authority, they shall adopt rules concerning the reception of requests, determine the accepted language for filling in petitions and forms, etc.[3]

*The Regulation emphasizes direct contacts between the courts*, thus each Member State is obligated to make a list of courts competent in taking evidence. *In Hungary the competent courts are the local courts functioning at the seat of the county courts and in Budapest the Central District Court of Buda.* The request must be transmitted by the requesting judicial authority to the court of the other Member State competent in taking evidence (Article 2).

The Member States shall appoint a Central Authority for the supply of their competent courts with information and for resolving problems arising in connection with the requests (Article 3). In Hungary the tasks of the Central Authority are performed by *the Ministry of Justice.* In the interest of "the highest degree" of transparency and legal security, requests about taking evidence shall be submitted *in a unified printed form* in the official language of the requested court or in another language accepted by the given Member State. Hungary accepts requests and the printed forms prescribed by the Regulation in the Hungarian and English languages. Requests may be delivered by mail, fax or e-mail as well.

The Regulation – pointing to the future – supports the use of *modern communication technology*, of video and telephone conferences. As their use may involve *extra costs*, the Regulation lays down who bears the costs of the fees of experts and interpreters. If the requested court requires the reimbursement of the enumerated costs, the requesting court shall arrange for it *without delay.* In the final analysis, costs are borne by the parties, with regard to the rules of liability for costs, the Regulation refers to the law applied by the requesting court (Article 18).

This Regulation is effective in all Member States of the European Union, except Denmark. (Denmark does not participate in the European area of justice as

[3] In Hungary these rules are contained partly in the Legislative Decree on International Private Law, partly in Government Resolution 1147/2002. (IX. 4.).

a consequence of her reservations concerning the Treaty of Amsterdam). In the matters falling within her scope of authority, she has priority over the provisions of The Hague Conventions of 1 March 1954 and 18 March 1970 and even over the provisions of the bilateral agreements signed between the Member States.

# Taking Evidence Abroad According to Finnish Law

*Laura Ervo*

## 1. The Code of Judicial Procedure

According to Chapter 17, Section 11 it is usually forbidden to use a private written statement drawn up for the purpose of a pending or imminent trial. It, however, may be possible in the case, where the court admits it for a special reason. One of the special reasons can be the fact that the witness is staying abroad.

In Section 11a it is said that separate provisions apply to the admission of evidence abroad. This means that the first thing is to find out, if there is some special legislation of treaties on the legal assistance and if not we have to decide if there is a special reason for allowing the use of a private written statement as a piece of evidence. If there is a special reason or not, depends on how important a piece of evidence is, how trustworthy the statement is, how expensive it would be to take the evidence abroad on the contrary to the value of the demands and how much time it would take to take the evidence abroad and lastly on the opinion of the opposite party.[1]

According to *Jokela* it would be possible to use written statements of private nature even in such a situation, where we have a treaty or separate provisions of other kind on legal assistance.[2] In my opinion, the legal assistance should be the primary solution because of the very important evidentiary principles that is orality and immediacy as well as parties' right to examine the witnesses. Even the evidentiary value will usually be lowered in written statements of private nature.

In case 1978 II 70, the Supreme Court decided that the district court should have used the legal assistance on the basis of the Nordic Convention on Legal Assistance instead of a statement of private nature. Even Jokela seems to accept this solution in Nordic connections.[3]

---

[1] Jokela 2004, p. 171–172.
[2] Jokela 2004, p. 172.
[3] Arg. Jokela 2004, pp. 171–172.

## 2. Treaties

Finland as well as other Nordic and European countries has ratified very many international treaties concerning the issue how to take evidence abroad and ask legal assistance in the matters of evidence. The most essential convention is the Hague Convention on Taking of Evidence Abroad in Civil or Commercial Matters from the year 1970.[4] However, Finland has made a reservation on the Hague Convention on the discovery. Finland does not accept the legal assistance for discovery and does not give legal assistance in cases, where the aim is to reveal the documents, which the opposite party has in his/her possession. The legal assistance in the situations of this kind presumes that the request is specialized.[5]

Finland has as well ratified the Nordic Convention on Legal Assistance, which includes also statutes in taking evidence. The situations, where we need legal assistance between Nordic countries are quite rare because of two facts. Firstly, because of the fact that distances between Scandinavian countries are short and especially because of the fact that according to specific legislation it is obligatory to appear by a person to the court even to another Nordic Country in order to give evidence in a situation, where it is very important to hear the witness in order to find out the material truth in the case. In consideration, the court takes into account the harms to the witness, that will follow of this kind of order for personal appearance.[6] However, this possibility to give the order for personal appearance is, of course, the primary one because of the aim at the best evidence including for instance the principles of orality and immediacy.

In addition Finland has a bilateral treaty with Russia concerning legal assistance including the evidentiary matters. However, this possibility is not very workable in practice because of slowness and bureaucracy as well as very wide public grounds for refusal.[7]

## 3. The European Union

In European Union the Hague Convention has been replaced by Council Regulation (EC) No 1206/2001 of 28 May 2001 on cooperation between the courts of the Member States in the taking of evidence in civil or commercial matters. It came into force on the 1st of January 2004.[8] The newest proposal among European Union is a proposal for a council framework decision on the European

[4] More on this topic in Koulu 2003, pp. 181–187.
[5] Koulu 2003b, p. 1142.
[6] Koulu 2003, pp. 191–192 and 2003b, p. 1143.
[7] Koulu 2003, pp. 192–193 and 2003b, p. 1143.
[8] Jokela 2004, p. 184, Koulu 2003, pp. 193–199 and 2003b, p. 1143.

Evidence Warrant for obtaining objects, documents and data for use in proceedings in criminal matters.[9]

This proposal for a Council Framework Decision applies the principle of mutual recognition to a European warrant for the purpose of obtaining objects, documents and data for use in proceedings in criminal matters. The European warrant is referred to hereafter as the European Evidence Warrant. It will result in quicker, more effective judicial co-operation in criminal matters and replace the existing mutual assistance regime in this area in line with the conclusions of the Tampere European Council. Minimum safeguards for such co-operation are also introduced.[10]

The proposal focuses on objects, documents or data obtained under procedural law measures such as production orders and search & seizure orders. It includes requests for copies of criminal records. It does not address taking statements (in whatever manner) from suspects, defendants, witnesses or victims. Nor does it address procedural investigative measures which involve obtaining evidence in real-time, such as the interception of communications and monitoring of bank accounts. Although this proposal does not cover the obtaining of these other types of evidence, the Commission considers it to be the first step towards replacing the existing regime of mutual assistance within the European Union by a single EU body of law based on mutual recognition and subject to minimum safeguards.[11]

The European Council reached consensus on the proposal on 1st and 2nd June 2006 in Luxembourg and the proposal was approved on October 21[rst] 2008.

## 4. Special, domestic statutes

In Finland there is still in force some rather old domestic statutes on taking evidence abroad from the year 1921 and on giving legal assistance in Finland from the year 1927. These statutes will be applied if there are no treaties between the concerned states that are, when the other state is not ratified the Hague Convention, is not a member State of European Union or is not a Nordic country or if there is no bilateral treaty as well. In practice these old domestic statutes will be applied rather rare, but they are not desuetudes yet.[12]

---

[9] Brussels 14.11.2003, COM(2003) 688 final 2003/0270 (CNS).

[10] Brussels 14.11.2003, COM(2003) 688 final 2003/0270 (CNS), p.2.

[11] Brussels 14.11.2003, COM(2003) 688 final 2003/0270 (CNS), p.2.

[12] Koulu 2003, p.200. More on this topic in Koulu 2003, pp.199–201, 2003b, p.1142 and Lappalainen 2001, p.257.

## 5. Problems and solutions

Taking evidence abroad with the help of legal assistance means not only help but also problems. Problems will arise in the light of the aim at the best evidence, which means that the pieces of evidence should be taken in an oral and immediate way and usually in a public hearing where all parties as well as judges who will decide the case are at present. In addition the parties should have a possibility to examine the witnesses. In situations, where the hearing happens abroad the personal appearance of all these people involved is usually impossible or in every case very difficult. The costs or even statutes can hide the appearance.

The members of the national court for instance don't normally have the competence to travel abroad in order to take evidence. The hearing is the task of the foreign court, which is giving legal assistance.[13] In such situations the evidence is, of course not, immediate at all.

In European Union these problems have been solved quite well, because according to Council Regulation (EC) No 1206/2001 (see above) the parties and their representatives have in most cases the right to be present at the performance of the taking of evidence by the requested court. Even representatives of the requesting court have the right to be present in the performance of the taking of evidence by the requested court. The situation is the same in many other treaties concerning taking evidence abroad as well.[14]

These possibilities doesn't, however, make the evidence immediate[15] and according to the Finnish Code of Judicial Procedure, Chapter 17, Section 8e evidence admitted outside of the main hearing shall be readmitted in the main hearing, unless there is an impediment to the same.

According to *Koulu* a piece of evidence should be readmitted in the main hearing in all cases, where the piece of evidence has been taken outside of the main hearing – for instance abroad – and it doesn't help if the parties and/or the representatives of the court have been at present in the requested court.[16] I disagree and agree with *Lappalainen*, who argues that the same reasons and circumstances usually occur still during the main hearing, which have incurred the need for the legal assistance and been the grounds for taking the evidence abroad. Therefore there is normally an impediment to the same and it is impossible and unnecessary to readmit the evidence. In such situations, the evidence is, however, not immediate but the court has to chase up the content of a piece of evidence from the minutes or the recording done by the foreign court.[17]

---

[13] Arg. Koulu 2003, p. 188.
[14] Koulu 2003, pp. 193–199 and 2003b, p. 1143.
[15] Lappalainen 2001, p. 256 and Koulu 2003, p. 196.
[16] Koulu 2003, p. 196.
[17] Lappalainen 2001, p. 259.

The possibility to the videoconference or to the teleconference will give some help to the problem of immediacy. According to Article 10 in the Council Regulation (EC) No 1206/2001 the requesting court may ask the requested court to use communications technology at the performance of the taking of evidence.[18] According to Finnish national law, the videoconference is a suitable way in organising the performance of the taking of evidence in situations, where 1) the witness cannot be at present in the main hearing because of his or her illness or other very special reason, 2) where the reality of the statement can be evaluated without his or her presence, 3) where this kind of system is needed because of the protection of the witness in some special situations or 4) if the witness is under 15 years old or mentally ill. The hearing can happen even by phone in situations 1–2 mentioned above. The parties should, however, have the possibility to examine the witness in all of these situations.[19] This right is very essential according to the Article 6 in the European Convention on Human Rights, which also Finland has ratified at the beginning of the nineties.

The real solution has, however, been made in Article 17 in the Council Regulation (EC) No 1206/2001. According to it, it is even possible to take evidence immediately abroad, which is a revolutionary novelty in international civil proceedings. Before that it has not been possible to the court to take evidence directly in another state.[20]

## Bibliography

| | |
|---|---|
| Jokela 2004 | Jokela, Antti: Oikeudenkäynti III. Jyväskylä 2004. |
| Koulu 2003 | Koulu, Risto: Kansainvälinen prosessioikeus pääpiirteittäin. Vantaa 2003. |
| Koulu 2003b | Koulu, Risto: Kansainvälinen siviiliprosessioikeus. In Prosessioikeus, pp. 1083–1163. Juva 2003. |
| Lappalainen 2001 | Lappalainen, Juha: Siviiliprosessioikeus II. Jyväskylä 2001. |

[18] Jokela 2004, p. 185, Koulu 2003, pp. 197–198 and Koulu2003b, 1143.
[19] Code of Judicial Procedure, Chapter 17, Section 34a.
[20] Jokela 2004, p. 185 and Koulu 2003, p. 198.

# Discussion

*Professor Kato:* I would like to ask the floor for comments or questions.

*Professor Trocker:* May I put a question to the audience? We have been talking about the conflicts under the Hague Convention, but I want to stress another aspect. The Hague Convention has been signed by all the major players in international trade, yet Japan has not signed the Hague Convention. Second proposition: the Hague Convention, apart from the 'troubles' that we have with some of the discovery requests, works well in most cases. So we should not consider the Hague Convention as an instrument which has not fulfilled its purpose and objectives. It is a fundamental instrument of cooperation. Therefore my question to the audience is: why is Japan hesitating to sign the Hague Convention on Evidence while, on the other side, not necessarily to everybody's satisfaction, the Service Convention has been adopted?

*Professor Taniguchi:* Well, I am not able to answer this question. This is exactly the kind of question I have been asking myself for a long time. I also have asked this question to many people, but nobody could give me a satisfactory answer. Of course, one reason given to me was the fear of American discovery, but there is Article 23 and many European countries acceded to the Convention, although they must have had the same kind of fear, so I don't understand it. And this is not limited to the Evidence Convention. There are many other important conventions which have not been acceded to by Japan like CISG, that is, Vienna Convention on the International Sale of Goods, which is a very important convention for a trading country like Japan. About 70 countries have acceded to the Vienna Convention, but the United Kingdom and Japan are important exceptions. Well, I don't understand that either. Japan's attitude has been criticized internationally. I think Professor Dogauchi, a great expert in this area, is the best person to answer the question, so I would like to turn to him.

Many countries enacted so-called 'blocking statutes' against American discovery. Many people have asked me why Japan don't enact such a statute and I answered: Well, we are afraid of American discovery, but we are politically in alliance with the United States, which would make the legislation politically incorrect, if not impossible. Yet, France enacted such a statute, and Australia and so forth, though we don't hear very much about this these days. My understanding is that such legislation has proved ineffective. It didn't work at all because American courts do not mind going ahead despite of this kind of statute in a foreign country. Even if you will be punished if you comply with American demands of discovery, this is no defence in an American court. I can say only this. Now I would like to turn to Professor Dogauchi to better answer your question.

*Professor Dogauchi:* Perhaps it is a pity at least for the lawyers who realize the necessity for harmonized management of international litigation. Perhaps all the lawyers here do not understand why Japan has not yet entered into such an important convention. Perhaps the Japanese business community does not understand the necessity, but it is true that they fear the American litigation in which they might be involved.

As Professor Trocker pointed out, the underlying problem in the field of taking evidence abroad, especially with regard to the taking evidence for the benefit of U.S. proceedings, is the jurisdictional issue; or to say it more directly, exorbitant exercise of jurisdiction by American courts. But the rules of the 1970 Hague Convention do not make it a condition that a resulting judgment of the proceedings pending abroad is to be recognized in the requested state. If the judgment were not recognized because of improper exercise of jurisdiction or improper type of process or even violation of policy, giving judicial assistance to such proceedings would be an injustice to the defendant there, especially if the defendant is a national of the requested state. Could you explain why these rules do not make the prospective recognition and enforcement of the resulting judgment one of the conditions for giving judicial assistance?

*Professor Trocker:* Well, let us put the taking of evidence abroad in the context that you have to consider it the objective to help the state or the court where the case is pending to resolve the dispute before that court without any implications that go beyond the resolution of that dispute within the forum state. And, therefore, the article that you were mentioning that judicial assistance at the level or at the stage of proof taking does not involve a recognition of the judgment is an established rule, which was already in the previous Hague conventions and is perfectly compatible with the purpose and task of taking evidence. My impression is that the tensions that we have with the United States upon the application of the Hague Convention sometimes overshadow and sometimes mislead the understanding of what the purpose of cooperation in the field of taking evidence is. It does not imply any obligation to recognize, just as it does not imply recognition of the jurisdiction that the court exercises. And this is simply due to the fact that the substantive law or the jurisdictional criteria may be very different in various parts of the world, or the countries that decide to cooperate with this perspective. These differences are difficult to overcome. However, they should not preclude judicial cooperation in the field of evidence or information gathering. Maybe in the future we will be able to harmonise the rules of jurisdiction to adjudicate and agree on common policies of jurisdiction to prescribe.

*Professor Stürner:* I think it is the prevailing opinion that the Hague Service Convention and the Hague Convention on the Taking of Evidence should be applied independently of possible recognition or non-recognition of later judgments of foreign courts. But surprisingly, most recently the German Constitutional Court came to another result. It was the *Bertelsmann* case where the Constitutional Court argued that the claim was clearly abusive and therefore judicial aid by service abroad should not be granted. In my opinion this decision is completely wrong, but it may be that this decision is the beginning of a development towards a more restrictive practice in cases of very excessive claims or in cases where the foreign court has a very excessive understanding of its jurisdiction. Mr. Trocker, I agree with your point of view, but it could be that the practice of European Supreme Courts will change or will be more unforeseeable and capricious.

Let me make a second remark. It is the European understanding that American jurisdiction is sometimes exorbitant and excessive. I think that the Europeans are not very honest when arguing on this basis. Take tort cases: the American courts restrict their jurisdiction by examining the purposefulness of the harmful act or by examining foreseeability when placing goods in the stream of commerce. These restrictions are unknown to European law. Under European law, the harmful act causing damages is enough to justify jurisdiction of the country where the harm occurred over the persons acting in foreign countries. There is no requirement of purposefulness or foreseeability, the same may be true in cases of unfair competition or even anti-trust law. Therefore, I am not sure whether it is really correct to say that the American understanding of jurisdiction is broader. American courts attracted more cases than European courts, and it is the number of cases which may have contributed to this picture of broad American and small European jurisdiction. But with the increase of European cases in the field of anti-trust we will begin to notice that the European understanding of jurisdiction is sometimes very broad too, and that there also exist long arm statutes under European law.

*Professor Trocker:* I think that the decision of the German Constitutional Court is very unfortunate and makes the court not very reliable in this area because they made a completely different decision not so long ago. And I think if we bring in public policy concerns at the service level we are really going in the wrong direction. So I hope this is an isolated accident. Cases like *Bertelsmann*, if they are considered abusive, should not be solved by putting pressure from a foreign state on the forum state. These kinds of cases should be solved by using a domestic instrument like 'striking out'. A clearly, manifestly unfounded case should end there, it should not involve policies of different countries. So, then there was the problem with the broad notions of jurisdiction. I agree obviously with Professor Stürner that in tort cases Europeans apply a very broad notion of jurisdiction. Our justification is a unilateral view of protecting the plaintiff as the weaker party. The concern of the American developments, *Volkswagen*, *Asahi* and all the other cases that we know, is that, – and I think the Swiss statute of private international law has incorporated part of this lesson – you also have to be concerned about the defendant and therefore he has to be somewhat purposefully involved. The accident in Oklahoma and so on is not enough in itself. Our problem in this area with a broad notion of jurisdiction to adjudicate is that, particularly as far as corporations are concerned, we still prefer as a connecting factor the seat or the place of activity, the English 'place of business', some sort of identifiable location, and we are not so comfortable with the 'economic' approach of the U.S. courts, you know: 'doing business'. We have some difficulties with this concept or notion, because there is an element of unpredictability, uncertainty, a case-by-case test involved, and it is this rather than the reasonableness in itself of the criterion that makes us somewhat uncomfortable.

*Professor Murray:* I just have a couple of comments, because I hear a strain that suggests somehow that the American need for proof abroad is somehow connected to a sense that American justice is in general exorbitant and stretches out its jurisdiction perhaps arbitrarily. That suggestion has been made many times. Professor Stürner, I think, pointed out that in many ways the actual provisions of American extraterritorial justice are no more extravagant or exorbitant than those which are used by other countries. Why is it that, and I take what Professor Trocker says, that the forms of American doctrine with extraterritorial jurisdiction are a little bit different from, and perhaps unfamiliar to, Europeans and hard for them to accept? But I think what is really hard to accept and what makes it very easy to say that American justice is exorbitant, is that the processes that American justice brings with it are so alien and are so much disliked by foreign defendants, particularly the prospect of punitive damages, which has been mentioned here several times as a matter of substantive law, and the unpredictability of the jury verdict as a matter of procedural law coupled with the tremendous costs that are involved on private litigants, often which cannot be recovered. Anytime that you are faced with that kind of procedure and you don't want it, it is very easy to feel that the jurisdiction is exorbitant. And if our processes were a little bit more like the European processes with which everyone is familiar or if our processes were not associated with jury trials and huge awards and punitive damages, I suspect that the exercise of American territorial jurisdiction would be much more an academic kind of debate among colleagues instead of a fierce resistance at any cost. So I think it is coupled a little bit with the American substantive law, with the American procedures and the alienness of those procedures to many Europeans and East Asians that makes any form of jurisdiction that extends those procedures over them unwelcome. And I think we have to concede that in our debate. I think that maybe that suggests that we should reform American procedures in general. But it is certainly the case that now many clients do anything to avoid American litigation, they would stand on their heads to avoid American litigation and any kind of a jurisdiction regime that makes them likely subject to American litigation is immediately questioned.

*Professor Andrews:* Could I bring to the attention of the panel a permutation which is not been examined because it lies outside your brief. This case went to the House of Lords. It has an interesting foreign evidential element. The case involved the well-known film director Polanski [*Polanski v Conde Nast Publications Ltd* [2005] UKHL 10]. As I understand it, he is currently in France, but is reluctant to go on Eurostar to London. If he were to land on English soil, he would be immediately arrested and extradited to the United States. It seems the Californian authorities would like to prosecute him for alleged rape a long time ago. So we had the remarkable case in England where Polanski sued a magazine. He claimed damages for defamation. Although he was the 'English' plaintiff, he could not for personal and 'practical' reasons attend in person at the trial that he had initiated. Question: whether it is acceptable for Polanski to give evidence by video link from Paris to be received in the High Court in London live? It was held that Polanski should be allowed to give such evidence. I think that on balance that is right. What it demonstrates is that the expansion of exciting technology has really broken down the whole concept of access to information and access to evidence in civil matters. I don't know if you have any comments on that.

*Professor Murray:* I would just in response to Professor Andrews comment say that I think you are absolutely right in the sense that the information technology as it has been adverted to by Dr. Ervo as well, and the ability to have videotaped conference calls, conference video, you name it, type of proceedings has made the obtaining of information abroad in forms which are useful in court much easier and also much less intrusive on the foreign sovereign. And so that doesn't mean there is necessarily, there is perhaps a technical or perhaps a real intrusion, but perhaps it is a kind of intrusion that can be dealt with by some kind of expedited process. If all you are going to do is conduct a conference call type of proof taking or something like that, it is not like you are sending a judge abroad to sit in all of his glory on the soil of another country. I think law professors could say no, but it is the same kind of idea and we can argue whether or not the electronic impulses are the same thing as sending a judge abroad. But as a practical matter, when we talk practically, the cost, the intrusion, the disturbance, the amount of a problem that is being caused to the foreign sovereign can be minimized tremendously and language problems and so forth can all be avoided or reduced by the use of this kind of electronic technology. And I think as it is indicated in the Scandinavian lands certainly and in other places that that does point to ways in which we can reduce old conflicts that came out of the old technology.

*Professor Takagi:* I would like to make comments from the point of view of a practitioner. I was a private lawyer for 25 years and became a judge 12 years ago. When I was in private practice, I was involved in civil litigation pending in the United States representing a Japanese client. I represented two cases. One was a class action. As a general observation, I think discovery is a very good tool to access the truth, reveal hiding facts or something like that. And I attended the depositions and also the production of documents like that. Though they were too broad sometimes, they were a very good tool to access the truth. And, after becoming a judge, I was very frustrated because the lawyers representing plaintiffs and defendants liked to hide the facts, the facts unfavourable to the client. Professor Murray mentioned cross examination in Japan. I sometimes, many times, intervened in cross examination, even sitting on the bench. I asked many questions even when I was judge. I made many direct examinations to find facts with very limited information. So my colleagues, lawyers, criticized me that I had betrayed my former colleagues by being too aggressive a judge to access the truth. So I think my opinion may be the minority in Japan, but I think Japanese courts have to cooperate with discovery to some extent.

Of course, there are several preconditions. For example, the Japanese court may reserve to refuse cooperation if the American jurisdiction is too broad. And, for example, American deposition may take place too broadly, so the Japanese court may request the American court, the American judge, to decide about the necessity of the deposition. And if the Japanese court thinks that the deposition is not necessary, the Japanese court can refuse it like that. There are many misleading questions and other hearsay questions. This is not good. So if the Japanese court allows the deposition in Japan, Japanese judges have to preside over the deposition restricting misleading questions. Of course we need to impose several restrictions, but I think it is better to cooperate with American discovery to some extent. Probably in Japan this is the minority opinion.

I would like to comment on another point again from the point of view of a bankruptcy specialist. As you know, Japan adopted the Cross Border Insolvency Act probably four or five years ago, mostly adopting the UNCITRAL Model Law on Cross Border Insolvency. But the Japanese statute opted out of one provision, which refers to direct court-to-court communication. I think it is because of language problems. But as far as corporate reorganisation case is concerned, direct court-to-court communication is a very useful tool. Inside the NAFTA countries, for example between Canada and the United States, there are several joint hearings to avoid contradicting decisions in parallel bankruptcy proceedings. So I would like to expect that before the end of the 21st century, even in civil litigation, direct court-to-court communication will be possible all over the world. And even sometimes joint hearings or something like that may be possible all over the world regardless of boundaries. Thank you.

*Professor Murray:* I would like to respond briefly to Professor Takagi's excellent observations. And specifically referring to what Professor Trocker said about the fact that often foreign parties confront American discovery in its unrefined and overbroad form, and of course you get these very broad discovery requests, all these plans or whatever it might be, and the foreign parties throw up their hands and say this is terrible. But of course as was the case in *Aerospatiale*, these discovery requests upon objection raised by the opposing party are subject to being pared down and tailored and otherwise made much more specific under the supervision of the judge. And that does happen and often when the requests are so pared down by the supervision of the judge, that is the American judge, then they become much more reasonable and better tailored. I think that when I tried in my modest proposal to suggest a way for international cooperation on the taking of evidence, I think many of the points which Professor Takagi also mentioned were similar, that is before you are shipping American broad requests for discovery abroad, they should be filtered by an American judge to make sure that they are not overbroad when you are shipping them abroad to a foreign colleague to ask for assistance, and that there should be judicial oversight of discovery and particularly on the depositions. And the proposal was that at the request of the party in Japan for instance that the deposition could be overseen by a Japanese judge to make sure that the person would not be subject to oppression or harassment and that any Japanese policies, not blocking statutes (I quickly say that I am glad that Japan has not enacted a blocking statute), but real privileges that exist in Japan, real confidentiality, interests that are public policy of Japan can be properly maintained in that process. I think that is the kind of cooperation and the attitude that you have is one that I think will support real cooperation of the kind that I perhaps naively put forward in my proposal that we could all do.

*Professor Andrews:* Professor Trocker paid a very high compliment to certain people in the room when he expressed admiration for one of the principles of the UNIDROIT/ALI document. And in particular of course he referred to the concept of 'access to information', which is contained in the relevant principle [*ALI/UNIDROIT: Principles of Transnational Civil Procedure* (Cambridge UP 2006), Principle 16]. I wonder if in fact he is not being unduly kind because the concept of access to information raises many more questions than it answers. Do you feel that in the context of the material that has been discussed this morning, that we are any closer to understanding answers to the following two puzzles which continue to bedevil English civil procedure? Question number 1: What is the threshold at which a pre-action application for information is to be castigated as 'fishing'? Secondly, should we hesitate, and if so to what extent, in obtaining information from non-parties prior to the trial? Those are the two areas of uncertainty in my legal system. And I think they represent general problems.

*Professor Trocker:* I would say the first question allows me to apply Professor Taniguchi's strategy in terms of passing the question to the audience. I mentioned and I am very positive about the trends that are developing in various countries to extend access to information prior to the beginning of a judicial action. Now, the question that I would like to pose to the audience – I know and I mentioned Professor Taniguchi's contribution and other articles that I have seen – how does the 2003 reform in Japan regulate specifically access to information prior to trial? I am using on purpose the expression 'information' and not evidence, because obviously the relevancy at this stage is a different one from the relevancy that applies to evidence once specific facts are pleaded. So, how broad can this information be at the pre-action stage? I am not familiar in detail with the new regulation in Japan, but since it is not only the English that have this problem within the pre-action protocols, but the French have also started to extend enormously their Article 145 with regard to the application of what they call 'preliminary instruction measures', Professor Andrew's question is of great interest and importance.

And here I see the striking and fascinating converging trend with American discovery because, as I tried to emphasize very briefly, if you want someone to be precise and rational once he starts litigation, he has to have information. And therefore, if you want to keep the fact pleading principle as a rigid principle, you have to allow access to information before the commencement of proceedings. In that respect – and it is not merely because I like and I have great admiration for the members of the drafting group of the ALI/UNIDROIT Principles of Transnational Civil Procedure that I mentioned – I find the drafting of Principle 11 extremely interesting in connection with Principle 16, because it gives you a point of reference and at the same time it opens the way for flexible criteria. I think, of course, that it requires a judge capable of operating in this area and making a distinction between abusive intrusion or some sort of attempt to find out industrial or business secrets, to distinguish this from legitimate information that one needs to file a claim. So I think this is an excellent question and if I may I would like to ask the audience to give me some understanding about the 'pre-action', let us call it this, information that in accordance with the 2003 amendments to the Code of Civil Procedure in Japan is admitted and how do the courts, because they ultimately are involved, handle this in order to determine a reasonable limit to information requests.

*Professor Takagi:* Thank you. In civil law countries including Japan, there is no distinction between hearing and trail or pre-trial and trial. In pre-trial proceedings including depositions and productions of documents, American judges control the pre-trial in limited extent. Therefore, Japanese judges and lawyers feel discoveries are too broad. It is best to provide some assistance for discovery. But of course as Professor Trocker said, if the production of documents is too broad by reference to the national domestic law, Japanese courts can refuse to cooperate with the production order like that. Of course, we need some limits to that.

And I would like to add to the comment I made about joint hearings. Joint hearings are held using video camera conference, which is very useful. Thank you.

*Professor Taniguchi:* As my report has been mentioned by Professor Trocker several times, I am obligated to say something. The 2003 amendment of the Code of Civil Procedure adopted this pre-action information gathering procedure with a court intervention and I don't know how effective this has been conducted in practice, and I want to ask a practitioner, like Professor Takagi. I am a counsel in a law firm, a litigation law firm in Tokyo, but I haven't heard that this has been used very actively. And the law itself is not drafted in a way that is very effective. This was originally influenced by a German amendment, I think. I don't remember when it was done, but Professor Stürner can explain. Expanded preservation of evidence, and then also I think this pre-action information gathering procedure, was adopted in Germany and then Japan was, I think, sort of influenced by that. I don't think this is very effective. There is a certain limitation when you read the text of the law. Because there is no Japanese report on this subject, I don't know why, I would like to ask Professor Kawano. I guess because in this area the Japanese law is not clear at all, so there is not much material you can depend on.

As far as I know, we have very simple statutes which were enacted more than 100 years ago about international judicial cooperation. So we accepted this traditional method of letters rogatory. But this has been very unsatisfactory, especially from an American point of view, because you have to go through diplomatic channels and you have to give a list of questions to be asked to Japanese witnesses and this will come to a competent court and the judge calls the witness and then just asks these questions and records the simple answer in a summary form, not a verbatim transcript. A very simple answer will come back and it doesn't help at all. So what Americans did was not to use this. I have seen the statistics on this: very few requests of letters rogatory. And so what Americans do is just to conduct the deposition. First, they wanted to do it in a hotel room and then the Japanese side objected that this was a violation of Japan's sovereignty. So when you stated the purpose of visit to Japan as deposition-taking, the visa was denied by the Japanese government so there was some turmoil. And then an agreement was reached so that the Americans could take the deposition in the American Embassy building. So there is a certain room assigned for that purpose and there is a long waiting list to use this facility. Of course, the American embassy is United States territory, so the Japanese government can't do anything.

But recently my law firm has been handling a very interesting big case in which letters rogatory came to Japan and many Japanese tax officers are being examined in various Japanese district courts in which the Japanese lawyers representing American parties are present and ask questions. And also American lawyers, though not entitled, are permitted to be present in the room. It is just an adversarial examination taking place there. But of course this was very difficult, because the public information privilege was raised, because these are public officials, so it did not go well. But I think there was some progress in this respect and verbatim records have been taken in that process. It is all up to the judge's discretion. So that is a present example.

*Professor Kato:* As the discussion time comes to an end, I would like to ask for one final comment by Professor Kawano.

*Professor Kawano:* I would like to explain very briefly about the new situation relating to the taking evidence or information problem in Japan. In 1998, we changed our civil procedure law. Before that, we had very slow justice in Japan. But at that time we tried to change our civil system and at the time of the preparation of these amendments, there were certain voices that called for accepting the American discovery system also in Japan. But there were some very difficult discussions. One of the most important policies was to accelerate our civil justice. For that purpose, we needed to encourage litigants and attorneys to prepare their case properly. However, if you prepare the case properly, you need information for leading their litigation. You should get information as soon as possible from the adversary parties, but at that time we limited that to pending procedures only. But it was not enough, so we made subsequently further changes. This time, we changed our legal system with regard to the stage before filing, so it is possible to get some kind of information before filing. Within 40 days before the notice of filing the case, it is possible to require the adversary party to submit some information relating to the procedural matters for preparing argument and evidence. The requirement doesn't have sanctions. It is only a relation between the two parties on voluntary bases. We are sceptical of a court conducting this process. It is a kind of trial to get some information. On the other hand, there is criticism about the function of this, but it is a new philosophy. Nobody knows whether it will be successful or not, but we have to observe and to consider further.

*Chapter 4*

# Preclusive Effects of Foreign Judgments

# Preclusive Effects of Foreign Judgments – The European Tradition

*Rolf Stürner*

## Introductory Remarks

The growing worldwide exchange of goods, services and ideas is more and more a source of international disputes which are determined by court judgments. A main issue of the law of transnational civil procedure is not only the question whether a foreign judgment should be recognized and enforced or not, it is also the scope of recognition which is often in dispute. Take the case that a Japanese court has to decide on the acknowledgement of an American judgment. Does Japanese recognition create effects of American claim and issue preclusion or are the effects of recognition restricted to the minor effects of a final Japanese judgment?

The following considerations discuss this question in three steps. The first step will be an analysis of the European development and its history from the beginning to the modern attempts of the European Court of Justice to resolve the described problem. The second step will be a short discussion of the U.S.-American and Japanese development. And the third and last part of this presentation will be a recommendation for a future worldwide conception.

## I. The European Development

### *1. The Principle of Finality*

All procedural laws have in common the principle that a decision should end the lawsuit whenever possible and demanded by the parties to litigation. The main purpose of a legal dispute is to realize the rights of the parties, thereby creating peace under the law. Realization of law without finality and legal certainty is hardly conceivable. Therefore, the guarantee of a fair and effective procedure and protection of individual rights according to Art. 6(1) ECHR (European Human Rights Convention) includes the guarantee of finality of judicial decision making. Hence, under Art. 6(2) EU-Treaty the finality of judicial decision making is common standard of the European Union, though the national procedural laws vary in detail.

### 2. *Basic Questions*

The principle of finality involves several basic questions, to which the national legal systems respond quite differently.

#### a) *Final Order and Underlying Issues*

The first basic question is, what shall be final: only the final court order or the determination of underlying issues as well? Underlying issues may be of legal or factual nature.

#### b) *Claim for Relief as Selected by the Claimant or All Claims Arising out of the Case?*

The second fundamental question attends to whether the final decision precludes all further claims arising out of the facts of the case and thus bars all further proceedings relating to the case or whether the parties define the scope of finality through selecting limited claims for relief.

#### c) *Personal Scope*

The third basic question concerns the persons, against whom the finality of a decision works: only the parties to litigation or also third persons?

### 3. *Common Sources of Legal History*

The present national rules governing the finality of decisions and the preclusive effects of decisions and their scope are mainly the result of the European reception of Roman law; especially in English law, however, Germanic roots have survived.

#### a) *Roman Law*

The Roman law already developed a legal theory of an action's estoppel ("bis eadem re agere non licet") and the exceptio rei iudicatae, handed down by the Codex Justinianum in manifold forms.[1] Regarding the scope of preclusive effects, especially one passage in the Digests should be mentioned that already describes all important coordinates of the later development and discussion: "Inspiciendum est, an idem corpus sit, quantitasque eadem, et idem ius et eadem

[1] The relation between consumption after litis contestatio with actiones in personam and exceptio rei iudicatae with other actions describe *Kaser/Hackl*, Das Römische Zivilprozeßrecht, 2nd ed. 1996, §§ 42 III, 43, 55 II, III with references; important recent literature: *Liebs* SZ RA 86 (1969), 169 ss.; *Kaser* SZ RA 101 (1984), 57 ss.; 103 (1986), 48; *Wieling* SZ RA 102 (1985), 291 ss.

causa petendi".[2] Such formulas have influenced the res iudicata doctrine of the German common process[3] as well as the tradition, from which art. 1351 of the French Code civil emerged:

"L'autorité de la chose jugée n'a lieu qu'a l'égard de ce qui a fait l'objet du jugement. Il faut que la chose demandée soit la même; que la demande soit fondée sur la même cause; que la demande soit entre les mêmes parties, et formée par elles et contre elles en la même qualité".

Even the English doctrine of the cause of action estoppel is in some respects a progeny of the Roman legal tradition of res iudicata as well.[4]

### *b) Germanic Law*

During the medieval period of the Germanic procedure, a legal theory had developed according to which a party must not contravene its own earlier procedural acts in subsequent proceedings, a rule that later extended to judicial findings reached through a party's responsible cooperation.[5] In the time of the common German process this legal tradition disappeared more and more, in English civil procedure, however, it created the doctrine of issue estoppel,[6] which until now predominates the Anglo-American understanding of res iudicata questions.

### *c) Unclear Legal Tradition*

Both starting points of procedural history cannot, however, be regarded as clearly contrasting doctrines, the tradition of "res iudicata" characterized by clear definition and the tradition of "estoppel" characterized by equity considerations. The classic and post-classic history of the Roman "res iudicata" doctrine and its later reception did not completely exclude considerations of equity with the consequence of remarkable uncertainty.[7] Not without good reason 19th century advocates of a broad res iudicata concept – e.g. *Savigny*[8] – referred to Roman sources as well as supporters of a very narrow and rigid view.[9]

---

[2] D. 44.2; pr. 12, 13.

[3] *Wetzell*, System des ordentlichen Civilprozesses, 3rd ed. 1878, pp. 580 ss.; as to the influence on art. 1351 C.c., see *Juliane de Van*, Dalloz Rép. civ., "Chose jugée", IV/1996.

[4] See *Andrews*, Principles of Civil Procedure, 1994, 17–002; *Millar* 35 Ill.L.Rev. 41 ss. (1941); *Spellenberg*, FS Henckel, 1995, pp. 841, 846 s.

[5] *Seelmann*, Der Rechtszug im älteren deutschen Recht, 1911, p. 188; *Gál* SZ GA 33 (1912), 316.

[6] *Millar* 35 Ill.L.Rev. 41, 54 (1941).

[7] *Kaser/Hackl*, Römisches Zivilprozeßrecht, §§ 55 III 2, 74 III 2.

[8] *Savigny*, System des heutigen römischen Rechts, Bd. IV, pp. 350–370, 439–443, 451, 452; to an even greater extent *Windscheid*, Lehrbuch des Pandektenrechts, 3rd ed., Bd. I, p. 396.

[9] E.g. *Wetzell*, Civilprozeß, 3rd ed. 1878, pp. 572 ss.

### 4. *Variations of the Res Iudicata Doctrine on the National Level*

After a survey over the historical roots of the res iudicata doctrine, we now analyze the present status of res iudicata in important European legal systems. In doing so, the restrictive understanding of the German legal family shall be compared with the generous English concept; followed by remarks on the procedures influenced by the French system with its cautious expansions of the res iudicata doctrine.

### 5. *The German Doctrine of Res Iudicata*

#### a) *Final Order and Underlying Legal or Factual Findings*

The drafters of the ZPO faced a common procedural law that was acquainted with all conceivable positions regarding the scope of res iudicata: the final order (Tenor) only, final order and underlying legal findings, final order and both legal and factual findings.[10] At last, the legislator with reference to the Prussian and French example decided for party autonomy and clarity as crucial standards. Decisive is alone the formally expressed will of the parties to litigation; if the parties want a binding determination of legal issues which are a necessary element of the court's judgment, they must apply formally for an interim declaratory judgment (Zwischenfeststellungsklage).

The present res iudicata doctrine strictly holds to the view of the 19th century legislator. Final is only the decision as contained in the court order (Tenor) to the extent that it adjudicates the parties' claim for relief (§ 322 [1] ZPO).[11] There are only some few concessions to a more extensive res iudicata concept. They can be found in the area of the so-called "contradictory opposite". Uncontested, however, even in this regard are only the clear cases that e.g. the awarded sum is demanded back as unjust enrichment or that, after an unrestricted damage award, the defendant seeks a declaratory judgment stating a lack of liability.[12] Controversial is the case that a claim for correction of the land register has been finally affirmed by court judgment and then subsequently the defendant demands for a declaratory judgment stating his ownership.[13] Even in case of reciprocal obligations in contracts[14] or in case of actions seeking only partial relief

---

[10] *Hahn*, Die gesamten Materialien zu den Reichsjustizgesetzen, Bd. 2, 2nd ed. 1983, Neudruck der Ausgabe Berlin 1881, pp. 290 s. with references; on the history of the res iudicata doctrine since *Savigny*, see *Gaul*, FS Flume, Bd. I, 1978, pp. 443 ss.

[11] For details, see *Rosenberg/Schwab/Gottwald*, Zivilprozeßrecht, 16th ed. 2004, § 153 with references; for a view favouring a more extensive res iudicata effect, see *Henckel*, Prozeßrecht und materielles Recht, 1970, pp. 149 ss.; *Zeuner*, Die objektiven Grenzen der Rechtskraft im Rahmen rechtlicher Sinnzusammenhänge, 1959.

[12] BGH LM Nr. 10 zu § 322 ZPO; RG HRR 1935, 216; similar BGH NJW 1995, 967.

[13] *Rosenberg/Schwab/Gottwald*, § 153 II 2 with references.

[14] Of different opinion *Zeuner*, Objektive Grenzen, p. 75; *Henckel*, Materielles Recht, pp. 198 ss.

(Teilklagen),[15] the prevailing opinion in Germany pursues its strict approach: no res iudicata effect for underlying issues.

*b) Claim for Relief as selected by the Claimant and other Claims Arising out of the Case – Party Autonomy*

According to the German conception, the finality of the decision does not cover all claims arising out of the case and its facts. Rather it is up to the parties to litigation to determine by means of their procedural applications precisely the scope of res iudicata. Thus, the subject matter of the proceedings and the scope of res iudicata are predominantly defined by the demands of the parties to litigation. If identical claims for relief are based on different facts, the subject matter of the proceedings and by the same token the scope of res iudicata will be different (so-called two-part subject matter conception – "zweigliedriger Streitgegenstand").[16] Within the limits of the claim for relief a party must completely exhaust all the facts and is not allowed to relitigate the dispute by introducing new facts and evidence.[17]

According to the present prevailing view, the party demand ("procedural claim") is *not* confined to certain legal bases (actions of substantive law),[18] to which the plaintiff refers. Hence, if different rules of law under different prerequisites yield the same result (concurrence of actions – "Anspruchskonkurrenz"),[19] the demand for relief covers the scrutiny of all applicable legal rules by the court. If in doing so, the court has not taken an individual legal rule into consideration, no new court action can be based on this rule.[20]

*c) Personal Scope of Res Iudicata*

German procedural law respects the personal limits of res iudicata effects relatively strictly: binding effect only *inter partes* and against successors of the par-

[15] BGH NJW 1994, 3165; 1997, 3019; BGHZ 135, 178; *Rosenberg/Schwab/Gottwald*, § 153 V; sceptical *Leipold*, Teilklagen und Rechtskraft, FS Zeuner, 1994, pp. 431 ss. with comparative references.

[16] For a discussion, see *Habscheid*, Der Streitgegenstand im Zivilprozeßrecht und im Streitverfahren der freiwilligen Gerichtsbarkeit, 1957; *Schwab*, Der Streitgegenstand im Zivilprozeß, 1954; *Rosenberg/Schwab/Gottwald*, § 92 III; § 153 I with references.

[17] Instructive BGHZ 123, 137, 141.

[18] *Windscheid*, Die actio des Römischen Civilprozessrechts, 1856, had defined the "claim" as a category of substantive law as opposed to the procedural remedy. Perhaps, the ZPO originally had in mind this substantive claim where it addresses the plaintiff's claim; on the former "substantive law theory", see *Rosenberg/Schwab/Gottwald*, § 92 III 1

[19] Recent doctrines combine several substantive claims that apply to the same subject to a single substantive claim and thus arrive at the substantive claim being the subject matter of the legal controversy; see *Rimmelspacher*, Materiellrechtlicher Anspruch und Streitgegenstandsprobleme im Zivilprozeß, 1970; *Henckel*, Parteilehre und Streitgegenstand im Zivilprozeß, 1961, pp. 262 ss.; *Georgiades*, Die Anspruchskonkurrenz im Zivilrecht und Zivilprozeßrecht, 1968, pp. 167 ss.

[20] Most recently, see BGHZ 117, 1, 5 ss.

ties (§§ 265, 325 ss. ZPO).[21] The most significant ground for this strict limitation is the constitutional right to be heard (Art. 103 [1] GG): nobody should be bound to the outcome of a proceeding if there was no opportunity of defence. Only he who fully succeeds to the legal position of a party to litigation may and must be bound down to the result a proceeding.

German procedural law provides for exceptions where in the public interest the res iudicata effect extends to everyone or at least to a group of persons. Standard examples are judgments determining paternity or decisions annulling a vote of the shareholders' assembly (§ 248 AktG). If according to substantive law the rights of a third person depend entirely on the rights of a party to litigation, the exceptio rei iudicatae may work in favour of this third person (e.g. the personal liability of the partner of a commercial partnership [OHG] that resembles the liability of the partnership itself; see § 129 HGB). The strict limitation of negative preclusive effects to parties to litigation has survived even the modern international tendency towards group actions with broad res iudicata effect against group members. In actions filed by consumer protection associations seeking a prohibitory injunction against the use of unfair contractual terms,[22] German law does not grant a judgment negative preclusive effects against individual consumers, only judgments in favour of the association may be given preclusive effect in a later action in favour of a claiming consumer. According to the most recently enacted Law on Test Procedures in Securities Litigation[23] a court's decision of the case chosen for test procedure will be given preclusive effect solely against the individual parties of other already pending cases which were correctly invited to intervene. Only under very rare and special circumstances German law permits notice by publication and the appointment or election of a representative of bondholders[24] or shareholders[25] who leads an action against the issuer of bonds or the shareholder's corporation in the interest of the group with full preclusive effects for all group members.

### 6. *Res Iudicata and Estoppel in England*

#### a) *Final Order and Underlying Issues*

For an English proceduralist, the question of whether the scope of the res iudicata effect is defined by the final order or by the judge's reasoning may be strange. For a helpful comparison with continental law, an answer should first try to understand the English conception as a whole. The English res iudicata

---

[21] In detail, see *Rosenberg/Schwab/Gottwald*, § 155 II 2 with references.

[22] Injunction Actions Law 2002.

[23] August 16, 2005 (BGBl. I, 2437), § 16.

[24] German Law on the Common Rights of Bondholders § 6.

[25] German Law on Special Corporation Procedures 2003 § 6(2) and German Law Regulating the Transformation of Companies § 26(2), 206.

doctrine traditionally differentiates between cause of action estoppel and issue estoppel.[26]

A cause of action estoppel arises where the "cause of action" in the later proceedings is identical to that in the earlier proceedings.[27] The "cause of action" describes the minimum facts the plaintiff according to the law must plead and – if necessary – prove to obtain the relief which he claims.[28] The final order of a judgment gives the judicial answer to the demand for relief as it is based on the "cause of action". Therefore, one may not be wrong in assuming that similar to a Continental "Tenor" or "dispositif", the final order circumscribes the scope of cause of action estoppel. English law, however, originally maintains the Roman legal concept[29] according to which the judgment creates a new legal title and the cause of action merges in the judgment (doctrine of merger).[30] Whether this doctrine reflects still the present prevailing point of view, may be debatable.[31]

Issue estoppel refers to the prerequisites, under which a cause of action can successfully be pursued in judicial proceedings. If such a prerequisite becomes an issue again in a subsequent cause of action, the preceding judicial finding as to this issue will be binding in the later proceedings, may it be based on evidence or mere admission.[32] The sole decisive question is whether the parties could and should have raised the issue[33] forming a necessary ingredient in the earlier cause of action.[34] "Issues" may refer to legal or factual questions; legal

---

[26] See, e.g., *Andrews*, Principles, n. 17–002; *Spencer Bower and Turner*, The Doctrine of Res Judicata, 2nd ed. 1969; in German language especially *Spellenberg*, FS Henckel, 1995, pp. 841 ss.; prior German literature: *Zeuner*, FS Zweigert, 1981, pp. 603 ss.; *Cohn*, FS Nipperdey, 1965, pp. 875 ss.

[27] House of Lords, Arnold v. National Westminster Bank plc [1991] 2 A.C. 93, 104 (per Lord Keith): "Cause of action estoppel arises, where the cause of action in the later proceedings is identical to that in the earlier proceedings..."

[28] Letang v. Cooper [1965] 1 Q.B. 232, 243, C.A. (per Diplock, L.J.): "... a cause of actions consists of the minimum facts which a plaintiff is required in law to plead and (if traversed) prove in order to obtain the relief which he claims". Very similar House of Lords, Republic of India v. India Steamship Co. Ltd. [1993] A.C. 410, 419 (per Lord Goff of Chieveley); furthermore Black v. Yates [1992] 1 Q.B. 526, 543 (per Potter, J.).

[29] On consumption and obligatio or actio iudicati in Roman law, see *Kaser/Hackl*, §§ 42 III, 43, 55 II, III; moreover, *Wetzell*, System, pp. 571, ss., 573.

[30] House of Lords, Republic of India v. India Steamship Co. Ltd. [1993] A.C. 410, 416, 417 (per Lord Goff of Chieveley): "... transit in rem iudicatam ..."

[31] Whereas foreign judgments rendered in favour of the plaintiff in former times did not constitute an obstacle to a renewed action in England for want of "merger" effect, this has been changed by the Civil Jurisdiction and Judgment Act 1982 sec. 34 where the doctrine of merger remains unmentioned; on this, see House of Lords a.a.O. 418 (per Lord Goff of Chieveley). *Andrews*, Principles, n. 17–001 ss. already leaves the doctrine of merger unmentioned.

[32] Following House of Lords, Republic of India v. India Steamship Co. Ltd. [1993] A.C. 410, 416/417 (per Lord Goff of Chieveley).

[33] House of Lords, Yat Tung Investment Co. Ltd. v. Dao Heng Back Ltd. [1975] A.C. 581, 590 (per Lord Kilbrandon).

[34] House of Lords, Arnold v. National Westminster Bank plc [1991] 2 A.C. 93, 105 (per

identity of issues requires that, despite of the different context, the legal inferences be similar in both proceedings.[35] The estoppel effect can be proved by means of the opinion of the judgment ("full reasoned judgment"), furthermore by the pleadings, the record or any other evidence, since the basis of estoppel is not judicial conduct but party conduct. Accordingly, considerations of fairness play a major role for issue estoppel. Therefore, no issue estoppel if a later decision or statute changes the underlying law or if a party has access to new evidence that was not accessible before.[36] Likewise, a judgment by default may often not be preceded by any conduct of the defaulting party that permits substantial inference with the consequence of a possible lack of issue estoppel.[37]

### *b) The Claimants Claim for Relief and Other Claims Arising out of the Case – Abuse of Process*

The procedure of the common law courts was originally initiated by strictly formalized writs.[38] According to this tradition a limitation of the scope of res iudicata to the plaintiff's "action" or formal relief would be a consequent solution in the eyes of a continental observer. Just the contrary is the case, however, the way the matter stands today. Since the 19th century, there has been a clear tendency to urge the litigants to dispose of the matter in dispute, as it arises from the facts, as comprehensively as possible. There is practically in force a rule against successive actions,[39] as well as against splitting into an action for property damage and one for personal injury[40] and against splitting into different

Lord Keith of Kinkel): "Issue estoppel may arise where a particular issue forming a necessary ingredient in a cause of action has been litigated and decided and in subsequent proceedings between the same parties involving a different cause of action to which the same issue is relevant one of the parties seeks to re-open that issue"; Henderson v. Henderson [1843] 3 Hare 100, 115.

[35] See the famous case of Thoday v. Thoday [1964] 2 W.L.R. 371 (C.A., per L.J. Diplock): divorce proceedings instituted by the wife on grounds of the husband's matrimonial offence and subsequent action by the husband for malicious desertion allegedly committed by the wife.

[36] House of Lords, Anrold v. National Westminster Bank plc [1991] 2 A.C. 93, 108 ss. (per Lord Keith of Kinkel), 111 per Lord Lowry; Phospate Sewage Co. v. Molleson [1879] 4 App. cas. 801, 814.

[37] New Brunswick Railway Co. v. British and French Trust Corporation Ltd. [1939] A.C. 1, 21, 28, 38.

[38] On the history of the "writs", see in detail *Millar*, Civil Procedure of the Trial Court in Historical Perspective, 1952, pp. 17 ss., 32, 43 ss.

[39] Brunsden v. Humphrey [1884] 14, Q.D.D., 141, 147 (per Bowen, L.J.): "Damages resulting from one and the same case of action must be assessed and recovered once and for all"; *Andrews*, Principles, p. 507: rule against successive actions; similar House of Lords, Republic of India v. India Steamship Co. Ltd. [1993] A.C. 410, 419 (per Lord Goff of Chieveley): no splitting into "action for damage to cargo" and "action for short delivery" after a ship accident.

[40] This is apparently the tendency displayed in Talbot v. Berkshire County Council (C.A.) [1994] Q.B. 290, 296; House of Lords, Republic of India v. India Steamship Co. Ltd. [1993]

forms of substantive actions.[41] As regards actions for damages, future damages are, in principle, precluded as well. A plaintiff must prove and receive damages arising out of the same cause of action once and for all.[42] An important exception is the award of provisional damages[43] where the claimant makes it clear that he applies only for compensation of that part of the damages which have already occurred and that further damages may develop in the future. If several parties are involved in the proceedings (third party proceedings), all litigants must seize the opportunity fully to dispose of the case, e.g. file a third party complaint.[44] This very broad application of the classical cause of action estoppel becomes increasingly intermingled with the new doctrine of abuse of process: the abuse lies in the fact that the court and the parties are asked repeatedly to deal with the identical matter and that the opponent is left in the dark about what he or she owes altogether. In the end, the doctrine of "abuse of process" may be a common basic idea, on which all kinds of res iudicata and estoppel are founded.

*c) Personal Scope of Res Iudicata and Issue Estoppel*

The personal scope of res iudicata and issue estoppel is determined by the adversarial principle and the principle of due process of law. A legal dispute's result is binding only on those parties that participated in the proceedings and on their privies and successors: heirs, the bankrupt succeeding the trustee in bankruptcy, singular successor etc.; since only they were given an opportunity to be heard. Partly different rules apply to paternity matters.[45]

The doctrine of "abuse of process", however, may permit results where a former litigant is bound to findings that become an issue (issue estoppel) in his relationship to third persons who were not involved in the first proceedings. He, who has been found guilty in criminal proceedings, should not be allowed to change this result straight away in a civil action.[46] Whether this non-mutual estoppel applies to civil proceedings as well, remains questionable. Former decisions answered this question in the affirmative,[47] more recent ones in the nega-

---

A.C. 410, 420 (per Lord Goff of Chieveley); formerly, it was differently held in Brundsen v. Humphrey [1884] 14. Q.B.D. 141.

[41] Black v. Yates [1992] 1 Q.B. 526, 544 (per Olter, J.): "cause of action" not equivalent to "form of action"; Letang v. Cooper [1965] 1 Q.B. 232, 243/244 (per Diplock, L.J.).

[42] Buckland v. Palmer [1984] 3 All.ER. 554 (C.A.).

[43] Part 41 CPR.

[44] Talbot v. Berkshire County Council [1994] Q.B. 290 (C.A.); on the entire subject, see *Andrews*, Principles, n. 17–006.

[45] On restrictions of the res iudicata, see Hager v. Osborne [1992] Fam. 94 (per Ward, J.).

[46] House of Lords, Hunter v. Chief Constable of West Midlands Police [1982] A.C. 529. However, *evidence to the contrary* is admissible except for defamation actions.

[47] Reichel v. Magrath [1889] 14 App.Cas. 62; Reichel v. Provost of Queens College ibid. Reichel had lost a suit for an ecclesiastical office. In subsequent proceedings instituted by his successor who was seeking an injunction against interference with the performance of his

tive[48] and the House of Lords acknowledged, in principle, non-mutual estoppel but restricted its scope of applicability to cases of clear abuse of process. Until now, the English courts, unlike other courts in the common law tradition, seem to be prone to disapprove of non-mutual offensive or defensive estoppel.[49]

Another exception have been the so-called "test actions". In complex disputes it has been conceivable to stay all other proceedings until one test case has been finally decided. If the other parties challenge the result of the test case, this may constitute abuse of process.[50] Similarly preclusive effects of judgments in modern group actions may work against all registered group members.[51] A further phenomenon of third party effect of English judgments is similarly pragmatic: in case of mandatory or prohibitory injunctions even non parties will be held in contempt of court if they intentionally support the defendant in disregarding the injunction or on their own initiative try to circumvent its effect.[52]

### 7. *Chose Jugée in the French Process*

#### a) *"Dispositif" and Underlying Issues*

Art. 455 [2] NCPC provides as follows: "Le jugement énonce la décision sous forme de dispositif". This rule had already been the basis of the prevailing doctrine before the Nouveau Code. However, simultaneously there have always been tendencies to advocate a more extensive binding effect of certain elements of the judgment[53] based on an extensive interpretation of the aforementioned Art. 1351 C.C. These tendencies have even survived the clear rule of art. 455 (2) NCPC until today.[54] The courts have always emphasized that even crucial elements of the judgment could only be consulted in construing the "dispositif", i.e., the final order, but could not have res iudicata effect themselves.[55] However,

---

duties, Reichel was bound to the outcome in the previous process. On the questionable qualification as status matter, see Bragg v. Ocenus Mutual Underwriting [1982] Lloyd's Rep. 132, 137 C.A. (per Caius, arguendo).

[48] For example Townsed v. Bishop [1939] 1 All. E.R. 805; Gleeson v. J. Wippel Co. Ltd. [1977] 1 W.L.R. 510 (Megarry V.C.).

[49] On the entire problem, see *Watson*, Issue Estoppel, Abuse of Process and Repetitive Litigation: the Death of Mutuality, in: Scott, International Perspectives of Civil Justice, 1990, p. 179 ss.

[50] Northwest Water Authority v. Binnie [1990] 3 All. E.R. 547; Ashmore v. National Coal Corp. [1990] 2 Q.B. 338.

[51] *Andrews*, English Civil Procedure, 2003.

[52] For example, Ltd. v. A-Z and AA-LL [1982] Q.B. 558 (C.A.); Attorney General v. Times Newspapers Ltd. [1992] A.C. 191 (House of Lords).

[53] Instructively, see *Motulsky*, Pour une délimitation plus précise de l'autorité de la chose jugée en matière civile, Dalloz 1958, chron. p. 1.

[54] For impressive more recent descriptions, see *Perrot/Fricéro*, Juris classeur, Fasc. 554, Autorité de la chose jugée, IX/1998, pp. 18 ss.; *J. de Van*, Dalloz, Rép. civ. Chose jugée, IV/1996, pp. 17 ss.

[55] For a more recent Decision, see, e.g., Cass. com., 17. 1. 1997, D 1997, rapp. Rémery.

the court practice eventually makes concessions, which – conceptually not always precisely distinguishable – involve the headwords "motifs décisoires", "motifs décisifs" and "soutien nécessaire du dispositif" and "décisions implicites" respectively.

In some instances there are elements missing in the "dispositif" of the decision that actually have been adjudicated upon application of the parties. In such cases the Cour de Cassation has from time to time permitted the completion of the "dispositif" by what was laid down in the court's reasoning (motifs décisoires).[56] Especially as to "jugements mixtes" (art. 544 NCPC) that render a decision on a part of the merits combined with an order to take evidence on the other part and with regard to interlocutory judgments (art. 480 NCPC), which may determine admissibility issues, the controversial question arises of the res iudicata effect of the "motifs décisoires", "qui sont le soutien nécessaire du dispositif". The judicial practice varies. Thus, in an action for payment based on a valid sales contract the determination that a party has no right of action shall have res iudicata effect for a counterclaim demanding for performance of the contract;[57] inversely, in similar cases recent decisions emphasize the irrelevancy of the "soutien nécessaire du dispositif".[58]

The courts partly assume that the res iudicata effect not only extends to the formal order but also to preliminary questions the judge had to answer necessarily to reach the final judgment and thus are its logical foundation. Unlike with the "motifs décisoires" or "motifs décisifs" this is not about assigning res iudicata effect to actually existent arguments of the court's reasoning, but tacit inferences shall be included into res iudicata ("virtuellement compris"). In fact, there are numerous examples for this phenomenon in past and more recent decisions. The losing plaintiff who has pursued only a part of the entire claim will be bound in subsequent proceedings for the rest of the claim by the negative decision on the causa (cause).[59] A judgment enjoining competitive conduct on contractual grounds has been considered to have res iudicata effect in reference to the enforceability of a corresponding contract clause in a following suit.[60] Occasionally, the courts have held, however, that the parties must not be unfairly surprised by the "décision implicite".[61]

---

[56] *Perrot/Fricéro*, Juris classeur, Procédure, Fasc. 554, n. 108.

[57] Cass. 3e civ., 27.4. 1982, JCP G 1982, IV, 236.

[58] Cass. com., 14.5. 1991, D. 1991, inf.rap. p. 162; Cass. 2e civ., 17.5. 1993, JCP G 1993, II, 22162, note E. Du Rusque; Cass. com. 12.1. 1993, Bull. civ., IV, n 4; *Héron*, Localisation de la chose jugée et rejet de l'autorité positive de la chose jugée, Melanges Perrot, 1996, p. 131.

[59] This appears to be the holding in Cass. civ., 17.8. 1870, DP 1870, I, p. 32; for a concurring view, see *Perrot/Fricéro*, J.C. Fasc. 554, n° 118. However, the remaining references for the rule "in toto pars continetur" do not appear pertinent.

[60] Cass. 3e civ., 20.3. 1978, Bull. civ. III n° 126; similar Cass. 3e civ., 13.11. 1986, Gaz. Pal. 1986, I, p. jurispr. p. 22.

[61] Cass. 2e civ., 24.2. 1988, JCP G 1988 II, 21090, note *L. Cadiet*.

### *b) The Claimant's Claim for Relief and Other Claims Arising out of the Case*

Art. 1351 C.c. requires identity of the "chose demandée" and identity of the "cause" as prerequisites of res iudicata. But French law rather generously allows the splitting-up of a case with its coherent factual basis.

There is a lack of "identité de chose demandée", e.g., where further damages are asked for in a second action,[62] a problem that must be clearly distinguished from the question already dealt with concerning a "décision implicite", especially of the *causa* (cause) through the earlier decision. The plaintiff may in different proceedings first demand a coercive fine ("astreinte") and then sue for damages, even though both are a consequence of the same breach of contract.[63]

The exact scope of the "identité de cause" is disputed in the French doctrine: legal grounds of the action, factual basis regardless of the applicable law,[64] the entirety of facts and legal grounds.[65] The court practice has not endorsed a stringent concept with respect to the "identité de cause". Hence, a differentiation between certain groups of cases seems to be necessary, it is not recommendable to rely on abstract rules.

In liability cases, the cause of action is always determined by the liability rule, on which the claimant's case is based. E.g., the plaintiff may sue on the basis of art. 1382 C.c. even though he failed with an earlier suit based on art. 1384 C.c.[66]

Likewise, there has been a strong tendency towards splitting-up the same case by means of singling out separate grounds for nullity of a contract with the "action en nullité des actes juridiques". E.g., who lost an action for a contract's invalidation based on hidden defects ("action en résolution d'une vente"), may sue a second time for annulment ("demande en annulation") on grounds of a violation of the law of hire purchase.[67] But – and this is a complication – sometimes various grounds for nullity are considered one single cause of action if they refer to the same factual element, e.g. various defects of form.[68]

### *c) Personal Scope of Res Iudicata*

Third persons are not subject to any res iudicata effect, though they have to respect the fact that the judgment is existent. There is an interesting development in the field of dependency of liability based on substantive law. A judgment entered against a debtor shall have res iudicata effect against a co-debtor; the

---

[62] E.g. Cass. 2e civ., 5. 1. 1994, Bull. civ. II n° 15; 30. 10. 1989, JCP G 1989. IV. 420.

[63] Cass. 1re civ., 28. 2. 1989, JCP G 1989. IV. 160.

[64] See, especially, *H. Motulsky*, La cause de la demande dans la délimitation de l'office du juge, Ecrits, p. 101 s.

[65] For an overview, see *Perrot/Fricéro*, Procédure Civile, Juris Classeur, Fasc. 554, n° 165.

[66] Cass. 2e civ., 24. 6. 1970, Bull. civ. II n° 221; for further references, see *Perrot/Fricéro* n° 172.

[67] Cass. com., 14. 3. 1972, Bull. civ. IV, n° 88.

[68] Cass. 1re civ., 31. 1. 1978, Bull. civ. I, n° 37.

same is true for a judgment against the principal debtor, since it shall be binding on the guarantor who is jointly liable.[69] The Cour de Cassation justifies this extension of the res iudicata effect referring to the "représentation" of the co-debtor and guarantor by the defendant of the earlier proceeding.

### *8. Subject Matter and Res Iudicata in the Jurisprudence of the European Court of Justice*

#### *a) The Brussels Convention and the Jurisdiction and Judgments Regulation*

The Brussels Convention and the new Jurisdiction and Judgements Regulation provide for an exception from recognition in case of "irreconcilability" with an earlier judgment of the state where recognition is sought. The ECJ has taken "irreconcilability" for granted if two decisions have contradictory legal consequences;[70] accordingly, a decision on marital support is irreconcilable with an earlier divorce decree.

Entirely consistently the ECJ with regard to the subject matter of litispendence proceeds on the premise of subject matter identity of an action for specific performance or payment on the one hand and underlying issues on the other. The action for payment of the purchase price has the same subject matter as an action seeking a declaration of nullity of the sales contract or an action for its rescission respectively.[71] Inversely, there is an identical subject matter in dispute of an action for a negative declaratory judgment determining that nothing is owed and of actions for payment,[72] even if actions for payment or specific performance include both "actions in personam" and "actions in rem" under English law. Under the jurisprudence of the ECJ the identity of the claims for relief does not determine the scope of the subject matter, it is the identity of the core issues ("core issue theory"). Some authors criticize the innovative character of the ECJ's subject matter doctrine and argue that this subject matter doctrine cannot be found in any member state's legal system.[73] This is true only to a very limited extent. The ECJ does adopt familiar patterns especially of the English res iudicata doctrine and the Court goes back behind the national continental codifications favouring the conception of the old common procedure and *Savigny*.

#### *b) Unclear Contour*

Because of the small number of cases that come before the ECJ, its subject matter conception necessarily lacks a clear contour. Thus, it is clear that an action

[69] Cass. civ., 18. 10. 1982, Bull. civ. IV, n° 316, p. 267.
[70] EGJD 1998, 645 = NJW 1988, 663 (Hoffmann/Krieg).
[71] ECJD 1987, 4871 ss. (Gubisch/Palumbo).
[72] ECJD 1994, 5460 ss. (The Tatry).
[73] *Geimer/Schütze*, Europäisches Zivilverfahrensrecht, 1997, Art. 21 n. 29.

for a declaratory judgment and an action for payment on the same claim result in an identity of the subject matter in dispute[74] and the same is true for the determination of payment actions and their underlying legal issues.[75] Whether the mere identity of the underlying legal basis of different claims suffices for the application of the "core issue"-doctrine, is an open question yet, e.g., when an action for payment of the purchase's price and an action for damages arising out of a breach of contract are based on the same sales agreement.[76] Similar configurations with an unclear result are actions for partial relief in courts of different EU member states and the relationship between a set off and an independent action in an EU member state.[77] All in all, the core issue-doctrine is more a jurisprudence of pragmatic equitableness than a doctrine in the sense of the traditional continental European system thinking.

### 9. *Effects of Recognition of Judgments within the EU*

It is probably the prevailing opinion and the point of view of the ECJ that the effect of recognition of a decision of a Member State's court should be the extension of the national res iudicata effect to the other EU member states.[78] This adherence to a national perspective stands in a peculiar contradiction to the endeavour of the ECJ to come to an autonomous all European subject matter conception. The present subject matter jurisprudence of the ECJ appears to be unsystematic and "open" in this regard, too.

## II. The American and Japanese Development

The European procedural systems are the origin of all other procedural systems of Western civilization worldwide. There is no variation of a res iudicata doctrine all over the world without European foundation. It seems therefore to be justified to give a detailed analysis of the European variety and the attempts of the European Court of Justice to harmonize or even unify the different diverging procedural systems. Before discussing the prospects of worldwide harmonization, it pays to give a short description of the res iudicata-doctrine of two

[74] As the ECJ, see H.R. 10.11. 1995, N.J. 1996 No. 259 (Netherlands); BGHZ 134, 201 = NJW 1997, 970 (Germany).

[75] As the ECJ, see BGH NJW 1995, 1758 (Germany); Cass., 15. 10. 1992, no. 11262, Riv.dir. int.priv.proc. 1994, 93 (Italy).

[76] See Cass. Rev. crit. 1978, 773 (France); differentiating *Schlosser*, EuGVÜ, Art. 27–29 n. 22.

[77] For a good overview, see *Geimer/Schütze*, Europäisches Zivilverfahrensrecht, Art. 21 n. 31 ss.

[78] ECJD 1988, 645 n. 11 (Hoffmann/Krieg); *Schlosser*, EuGVÜ, Art. 26 n. 2; report *Jenard* on Art. 26; report *Schlosser* n. 191.

economically very important countries which are the progenies of different European systems: the U.S. and Japan.

The American understanding of res iudicata is a very broad one – the consequence of the English influence on the development of the law of the former American colonies and of the vitality of the political and legal culture of American citizens of English origin. All claims derived from the same factual basis must, in principle, be asserted at once in the same proceedings, and hence, later additional actions or partial suits are ordinarily not permitted ("claim preclusion"). Factual or legal issues determined by the court as a necessary element of its judgment should generally not be re-examined in a subsequent dispute in which the same issue is also presented ("issue preclusion"). The most significant difference to the English doctrine is the very generous application of non mutual estoppel, some American authors call it "the death of mutuality". A party to litigation may be bound to findings of an earlier proceeding that are the consequence of that party's procedural activity and become again an issue in a second proceedings with a third person who was not involved in the first dispute. It is not wrong to state that the American conception of res iudicata creates the most rigid preclusive effect worldwide.

In the eyes of a foreign observer, Japan's procedural system could be described as a hybrid system which has been originally influenced mainly by German law and has come under additional American influence after the Second World War and during the last decades of American hegemony and legal missionarism. Many new developments realize conceptions of genuine Japanese origin and character. Nevertheless – in the field of res iudicata the original German doctrine stands relatively undisturbed, and attempts to implant elements of the American doctrine of claim and issue preclusion were not very successful. The Japanese Supreme Court, however, took some steps towards a limited form of "issue preclusion" when determining that a party to litigation may act in bad faith through contradicting its own statements made in an earlier dispute. Whether this form of preclusion is a rare exception based on equity considerations or an approximation to Anglo-American ideas of issue preclusion is still in dispute though the prevailing opinion seems not to be keen on the reception of elements of the Anglo-American doctrine of "issue preclusion".

## III. Prospects of Worldwide Harmonizations

The Principles of Transnational Civil Procedure, which were unanimously affirmed in 2004 by Unidroit, Rome, and the ALI in Washington, are a first important step towards a worldwide harmonization of procedural law. Principle 28 suggests a solution that gives the parties as much freedom as possible to determine the scope of the dispute themselves. This is probably the best way to establish clarity and certainty about the scope of earlier disputes and their significance for subsequent proceedings in the field of transnational litigation. All in all, the "Principles"[79] prefer the continental European concept as originally developed by the modern German doctrine[80] and in recent times more and more adopted by the Romanic legal systems. According to this concept the parties' formal claim for relief determines the scope of the subject matter in dispute which is decisive for questions of lis pendens and res adjudicata. A judgment will be given res iudicata effect with respect to its necessary elements only in exceptional cases when renewed dispute over earlier determined factual or legal issues would be clearly abusive. As a result, the "Principles" suggest a rather limited form of claim preclusion and do not, in principle, recognize issue preclusion. This sparing solution takes into account that the judges of a court recognizing a foreign judgment would need to have remarkably good knowledge of foreign law if they would have to determine the scope of a claim or issue preclusion according to the common law model, accepted with restrictive modifications in some civil law countries. Such knowledge would generally require intensive and expensive expert assessment which nonetheless may not always be correct and reliable. All this speaks well for a more modest solution casting the formal claims for relief as a relatively clear and uncomplicated standard.

It is true that the solution of the Principles does neither harmonize with the jurisprudence of the EJC nor with the most recent American Uniform Law on Jurisdiction and Recognition as affirmed by the ALI in 2005. Nevertheless – and it may not be surprising that a reporter of the Principles holds for the superiority of their suggestion – the better arguments may struggle for the Principles. It is indeed not recommendable to complicate transnational disputes as did especially the ECJ with its unclear innovations. This may be in the interest of international law firms, not of their clients. A broad scope of res iudicata in transnational disputes could be a threatening machinery for a worldwide dis-

---

[79] Principle 28.

[80] The German legislature of the 19th century did not realize the conception of res adjudicata as developed by the "common procedure" in many German individual states and approved by *Carl Friedrich von Savigny* (see *Gaul*, Festschrift Flume, Vol. I, 1978, p. 443 ff.). This conception had much similarity with the common law doctrine of res adjudicata. The legislature preferred complete party control over the scope of res adjudicata (see *Hahn*, Die gesammelten Materialien zu den Reichsjustizgesetzen, Vol. 2, 2nd ed. 1983 [Reprint of the edition Berlin 1881], p. 290 f.). Issue preclusion requires a special claim for declaratory relief (see sec. 256[2] German Civil Procedure Code and *Murray/Stürner*, German Civil Justice, Ch. 9(F)(2)(a) and (3), p. 358 f., 361). For similar solutions in other European countries see art. 34 Italian Civil Procedure Code and art. 408(2) and (3) Spanish Civil Procedure Code. The Greek Civil procedure has in some respects preserved the traditional concept of collateral estoppel of the German "common procedure", see art. 331 Greek Civil Procedure Code; *Kerameus* 157 AcP 241 ff. (1967); *Yessiou-Faltsi*, Civil Procedure in Hellas, 1996, p. 241 No. 269; *Tsikrikas*, Die Wirkungen der Urteile des Europäischen Gerichtshofs im Vertragsverletzungsverfahren, 1990, p. 57 ff.

semination of judicial errors. The quality of courts is not equal all over the world and it is one of the fundamental errors of the EU and its ECJ to take equality of all courts of the individual states of the Union for granted. Let me finish with a compliment to our host. The solution of the Principles follows the Japanese example: clear and narrow scope of res iudicata as a rule, but room for equity based exceptions in extraordinary cases.

# Preclusive Effects of Foreign Judgments According to Finnish Law

*Laura Ervo*

## 1. Res judicata

The traditional starting point in Finland has been that the foreign judgment does not have any res judicata effect in Finland[1], but today this situation has been dramatically changed because of European Union and its legislation and very many other international treaties.[2] The trend in the future will be expanding.

The precluding effect of other Nordic judgments in civil cases has the oldest and widest tradition in the Finnish legislation. In addition Finland has ratified very many other international treaties concerning the jurisdiction and enforcement of foreign judgments. In 1983, Finland acceded to the Convention on the Recognition and Enforcement of Decisions Relating to Maintenance Obligations, done at The Hague on 2 October 1973 (SopS 35/1983), and in 1994 Finland acceded to the European Convention on the recognition and enforcement of decisions concerning the custody of children and on the restoration of custody of children (SopS 56/1994), done in Luxembourg on 20 May 1980. In 1993, Finland acceded to the Lugano Convention and in 1999 in Brussels convention. In 2001, in Finland came into force European Council Regulation (EC) No 2201/2003 concerning jurisdiction and the recognition and enforcement of judgments in matrimonial matters and in the matters of parental responsibility, repealing Regulation (EC) No 1347/2000.[3]

The Nordic judgments have had automatically precluding effect in Finland. The situation is the same based on the Lugano and Brussels conventions. However, there is even the possibility to ask recognition on the basis of these conventions in some special situations.[4]

---

[1] Tirkkonen 1974, pp. 154–155.

[2] Similarly Jokela 2004, p. 432.

[3] The treaties can be found in Finnish in Johansson 2002.

[4] Koulu 2003b, p. 1148–1149.

The precluding effect based on a foreign judgment is as wide as it would be in an original country. So, the res judicata-effect is identical to the legislation of the state where the judgment has been given.[5]

Even if some foreign judgment would not have res judicata-effect in Finland, it may have weight as evidence according to the free evaluation of evidence. The court may then decide the value of foreign judgment as a piece of evidence. According to Koulu the default judgment has, however, normally no value as evidence.[6] In my opinion even judgments given by default may have some value as an evidence, but – of course – the judgment given after normal, adversarial proceedings usually has more value as a piece of evidence. The default judgment for instance can tell us that the opposite party has neglected his or her rights. Even this news may be important and have some value in some special situations. In short, foreign judgments can be valuable and important in Finnish jurisdiction even if they would not have res judicata effect.

## 2. Lis pendens

In Finland lis pendens-effect is based on res judicata-effect. In the case where the foreign judgment will get res judicata-effect in Finland, it has even lis pendens-effect, otherwise not. So, in order to know, if the effect is precluding effect already on the basis of the pendency, we have to test, if the judgment, which probably will be given in the future on the ground of this action, will get res judicata-effect or not.[7]

Traditionally only Nordic judgments have had lis pendens-effect in Finland. Nowadays, with the Lugano and Brussels treaties the lis pendens-effect covers, however, all European judgments. The only requirement is that the hypothetical foreign judgment would be placed on the scope of application of the treaties mentioned above.[8]

Wide lis pendens-effect allows even abuse of proceedings. The party can have for instance interest to get lex fori-benefit and therefore make summons very rapidly without any negotiations in order to achieve friendly settlement. The problem is called "forum running". The other example of it is the situation, where the party brings a suit of negative action for declaratory judgment against the opposite party in order to bind his or her hands with the lis pendens-effect. In spite of these possibilities to abuse the system, it is said in the case law of EC

[5] Koulu 2003b, p. 1148–1149.

[6] Koulu 2003, p. 212–213 and 2003b, p. 1149.

[7] Koulu 2001, p. 46–48, 2003, p. 207 and 2003b, p. 1146.

[8] Koulu 2003, p. 208 and 2003b, p. 1146 as well as Lappalainen 1995, p. 259–260.

that the pure doubt of abusing the norms is not enough in order to make an exception to the lis pendens-rule at national level.[9]

## 3. Foreign arbitral awards

Finland acceded in 1962 to the New York Convention on Recognition and Enforcement of Foreign Arbitral Awards. Later these norms have been similarly included in Finnish Arbitration Act.[10] Because of this treaty, the foreign arbitral awards are very widely recognised. An arbitral award which has been made in a foreign state by the virtue of an arbitration agreement made in compliance with the similar Finnish norms shall be recognised in Finland. The Finnish Act covers in that way all foreign arbitral awards based on written arbitration agreement and they are automatically recognised in Finland.[11] However, it will not be recognised to the extent that it is contrary to the public policy in Finland.[12] These exceptions based on ordre public can be in question when there is an error in the foreign arbitral award in its facts or in the judicial points of view.[13] The court will take ex officio into consideration if there is an ordre public reason in the arbitral award. However, there is so little case-law on this subject, that the interpretation is not established.[14]

The Finnish court does not, however, take the res judicata effect into consideration ex officio, if it is based on a foreign arbitral award. In these situations, the party has a duty to request on it during proceedings.[15] If the party would like to request to a negative res judicata effect based on a foreign arbitral award, it must be done when a party avails his or her right of action at the first time during the process.[16] If the party would like to request to a positive res judicata effect based on a foreign arbitral award, he or she must take the rules of preclusion into consideration and usually do it during the pre-trial stage.[17]

According to Section 53, an arbitral award shall, however, not be recognised in Finland against a party who furnishes proof that 1) he did not have the capacity to enter into the arbitration agreement or that he was not properly represented when the arbitration agreement was entered into, or that an arbitration agreement which complies with the form of the arbitration agreement is not valid under the law to which the parties have subjected it, or failing any indica-

[9] Koulu 2003, p. 208–210 and 2003b, p. 1147–1148.
[10] Jokela 2004, p. 434.
[11] Koulu 2003b, p. 1156.
[12] Section 52 in Arbitration Act.
[13] Jokela 2004, p. 434, Koulu 2003, s. 225 and Koulu 2003b, p. 1156.
[14] Koulu 2003b, p. 1156.
[15] Jokela 2004, p. 434 and Lappalainen 2001, p. 425.
[16] Lappalainen 2001, p. 416.
[17] Lappalainen 2001, p. 416, footnote 58.

tion thereon, under the law of the state where the award was made; 2) he was not given a proper notice of the appointment of the arbitrator or of the arbitration proceedings or was otherwise unable to present his case; 3) the arbitral tribunal has exceeded its authority; 4) the composition of the arbitral tribunal or the arbitral proceedings substantially deviated form the agreement of the parties of, failing such agreement, from the law of the state where the arbitration took place; or 5) the arbitral award has not yet become binding on the parties or it has been declared null and void or set aside or suspended in the state in which, or under the law of which, that award was made. So, it is the party, who has the burden of proof in situations mentioned above.[18]

In Finnish Arbitration Act there is no rule based on point in an article 5(2) in the New York Convention on Recognition and Enforcement of Foreign Arbitral Awards. Therefore Finnish courts have to recognise even such foreign arbitral awards, where the solved matter would not have been able to solve in arbitration according to Finnish law. The only excuse is, if the reason is at the same time against Finnish public policy.[19] In my opinion there is always that kind of ordre public reason and therefore the fail in Finnish Arbitration Act is without any sense. According to Section 2 in Finnish Arbitration Act arbitrators may solve only non-mandatory civil matters. It is said in Section 2 that "any dispute in a civil or commercial matter which can be settled by agreement between the parties may be referred to final decision by one or more arbitrators". In mandatory civil matters or in criminal cases there are always some, wider interest, which the court have to take into consideration. In non-mandatory civil matters, the only interest is the interest of the parties. In mandatory matters there can be for example the interests of a child or other kind of important interests in society, which the court have to take into consideration. Therefore cases of that kind must be solved by State courts only. Abroad the recognition of a Finnish arbitral award may of course be hindered because of this reason based on the point in an article 5(2) in the New York treaty.[20]

## 4. Enforcement

So, the main principle is nowadays, that the foreign judgment in civil cases has a very wide res judicata effect in Finland in every case concerning Nordic and other European judgments. In spite of this, the enforcement of foreign judg-

[18] Koulu 2003b, p. 1156. In a case solved by the Finnish Supreme Court 192:112 the party could not testify that the German court of arbitration would have gone further in its jurisdiction than the German legislation admits.

[19] Koulu 2003b, p. 1157.

[20] Koulu 2003b, p. 1157.

ment is not directly possible. The district court decides the enforceability[21] of the judgment on the request of the party.[22] The proceedings in such cases are one part of non-contentious jurisdiction and therefore quite easy and rather expeditious. However, from 21st October 2005 on, the enforcement on the basis of unchallenged European grounds for execution is possible directly.[23] The Regulation created a European enforcement order for uncontested claims. Thanks to the introduction of minimum standards, the instrument allows the free movement of decisions, out-of-court settlements or authentic instruments concerning uncontested claims in all the Member States. It is no longer necessary to use an intermediate procedure in the Member State of enforcement prior to recognition and enforcement. So, this very important reform is simplifying the enforcement system among European Union in a radical way.

In addition according to the new regulation on the European Small Claims Procedure, a judgment delivered in a European Small Claims Procedure shall be enforced under the same conditions as a judgment handed down in the Member State of enforcement. This rule in article 21 shall apply from 1 January 2009.

An arbitral award which has been made in a foreign state and which will be recognised in Finland will be enforced upon request. An application for enforcement will be submitted to the court of first instance.[24] The hearing is based on adversarial proceedings – on the contrary to the New York Treaty[25] – and therefore before the arbitral award made abroad is declared enforceable, the court shall give the party against whom the enforcement is sought an opportunity to be heard, unless there is a special reason to the contrary.[26] That kind of special reason can for instance be that the address of the opposite party is not known.[27] In my opinion the reason like this is perhaps not enough in order to skip hearing because it is always possible to perform the service by way of a public notice, which is also the usual way to act in civil proceedings if the whereabouts of the recipient or a person empowered by him or her to receive service cannot be discovered.[28]

---

[21] About the enforceability see Koulu 2003, p. 214–217.

[22] Jokela 2004, p. 433. About the proceedings see Koulu 1996, p. 121–179 and 2001, p. 46–81.

[23] Parliament and Council Regulation of 21 April 2004 creating a European enforcement order for uncontested claims.

[24] Section 54 in Arbitration Act.

[25] Koulu 2003b, p. 1157.

[26] Section 54 in Arbitration Act.

[27] Koulu 2003b, p. 1157.

[28] Chapter 11, Section 9 in the Code of Judicial Procedure.

## Bibliography

| | |
|---|---|
| Johansson 2002 | Johansson, Sirpa (ed.): Kansainvälisen siviiliprosessioikeuden käsikirja. Vantaa 2002. |
| Jokela 2004 | Jokela, Antti: Oikeudenkäynti III. Jyväskylä 2004. |
| Koulu 1996 | Koulu, Risto: Täytäntöönpano Luganon ja Brysselin sopimuksen perusteella. Jyväskylä 1996. |
| Koulu 2001 | Koulu, Risto: Kansainvälisen prosessi- ja insolvenssioikeuden pääpiirteet. Jyväskylä 2001. |
| Koulu 2003 | Koulu, Risto: Kansainvälinen prosessioikeus pääpiirteittäin. Vantaa 2003. |
| Koulu 2003b | Koulu, Risto: Kansainvälinen siviiliprosessioikeus. In Prosessioikeus, pp. 1083–1163. Juva 2003. |
| Lappalainen 1995 | Lappalainen, Juha: Siviiliprosessioikeus I. Jyväskylä 1995. |
| Lappalainen 2001 | Lappalainen, Juha: Siviiliprosessioikeus II. Jyväskylä 2001. |
| Tirkkonen 1974 | Tirkkonen, Tauno: Suomen siviiliprosessioikeus I. 2nd edition. Porvoo 1974. |

# Discussion

*Professor Kato:* I would like to ask for comments and questions on the two speeches. Professor Andrews, please.

*Professor Andrews:* Thank you very much indeed. I would like to begin by asking the distinguished speakers if they can clarify what the conceptual or policy argument is supporting *res judicata*. There seemed to be some hesitation in pinpointing it. But I was particularly intrigued by Professor Stürner's suggestion that perhaps the root concept is a notion of abuse of process. And perhaps Professor Stürner would like to expand upon that.

*Professor Stürner:* The argument of abuse of process is a very general one. It is more a principle of the law as a whole. It may be necessary to argue on the basis of more specific legal principles, e.g., finality as an element of rule of law, certainty as a phenomenon of rule of law. But, indeed, the more general topic is abuse of process, and it is not without reason that English courts have gone back to this more general argument in the last ten, twenty years. But, nevertheless, it may be a bit dangerous to use this argument, because it is very broad, depends much on equitableness and has no real clear contours.

*Professor Andrews:* When I first approached this subject I was struck by the profusion of Latin maxims. And if you recall, one of them translated is 'no one is to be vexed or disturbed twice in the same matter'. And I think that expresses a private perspective. The other one is that it is in the public interest that there should be an end to civil disputes. So that gives us a public dimension. And I think the truth of the matter is that there are these two dimensions to this whole question of the platform or the foundation of *res judicata*. It is not just a question of justice between the parties, but there is a public order dimension. Would you agree with that?

*Professor Stürner:* In principle, yes. But let me say that in Anglo-American tradition the argument of public interest may have more weight than in civil law countries. To organize a jury trial, that is a lot. But to organize a decision by an alone sitting judge, for example, does not have the same dimensions which a jury trial has. Therefore, a judgment rendered after a jury trial has more significance in Anglo-American legal culture than a judgment given by a civil law judge, who is traditionally more a form of an officer.The number of judges in civil law countries is very high compared with the number of judges in common law countries and the number of judgments rendered by Anglo-American courts after trial. It is true, that in all legal cultures res judicata has a private and public dimension, but the weight of each dimension is different according to the peculiarities of the administration of justice.

*Professor Andrews:* Another consideration, which is particularly important in England, is the principle that the parties must bring all relevant disputes together under the umbrella of a single action. If they fail to raise a claim or matter which is sufficiently closely connected with the initial dispute, they are precluded from raising that issue in subsequent proceedings. I regard that as an efficient and attractive principle. But I sense that in different parts of the world it is not regarded as satisfactory. Do you have any comments on that aspect of *res judicata*?

*Professor Stürner:* I think that the origin of this broad scope of claim preclusion or cause of action estoppel is also the jury trial. This trial causes a lot of organisational trouble, it is a political event. If a party applies to this board of lay judges led by a professional judge, a party to litigation should do all, that the dispute which arose out of the facts will be resolved once and for all. If a party applies to a form of a judicial officer only, like the *praetor* in ancient Rome or the *judex*, it is not so important whether you may have one or three different proceedings. Each proceeding is more a private procedure in chambers, you could say, and not a big event.

*Professor Trocker:* I agree with Professor Andrews that this concern about rationalizing resources is very important in English and American law. But I think in the continental tradition there is a strong perception of party initiative and a concern of how the parties have defined the object, the '*Streitgegenstand*', and this is the determining factor, not the potential influence of related factors. In order to have cumulative actions we need a strict legal relationship. I mean our concept of *connexitas* is a very strict one as compared to the one that they use in common law countries. This obviously has a cost and ends up as the French did to some extent, although they tried to narrow it, that you can file in succession various claims based on different factual and legal bases even if they are related. I think that the European Court's approach rationalizes all this to some extent and a concept like the 'core issue' has some sense.

*Professor Stürner:* At first glance it seems to be more economical to do all at once. But it was the experience of the common procedures that this concept of doing all at once and for ever produced very lengthy proceedings, which took many years to resolve the whole dispute. Parties were afraid to be precluded, consequently their pleadings were broad and extensive. The idea of the German legislature of the 19$^{th}$ century was party disposition and procedural economy. The intention was to keep the dispute as narrow as possible. If one important issue of a broader dispute is determined by the court, there is a good chance that the parties will settle the dispute on other issues. Take the "Teilklage", the partial claim. If you have a contract over 100.000,– Euro, the plaintiff may be permitted to demand for 10.000,– Euro only without any threat of a later preclusion regarding the remaining contractual amount. If the court determines the smaller dispute, which is less expensive and risky under German cost law, there will regularly be no further dispute over the legal basis of the claim, if the claim was dismissed. If the court renders a judgment in favour of the claimant, the defendant will often pay the rest without further legal dispute. The idea of a limited scope of proceedings has many advantages. German procedures need only half a year for each instance, and their limited scope is one of the reasons for timely justice.

*Professor Trocker:* You are perfectly right if you see it from one perspective. But if you consider all the adjustments that we are making in order to prevent multiplicity of suits, already at a conceptual level we speak about the "implicit objective reach" of *res judicata*, for example in Italy. And we have invented the distinction between logical and legal prejudicial issues, probably legal relationships, in order to adjust to some extent the excessive emphasis on party delimitation and to rationalize judicial resources. So our jurisprudence is certainly going in the direction of extending the effects of *res judicata*. We have expanded it in relation to third parties, and not only on a formal theoretical basis, beyond the specific examples that we have like the ones that you were mentioning with regard to Germany, and we have even developed a sort of general principle according to which judgments are binding vis-à-vis third parties if there is a 'prejudicial dependency' of their legal relationship upon the one that is in dispute between the parties. So we are making adjustments without changing the basic rule, because I think that there is also a rationalizing aspect in that and an expectation not to waste resources. So this is just another part of the explanation that we are using for this very intriguing and very complicated topic.

*Professor Stürner:* As a judge of the court of appeals, whose responsibility were decisions on appeals against recognition and enforcement of foreign judgments, I made some knowledge of French and Italian res judicata-doctrines. To be honest, they seem to be more complicated than the Anglo-American or German solution. The German solution with its very limited scope as applied by the courts – not the academic discussion, which is terribly confusing – is relatively clear and easy to be explained. The same is correct for the Anglo-American solution with its very broad scope of issue and claim preclusion. But the Italian doctrine ("presupposto in senso logico e tecnico") with its difficult differentiations is not easily understandable and the same is true for the traditional French doctrine. There are forms of limited issue or claim preclusion, and for foreign judges it is nearly impossible to draw the correct line in due time when studying a lot of complicated case law. This may be true even for domestic lawyers.

*Professor Murray:* I have two questions actually. One is I was just trying to think through in international process the way that Germany or Japan would treat a judgment that was rendered by a court in an Anglo-American land in terms of preclusive effect in Germany or Japan by recognition of the foreign judgment. Would that be recognized only to the extent a German or Japanese judgment would have been recognized in terms of the actual claims of the parties in the foreign judgment or would it be recognized to the same extent that a court in the country which rendered the judgment would have recognized the foreign judgment in the broad sense that the American judgment would be?

*Professor Stürner:* This is a very complicated question. The starting point is that a judgment has the effects of the law of the country where the judgment was rendered. This is also the point of view of the European Court of Justice and it is the prevailing European opinion under the European Regulation on Jurisdiction and Enforcement. But there are legal systems, like in Germany, where the effects of foreign judgments are restricted if they do not harmonize with national public policy. The question is how to define public policy. Take the example of issue preclusion, is it against German public policy? We have no judgment of our Federal Supreme Court on this issue. Some academics argue that the exclusion of issue preclusion is covered by German public policy as a fundamental principle of the German res judicata doctrine. Other academics refer to issue preclusion under German law in case of tender of defence, concluding that a legal instrumentality provided by domestic law under special circumstances could not infringe fundamental principles of German law. In international cases it is always difficult to determine questions of claim or issue preclusion under foreign substantive law. What are the claims which could arise out of the cases' facts? What is the logical fundament of a case? You need a very good knowledge of foreign substantive law or the help of experts. In the end you need weeks or months to determine questions of preclusion. That is not very pragmatic. This is the reason why the Principles of Transnational Civil Procedure provide a very restricted scope of claim and issue preclusion following the modern French and the German example.

*Professor Murray:* That brings me to the second question. Because, as you point out, if you take the general principle that the foreign judgment should be given the same effect it would be given in the country where it was rendered and then you try to use *ordre public*, so to speak to say: well, we don't have that here, and then finding out whether in fact there is a different meaning results in a detailed inquiry. Does that suggest as you suggest in part in the Principles that there should be some middle ground? You just said a minute ago that there is no middle ground theoretically possible and that certainly seems to appeal, but then you say, well maybe with respect to maybe estoppel action by the parties, equitable considerations in issue preclusion and in Principle Number 28.3, that it should be applied only to prevent substantial injustice, how about that?

*Professor Stürner:* Let met say that there is no rule of law without exception. If you make a rule of law without exception it is in the end not tolerable. Take the Japanese development. It was my pattern when we drafted this principle. The Japanese took the German example as their starting point. But there may be cases where it is not tolerable that a party acts in complete contradiction to the result of a former taking of evidence. And for these cases we need an exception of acting in bad faith. Sanctioning acting in bad faith is a general principle of law. It wouldn't have been tolerable to exclude this exception. It should be mentioned. The solution of the Principles is not the solution of most European countries. It was necessary to find a simple worldwide common standard for recognition of judgments. This was not the varying scope of the domestic effects of judgments. The principles make the attempt to formulate a general standard, which is pragmatic and easy to be adjudicated by foreign judges who are not familiar with the peculiarities of foreign substantive law.

*Professor Murray:* I think that your suggestion that the limited effect of claim preclusion is justified as a policy matter because the non-jury continental type of proceeding is relatively inexpensive and easy to invoke, maybe even according to the kinds of proceedings that are involved in these Principles. Any legal proceeding is a big deal in a sense. And so to suggest that litigants should be permitted to come in pretty much whenever they feel like presenting a claim may be understating. Do you think of the burden on the state and on the opposite party by this kind of repeated litigation of related issues?

*Professor Stürner:* First, cases with repeated litigation are extremely rare, because the effect on the parties is that they will settle the case on the basis of the first rendered judgment. And second, the other party is free to apply for a negative declaratory judgment. If the threat of a follow up dispute is a burden for the other party …

*Professor Murray:* ... the other party has the right to expand the scope of the proceedings.

*Professor Stürner:* And there is another point we should perhaps mention. In many European jurisdictions the court can give a judgment on the legal basis or "ground" of a claim *ex officio* without application of the parties. If the court has the feeling that there will be a sequence of partial claims with a repetition of disputes regarding the legal basis, the court may render what we call a '*Grundurteil*', and this is the same in France or Italy and can be done mostly *ex officio.* So the court could stop an abuse of process. But it is very rare that this is necessary.

*Professor Murray:* If this system is so efficient and desirable, to what do you attribute the efforts of many jurisdictions or some jurisdictions at least to try to find a middle ground? Such as the French for instance, possibly the Italians, where there is some effort. In other words they are unwilling to stay with the clean and clear German/Japanese solution. Are they just wandering in the darkness?

*Professor Stürner:* No, no. I wouldn't say it is a wandering in the darkness, but it is another understanding of justice. You have to make your choice between justice and certainty. Certainty is a form of justice and these legal cultures prefer justice in a more material sense and the Germans and Japanese prefer justice in the form of certainty. And I wouldn't be antagonistic to other legal cultures. Their solutions are in part our own German history too. Hundred years ago we had the same solutions. But I think for international cases it is a real burden for parties to litigation to analyze the substantive law of the relevant country as a whole.

*Professor de Cristofaro:* The topic is very difficult. And I think that whatever problem the topic of *res judicata* goes to, the parties will have to ask for council and they will have to ask for experts to give them some information. The same principle of finality has a different understanding in civil law countries in comparison to common law countries. For Italy, for Germany, the judgment is final only when it has been approved by the court of last instance. In the United States, and also in England, the judgment is final when the judge has decided the whole matter which is pending before him and so the first instance judgment is final. I had the occasion to follow a case where an American judgment had to be recognized in Italy. It was easy to persuade the Italian judge that the first instance Michigan judgment was not final from an Italian point of view. But if you look at the American law, maybe the Michigan first instance judgment was already final from an American point of view.

Also the substantive law is very important in this field. For instance the question of the nullity or voidability of a contract has a different impact in Italy and in Germany because, in German law, you cannot dispute the voidability of a contract after you have a first judgment which says the contract is valid. In Italy, you may still dispute the voidability of the contract even if you have a first judgment which says that the contract is valid. But this is because in Italy voidability is an effect of the judgment, is an effect of the '*Gestaltungsklagerecht*', while in Germany the voidability is the effect of a declaration of the party and then the judge has to decide in a declaratory judgment whether the declaration was effective or not, depending upon its substantive law. So, you always need some expert to understand, to let the judges from one country understand the peculiarities of the *res judicata* of another system. The European Court of Justice adopted a sort of large notion not of *res judicata*, but of *lis pendens* actually.

And it followed maybe the necessity of rationalizing economic considerations. We thought that in Japan they adopted a strict rule on *res judicata* effects, but they are open to accept also abuse of process considerations.

I refer to the famous *Gubisch* case, the first case where the European Court of Justice rendered a judgment on '*Streitgegenstand*', on the object of the process. There was a clear abuse by the Italian defendant in Germany because, after a couple of years of litigation in Germany, the Italian defendant, who had raised in Germany an objection voidability of the contract, began a fresh action in Italy claiming for the voidability of the contract. And the preliminary reference went to the Court of Justice not from an English judge or from an Irish judge, but from the Italian Supreme Court of Cassation, because the Italian Supreme Court felt that it was absurd to say in this case that there is a difference of the actions and the second action should proceed in parallel with the first one, even though they involve the same questions.

*Professor Stürner:* Yes, but first let me say that each solution has its weak points and some of the problems we have discussed in our ALI/Unidroit working group many times. But not all points you have now chosen as a basis of your attack are really weak. First, what is a final judgment? We didn't decide in the Principles what is final. We described only the scope of *res judicata* when a judgment is final. We discussed whether we should make a rule or a principle on finality, but we discovered what you analyzed now and here. It is very different: in France, for example, a judgment of first instance has *chose jugée* in the sense of '*materielle Rechtskraft*' but it is not final. Therefore our conclusion was that we should not define what is final, but we wanted to define the scope of *res judicata* in case of finality. I think you met the point, but please understand, it was not our intention to formulate any principle on finality.

The second point was the question of nullity, claims for rescission or nullity. According to the Principles, it is a party's claim for relief which defines the scope of *res judicata*. In case of claims for nullity or rescission it may be necessary to interpret the claim on the basis of the legal foundation of the claim. It seems to be reasonable to limit the scope of res judicata to the lack of form if the claim was clearly based on form provisions. The party would be free to initiate a new proceeding demanding for rescission based on error. The idea is that it is the party's disposition which is the basis of the limitation of the scope of *res judicata*. So, if I understood you correctly, the Principles would follow the Italian doctrine in this case. And I think it is reasonable, because you don't need any experts if you determine questions of claim preclusion on the formal basis of the plaintiff's claim for relief only.

You defended the lis pendens doctrine of the European Court of Justice. Let me answer that the opponent of the later Italian claimant was free to apply for a declaratory judgment in Germany to avoid a second dispute in Italy. Was it really correct and necessary to take procedural malpractice as a ground to develop a new lis pendens doctrine? The problem is perhaps the lack of flexibility of the European lis pendens rules.

*Professor Andrews:* I would like to ask about the nature of judgment that underpins this. I have just noted down a few categories here. I wonder if you can help me to try to work out in the transnational context how these various categories would or should be treated. Obviously one would start with the decision on the merits after all the evidence has been considered. Another category would be where there is a consent judgment between the parties. Another category is default judgment where the defendant has failed to enter a defence, or there has been some other procedural shortcoming on his part. Another category is where there is final judgment on the merits where there has been a summary judgment on the merits, but without examination of witnesses. Also I think one might include the question concerning the status of decisions on interim or provisional matters, but not concerning the substance of the main claim. You can see there are many types of judgment that need to be differentiated. Which of those in your view counts as a solid basis for *res judicata* in the context of transnational litigation?

*Professor Stürner:* If you take the decision on the claim for relief, all of them. If you discuss issue preclusion, you have a lot of problems which cannot be resolved. And so I think your analysis is more an argument for the solution we have chosen. If you restrict this form of international *res judicata* to the claim for relief as formulated by the parties to litigation and avoid having any form of issue preclusion, it will work relatively well. If you go further, we will have a lot of problems indeed.

*Professor Kato:* As a Japanese lawyer I know that Japan has a very strict idea of *res judicata*. But I am still attracted to the idea of the middle ground type of concept which Professor Murray referred to. And as far as a foreign judgment is concerned, of course, it is almost impossible to give effect to strict *res judicata* because the substantive law itself is different and some part of a foreign law might be against the public order of a different country. The procedure might be different. So we would like to give a different effect for a foreign final judgment. Even the civil law countries have *bona fide* principles. If a second law suit is brought in a different country and is against the final decision of the first country, this *bona fide* principle idea should be applied. If such a foreign decision is made in the case of default, well of course there are different assertions. The *bona fide* idea is very malleable, so such kind of idea is very suitable to the effect of a foreign judgment.

Any comments or questions from the floor?

*Professor Andrews:* Do you have any thoughts on the problem of 'new facts'? These concern facts arising subsequent to the original decision. Might one relax the doctrine of *res judicata* in the light of a party's genuine plea that new facts have arisen or been discovered? Might broad factors of equity justify re-opening that decision?

*Professor Stürner:* As you know, we made no principle on the temporal limitations of *res judicata*. But I think it is the worldwide prevailing opinion that facts which could have been pleaded in the last oral hearing are precluded and that only in exceptional cases of fraud etc. you could apply for a new hearing. And facts happening afterwards, they could be a reason for a new hearing or even a new procedure. But indeed we made no remarks and no specific rules on this topic. That is a white part of our map.

*Professor Kawano:* I would like to talk very briefly about Japanese treatment of *res judicata* problems. In Japan there is some kind of influence from U.S. thinking, especially the view of due process, but also views on these problems. If there are difficulties regarding points which should have been presented at an earlier stage, there are possibilities to consider fundamental rights. In Japan, though such considerations are sometimes argued, in principle there is a very mechanical operation of the judgment's effect, the effect of the former judgment itself. But now we have to consider certain possibilities or the rights of people. Maybe this relates to the last point which Professor Andrews made. So if you find new facts, traditionally we have thought this is subject to the temporal limitation or certain considerations in accordance with the *res judicata* way of thinking.

*Professor Murray:* As I consider the application of the issue of claim preclusion based upon the claims themselves, it makes me think that probably American pleading practices and trial preparation practices would have to be made somewhat more rigorous, because often for instance our complaints don't have any particular claims. They ask for "whatever relief we might be entitled to". There are also various kinds of doctrines that say that the pleadings are automatically amended to conform to the proof. And so that is all based upon a procedural law backdrop that gives this very broad effect to *res judicata*. So therefore it doesn't matter too much as to what the claims are or whether for instance a defendant goes through the trouble of pleading in a negative declaratory judgment case, because automatically everything that could have been pleaded is automatically adjudicated regardless of what the particular claims are. So that in order to go to this kind of a system we would have to sharpen up our pleading not only to the fact of having somewhat more extensive fact pleading, but also being much more disciplined about the matter of setting forth exactly what relief is sought and the basis for the relief in a way so that the court could look at relatively few papers to decide what the factual claims were rather than to have to look at the whole record of the case to see what actually happened under our current, rather sloppy practice.

*Professor Stürner:* Indeed the Principles wanted to encourage parties to international litigation to formulate clear claims for relief, and if you read the text you can see that we inserted 'as amended', to give due regard to amendments during the procedure, or clarifications. The latest formulation of the claim is the decisive one. But it is not only the United States that are very generous regarding claims for relief. Many European states have a very liberal practice. There are judgments from some countries where a judge doesn't say anything about interests. You have to read the full text, the full reasoning. Or where the judge says nothing on costs. Or where the judge deletes a part regarding the amount for which the defendant is due with the consequence that you must read the reasoning to calculate the amount etc. But, indeed, the Principles want to make it clear that it would be favourable to have clear and exact claims for relief. An exact formulation of the claim for relief and the corresponding court order is also important for the enforcement, because it is difficult to enforce judgments with an unclear content.

*Professor Murray:* I think that we are talking about partly the judgment, but it is also partly the claims that were adjudicated. For instance with a jury verdict, the plaintiff may ultimately by way of discovery and actually by way of the procedure before the jury may have asked for who knows what compared to what was in any written pleading and the judgment may be just for a certain amount of money. In which case what relationship does that judgment bear to the claims that were asserted? That is often very unclear from American process because we only know what the relationship of the judgment to the claims was when we listen to the arguments of the lawyers that were made to the jury and we go back and look at the various processes. Often there are no amendments, because the claims are very general to begin with. So that we only know what has been awarded by listening to what arguments were made to the jury and often the jury's amount is not reconcilable even then. It is just an award. So we would have to perhaps sharpen up that whole practice, so that we would know exactly what was placed to the jury and then the judgment would say what the result of that was.

*Professor Andrews:* Going back to your point about abuse of process, Professor Stürner, one half of me thinks that you are right and that to embrace a broad concept of abuse of process is unsatisfactory and could lead to capricious and unpredictable results. On the other hand, perhaps it would be a prudent thing to keep this doctrine as broad as possible in order to provide some way of countering bad faith in various contexts.

So I will give you a couple of examples. Recently someone made a whole series of applications to the Commercial Court in London in which they were seeking freezing injunctive relief. They petitioned four different judges obviously on different days and without the respective judges actually being aware of the fact that there were serial applications essentially on the same facts for the same relief. Eventually one of these judges realized that there had been multiple applications for the same relief and he said that this is an abuse of process. Once a judge realizes what is going on, the application can be dismissed forthwith. You cannot really explain that on the basis of traditional *res judicata* principles for the simple reason that there has not been a decision *inter partes*. This is because the application is made 'without notice', that is, *ex parte*. So that is one example of what can go on.

A second example, known in England as the problem of the 'vexatious litigant', is the person who makes repeated or even a whole series of claims. There must be a mechanism to stop such abuse. In England such a person can even be stopped from bringing any civil claims without official permission. Obviously there are human rights implications (namely, regard for the right of 'access to justice', implied in Europe by the Strasbourg Court under Art 6(1) of the European Convention on Human Rights, 1950). And there might be national constitutional rights of access to court. But, again, I think that a legal system needs to protect itself against this sort of extreme behaviour. And no doubt there might be a need to do so in the cross-border context.

In the light of my two examples of English controls on bad faith petitions and claims, might not other nations recognise also the need to adopt a broad concept of abuse of process rather than a narrow doctrine of *res judicata*?

*Professor Stürner:* The English starting point of *res judicata* is relatively narrow, because it is the idea of estoppel, of *venire contra factum proprium*. The continental starting point is much broader. It is not only the idea of estoppel. It is the idea of *ne bis in idem*. Indeed, I think that the English *res judicata* doctrine based on estoppel needs a form of extension. Your theory of abuse of process resolves cases which could on the continent be resolved by means of the traditional *res judicata* doctrine. Other cases where you have no identity of the subject matter, may be cases of abuse. Each legal culture develops some legal instrumentalities to get rid of those cases. In Germany, we would argue that there is no legitimate interest to bring this action to the courts. But we should be very cautious when using those legal instrumentalities, because they could also be abused by judges and by courts. The English experience with abuse of judicial power is not so bad, but on the continent we have had very bad experiences. And therefore, it is, in the eyes of continental or Japanese observers, very dangerous to have a too broad understanding of abuse of process. But there are two forms in England according to my understanding. One form is to compensate for the narrow scope of the traditional *res judicata* doctrine. This function is on the continent covered by the broader continental approach to res judicata. The other one has nothing to do with *res judicata*. It is a more general rule and countries with a very democratic tradition and without the experience of a complete breakdown of their legal culture will be more generous in granting those powers to courts. The continental tradition is very reluctant to do this.

*Professor Kato:* Lastly, we hope that all of you have enjoyed the lively discussion over these two days. We owe this to the organizer and the distinguished speakers. We would like to show our appreciation to everyone. First, the organizer Professor Kawano. Thank you very much. And I would like to say again now a special thank you to our speakers: Professor Stürner, Professor Murray, Professor Andrews, Professor Trocker, Professor Kengyel, Professor de Cristofaro, and Dr. Ervo. And we would like to say a special thanks to our staff, Tohko Hakayawa and Dr. Natalie Konomi. Thank you very much to all of you.

# Speakers' Profile

*Professor Neil H. Andrews*
Neil Andrews studied law at Oxford University. He took his BCL degree from the University of Oxford in 1982. Since 1981 he has been a Member of the Bar, Middle Temple, and he has taught law at the University of Cambridge since 1983. In 1995 his book "Principles of Civil Procedure" won the SPTL Prize for Outstanding Legal Scholarship. From 1999–2004, he was the English representative of the drafting committee of the American Law Institute's and UNIDROIT's joint project on "Principles of Transnational Civil Procedure". Since 2000 he has been a member of the American Law Institute and since 2003 a council member of the International Association of Procedural Law.

*Professor Marco de Cristofaro*
Marco de Cristofaro has been Professor of Civil Procedure at the University of Padova since 2002 and Director of the Department for Public, International and European Law since 2003. He has served as a Coordinator of Department Directors of the University of Padova since 2008. He is editor of the first and unique Italian Law Review for International Litigation (Int'l Lis).

*Professor Dr. Laura Ervo*
Laura Ervo is Professor of Law (Vic.) at the University of Helsinki, Faculty of Law. She is the Head of Department at Vaasa Unit for Legal Studies and is also lecturer at the Universities of Turku (2005), Helsinki (2006) and Joensuu (2008). She holds a Doctor of Law from the University of Turku (2005) and the title "Trained on the Bench" granted by the Court of Appeal of Turku (1998). Laura Ervo is a member of the International Association of Procedural Law and a council member of the Association of Nordic Procedural Law. Her main field of research is procedural law, especially human rights in civil procedure and the law of evidence.

*Professor Dr. Masanori Kawano*
Masanori Kawano has been teacher of civil procedure law in Japan since 1973 and holds a Doctor of Law from Kyushu University (1995). He joined Nagoya University Graduate School of Law in 1999, where he was Dean for the period 2002–2004. His main fields of research are civil procedure, bankruptcy and arbitration. He is a member of the International Association of Procedural Law. He was also a member of the joint American Law Institute/UNIDROIT Study Group and contributed to the preparation of the "Principles of Transnational Civil Procedure" from 2000–2003.

*Professor Dr. Miklós Kengyel*
Miklós Kengyel habilitated at the Law Faculty of the University of Pécs in 1994. He became a Professor of Law at the University of Pécs in 1994 and at the Andrássy German

Speaking University of Budapest in 2003. He was Dean of the Law Faculty in Pécs for the period of 1993–1999 and Rector of the Andrássy University from 2003–2008. His main fields of research are national civil procedure, international and European civil procedure, legal cultura. He is member of the International Association of Procedural Law.

*Professor Peter Loos Murray*
Peter L. Murray is Robert Braucher Visiting Professor of Law from Practice, Edward R. Johnston Lecturer of Law, Harvard Law School, Cambridge, M.A. He received his LL.B. from Harvard Law School, and was admitted to the Bar. He has 28 years of experience in general and trial practice in State and Federal Courts in Maine including civil and criminal jury and non-jury trials, appeals and administrative proceedings. He published "German Civil Justice" with Professor Dr. Rolf Stürner, University of Freiburg. He is a member of the American Law Institute and the American Bar Association.

*Professor Dr. Rolf Stürner*
Rolf Stürner habilitated at the Faculty of Law of the University of Tübingen (1976) and became a Professor of Law at the University of Konstanz in 1976. Since 1992 he has been a Director of the Institute for German and Comparative Civil Procedure, University of Freiburg. He was Visiting Professor at the University of Geneva (1986–1988) and at Harvard Law School (2001, 2003, 2005) and judge of the State Courts of Appeal in Stuttgart and Karlsruhe (1980–2008). He was President of the Association of German, Austrian and Swiss Proceduralists and he is a member of the American Law Institute, a corresponding member of UNIDROIT, Rome, a member of the Academy of Humanities and Sciences, Heidelberg and a member of the Council of the International Association of Procedural Law. He was co-reporter for the joint project "Principles of Transnational Civil Procedure" of UNIDROIT and the American Law Institute. In 2004 he published the book "German Civil Justice" together with Professor Peter L. Murray, Harvard Law School.

*Professor Dr. Nicolò Trocker*
Nicolò Trocker has been a Professor of Civil Procedure at the University of Florence Law School since 1986. He studied at the Universities of Munich (Germany) and Florence (Italy), where he earned his J.D. degree (1967) and at the European University Institute, where he received a Jean Monnet fellowship. In 1993 he taught as a Visiting Professor at Chuo University, Tokyo. Since 1990, he has been a member of the Académie Internationale de Droit Comparé. 2002–2005 he was a Visiting Professor at the University of Miami, where he taught transnational litigation.